IFIP – The International Federation for Information Processing

IFIP was founded in 1960 under the auspices of UNESCO, following the First World Computer Congress held in Paris the previous year. An umbrella organization for societies working in information processing, IFIP's aim is two-fold: to support information processing within its member countries and to encourage technology transfer to developing nations. As its mission statement clearly states,

> *IFIP's mission is to be the leading, truly international, apolitical organization which encourages and assists in the development, exploitation and application of information technology for the benefit of all people.*

IFIP is a non-profitmaking organization, run almost solely by 2500 volunteers. It operates through a number of technical committees, which organize events and publications. IFIP's events range from an international congress to local seminars, but the most important are:

- The IFIP World Computer Congress, held every second year;
- Open conferences;
- Working conferences.

The flagship event is the IFIP World Computer Congress, at which both invited and contributed papers are presented. Contributed papers are rigorously refereed and the rejection rate is high.

As with the Congress, participation in the open conferences is open to all and papers may be invited or submitted. Again, submitted papers are stringently refereed.

The working conferences are structured differently. They are usually run by a working group and attendance is small and by invitation only. Their purpose is to create an atmosphere conducive to innovation and development. Refereeing is less rigorous and papers are subjected to extensive group discussion.

Publications arising from IFIP events vary. The papers presented at the IFIP World Computer Congress and at open conferences are published as conference proceedings, while the results of the working conferences are often published as collections of selected and edited papers.

Any national society whose primary activity is in information may apply to become a full member of IFIP, although full membership is restricted to one society per country. Full members are entitled to vote at the annual General Assembly, National societies preferring a less committed involvement may apply for associate or corresponding membership. Associate members enjoy the same benefits as full members, but without voting rights. Corresponding members are not represented in IFIP bodies. Affiliated membership is open to non-national societies, and individual and honorary membership schemes are also offered.

John Impagliazzo   Timo Järvi
Petri Paju (Eds.)

History
of Nordic Computing 2

Second IFIP WG 9.7 Conference, HiNC2
Turku, Finland, August 21-23, 2007
Revised Selected Papers

 Springer

Volume Editors

John Impagliazzo
Qatar University, Department of Computer Science and Engineering
2713 Doha, Qatar
E-mail: john@qu.edu.qa

Timo Järvi
University of Turku, Department of Computer Science
20014 Turku, Finland
E-mail: timojarvi@gmail.com

Petri Paju
University of Turku, Department of Cultural History
20014 Turku, Finland
E-mail: petpaju@utu.fi

CR Subject Classification (1998): K.2, K.1, K.3, K.7

ISSN   1868-4238
ISBN   978-3-642-26039-1 Springer Berlin Heidelberg New York

This work is subject to copyright. All rights are reserved, whether the whole or part of the material is
concerned, specifically the rights of translation, reprinting, re-use of illustrations, recitation, broadcasting,
reproduction on microfilms or in any other way, and storage in data banks. Duplication of this publication
or parts thereof is permitted only under the provisions of the German Copyright Law of September 9, 1965,
in its current version, and permission for use must always be obtained from Springer. Violations are liable
to prosecution under the German Copyright Law.

springer.com

© IFIP International Federation for Information Processing 2009
Softcover reprint of the hardcover 1st edition 2009

Typesetting: Camera-ready by author, data conversion by Scientific Publishing Services, Chennai, India
Printed on acid-free paper   SPIN: 12737352   06/3180   5 4 3 2 1 0

Dedication

We dedicate this book

to the men and women who seek to preserve the legacy of the computing profession, particularly those from the Nordic countries, whose accomplishments and dedication to computing have propelled the work of their colleagues and have enhanced the computing profession around the world.

Preface

The First Conference on the History of Nordic Computing (HiNC1) was organized in Trondheim, in June 2003. The HiNC1 event focused on the early years of computing, that is the years from the 1940s through the 1960s, although it formally extended to year 1985. In the preface of the proceedings of HiNC1, Janis Bubenko, Jr., John Impagliazzo, and Arne Sølvberg describe well the peculiarities of early Nordic computing [1]. While developing hardware was a necessity for the first professionals, quite soon the computer became an industrial product. Computer scientists, among others, grew increasingly interested in programming and application software. Progress in these areas from the 1960s to the 1980s was experienced as astonishing. The developments during these decades were taken as the focus of HiNC2.

During those decades computers arrived to every branch of large and medium-sized businesses and the users of the computer systems were no longer only computer specialists but also people with other main duties. Compared to the early years of computing before 1960, where the number of computer projects and applications was small, capturing a holistic view of the history between the 1960s and the 1980s is considerably more difficult. The HiNC2 conference attempted to help in this endeavor. First, people who worked with the systems and applications of that time may feel that they have not done something historically important, but just been a part of the technical or sociological development. On the other hand there are historians who try to capture the history in Scandinavia as well as in the rest of the world. HiNC2 brought these people together, with the hope that presentations from both perspectives would raise a fruitful discussion, and increase the understanding of history.

The HiNC2 conference in Turku, August 2007, raised a rather wide interest; there were speakers from all Nordic countries and from the United States and Estonia. The Program Committee had the idea of extending the geographical area from the Nordic countries to the Baltic countries as well, since Finland in particular had plenty of cooperation with the Soviet Union and its Baltic member states, particularly Estonia, during the last decade of the Soviet Union. Most speakers have a computer science background but we also had speakers from industry, public administration and museums or departments of history.

In the closing discussion of the first HiNC conference in Trondheim, the next organizer was left open. After Trondheim, the Finnish members of the IFIP Working Group 9.7 kept discussing the need to arrange a second conference, and in early spring 2006, they decided to take the initiative toward an HiNC2 in Finland. The first meeting and planning session was held at the University of Turku in April 2006, where the HiNC2 arrangement mainlines were agreed. Thereafter both the Program Committee and the Organizing Committee worked fruitfully until the days of the conference.

With a post-conference publication, the Organizing Committee gave the authors the opportunity to modify their papers after the comments received in the conference and to improve the accuracy of their historical writing. This has made the work of the editors more tedious, as they had to wait for the modified manuscripts to come in, and then suggest improvements, then receive the corrected manuscripts, and finally edit them to become a book. We hope that the result of this effort will capture history more accurately.

When looking at the themes in the conference we discover that authors had already presented many of them at the HiNC1 conference. A new topic considered the ways in which to conserve the history of information technology. In addition, computer games became part of the program. New practical computer applications rose during 1960–1980, which later became a necessity.

Unfortunately, the editors could not publish two of the talks presented at the conference. One talk was on the "Birth and Development of the Finnish Software Entrepreneurship" by Kirsti Roine, which would have appeared in the "Software Histories" section. An abstract of this talk appears elsewhere [2, pp 55-57]. Raimo Ollila, representing a main sponsor of the conference, gave the second talk titled "Challenges of ICT on the Newspaper and Publishing Industry." We cannot refer to it, because he could not submit a manuscript.

In the closing session, the future of this conference series was discussed. Both Sweden and Iceland were mentioned as future arrangers of the HiNC3.

June 2009   John Impagliazzo
                                                         Timo Järvi
                                                         Petri Paju

References

[1] Bubenko Jr., Janis & Impagliazzo, John & Arne Sølvberg (eds.): *History of Nordic Computing*. IFIP WG9.7 First Working Conference on the History of Nordic Computing (HiNC1), June 16-18, 2003, Trondheim, Norway. Springer: New York 2005
[2] Paju, Petri, Kivinen, Nina, Järvi, Timo and Ruissalo, Jouko (eds.): *History of Nordic Computing - HiNC2. Extended abstracts*. Turku Centre for Computer Science, General Publications No 42. Turku 2007

HiNC2 Conference Organization

Executive Committee

Organizing Chair	Timo Järvi
Program Committee Chair	Jouko Ruissalo
IFIP WG 9.7 Chair	John Impagliazzo
General Secretary	Petri Paju

Organizing Committee

Leena Järvelä	Museum of Electronics, Salo, Finland
Timo Järvi	University of Turku, Finland
Eija Karsten	University of Turku, Finland
Jaana Lindgren	The Congress Office, University of Turku, Finland
Sanna Mustonen	The Congress Office, University of Turku, Finland
Petri Paju	University of Turku, Finland
Petri Saarikoski	University of Turku, Finland
Reima Suomi	Turku School of Economics, Finland
Kaisa Sere	Åbo Akademi University, Finland

Organizers

International Federation for Information Processing
TC 9, WG 9.7, History of Computing

University of Turku
Department of Information Technology
School of History
School of Cultural Production and Landscape Studies

Åbo Akademi University
Department of Information Technologies

Turku School of Economics
Institute of Information Systems Sciences

Turku Centre for Computer Science

HiNC2 Program Committee

Chair: Jouko Ruissalo | Formerly the Finnish Information Processing Association
Secretary: Petri Paju | University of Turku, Finland
John Impagliazzo | IFIP WG 9.7 (History of Computing), Qatar University, Qatar
Hans Andersin | Helsinki University of Technology, Finland
Oddur Benediktsson | University of Iceland, Iceland
Janis Bubenko, Jr. | Royal Institute of Technology and Stockholm University, Sweden
Kjell Bratbergsengen | Norwegian University of Science and Technology, Norway
Jóhann Gunnarsson | The Icelandic Society for Information Processing, Iceland
Lars Heide | Copenhagen Business School, Denmark
Anker Helms Jørgensen | IT University of Copenhagen, Denmark
Per Lundin | Royal Institute of Technology, Sweden
Markku Nurminen | University of Turku, Finland
Lena Olsson | Stockholm Institute of Education, Sweden
Arne Sølvberg | Norwegian University of Science and Technology, Norway
Jaakko Suominen | University of Turku, Finland
Martti Tienari | University of Helsinki, Finland
Aimo Törn | Åbo Akademi University, Finland
Marja Vehviläinen | University of Tampere, Finland

Acknowledgments

The conference was organized by the International Federation for Information Processing (IFIP) Working Group 9.7 (History of Computing) of its Technical Committee 9 (Relationship between Computers and Society). The Organization Committee of the Second Conference on the History of the Nordic Computing wishes to extend its appreciation to the following groups:

- University of Turku for hosting the conference and for help in the arrangements
- Åbo Akademi University for co-hosting the conference
- Turku School of Economics for co-hosting the conference
- Turku Centre for Computer Science for practical help and economical guarantee

We thank the following donors for monetary or other support. Without them, the conference could not have occurred.

- Academy of Finland
- Turku University Foundation
- City of Turku
- IBM
- PerkinElmer
- Teleste Corporation
- Turun Sanomat

Table of Contents

1. Keynote Addresses

2. Working with History and Its Usability

3. Computer System Perspectives

4. University Computing

5. University Education

6. Computers, Policies and Politics

7. Perspectives on Computer Applications

8. Publishing and Communication Applications

9. Software Histories

10. History of Computer Playing

11. Panel Discussions

Organizing the History of Computing

'Lessons Learned' at the Charles Babbage Institute

Thomas J. Misa

Charles Babbage Institute, University of Minnesota, Minneapolis Minnesota 55455 USA
www.cbi.umn.edu

Abstract. This paper tries to distill some of the 'lessons learned' from the Charles Babbage Institute's quarter-century experience (1980-present) in organizing the history of computing. It draws on the author's (recent) experience as CBI director; conversations with Arthur Norberg, CBI's long-time founding director; and papers delivered at a special symposium appraising CBI's role in computing history, which appeared in the *IEEE Annals of the History of Computing* 29 no. 4 (October-December 2007).

Keywords: Charles Babbage Institute, oral history, archiving practices, electronic documentation, history of computing.

1 Introduction

When the Charles Babbage Institute (CBI) came to the University of Minnesota in 1980 (its origins were a few years earlier in California), no one knew what a research center in the history of computing should look like. Disciplinary research centers at the American Institute of Physics (founded 1961) and IEEE (also opened in 1980) were the closest peer institutions; there was also the Boston Computer Museum (f.1979) although the museum's relocation to the West Coast, let alone its present incarnation in Mountain View, California, was yet some years off.[1] The *Annals of the History of Computing*, then sponsored by the American Federation of Information Processing Societies (AFIPS), had started publishing in 1979. Arthur Norberg, with experience as a research historian at the Bancroft Library at U.C. Berkeley and at the National Science Foundation, arrived in Minnesota as CBI's first permanent director in 1981. He initially planned a full suite of activities, including doing oral histories, developing archival collections, conducting historical research, collecting economic data, engaging in policy work, and conducting educational and outreach activities. In fact, CBI has focused nearly all of its energies on the first three areas—oral histories, archival collections, and historical research. This paper will discuss each of these in turn, spotlighting choices that were made, assessing the consequences, and outlining challenges for the future.

---

[1] The UK's National Archive for the History of Computing (Manchester) was created in 1987; see [18].

J. Impagliazzo, T. Järvi, and P. Paju (Eds.): HiNC 2, IFIP AICT 303, pp. 1–12, 2009.
© IFIP International Federation for Information Processing 2009

2 Developing Oral History Methods

Oral history as an identifiable field in the U.S. stretches back to the early days of folk-lore studies. In the past thirty years or so, the American Institute of Physics, the Smithsonian Institution, the Charles Babbage Institute, the Chemical Heritage Foundation, and several universities have developed oral history as a distinct method for conducting research in the recent history of science and technology. It is especially valuable when researchers have direct access to historical actors and/or where traditional documentary evidence is insufficient or unavailable. As Lillian Hoddeson recently emphasized, conducting oral histories requires the interplay of numerous skills: establishing trust with an interviewee, yet also being able at the right moment to ask probing, possibly difficult questions; relying on an interviewee's memory, yet also bringing documents that can help activate or sharpen memories (or establishing lines of questioning that can do the same).[2]

The "research grade" oral histories developed at CBI utilize a specific method and involve extensive interaction with the interviewee. They are nothing like a newspaper reporter fishing for a quotable anecdote or the popular free-form "reminiscence". CBI oral histories require extensive research beforehand by the interviewer, a substantial block of time for the tape-recorded interview itself (2-3 or more hours), and additional time for the subsequent process of transcription and editing. The interviewee has an opportunity to review the audiotape transcription, correcting mistakes and clarifying ambiguities. However, the goal is not to create a fluid, easy-to-read document ready for publishing in a popular magazine; rather, the goal is to preserve the nuances of the original conversation, while correcting obvious mistakes.[3] For better or worse, the edited transcript becomes the official version, and this is what is widely cited (we are recording 20,000 downloads a year from our online oral-history database). The audio recordings are retained, but in practice, researchers have rarely asked for them. The extensive time requirements for preparing, transcribing, editing, and (if permitted) web-publishing these oral histories make them an ideal research method for the study of certain key persons, who really need to be asked detailed questions about their activities, thoughts and motivations.

Ideally, interviewers bring contemporaneous documents and/or artifacts in order to encourage or stimulate the interviewee's memory. "Can you recall what you were thinking about in *this* memo . . . or in *this* diagram?" are such memory-invigorating questions. Hoddeson relates how an interview she did with physicist Richard Feynman, then 61, was going poorly owing to his recent surgery. He simply could not remember details of his wartime work, even when shown written documents he had drafted and personally signed. At last Hoddenson showed him a blueprint of the Oak Ridge (Tennessee) atomic facility, and this prompted one of Feynman's well-told "genius stories," in this instance about how he had spotted a crucial weakness in the complex system of pipes and pumps in the atomic facility's chemical plant (p. 193). Telling this story seemed literally to activate his memory, and soon additional stories and recollections were readily forthcoming. [8]

---

[2] See the AIP's guidelines <www.aip.org/history/oral_history/conducting.html> and [16] For connections to historical methods, see [8] and [17].

[3] For recent reflections on editing oral history manuscripts and preparing them for publication, see [9].

In addition to documents, key artifacts or even close colleagues can be helpful in jogging or jolting the interviewee's memory. Doing a group interview with colleagues has several obvious attractions, not least the pleasant social time and opportunity to reminisce with friends; yet it is important to keep in mind *why* one does the interview. If there are a specific set of research questions, then the interviewer must work extra hard to keep two or more interviewees on track and focused. Having a chance to sit around and record some of the "old stories" is frequently attractive to the interviewees, but then the interviewer needs to take special care. Researchers studying the complex phenomena of memory suggest that we do not really directly remember the original (ur–)memory; rather, we recall the last re-telling or recollection of that memory. If, somewhere down the years, the re-told story has wandered away from the original, then the oral historian's elaborate process of recording, transcribing, and validating of this more-or-less accurate storytelling as a "historical fact" can be seriously in error.

Controversies surrounding oral histories tend to crop up when someone asserts too much for the genre. The historian of modern biology Horace Freeland Judson, whose *The Eighth Day of Creation* (1979) depended heavily on oral histories with colorful pioneering figures in molecular biology, has been criticized in these terms [10]. (An additional liability is that researchers may consult his 52 oral histories, deposited at the American Philosophical Society, "only with the prior written permission" of Judson; moreover, several of them are "closed indefinitely to researchers."[4]) After significant time spent with pioneering figures in a field, it is certainly tempting to see their retrospective accounts in a favorable, even privileged light. A better approach recognizes that oral histories are one subjective source—no worse but certainly no better than any other single source. The pragmatic solution when faced with this seemingly intractable problem is to rely on the historian's fundamental methods of *source criticism* (paying careful attention to the perspective and potential bias of any source, as well as examining its reliability, authenticity, and distance from events) and *triangulation* (seeking to find corroboration among varied sources, whether documents, published accounts, artifacts or oral histories). It goes without saying that open access to all relevant documents—including, ideally, interviews and transcripts—is necessary for such triangulation.

It is important to emphasize that different modes of interviews, and other complementary research methods and sources, will be necessary to keep pace with changing questions and themes in the history of computing, especially the recent interest in the users of computing and the emerging awareness of the important roles played by non-pioneering figures. It certainly makes sense to invest many hours of intensive research and preparation time to be able to ask insightful questions of a pioneering figure. These figures can be the most valuable interviewees—and, sometimes, also the most troublesome. Often, people who have been in the public eye as a prominent scientist, engineer, or business executive have already experienced all the "usual questions" and have already formulated answers to them; consciously or not, they have erected or constructed a "mask", and it may not be easy to go beyond their public persona or identity. A careful oral historian can choose to avoid posing the usual questions, or to ask knowledgeable follow-up questions in the case of a pat reply. Hoddeson relates her mistake in interviewing a certain Bell Laboratories executive in his office, where over

---

[4] See <www.amphilsoc.org/library/mole/j/judson.htm>.

the years he had held numerous interviews and where his "mask" was secure: she conducted a well-paced interview, and recorded all the "usual stories" that he'd already re-
told many times before.

Over the years, CBI researchers have done nearly 300 interviews, and, including
those done by our collaborators and colleagues, our on-line database contains nearly
400 interviews. You can directly query the database by name or subject; for a sugges-
tive listing see <www.cbi.umn.edu/oh/subject.phtml>; most of the interviews are
available on-line as PDFs. Looking down the subject list at "X" there are entries for
Xerox Data Systems and Xerox's Palo Alto Research Center that lead to a 52-page
interview with Paul A. Strassmann, who was chief computer executive at Xerox.
From his vantage point in 1989, Strausmann described the interactions between
Xerox's mainframe-oriented Data Systems (XDS), and Xerox's established copier
business, as well as the growth of Xerox Palo Alto Research Center (Xerox PARC)
and its development of the Alto and Star computers. Staussman recalls Xerox's decision to embrace an integrated view of information technology and to distance itself
from computers per se. A listing under "XML" leads to a 36-page interview with Don
Chamberlin, who in 2001 was a researcher at IBM–San Jose. Chamberlin recounted
his early life, his education at Harvey Mudd College and Stanford University, and his
work on relational database technology. Together with Ray Boyce, Chamberlin developed the SQL database language. He also briefly discussed his recent research on
XML query languages. While Chamberlin's interview is something like a career
summary, Strassmann's interview is more focused on a specific phase of his career.

CBI's established model of oral histories, a particular model to be sure, has been so
successful that only recently have we seriously considered other types and modes of
interviews. At CBI, we have several different types of experiments for a research project on the National Science Foundation's FastLane system. Today, FastLane forms a
comprehensive information infrastructure used in all phases of NSF's grant making,
its core mission. To deal with the large number of legacy users at NSF as well as
sponsored projects staff and researchers at universities, we plan shorter, targeted interviews with non-pioneering figures (combined with longer, traditional interviews
with the key FastLane designers). We have a plan for a semi-automated transcription
technique, using voice-recognition software; unfortunately, you cannot (yet) have
your interviewee speak directly into a computer to produce a transcript, since the
software needs to be 'trained' for a certain voice.

We also are developing a web-based interview platform for our research. This
activity connects a web-based front end to a database for recording respondents'
answers to semi-structured interview questions as well as their own unstructured an-
ecdotes or stories (the capacity to do binary-format uploads will allow a degree of
self-archiving, since users will be able to upload images, documents, and even binary
files of their own spoken interview answers). We also are experimenting with a wiki
to facilitate our interviewees participating in the writing of history.[5]

Our goal with these new methods is to gain access to people and sources that, practically speaking, were not available using our traditional, time-intensive oral history
methods. We hope the new methods might better 'scale' with a larger numbers of

[5] Various experiments in Web-based history have been funded by the Sloan Foundation. For
candid reports, see [6,7]. Early results were reported in [12].

interviewees. Again, this is a good example of the interplay of changing historical questions with new research methods and tools. Time-intensive oral histories made sense when our research questions concerned a limited number of pioneering figures. We need new research methods to understand a larger and more diverse group of individuals.

3   Evolving Archiving Practices

A second activity is archiving the papers of individuals, institutions, companies, and professional groups, which was a priority of CBI from the start. Here too Arthur Norberg and his colleagues (for most of its history CBI has had both professional historians and professional archivists on staff) faced some difficult choices. While the industry and professional groups advising CBI initially advocated a strategy of "saving everything", CBI's actual collections strategy was much more focused. Bill Aspray has recently described these debates, noting the several shortcomings in the save-everything collecting strategy. These involve numerous practical and intellectual problems: vexing problems of space, cost, appraisal, preservation, indexing, provenance, and (not least) effective cooperation with other peer organizations and institutions.[2]

In time, CBI evolved into a true physical archive, with extensive on-site storage, active collections development, professional archiving, and full-service accommodations for researchers. As far as I know, little thought was ever given to CBI serving as an archival clearinghouse such as the Oxford–Bath archives of contemporary science. The problem was not one of coordinating existing collections. Rather, there was a pressing need for some *place* that would collect, preserve, and make publicly accessible records and documentation on the history of computing (most university libraries in the U.S. are rather reluctant to take non-literary materials from beyond their own campuses), and a salutary awareness of that need on the part of the technical-professional community. The thought was that an important part of the history of computing had just occurred, and that it would likely be lost unless some institution such as CBI collected that history. Even today, CBI often seems to serve as a sort of "last chance" for computer history records, especially those held by individuals.

CBI's active collecting policy and practices took form with intellectual input from the technical community, Norberg, and Bruce Bruemmer, CBI's first professional archivist who served from 1984 to 1997. (Subsequently, CBI's full-time archivists have been Elisabeth Kaplan from 1999-2005 and Arvid Nelsen, hired in April 2007.[6]) For several years, CBI had the typical archival storage in the basement of an older building (in the University of Minnesota's Engineering Library). In 2000, CBI moved into a new, purpose-built special collections library. Andersen Library features office suites and reading rooms for the University's archives and special collections units as well as state-of-the-art climate-controlled archival storage space underground. The facility exploits the geological fact along the Mississippi River basin that layers of soft sandstone alternate with layers of hard limestone; the underground storage cavern was created when two 600-foot-long holes were bored through the sandstone layer,

---

[6] For a more detailed history, see [3].

and then reinforced with a concrete tube structure. Not only were construction costs quite reasonable, but also the ongoing energy costs are low since little temperature regulation needs to be done for the underground space (corrections to humidity are still needed). The facility was built with a special appropriation of Minnesota-state funding since the state needed large-scale remote storage when constructing or moving an entire library; accordingly, you can back a large U.S.-size "tractor-trailer" unit right into the loading area, offload boxes onto a gravity-slide conveyor ramp, and then store boxes on metal racks that stretch nearly two stories high.[7]

There are many irreplaceable gems in CBI's archives, but not every computer manual could—or should—be given the exacting archive-grade preservation required for the most valuable historical materials. Generally CBI followed the standards of the professional archiving community, which embraced a high degree of physical preservation, a detailed level of collections processing, extensive indexing of the collection, and broad dissemination of the resulting finding guides. Consequently, most of the archival material in CBI's 250 collections—including its two largest corporate collections (Burroughs and Control Data)—are processed down to the "folder" level. Researchers have access to these collections through a keyword search tool <http://discover.lib.umn.edu/findaid>. A recent update permits detailed and accurate searching across CBI's collections (as well as across the University's other archival collections as desired). Really, for the first time, we have gained practical access to the 731 boxes of the United States National Bureau of Standards sprawling collection of computer literature (1956-1978). CBI's U.S.-oriented collections are well known to computer historians, but recently we made a survey of our surprisingly wide international holdings (including founding documents on IFIP, documentation on ALGOL, information on Soviet bloc computing, and other topics, as well as the only WorldCat-listed copy of James Connolly's *History of Computing in Europe* [published by IBM World Trade Corporation in 1967]). [5, 20]

One challenge we are confronting today in archiving is the tradeoff between processing and accessibility. Put simply, with the accepted model of extensive processing, our collections have not typically been available to researchers until after we process them—sometimes for many years. Archivists in the U.S. have lately favored a model of "minimal" processing with an acceptance of describing collections, at least initially, at the overview box-level rather than at the more detailed folder level. Collections are more quickly made available to researchers, even though they may later undergo further processing (at the folder level). Another challenge we face is continuing to round out our existing collections from the "mainframe" era while starting or expanding more-recent collections documenting the personal computer, networking, graphics, office automation, internet, and mobile computing.

It will be interesting to observe the interactions between archival theory and practices in the age of electronic and born digital records. There are certainly numerous collections of scanned documents available on-line today.[8] One solution, it may well

---

[7] Information on the Andersen Library building, including construction photographs, may be found at <andersen.lib.umn.edu/aboutandersen.html>.

[8] See (e.g.) the Alan Turing Archive for the History of Computing <www.alanturing.net/>; Mike Muuss' History of Computing Information <ftp.arl.mil/~mike/comphist/>; and J. A. N. Lee's materials <ei.cs.vt.edu/~history/>.

appear, to the practical problem of where to store large volumes of records is simply to digitize the whole lot and throw out the bulky paper originals. More than one person has observed to me that if Google can effectively search the entire world wide web, then certainly a decent search engine could retrieve scanned, digitized documents in an archive such as CBI. I think the problem may be more complex than it first appears. To begin, a digitized image of a document—a memo, research report, or drawing—is not searchable unless it has been OCR-ed and/or someone has assigned metadata to it (and both of these are time-intensive processes). There is the attractive hybrid, raw-OCR-plus-image model used by the "Making of America" project at Michigan and Cornell. This project gives its scanned books, journal articles, and other documentation from the 19th century a raw OCR (with around 99% but not 100% accuracy); the OCR-text results are entered into a searchable database; and these entries are linked to high-quality scanned images of the original pages. Yet even with substantial funding by the Mellon Foundation, and a decade of large-scale university effort at Cornell and Michigan starting in 1995, the total number of pages has reached just 3.8 million.[9]

At CBI, we face a numbers-and-resource-allocation question. CBI presently holds around 5,000 shelf feet of paper documents, or more than 5 million pages, in addition to a growing electronic archive. Our documentation is very diverse: loose handwritten notes, formal research reports, market surveys, laboratory notebooks, bound and unbound journals and books. Some of these "pages" are viewed regularly, at least as archival collections go, but many of them might be called up and examined only once in a very long time. Digitizing each and every of these pages would represent an enormous commitment in staff time, not only for the scanning itself, but more importantly for describing the documents, indexing them, and setting up and maintaining a database retrieval scheme. We estimate that such archival grade scanning costs us around $1 per page (although, like Google, we can scan second copies of book pages at lower cost). Corporate lawyers might have the resources to do this and to make large datasets of trial documents available and retrievable, even on-line; but it is not clear that this would be an effective use of archiving resources at CBI's (modest) scale of operations. If we made a full-scale commitment to digitizing our present collection, our collecting of new materials would probably grind to a halt.

Now, consider the status of a document not merely as a container for "information" but also as an artifact. CBI has a very large collection of computer manuals and other printed documentation, more than 500 boxes total, of which approximately half is processed and half unprocessed.[10] We are under some institutional pressure to reduce the size of the so-called unprocessed collections. Computer manuals are by no means unique; and there are catalogues of on-line computer manuals.[11] Yet a preliminary investigation of our users suggests that the computer manuals have received far more use than we had assumed. Then, too, taking (say) one of the three-ring notebook binders out of its box, and examining how it was used (colored tabs); even the smell of the

---

[9] See <quod.lib.umich.edu/m/moagrp/index.html> and <cdl.library.cornell.edu/moa/>. The current page count (June 2007) is at <quod.lib.umich.edu/m/moagrp/>.

[10] For the Computer Product Manuals Collection (1940s to 1980s) see <www.cbi.umn.edu/collections/inv/cbi00060.html> or <special.lib.umn.edu/findaid/xml/cbi00060.xml>.

[11] For the Manx catalogue, see <vt100.net/manx/>; a collection of documentation and software can be found at <www.bitsavers.org/>.

cheap plastic (no fine leather bindings here) tells you something about the social and cultural history of computing. If we digitized the "content" of the computer manuals and purged them as artifacts, we would certainly gain some open shelf-feet but we would also have lost the contextual information of the artifact itself, with clues to how and why programmers used it.

Finally, let me conclude this section with some thoughts on the "migration model" for electronic or born-digital records. A National Archives document categorizes the many on-going experiments in preserving digital records into five broad areas:[12]

    (a) preserving the original technology used to create or store the records;
    (b) emulating the original technology on new platforms;
    (c) migrating the software necessary to retrieve, deliver, and use the records;
    (d) migrating the records to up-to-date formats;
    (e) converting records to standard forms.

The migration model focuses on (c) and (d) of these options. (The "Making of America" project mentioned above stores its scanned book and magazine pages in 600 dpi TIFF images, a stable and standard non-compressed form, as in (e); and then converts the huge TIFF files on-demand to compressed GIF images for delivery over the WWW.)

One certain liability of paper records is their physical bulk and the costs needed to store them securely over the long term. Yet one advantage is that once the paper records have been processed they are stable: during IBM's crisis in the 1990s it was forced to close its archives for a number of years, but, when the company's economic prospects improved, all that was needed was to unlock the IBM archive's doors and re-open the facility. Its paper records were still there waiting patiently. Electronic records may not so successfully survive such a temporary closure. Archiving experts are exploring the "migration model" to store electronic records over time. Records stored in yesterday's obsolete format need to be "migrated" to today's standard format to ensure continued accessibility; alternately, software capable of reading and interpreting the ancient data will need to be migrated onto up-to-date hardware. In the future, with the assumption of changing software and/or data formats, there will be the need for further migrations—a little-acknowledged downside to the seemingly relentless march of Moore's Law.[13]

It seems to me that the "migration model" entirely transforms electronic archiving: it was supposed to be a low-cost enterprise, but instead it might be one with surprisingly high and recurrent costs. Here are some considerations to migrating records themselves. First, since no piece of software can be perfect, the downstream or migrated records will have some minor but essentially undetectable errors; consequently, it seems very risky to dispose of the original records, and quite likely the same for the second and subsequent generations as well. So instead of having a single-generation electronic archive, we are likely to have multiple-generation archives, one for each of the migration generations. Over time a single collection of electronic records, which

---

[12] See Kenneth Thibodeau, "Preservation and Migration of Electronic Records: The State of the Issue" <www.archives.gov/era/papers/preservation.html> (accessed May 2007).

[13] Or worse, as the Thibodeau (supra) suggests: "the market has tended to exacerbate the problem of preserving electronic records. The pressures of competition have led the [IT] industry to obey Moore's law, replacing both hardware and software on a frequency of two years or less."

might have been stored in a fixed number of traditional archival boxes, will actually grow in size and complexity. Second, I think the migration model typically assumes a linear progression: you start with the "1st" generation of original records and migrate from there to the "2nd" generation and from the "2nd" to the "3rd", and so on. Remember each migration is more or less forced by soon-to-be obsolete formats (we are entirely assuming stable storage media and/or well-secured servers, another cost that should not be forgotten). If an archive is unable to conduct one of these generational migrations, it seems in great danger of having its collections slip off the standard migration pipeline. Hypothetically, what if an archive was forced to be dormant for ten years—or for any reason simply forced to skip one or more required migrations? Now, think about the next 75 or 150 years. Given these problems, some archival specialists reasonably advocate just printing out emails or other electronics documents and archiving them based on the well-tried paper models.

4 Conducting Historical Research

Third, CBI has conducted an active research program throughout the past quarter century. Indeed, you can chart CBI's longer-term research projects and find a close correspondence with shifting emphases in the oral histories conducted and even in the specific collections taken in. This, too, is part of the CBI model: our research projects have led to oral histories and networking in various communities, which in turn has frequently led to collection development in those communities, and, in the longer term, the creation of an entire infrastructure for research. For example, during the years when CBI did a NSF project on the "Computer as a Scientific Instrument" (1998-2001) CBI's oral histories focused in complementary fashion on NSF staffers and computer researchers active in the area; and similarly for another NSF-funded project on "Building a Future for Software History" (1999-2003). Several important archival collections in early networking and computer science came during the (sponsored) project that examined DARPA's influence on computer science, and which resulted in Norberg and Judy O'Neill's *Transforming Computer Technology: Information Processing for the Pentagon, 1962-1986* [14]. Norberg's own research on Minnesota's pioneering computer industry, including numerous oral histories and many individual and company collections, was published as *Computers and Commerce* [15]. Capitalizing in part on CBI's accumulated records, Jeffrey Yost, CBI's associate director, recently published a valuable overview titled *The Computer Industry* [19]. In short, there has been a continual interplay between research, oral history, and archiving activities, and it is difficult to imagine CBI today not having all of these functions.

The archives staff, too, has conducted substantial field-shaping projects, in addition to the processing of collections, the handling of reference questions, and the provision of research assistance. *The High-Technology Company: A Historical Research and Archival Guide* (written by CBI staffers Bruce Bruemmer and Sheldon Hochheiser and published in 1989) was for some years the best and indeed only resource concerning this sector, and distributed by the Society of American Archivists [4]. Recently, CBI staff conducted a study "Documenting Internet2: A Collaborative Model for Developing Electronic Records Capacities in the Small Archival Repository."[14]

---

[14] A list of CBI's publications is at <www.cbi.umn.edu/research/staff_publications.pdf>.

Support for scholars working on their Ph.D. in the field has also been an important on-going activity through the CBI–Tomash Fellowship. Awarded annually since 1978, the list-to-date of 28 fellows reads something like a who's who in computing history.[15] Collectively, they have published highly respected works in all areas of the history of computing. In scholarly terms, the CBI–Tomash dissertations have resulted in the two best books on Silicon Valley, the definitive study of the internet, key studies of computing in organizations, the corporate and Cold War contexts, and several scientific disciplines, the key study of magnetic recording technology, as well as pioneering studies of computing in Chile and Italy, and comparative studies with Japan and England. The recent volume from MIT Press on the commercial internet has chapters written by no less than six former CBI–Tomash fellows, including those of both co-editors (William Aspray and Paul Ceruzzi) [1].

5 Conclusion

In conclusion, here are three items in my personal "wish list" of initiatives for the history of computing. One, I would like to develop a software tool for archiving email: it would permit the capture, sorting, editing, and archiving of emails, which currently arrive at our shop on 5.25 floppies, 3.5 floppies, as electronic files, and on CDs in a wide variety of formats. I think it is a good bet that emails will have high research value in the universe of "born digital" records. Emails frequently contain a heterogeneous mixture of content, even in the same message: personal or private comments, professional business, a bit of gossip here and there, as well as binary-code attachments such as images or Word documents or Excel spreadsheets. I believe that potential email donors would respond positively if we had an effective means for removing their private content, just as slips of paper with private comments were certainly removed from traditional paper archives, while leaving intact their professional, technical, or public content. Such privacy concerns are prominent in collections of emails we are working on now. Of course, at a certain moment, the edited content in such a database would need stability, to be locked down, so that subsequent users of the email database do not continue the editing process. Emails also contain a wealth of useful meta-data about how and when and where the message was sent. So for these reasons there are several obvious shortcomings with (say) creating PDF files from emails with the personal bits blacked out,[16] or just printing them out.

I also would like an institutional or collective means of "finding good homes" for archival collections that might not fit our collecting priorities but that still ought to be preserved somewhere (we have several of these in process right now). And, finally, I would like to think prospectively about how changes in our field's topics, themes, and

---

[15] The CBI-Tomash fellows are listed at <www.cbi.umn.edu/research/recipients.html>.

[16] For problems with improperly "redacted" or blacked-out text in PDF documents, see the well-publicized travails of the CIA, AT&T, and others: <cryptome.org/cia-iran.htm>, <it.slashdot.org/it/06/06/22/138210.shtml>, <news.com.com/2100-1028_3-6077353.html>. The NSA advises "any sensitive information must be removed from the document through deletion"; see [13] p. 4.

research questions might shape and direct our archiving strategies and practices [11]. I welcome continuing opportunities to share and discuss our experiences.

References

[1] Aspray, W., Ceruzzi, P.E. (eds.): The Internet and American Business. MIT Press, Cambridge (2008)

[2] Aspray, W.: Leadership in Computing History: Arthur Norberg and the Charles Babbage Institute. IEEE Annals of the History of Computing 29(4), 16–26 (2007)

[3] Bruemmer, B., Kaplan, E.: Realizing the Concept: A History of the CBI Archives. IEEE Annals of the History of Computing 23(4), 29–38 (2001)

[4] Bruemmer, B., Hochheiser, S.: The High-Technology Company: A Historical Research and Archival Guide. Charles Babbage Institute, Minneapolis (1989), Available on-line, along with other research resources,
http://www.cbi.umn.edu/hostedpublications/

[5] Connolly, J.: History of Computing in Europe. IBM World Trade Corporation (1967)

[6] Hessenbruch, A.: The Trials and Promise of a Web-History of Materials Research. In: Grandin, K., Wormbs, N., Widmalm, S. (eds.) The Science–Industry Nexus, pp. 397–413. Science History Publications, Sagamore Beach (2004)

[7] Hessenbruch, A.: 'The Mutt Historian': The Perils and Opportunities of Doing History of Science On-line. In: Doel, R.E., Söderqvist, T. (eds.) The Historiograhy of Contemporary Science, Technology, and Medicine, pp. 279–298. Routledge, New York (2006)

[8] Hoddeson, L.: The Conflict of Memories and Documents: Dilemmas and Pragmatics of Oral History. In: Doel, R.E., Söderqvist, T. (eds.) The Historiography of Contemporary Science, Technology, and Medicine, pp. 187–200. Routledge, New York (2006)

[9] Jones, R.: Blended Voices: Crafting a Narrative from Oral History Interviews. Oral History Review 31(1), 23–42 (2004)

[10] Judson, H.F.: The Eighth Day of Creation: Makers of the Revolution in Biology. Simon and Schuster, New York (1979)

[11] Misa, T.: Understanding How Computing Has Changed the World. IEEE Annals of the History of Computing 29(4), 52–63 (2007)

[12] Misa, T., Zepcevski, J.: Realizing user-centered computer history: Designing and using NSF's FastLane (1990-present). Paper to annual meeting of the Society for the History of Technology, Lisbon, October 12-14 (2008),
http://netfiles.umn.edu/users/tmisa/www/papers/
FastLane_SHOT-2008.pdf

[13] National Security Agency. Redacting with Confidence: How to Safely Publish Sanitized Reports Converted From Word to PDF (NSA Information Assurance Directorate Report # I333-015R-2005),
http://www.fas.org/sgp/othergov/dod/nsa-redact.pdf

[14] Norberg, A., O'Neill, J.: Transforming Computer Technology: Information Processing for the Pentagon, pp. 1962–1986. Johns Hopkins University Press, Baltimore (1996)

[15] Norberg, A.: Computers and Commerce: A Study of Technology and Management at Eckert-Mauchly Computer Company, Engineering Research Associates, and Remington Rand, pp. 1946–1957. MIT Press, Cambridge (2005)

[16] Norberg, A.: How to Conduct and Preserve an Oral History, IT History Society (2008),
http://www.ithistory.org/resources/norberg-article.pdf

[17] Thomson, A.: Four Paradigm Transformations in Oral History. Oral History Review 34(1), 49–70 (2006)
[18] Tweedale, G.: The National Archive for the History of Computing. Journal of the Society of Archivists 10(1), 1–8 (1989)
[19] Yost, J.R.: The Computer Industry. Greenwood Press, Westport (2005)
[20] Yost, J.R.: Exploring the Archives—Part One: International Records. CBI Newsletter 29(1), 8–11 (Spring 2007),
    http://www.cbi.umn.edu/about/ns1/v29n1graphics.pdf

Provisioning of Safe Train Control in Nordic Countries

Harold 'Bud' Lawson

Lawson Konsult AB, Albavägen 25, Lidingö, Sweden
bud@lawson.se

Abstract. The safety of train traffic is a vital societal function. During the mid-1970s, the availability of inexpensive microprocessors and electronic components led to the first computer-based systems solution to this critical function. Sweden was the first country in the world to develop and deploy a computer-based solution for Automatic Train Control (ATC). The major suppliers Ericsson Signal Systems and ITT Standard Radio developed solutions for both of the functions required; namely the track to train transmission system as well as the onboard system. Both system functions have been further developed by companies that have taken over ownership of these system products; namely, Bombardier, respectively Ansaldo. In the original delivery to the Swedish Railways (SJ), Ericsson Signal delivered the track-to-train transmission system; whereas, Standard Radio the onboard system for SJ trains and Ericsson Signal delivered the onboard system for the Stockholm Local Traffic (SL) trains. We describe the functions provided by both systems; however, we place focus upon the unique properties of the Standard Radio onboard system that has had a stable architecture for over twenty-eight years. The two track-to-train transmission systems delivered by Bombardier and Ansaldo are compatible; in Norway, both suppliers have delivered their products for both of the functions. Further, the X2000 and Öresund bridge trains that travel between Sweden and Denmark utilize the Ansaldo onboard and track to train transmission products in combination with a Siemens system. In addition to the details of the Swedish ATC solution, a brief historical perspective of train control as well as the implementation of train control in the other Nordic countries is provided. The need for a holistic view of train control is cited in examining two actual train accidents in Sweden and Norway. Finally, we discuss the movements toward a European Rail Traffic Management System standard in respect to interoperability of train control.

Keywords: Automatic train control (ATC), real-time systems, safety-critical, systems engineering.

1 Introduction

The safety of millions of train passengers is dependent upon reliable safety related equipment and functions in the entire railway system. One of the most important functions is the monitoring of the behavior of train drivers; that is, assuring that they abide by speed limits, signal status, and other conditions. There have been numerous train accidents in Europe and elsewhere in the past where the availability and proper operation of this function would have hindered these incidents. This function, now often referred to as Automatic Train Protection (ATP), came into being since 1980s in Sweden as the Automatic Train Control (ATC) system.

J. Impagliazzo, T. Järvi, and P. Paju (Eds.): HiNC 2, IFIP AICT 303, pp. 13–28, 2009.
© IFIP International Federation for Information Processing 2009

In this paper, we present key properties of the Swedish ATC system. We place particular focus upon the onboard system conceived and developed by Standard Radio and Telefon AB, now owned by AnsaldoSTS (Ansaldo Sweden), and further developed and maintained by Teknogram AB of Hedemora, Sweden. We cite the major reasons for the success of this onboard system in providing safe train control for over twenty-eight years. In addition, we discuss the utilization of the Swedish solution in Norway and partially in Denmark as well as the solution utilized in Finland. The reasons for two train accidents in Sweden and Norway are presented. These accidents highlight the need for a holistic perspective concerning the technical and non-technical issues related to ATC and its deployment. Finally, we introduce developments concerning the European Rail Traffic Management System.

Harold Lawson, Sivert Wallin, Berit Bryntse and Bertil Friman, all were key players in the Standard Radio ATC onboard system solution; namely, as architect, developers and maintainers, and verifier of the later versions of the software. After twenty years of successful operation, they wrote about the properties of the Standard Radio onboard system [10]. Some parts of the current paper include that earlier presentation.

2 Train Safety: A Brief Historic Perspective

Railways as we know them today had their origin in the United Kingdom with the first public railway in 1825. At that time, there were 25 miles of track and two locomotives. In 1829, Stevenson introduced the steam engine called "The Rocket" and in competition with other engines, it attained a speed of 29 mph (unloaded) and 25 mph hauling 13 tons of wagons. This catalyst led to the rapid development of railroads around the world. By 1875, there were approximately 160,000 miles of track and 70,000 locomotives in the world. This is an astounding development especially considering the primitive means of international transportation and communication available at that time. It is interesting to compare this with the rapid expansion of automotive traffic as well as computing technology and the internet.

Early accidents due to human errors in the UK and elsewhere rapidly led to the development of signaling to control traffic. To provide this critical function, several mechanical interlocking solutions where developed in order to prevent signalmen from accidentally setting conflicting routes. Interlocking developments then proceeded through generations of an ingenious variety of more complex mechanical and electromechanical systems.

3 Automatic Train Control in Sweden

The availability of inexpensive microprocessors and electronics in the mid-1970s offered new solution possibilities for interlocking as well as for protecting against driver errors. The Swedish National Railways (SJ) was quick to exploit these new possibilities and developed the worlds first computer-based interlocking and speed control system. The investment in this solution was motivated as follows:

To meet demands of increased efficiency of railway transportation on both existing and new tracks, the train speed must be increased and the trains must operate with shorter intervals. This requirement increases the demands on both the safety system and the train drivers thus leaving little room for human errors. The high degree of accuracy of the ATC system minimizes the risks for driver error.

Initially (in 1980 when the first ATC systems where installed), the plan for the Swedish State Railways (SJ) was that the train should be driven entirely according to the external optical signals, and that the ATC system should be considered only as a safety back up. With the advent of the X2000 high-speed trains (200 km/h), it turned out that the optical system was insufficient for presentation of all information needed, e.g. earlier warning for restrictions ahead, and different speeds for various train types. In addition, after they accumulated operational experience with the ATC system, it turned out that the ATC system could be trusted for presentation of information not otherwise available along the track. The resulting system nowadays is a very efficient, robust, and safe combination, well matching more expensive and more complicated systems used elsewhere in the world.

If the driver should lose concentration for a moment, the ATC will then take over the control of the train by applying the brakes. This brake application continues until the driver manually acknowledges to the system that he is once more capable of controlling the train. If the driver should fail to regain control, the ATC will continue to brake the train to a standstill.

The two major technical function constituents of the ATC system are the track to train transmission system product and the onboard system product.

3.1 Track-to-Train Transmission System

The wayside equipment consists of track-mounted transponders (called balises) transmitting messages (telegrams) to the vehicle when activated by the antenna mounted on the vehicle (see Figure 1). The information transmitted includes signal status as well as the speed limit followed until the next transponder group. Each type of information generates a unique message (telegram). The transponders combine into groups of minimum two and maximum five transponders. A transponder group can be valid for the current or the opposite direction of travel, or for both travel directions.

The transponders in a group either can have a fixed code or coded by an encoder connected between the signaling system and the transponder, in such a way that the transponder group can give information corresponding to the current signal aspect to the onboard equipment.

Fig. 1. ATC Track to Train Transmission System

When a vehicle with an active ATC travels over a transponder group, each transponder activates from the energy received from the antenna of the vehicle. The coded message is continuously transmitted to the vehicle equipment as long as the transponder is active. A valid combination of transponders will transmit all the information necessary for the vehicle equipment to evaluate the message and take the required action. The onboard equipment will detect either a faulty message or an invalid combination of transponders and notify the driver accordingly.

3.2 The Onboard System

Figure 2 portrays the vehicle onboard equipment and it consists of the following major components:

It uses an antenna mounted underneath the vehicle that activates the track equipment (transponders) by continuously transmitting a powering signal and receiving transponder messages that the system will evaluate and use to supervise the safe travel of the train.

It contains a set of computer equipment that evaluates the transponder messages. It presents the information to the driver that will break the train to a safe speed level if the driver should fail to take the correct actions. That is, if the driver does not brake the train or exceeds speed limits. The driver has to cancel manually each ATC brake application by pushing a brake release button.

It contains cab equipment consisting of a driver's ATC panel used by the driver to enter into the ATC system the data that is relevant to that specific train, and all other communication with the ATC equipment. The panel also keeps the driver informed of current speed limits and target speed limits at speedboards and signals ahead.

It includes vehicle-interfacing devices such as a speedometer connection, a main-brake pipe-pressure sensor, and one or more brake valves.

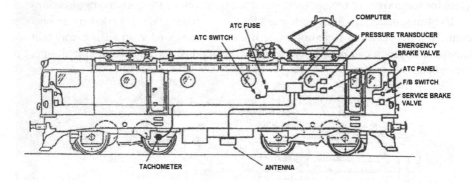

Fig. 2. Onboard ATC System Product

To provide for fault-tolerance, a three-processor solution with majority logic comparison of outputs was utilized for the early versions of the onboard system. In the Standard Radio onboard system, the same program executes on all three processors thus the redundancy protects primarily against processor hardware failures. Due to the observed high reliability of the hardware based upon many years of operation, later versions of the onboard system only utilize two processors.

4 Time Line for the Onboard System Product

The Standard Radio ATC product became the property of ATSS (Ansaldo Transporti Signal System) in 1990. Since 1984, they contracted a significant part of the further development of the product and maintenance to Teknogram AB. Appendix A illustrates a timeline highlighting the major product events.

The two latter developments of the system led to ATC2.1 developed especially for the Västervik line where they employed a radio-based control instead of the balise transponder system. Further, they integrated ATC2.2 in the X2000 train sets and freight locomotives that travel over the Öresund Bridge. In this case, Teknogram also developed an interface PC-board and software based upon the same operating system as ATC2 for communication with the Siemens solution utilized on the Danish railways. This system began operation during the summer of 2000 when the bridge officially opened. Now, even the line between Helsingor in Denmark and Helsingborg in Sweden also deploy this dual solution. The different software versions are fully backwards compatible, i.e. ATC2.2 could be used in any train in Sweden and Norway if desired.

In addition to the main ATC onboard product, they developed a separate PC-board and software running under the same operating system solution to function as the "black box" recorder for ATC. The recorder collects information for up to three days of train operation and includes telegram information and all transitions of speed greater than 2 km per hour. The most recent version of the recorder utilizes flash memories. Earlier versions utilized solid-state memories that required constant power (battery back up).

Standard Radio hoped that ATC would be an export product. Unfortunately, this market did not fully materialize until later and only a small project in Perth, Australia, utilized ATC1 (and it is still operating and expanding). Several potential customers, including British Railways examined the product, but decided not to buy it. This was very unfortunate since we now know that it has worked reliably for train traffic for over 28 years. This is a truly impressive record. The cost of one single serious accident would most likely pay for the installation of the system not to mention the personal loss and suffering associated with such accidents.

Since 1990, further exploited by Ansaldo (ASTS) and supported by Teknogram, the solutions utilized in ATC1 and ATC2 have been applied in several installations of ATC. The installations have included an ATP (Automatic Train Protection) system for Keretapi Tanah Melayu Berhard of Malaysia (installation 1996), ATP for Hammersley Iron Ore Railways in Australia (installation 1998), the ATC system for Roslagsbanan in suburban Stockholm (installation during 2000), ASES (Advanced Speed Enforcement System) for New Jersey Transit in USA, and the monorail system for Kuala Lumpur, Malaysia. All of these onboard systems have the same architecture and operating system core solution. However, the programs for the latter solutions are in the Ada programming language.

Further, Teknogram AB has successfully utilized the same architecture and operating system to develop and market more than twenty train simulators. Consequently, the ATC architecture has been the basis for the Teknogram business concept. For Teknogram and Ansaldo, this represents a truly exceptional example of the reuse of architectural concepts and operating system core for the implementation of new system products.

5 ATC Software Statistics

As indicated in the timeline of Appendix A, there have been two major versions developed and two minor variations on the second version that they developed for utilization by the Swedish Railways (SJ). The size in terms of number of procedures, lines of assembly code and number of memory bytes are as follows.

Version	Number of Procedures	Number of Instructions	Number of Bytes
ATC1	157	4116	10365*
ATC2	308	10281	26284**
ATC2.1	313	10523	27029**
ATC2.2	339	11178	29522**

* Motorola 6800 microprocessors
** Motorola 68HC11 microprocessors

The small size, clear structure, and simplicity of the software solution have led to many advantages in respect to verification as well as further development and maintenance as described below. We should note that even the Ada programming language solution developed by Ansaldo subsidiary Union Switch and Signal in Pittsburgh, Pennsylvania is very compact by Ada standards as reported by Alan Swiss, one of the developers of this version.

5.1 Evolution of the Architectural Concepts

In 1975, Standard Radio contracted the consultant services of Harold Lawson to assist Roger Andersson, project leader, and Sivert Wallin, chief designer, in the conceptualization of the architecture. Following a review of the work done to date on the software, Harold Lawson and Sivert Wallin re-examined the fundamental requirements of the ATC function and developed the problem oriented architecture concepts that has successfully provided product stability as well as a sound basis for further development under the entire life cycle of the ATC onboard system product.

The following three core concepts were developed and have been driving factors during the product life cycle.

Time Driven: The major conceptual aspect of the design is the treatment of the system as being continuous in time as opposed to being discrete event driven. Motivation - Given the fact that a 250 millisecond resolution (dT) of the state of the train in respect to its environment was determined to be sufficient to maintain stability, it became clear that the simplest approach was to simply execute all relevant processes (procedures) during this period of time.

Software Circuit[1]: As a result of the time driven concept a cyclic time driven approach became the basis for the solution where short well-defined software procedures behave like circuits.

Black-Board Memory: In order for Software Circuits to have access to key information, variables are retained in a black-board where both reading and writing are permitted.

This simplification of concepts led to the fact that the processors only needed to be interrupted by two events. One interrupt to keep track of time (1 millisecond) and one interrupt when information from a transponder is available. The time in the 250ms *dT* is more than adequate to perform all processing. Adding more structure to the problem, for example, via the use of an event driven operating system approach would have had negative consequences in terms of complexity, cost as well as reliability and risk thus affecting safety. In 1975, Lawson documented the fundamentals of the approach [4]. Figure 3 illustrates the operating system.

The "circuit like" structure of software led to highly simplified coding of processes (procedures). While it would have been useful to deploy a higher-level language in the solution, we deemed it unnecessary due to the low volume of code that was expected. Experience has indicated that this was a reasonable decision at that time. On the other hand, we decided to comment the code in a higher-level language. In earlier versions of the product, we employed the Motorola MPL language, a PL/I derivative. In later versions, we consistently employed a more Pascal-like annotation. In system tests, MPL, respective Pascal versions where executed in parallel with the execution of the assembly language version in order to achieve system verification.

As the concepts evolved, the more global implications of the concepts became evident as documented in a comprehensive software plan [5].

> "A comprehensive plan for the specification, development, testing, verification, production and maintenance of the software components of the ATC project is presented. The goal is to produce reliable software parts to complement the three processor Motorola 6800 system so that a trustworthy total system is provided. A further goal is to assure that the software constituent remains reliable under the lifetime of the product. That is, that future modifications to the software will not affect the reliability due to oversights concerning design features and software component interrelationships."
>
> ...
>
> "The key to a successful software product lies in the ability to decompose the system to be implemented into well defined units such as processes, procedures, blocks, etc. Further, the operation, inputs, and outputs of these units must be well specified and the specification must serve as a control over the implementation, testing, production, and maintenance."
>
> ...
>
> "In the ATC project, the process is the unit to which the system structure has been decomposed. A process should be viewed as a testable component,

---

[1] The naming of this concept was developed later when the concepts of the architecture were applied in a Swedish research and development project for local area networks in vehicles [2] and [3]. In the later Ada programming language solutions they are called objects.

precisely as a hardware component (integrated circuit). It must have a clear specification and have a well defined component test procedures."

...

"A system can never be more reliable than its components and their interconnections. Assuming that each software component has been tested, the interconnections of subsystems of components and finally the total system must be developed, tested, and verified systematically."

Thus, it is clear that even at this early point in the product history conceptualization, we clearly identified the importance of architecture as a controlling factor for the life cycle of the product. Even though the owners of the product and development and maintenance has changed management, the fundamental concepts established in the mid-1970s are still in place and have led to a successful solution for train safety not only in Sweden, but in other countries.

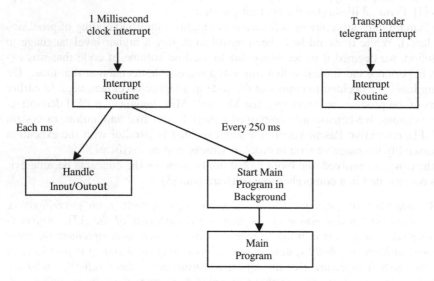

Fig. 3. Operating System Structure

5.2 Development and Maintenance Principles

The early development work was based upon using a PDP-15 computer both for simulation as well as for assembly language translation. The target system based upon Motorola 6800 processors was connected to the PDP-15 so that both procedure and system testing could be well controlled.

Due to the simplicity of the architecture, we discovered many advantages and principles that guided both development and maintenance. We established them as follows.

Utilize the clear points of built-in controls provided in the short procedures as an aid in the instrumentation of testing and in fault isolation.

As a general control of proper cycle execution, the stack pointer must be returned to the same point in each execution cycle.

By following code discipline, no wild loops can occur.

No backward jumps are permitted other than in well controlled loops in procedures.

By keeping the solution simple, quick reliable changes can be made and verified thus reducing costs.

The operating system core can easily be reused by removing procedures and incorporating new procedures for new functionality (recorder, simulator).

Following these principles has led both a reliable and stable onboard system product as well as a basis for the reuse of code.

5.3 Verification Perspective

We carried out verification via module testing, code inspection, and system test. Early verifications of ATC1 where carried out by the Foundation for Scientific and Industrial Research (in Norwegian: *Stiftelsen for industriell og teknisk forskning*, or SINTEF) at the Technical University in Trondheim, Norway. Bertil Friman was involved in verification of ATC2 as reported in [1]. The report describes the verification of the ATC2.2 version that is used for trains crossing the Öresunds Bridge.

5.3.1 Module Testing
Since the beginning of the ATC project, we tested the software circuit-like procedures of the ATC system by running them in parallel with equivalent software circuits written in a high-level language, and comparing the results. Back in 1975-76 when the original ATC was developed, we did this by connecting the target system (6800-based) directly to the bus of a minicomputer (PDP-15). We then ran the high-level version on a minicomputer that we also used to control the execution of the target system and to compare the results. The same principle, although more refined, is also in use today. The high-level version is now written in Pascal and runs on a PC computer. The PC computer has direct read/write access to the 64k byte memory space of the target system based upon 68HC11. This configuration makes it possible to test approximately 1000 value combinations per second. They can test two million combinations in roughly half an hour. If a software circuit has a small number of input variables, then they can test it exhaustively. If the number of input variables is large, then the value ranges are limited to values around min, max and close to the decision points in the code.

5.3.2 Code Inspection
Back in 1988, when they started the major revision of ATC that resulted in ATC2, they decided that because of the increased complexity of the program, it would be subject to a thorough and detailed inspection. They contracted Friman Datakonsult AB to do the inspection, which they mainly did by the use of informal proof techniques. They defined a goal, and then they built up an informal proof to see if they satisfied the goal.

They soon noticed that most goals were associated with variables and their contents. A (simplified) goal could for instance be that the variable HS (main signal speed) should always be zero after the passage of a stop signal transponder. Since most goals were associated with variables, the goal-proof-technique was successively replaced by a systematic analysis of individual variables. They did this analysis by tracing all places where a variable could be assigned a new value, and for each such place, finding out the real world conditions that were associated with the variable change. They could often check directly these real world conditions against sentences in the requirement specification.

Associating real world conditions to places in the code where a variable changes value requires an incremental analysis of variables. First variables that only depend on hardware inputs must be analyzed. Then variables that depend on these variables can be analyzed and so on. Sometimes two or more variables can be dependent on each other in a circular fashion. Analyzing such a loop requires more effort because they have to analyze all involved variables together. The variable based inspection method has been very successful both for ironing out special case errors and for enhancing the confidence in the ATC system.

Johan Fredrik Lindeberg and Øystein Skogstad at SINTEF in Norway encouraged at an early stage the development of CASE tools to support the code inspection. They developed several such tools. The most important was VTR (Variable TRacer) which is directly associated with the variable based inspection method.

5.3.3 System Testing
They did the bulk of the system testing of ATC with the use of a simulator. They tested the ATC system by simulating the train start-up and travel on the rails that are equipped with transponders. The simulator has handles, buttons and indicators that correspond to handles, and buttons and indicators in the locomotive cabin. They simulated the transponders with a file that contains their positions (from the starting point) and telegrams. They tested a new scenario (use case) by editing a track file and executing the new version on the simulator. After they changed a track file, they ran it on the simulator instantly. On some occasions, an interesting scenario has been discussed on the phone and at the same time been tested on the simulator. This was a superb trouble shooting mechanism. Many parties have contributed track files including Teknogram, ATSS, Banverket and Adtranz. Each track file is accompanied by a specification of how the ATC system shall react at each place on the route. ATSS has an archive containing hundreds of track files that can be used for the validation of new versions of the ATC system.

Quick cycle-time simulation has been a key ingredient in the ATC project since its beginning. The first simulator was a program that ran on the same PDP-15 mini computer that they used to assemble the code. It was directly, over the PDP-15-bus, connected to the development version of the ATC system. Today, the simulator uses a 68HC11 CPU with essentially the same operating system and program structure as the ATC program itself. They used a PC for storing the track files and for controlling the parameters of the simulation through the screen and keyboard.

6 Lessons Learned

We can learn several lessons from the Standard Radio ATC onboard system product experience. We could well apply these lessons in other products, particularly safety critical computer-based systems. Some of the most significant lessons are as follows.

6.1 Architecture Is a Key Aspect
The definition and consequent deployment of a problem relevant architecture is a key factor for success. While it is important to have well defined work processes for all

life cycle stages of a product, a good architecture reduces the need for heavy processes with multiple activities and tasks. One can simplify decision-making when we bound decisions by the architectural concepts as described by Lawson [11].

6.2   An Engineering Viewpoint Is Superior to a Software Viewpoint

Instead of creating significant quantities of software, an engineering view of the functions to be performed was taken. The analogy between hardware circuits and the logic of the software, later identified as software circuits provides a strong, simplifying solution. We can conclude that software, especially in large quantities, is dangerous, but we can control it with the proper engineering viewpoint.

6.3   Do Not Add More Structure Than Is Necessary

Adding more structure to a solution than necessary for achieving desired behaviors leads to unnecessary complexity that adds to costs and risks. This pitfall is very common, even for safety critical systems. Operating systems and programming languages that provide elaborate structures such as for interrupt handling and multitasking could complicate verification, further development, and especially maintenance. In addition, they can deploy complex methods and tools. All of these supporting methods and tools implicitly become a part of the product. Together they often are an overkill solution leading to increased cost and risk.

6.4   Verification Is a Vital Aspect of Safety Critical Systems

One must verify all safety critical systems with respect to their specifications and safe behavior in various situations. The combination of module testing, code inspection, and system test via simulation has proven to be an adequate approach for ATC. Simplicity in the architecture and code structure simplifies verification and contributes significantly to safety verification.

6.5   A Good Technical Solution Is Essential But Does Not In and Of Itself
Guarantee Safety

The technical solution is only one component of the total system. There are many other factors, including investment decisions, human factors, operation management, and so on, that can and have affected the utilization of the ATC safety system.

7   Train Control in Other Nordic Countries

The Swedish ATC computer-based solution was the first in the world. Norway was also quick to see the benefits of the Swedish ATC solution. Ericsson Signal originally provided the track-to-train transmission system solution in Norway, which was the same as in Sweden. Due to a perceived need to have one supplier, Ericsson Signal also delivered the onboard system solution based upon their product delivered for Stockholm's Local Traffic commuter trains. In the past few years however, due to problems arising in that onboard system now supplied by Bombardier, Norway is partially converting its onboard solution to the ATC2 system now supplied by Ansaldo.

Further, in later years Ansaldo has also installed their track to train transmission system product in parts of Norway.

In Finland in the mid-1990s, Bombardier delivered a modified version of the original Ericsson Signal track-to-train transmission system and the onboard system. As a coincidence, when Harold Lawson delivered his keynote speech at HINC2 in Turku, Finland, the day before there had been significant failures in this system and the local press interviewed him about ATC and its implementation.

Siemens supplied both infrastructure and onboard systems solutions for the Danish railways beginning in 1993. The Öresunds Bridge project led to a mixed solution for the new Öresund trains plus some X2000 train sets running between Sweden and Denmark. Since 2002, the first fully automatic (unmanned) trains in the Copenhagen underground where delivered by Ansaldo's subsidiary Union Switch and Signal of Pittsburgh, Pennsylvania. However, they did not base the solution utilized in this application upon the Swedish ATC system.

8   The Need for a Holistic System Perspective

As mentioned above, the technical product is only one part of the system. One must take a holistic systems engineering perspective to achieve the safety function to be provided in Automatic Train Control. These non-technical factors become evident by examining the following two accidents.

8.1   Borlänge, Sweden Accident

On 9 April 2000, six freight cars filled with Liquefied Petroleum Gas derailed and tipped over at 70 km/h in the Borlänge station. The speed limit in the area was 40 km/h. The authorities declared the station and central Borlänge off-limits to the public. As a result, 650 people evacuated for a week while they emptied the train of its contents.

The ATC braked the train three times in the 30 kilometers before the train crashed in Borlänge station. Unfortunately, the ATC infrastructure with balises does not cover the Borlänge station itself. They believe the driver had passed a restrictive optical signal just ahead of the turnout at which the train derailed. It turned out that the driver was drunk and tests showed that he had 1.0 per mille of alcohol in his blood.

Thus, ATC functioned exactly as it was programmed to behave. However, two non-technical factors were at work. Firstly, the earlier decision not to invest in placing ATC balises in the Borlänge station area. Secondly, the human factors aspect of a drunken train driver.

8.2   Aasta, Norway Accident

On January 4, 2000, nineteen people were killed and several more injured when an express train from Trondheim to Oslo carrying 83 passengers collided head-on with a local train carrying 17 passengers heading from Hamar to Rena about 150km North of Oslo.

The Norwegian National Rail Administration stated that the probable cause of the accident was the northbound train passing the main exit signal at Rudstad station while it was showing red. The trains were equipped with ATC, but the permanent infrastructure along this stretch of track on the Røros line was not equipped with this system. The *total* system was therefore not equipped with ATC.

Safe train control involves many aspects (technical and non-technical) including strategic planning, finance, resource allocation, human factors, management, administration, maintenance, training and education, catastrophe procedures, laws and regulations and more.

Thus, a holistic development and deployment of this critical train safety function involves the use of system thinking to build and analyze models for identifying and relating important multiple technical and non-technical aspects (problems and opportunities). This also relates to prudent decision-making in all aspects and the use of system engineering in respect to the life-cycle management of the system assets. Hence, the stakeholders must develop the capability to "think" and "act" in terms of systems as described by Lawson [11].

8.3 European Rail Traffic Management System

Many different train solutions have evolved in European countries starting in the 1800s resulting in incompatibilities, expensive maintenance, and traffic limitations. To improve upon this situation the European Rail Traffic Management System (ERTMS) standard sponsored by the European Union came into existence with the goal to achieve interoperability and more effectively develop and operate trains in Europe.

The European Train Control System (ETCS) is that part of ERTMS specifying control system standards for train to track communication and onboard system protocols. It also specifies the levels of equipment configurations including the use of radio communication. Six major suppliers both compete and cooperate to develop ERTMS and ETCS, namely Alstom, Alcatel, Ansaldo, Bombardier, Invensys and Siemens.

While these steps should help in treating more system related aspects, there is much, <u>much</u> more to do to achieve the holistic system safety perspective that is needed for this vital societal function.

9   Further Development of the Onboard System Concepts

The architectural concepts developed for ATC onboard system product is used in other projects in Sweden. During the early 1990s, Harold Lawson, the ATC architect, participated in the Swedish Nutek research funding agency sponsored Prometheus project for the automotive industry. They again proposed the engineering view of software as a means of developing the logic for safety critical functions in vehicles in the BASEMENT system [2 and 3]). A methodology based upon the use of "software circuits" evolved during this project.

The work on BASEMENT also led to the development, by Arcticus AB of an operating system concept called Rubus [12]. Rubus identifies the performance of two types of tasks: time driven (called Red) and event driven (called Blue). In relationship to the ATC solution, execution is carried out in time intervals (dT) where the Red tasks are always executed first and time remaining in dT is available for Blue task execution. They have successfully applied Rubus in developing several embedded system products including the Limited Slip Coupling device developed by Haldex Traction AB and now incorporated in all new Volkswagen automobiles as well as for medical equipment at Siemens-Elema AB. Arcticus has also produced supporting development tools and has utilized them by providing embedded systems solutions for Volvo Construction Equipment AB and for military vehicles produced by BAE Systems (Hägglunds).

Lawson reported [6 and 8] on the importance of architectural philosophy as a key to the engineering of computer-based systems. The articles cited ATC as one of the case studies in these articles. Lawson has reported on a further development related to ways of evolving the concepts into a complete resource adequate model called CY-CLONE [7]. Lawson together with Svensson further development of the CY-CLONE model for distributed and parallel execution [9].

10   Conclusions

The Automatic Train Control onboard system product developed by Standard Radio in the late 1970s has proven to be a highly successful product. It is based upon an engineering view of the problem domain that led to a straightforward architecture. The architectural concepts have been a key factor in relation to further development, maintenance, and verification of the product. The concepts used in this ATC product have been further developed in other real-time environments. Given the success of the approach, it is surprising that more safety critical systems were not constructed in a similar manner.

Acknowledgements

Several people have had important roles related to ATC and in particular the onboard system originally developed by Standard Radio. In this regard, the author gratefully acknowledges the contributions of the following people.

- o Sivert Wallin for his pioneering work at Standard Radio in developing the first onboard system. Founder and president of Teknogram AB, Hedemora, Sweden.
- o Bengt Sterner at SJ/Banverket for his vision of need for as well as the feasibility of providing ATC in Sweden.
- o Bengt Wenning at SJ for his vision on usability and ergonomics of ATC.
- o Johann F. Lindeberg and Øystein Skogstad of Norways Technical University for providing insights in the programming of ATC.
- o Berit Bryntse and others at Teknogram for their continued further development of the onboard system products.
- o Bertil Friman now employed at Ansaldo Sweden for his work in developing the verification strategy for ATC2.
- o Bertil Sjöbergh of Ansaldo Sweden for further development and marketing of ATC.
- o Denny Pascoe and Alan Swiss of Union Switch & Signal for providing information on the New Jersey Transit system and the Copenhagen underground.

References

[1] Friman, B.: Software Validation Inspection Report for Combined Danish-Swedish ATC System Version 2.2, Validation report, June 4 (1999) (ATSS Company Confidential)

[2] Hansson, H., Lawson, H.W., Strömberg, M., Larsson, S.: BASEMENT: A Distributed Real-Time Architecture for Vehicle Application, Real Time Systems. The International Journal of Time-Critical Computing Systems 11(3) (November 1996)

[3] Hansson, H., Lawson, H.W., Bridal, O., Eriksson, C., Larsson, S., Lön, H., Strömberg, M.: BASEMENT: An Architecture and Methodology for Distributed Automotive Real-Time Systems. IEEE Transactions on Computers 46(9) (September 1997)

[4] Lawson, H.W.: Recommendations for Software Organization and Execution Control for the MPU, Consultants Report to Standard Radio and Telefon AB, October 23 (1975)

[5] Lawson, H.W.: Preliminary Proposal for a Comprehensive Software Plan for ATC, Consultants Report to Standard Radio and Telefon AB, November 9 (1976)

[6] Lawson, H.W.: Philosophies for Engineering Computer-Based Systems. IEEE Computer 23(12), 52–63 (1990)

[7] Lawson, H.W.: CY-CLONE - An Approach to the Engineering of Resource Adequate Cyclic Real-Time Systems, Real Time Systems. The International Journal of Time-Critical Computing Systems 4(1) (February 1992)

[8] Lawson, H.W.: Engineering Predictable Real-Time Systems, appearing in Real Time Computing, October 1992. Lectures from a NATO Advanced Study Institute (1994)

[9] Lawson, H.W., Svensson, B.: An Architecture for Time-Critical Distributed/Parallel Processing. In: Proceedings of the EUROMICRO Workshop on Parallel and Distributed Processing. IEEE Computer Society Press, Los Alamitos (1993)

[10] Lawson, H.W., Wallin, S., Bryntse, B., Friman, B.: Twenty Years of Safe Train Control in Sweden. In: Proceedings of the Symposium on the Engineering of Com puter-Based Systems, Washington, DC (2000)

[11] Lawson, H.W.: A Journey Through the Systems Landscape. Version 8.0 – A book in preparation for publication (2007)

[12] Lundbäck, K.-L., Eriksson, C., Lawson, H.W.: A Real-Time Kernel Integrated with an Off-Line Scheduler. In: Proceedings of the 3rd IFAC/IFIP Workshop on Algorithms and Architectures for Real-Time Control, Ostend-Belgium (1995)

Appendix A

Historical Timeline

1973	Standard Radio decides to enter the train control market place Swedish State Railways (SJ) requests proposals on a transmission system
1974	Standard Radio, Philips, Ericsson Signal develop transmission solutions
1975	SJ selects the Ericsson Signal approach for the transmission system Standard Radio starts work on an onboard system concept SJ favors the Standard Radio onboard mechanical structure Work on the software architecture concept begins
1976	A problem related architecture evolves Guidance for development, production, testing, and maintenance
1977-79	Standard Radio selected for the onboard system for SJ trains Development, testing and verification Contract to Ericsson Signal for onboard system for SL trains only[1] Integration of transmission and onboard systems followed by validation
1980	Installation of ATC1 on SJ locomotives
1980-93	ATC1 operates successfully without any changes in software
1988-92	ATC2 plan: SJ, NSB[2], EB-Signal, Standard Radio-ATSS, Teknogram Further development based upon ATC1, testing, verification, validation
1993	Installation of ATC2
1995	Radio block solution introduced Linköping-Västervik line (ATC2.1)
1997-2000	Development and installation of Öresunds bridge system solution (ATC2.2)

1. SL – Stockholm's Local Traffic. Utilizes a different onboard solution based upon N-version programming. Different program solutions deployed and output results compared. This solution was inherited by Elektrisk Byrå AB, ABB Signal AB, Adtranz AB and finally Bombardier.
2. NSB - Norwegian State Railways

Computing and Computer Science in the Soviet Baltic Region

Enn Tyugu

Institute of Cybernetics of Tallinn University of Technology
tyugu@ieee.org

Abstract. This work includes references at events, people, and trends in computing in the three Baltic States: Latvia, Lithuania, and Estonia during their Soviet period. The Soviet computing science and practice could be divided into league A and league B. The first was for defense industry and power structures, the second for wide public. Although the Baltic computing belonged in essence to the league B, its scientific results were on the level with the league A.

Keywords: Baltic computing, computing history, Soviet computing.

1 Introduction

The title of the work sets the period of the subject – until fall of the Soviet Union, practically in the end of the 1980s. The geographical focus is on three Baltic republics: Latvia, Lithuania, Estonia, and to some extent on Leningrad as well. My personal experiences relate to Estonian computer engineering and science. Therefore, we will consider computing in this small country in more detail, including even some relations with Danish, Finnish, Norwegian, and Swedish computer scientists.

Computing in the Soviet Union was considered as a part of cybernetics – a "capitalist pseudoscience" in 1950s; hence, publicly was nonexistent although they used computers by physicists and space engineers. Nikita Khruschov in 1958 suddenly decided that the country urgently needed a larger number of computer engineers and mathematicians with computing skills for defense and space industry. Several hundreds young physicists, mathematicians and electronic engineers were reeducated in two years in Leningrad Technical University and Moscow Institute of Energy providing them as good education in computing as it was possible in those days. It may be interesting to look at the computer science curriculum of those days.

Below is the complete list of courses together with number of hours of supervised work – lectures and applications (taken from the course list of the author) given to the computer specialists in Moscow and Leningrad.

Ordinary differential equations – 90
Algebra – 90
Functions of a complex variable – 90
Probability theory and statistics – 105
Partial differential equations – 30
Numeric methods – 60

J. Impagliazzo, T. Järvi, and P. Paju (Eds.): HiNC 2, IFIP AICT 303, pp. 29–37, 2009.
© IFIP International Federation for Information Processing 2009

Programming – 55
Control theory and tracking systems – 204
Semiconductors and magnetic elements – 60
Electronic devices – 150
Theory of electric circuits – 60
Arithmetic and logic of computers – 45
Theory and design of analog computers – 90+180
Theory and design of digital computers – 108+206

The last two courses included many hours of practical work (180 and 206 respectively). One can notice the absence of logic and discrete mathematics, although the curriculum was rather mathematically oriented. In addition, they only offered a single rather short course in programming. The education was strongly oriented at hardware design and applied mathematics, because they knew little about programming. The term "software" did not exist yet.

2 First Years of Baltic Computing

Among the graduates of the classes given in Moscow and Leningrad were ten Estonians and even a larger number of Lithuanians who then returned to their countries. This was the first source of expertise in computing in the Soviet Baltic countries. Another input in this branch came from some enthusiastic mathematicians of Tartu University and Riga. At the end of the 1950s, Ülo Kaasik at the University of Tartu initiated mathematically oriented computer science education and its first graduates came in 1960. Leo Võhandu, who later moved to Tallinn Technical University, soon joined Ülo Kaasik in Tartu.

Lithuanian computing graduates from the Leningrad Technical University became the key players in a newly founded computer plant in Vilnius, and therefore they were not immediately visible in science. The computer plant, later known under the name "Sigma", became one of the major computing equipment producers for non-military computer systems. The Ruta 110 computer designed and produced in "Sigma" was widely used in the Soviet Union. There were two Lithuanian centers of computer science research – one in Vilnius and another in Kaunas. The leader of the center in Kaunas became Henrikas Pranevičius who graduated Kaunas Polytechnic Institute as a radio engineer in 1964. People know him for his works in formal methods and simulation applied to distributed systems. Albertas Caplinskas and Olegas Vasilecas worked in the field of knowledge-based software in Vilnius.

A *Latvian* young mathematician Janis Bardins from Riga was a graduate student of Boris Trakhtenbrot in Novosibirsk, a well-known expert in automata theory in the sixties. Barzdins became the leader of computer science in Latvia. Janis Barzdins obtained fundamental results in inductive inference, and later applied his experiences in inductive program synthesis. Besides these works, they did more research on the border of logic and computing at the University of Latvia. An active group of researcher in computer science grew around Janis Barzdins, including I. Etmane, R. Freivalds and others. Their research focused on logic and included various methods of synthesis of programs. Another research direction in the University of Latvia was automatic test case generation (Janis Bicevskis, Audris Kalnins, Juris Borzovs). Interesting research was carried out in the Riga Technical University in the field of fuzzy sets (Janis Osis had spent a year with Zadeh at Berkeley University) and system analysis by means of topological models.

Early *Estonian* computing was influenced by the fact that Institute of Cybernetics was founded in Tallinn in 1960, primarily by initiative of Nikolai Alumäe, who needed computers for his research in dynamics of thin shells (submarine hulls). This institute was the place where they built the first digital computer M-3 in Estonia in 1960. Its original design had come from Minsk, but they improved it significantly by adding a core memory instead of a much slower magnetic drum. This increased the performance of the computer considerably. The Institute of Cybernetics became a leading research center in computer science and computer applications in the Soviet Baltic region.

Fig. 1. STEM minicomputer in 1964

The first minicomputer called STEM, see Figure 1, was designed and built very early in Estonia – in years 1962 – 1964 at the Electrotechnical Research Institute in Tallinn. It had 16-bit words, small core memory, large ROM, and interactive input-output through electric typewriter. This computer was unusually reliable for those days. They used it in a technology department of Putilov factory in Leningrad and not in a computing center, because it did not require technical support around the clock that was then a common requirement. They used STEM in Putilov factory for engineering calculations during many years. More computers of this kind, but on different component base they built them for other large plants in the Soviet Union.

Fig. 2. The first analog computer built in Estonia

Neither the M-3 nor the STEM were the first computers built in Estonia. The very first was an analog computer designed and built in 1959 by electrical engineers of the Tallinn Technical University for the purpose of modeling and simulation of large power networks. This computer appears in Figure 2.

3   Computer Science in Estonia

Early research in computer science in Estonia was mainly in programming languages. This was language design and syntactic analysis. Malle Kotli developed a language called MALGOL (modular Algol) and it was widely used on popular Minsk computers. Mati Tombak became the leader of research in syntactic analysis, and he supervised a number of Ph.D. theses in this area. Success in syntactic approach inhibited deeper interest in semantics of computations for years. The situation changed in the end of the 1970s, when Merik Meriste and Jaan Penjam proposed new efficient methods of implementation of attribute semantics, and wider interest in automatic program construction appeared.

In the beginning of 1970s, Wilhelm Kracht introduced automata theory in his seminars to young scientists. Soon it gave output in the form of Ph.D. theses on decomposition of automata (Gabriel Jakobson, Andres Keevallik, Paul Leis). This research domain became practically widely recognized many years later, when fast computers and new challenges in chip design appeared. Many theses were written in the Institute of Cybernetics on the border between computer science, numeric methods and statistics. Leaders from the math side were Ivar Petersen and Sulev Ulm. A brief survey of research topics in 1970s and 1980s in Estonia is as follows.

o Research in databases (Ain Isotamm, Anne Villems, Enn Tyugu, Ahto Kalja, Hele-Mai Haav).
o Control theory and computer control (Ülle Kotta, Raul Tavast, Leo Mõtus).
o Systolic algorithms and FFT (Ilmar Arro, Toomas Plaks).
o Synthesis of programs (Enn Tõugu, Grigori Mints).
o Attribute grammars (Jaan Penjam, Merik Meriste).
o Expert systems and knowledge representation (Jaak Tepandi, Enn Tõugu, Mare Koit).
o Logic, in particular, proof theory, realizability, model checking (Grigori Mints, Tanel Tammet, Sergei Tupailo).
o Software environments (Boris Tamm, Jaan Pruuden, Mihail Matskin, Aleksander Shmundak).
o Test generation (Raimund Ubar).

4 Software Tools and Applications

On the software side, the first remarkable result was the development of a language and environment SAP-2 for numeric control of machine tools in Estonia in the beginning of the 1960s. The system SAP-2 was introduced in the Soviet aviation industry and gave a good position for its main developer Boris Tamm in the Soviet computing. Another group of researchers (Enn Tyugu et al) developed and applied in industry a modular programming environment SMP in the end of 1960s. This became a starting point for research in software engineering here, because SMP supported a well-defined software technology and documentation. This research direction was continued by development of structural synthesis of programs and its implementation in several software tools (PRIZ, MicroPRIZ, NUT). They used these tools in the development of CAD/CAM applications. The first engineering applications were optimization programs for machine tools such as cutting conditions and processing time for the Putilov plant in Leningrad in the 1960s. They developed larger applications for Elektrosila plant in Leningrad and rocket engines plant in Dnepropetrovsk in the 1970s. They also developed numerous applications in power semiconductor design and technology for Tallinn Electrotechnical plant in the 1980s under supervision of Valeri Grigorenko.

On the data processing side, there was an information system project for a large wholesale warehouse of Estonian Consumers Cooperative Society (ETKVL) that was completed already in the 1960s. The ETKVL administration well supported this project and it attracted good software developers due to strong working conditions and salaries; it became a success case of a large information system development in the Soviet Union. Another long-lasting and quite successful information technology project in Estonia was computer control of chemical processes in the oil shale chemistry, done by researchers of the Institute of Cybernetics and supervised by Raul Tavast in 1970s.

5 Computer Design Office

An important milestone of computing in Estonia was founding of the Computer Design Office (EKTA) of the Institute of Cybernetics in 1976. It had been a dream of Harry Tani, an outstanding computer engineer, who became the director of research of EKTA. Due to his personal contacts with German engineers as well as with researchers in the Soviet Union, EKTA got advanced microprocessors and printed circuits technology, and it evolved into a leading center in design and application of microprocessor systems in the Soviet Union. The Computer Design office designed and manufactured a small number of personal computers "Juku" for Estonian schools in 1988. It was a dream that success of this project would have the influence on education in Estonia comparable to the publication of bible in the native language in the eighteenth century. Unfortunately, manufacturing of these computers in larger numbers was impossible because of shortage of reliable components and devices like disk drives in the Soviet Union.

6   Computing in Leningrad

Leningrad had strong computer science and engineering education in many universities. However, paradoxically, not too many widely known results in computer science came out. Probably, the main reason was the confidentiality of many works performed in military institutions of this city. This kind of institution was, for example, a Construction Bureau-2 (KB-2) of Electronic Technology headed by Philip Staros (Alfred Sarant), who developed the lightweight computers for space, and it was the first to develop pocket calculators in the Eastern Block in seventies. Still, we remember a number of very interesting and pleasant people from Leningrad closely related to Estonia. Svjatoslav Lavrov and Viktor Varshawski were most supportive to young Estonian researchers. A special relation was between the Institute of Cybernetics and Leningrad Division of Mathematical Institute of the Soviet Academy of Sciences (LOMI). A strict constructivist logician Nikolai Shanin and his group had a strong influence on Estonian computer science. The members of this group Sergei Maslov (proof theory), Anatol Slisenko (recursion theory), Grigori Mints (proof theory), Yuri Matijasevich (algebra and logic) have all strongly influenced Estonian theoretical computer scientists. Grigori Mints worked as a researcher in the Institute of Cybernetics for ten years before taking a position of professor at Stanford University in the USA.

7   Western Contacts

Although Estonia was behind the iron curtain, the country had better scientific contacts with the West than most parts of the Soviet Union. There was a special agreement on scientific cooperation between the Soviet Union and Finland in the field of computer science. Estonian scientists mainly handled this without interference from Moscow, and beginning from 1988, it became an Estonian-Finnish agreement. Finnish scientists (Reino Kurki-Suonio, Markku Syrjänen, Hannu Jaakkola, Timo Järvi, Esko Ukkonen and many others) were frequent visitors to Estonia. Jaak Henno received a postdoc position with A. Salomaa's group in 1976; he worked on the complexity of multiplace functions and even published together with Salomaa. Good contacts were established with Denmark (Dines Björner) and Sweden (Bengt Nordström's group and Jan Smith in particular, Per Martin-Löf) in the 1980s. Eric Sandevall from Linköping sent a source code of Interlisp when it was a popular AI programming tool to the Institute of Cybernetics, and helped in this way the researchers in artificial intelligence to become a part of international AI community. Estonia became a meeting place of western and eastern computer scientists where they held numerous meetings because it was easily accessible from both sides, especially by ferry from Helsinki from the West.

8 Two Leagues of the Soviet Computing

Speaking about the computer science in the context of the Soviet Union, one has to bear in mind that it had been from the very beginning closely related to the Soviet power structures (defense industry and military people). This continued even later when usage of data processing became widely available. Due to shortage of resources, the computing industry and science could be divided roughly into league A that had better resources (including practically unlimited number of people in the research groups) and served the power structures, and league B that had shortage of resources, but more openness and some freedom of research. Attributes of league A were computers M-20, BESM-4, BESM-6 and later Elbrus. League B had the popular Minsk computers, and from the end of the 1970s, also Rjad (in Russian ES) computers that were copied from the IBM 360/370 mainframes. (Computers mattered in those days, because software was very much dependent on a hardware platform.)

Estonian computer science belonged to the league B, especially; there was no BESM computer in Estonia except in some military institutions that were completely closed to researchers. It seems now that this was a clever decision of the leaders of local institutes, in particular, of Boris Tamm and Nikolai Alumäe who were in the position of influencing the decision-making on high level. This gave more freedom in communication with West and more openness. However, already from the beginning of seventies, Estonian researchers established good contacts with the researchers from league A. This happened due to regular winter and summer schools organized in summer and winter resorts of Estonia jointly by universities and the Academy of Sciences with good programs and participation of research leaders of most of the league A groups. Finally, we started feeling like belonging to the league A, except that we did not have the right computers. Finally, they made a decision at the end of the 1970s that we should try to obtain a new Soviet supercomputer Elbrus-1. It happened that Elbrus-1 with serial number 10 was planned for delivery to the Institute of Cybernetics in 1979-1980. They also provided financing – almost 11 million rubles. Only the computer did not appear in time. It did not appear even a year later, and became operational only in 1987. Then we had already workstations that made simple arithmetic operations with short numbers faster than Elbrus-1 with its long words and very complex CPU.

9 The Start Project

START was a large computer hardware and software project in the Soviet Union in the 1980s where Estonian researchers actively participated. This project was initiated by researchers from Moscow (Viktor Brjabrin), Novosibirsk (Vadim Kotov and Aleksandr Narinyani) and Tallinn (Enn Tyugu) as a late response to the Japanese Fifth Generation Computer Project. There had been some attempts to establish a cooperative fifth generation computer project in the Eastern Block as a response to the respective Japanese project. These attempts were not successful, and this gave an opportunity for the researchers with good contacts to Guri Marchuk (the Chairman of the State Committee for Science and Technology and President of the Academy of Sciences) to propose the project START. Its intent was a completely open (non-secret) virtual research enterprise, contrary to several other similar Soviet projects. The aim of the initiators of the project was obviously to get better resources for testing their ideas in computer architecture (Vadim Kotov), software (Viktor Brjabrin) and artificial intelligence (Aleksandr Narinyani, Enn Tyugu). Due to the direct support from the president of the Soviet Academy of Sciences, the project enjoyed good resources. A special issue of the *Communications of the ACM* [1] described the outcome of the project START. About thirty persons participated in the project from the Estonian side. The main results in Tallinn were a workstation PIRS with a 32-bit processor KRONOS (processor developed in Novosibirsk), including software of the workstation (C compiler, UNIX installation, and a windowing system) and an intelligent programming environment Nut written in C. Later on, the Nut system appeared on many workstations and PCs; they used it for the simulation of large projects such as hydraulic systems and the radar coverage of Estonia.

10 Restructuring of the Research

The START project gave some resources to researchers in the end of eighties, when the international embargo on hardware and software was very restrictive. In addition, EKTA had its contacts with partners from West. This helped the research in computer science to survive until the end of the Soviet Union, when the situation changed abruptly. This is visible from the Figure 3 where one sees almost constant growth of the number of employees of Institute of Cybernetics and EKTA until the collapse of the Soviet Union [2]. The only disruption of the linear growth is from building up EKTA in 1976-1978.

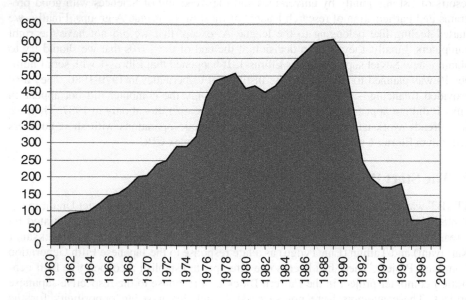

Fig. 3. Number of employees in the Institute of Cybernetics and EKTA

What happened later is another story. Briefly, the banks and other rapidly developing enterprises attracted clever people, and a number of researchers with good credentials left to other countries. EKTA became a small independent high-tech company; additionally, some other application-oriented groups of the institute had left. The institute has been incorporated in the Tallinn University of Technology, and it continues with almost constant number of employees, including some very bright young researchers, as a typical Western research center now.

References

[1] Communications of the ACM 34(6), 46–59 (1991)
[2] Institute of Cybernetics in changing times (In Estonian: Küberneetika Instituut muutuvas ajas) Institute of Cybernetics, Tallinn (2000) ISBN 9985-894-25-1

What Do IT-People Know about the Nordic History of Computers and User Interfaces?

A Preliminary Survey

Anker Helms Jørgensen

IT University of Copenhagen, DK-2300 Copenhagen S Denmark
anker@itu.dk

Abstract. This paper reports a preliminary, empirical exploration of what IT-people know about the history of computers and user interfaces. The principal motivation for the study is that the younger generations such as students in IT seem to know very little about these topics. The study employed a free association method administered as email. Eight students and four researchers participated, between 26-34 and 48-64 years of age, respectively. Responses totaled 222 and we analyzed and categorized them. First, the Nordic touch was extremely limited. Secondly, the knowledge of both students and researchers seems heavily based on personal experience so that the researchers know much more about the earlier days of computing and interfaces. Thirdly, there is a tendency amongst the students to conceptualize the history of *computers* in *interface* features and concepts. Hence, the interface seems to become the designation or even the icon for the computer. In other words, one of the key focal points in the area of human-computer interaction: to make the *computer* as such *invisible* seems to have been successful.

Keywords: User interface history, computer history, knowledge.

1   Exploring User Interface History

In the last years, I have become interested in the history of user interfaces to computers [4, 5]. My motivation is primarily the scarcity of the literature on this topic and a strong impression that young IT-people know very little about the history of user interfaces – and apparently also about the history of computers. They seem to believe that the PC was the first computer and that Windows was the first user interface. My exploration of the history of user interfaces is fascinating, and being a newcomer with a background in computer science and human-computer interaction (HCI), I have to adopt historians' practices and discourses [3].

The target audience for my research in user interface history consists of three main segments: historians of technology, researchers in IT and HCI, and students of IT and HCI. In accordance with good practice in HCI – know thy user – I would like to know more about the target audience. Getting to know the historians' practice and discourse

J. Impagliazzo, T. Järvi, and P. Paju (Eds.): HiNC 2, IFIP AICT 303, pp. 38–44, 2009.
© IFIP International Federation for Information Processing 2009

takes place through networking and studies of the literature. I do know IT-researchers and IT-students quite well in general, but my understanding of their knowledge of the history of computers and interfaces is rudimentary. Therefore, I conducted an exploratory survey of what the two groups know about these topics. This will help me sharpen my research questions and communicate my results more succinctly.

2 Probing Researchers' and Students' Knowledge

Given the nature of this unchartered territory, I included the broader history of computers in order to contextualize the interface issue. As computing is an international phenomenon I decided only to address the Nordic touch implicitly. I employed an open-ended data collection method: free associations. In addition, I recruited informants in my immediate vicinity. The researchers were four colleagues: two university researchers and two from industry with considerable research experience. They were all computer scientists and knowledgeable or experts in HCI, between 48 and 64 years of age. I recruited the students among the ones I supervised at the master level at the IT University in the fall of 2006. I asked fourteen students and received eight answers. Their median study time at the IT University was 1.5 years. They all had a baccalaureate degree in various areas, including media technology, IT-studies, and Danish. Their age varied between 26 and 34 years. The specific wording of the free association task was as follows.

> *Please complete a brief, free association task on the following question:*
> *When I say the history of computers, what do you say?*
> *Write down 5-10 points, names, events, systems, paradigms, etc.*

There was a similar question on the interface. I administered the survey by email. The respondents returned 222 answers, on average 28 for the researchers and 14 for the students, about equally distributed between computer and interface history. The respondents spent between 10-15 minutes and one hour in responding. One respondent in each group returned a 1-page essay, while the remaining respondents returned a list of words or short statements. The lengthy responses were condensed. I categorized all answers twice, with several weeks between to achieve some robustness (inter-rater reliability over time), in categories derived from the data that reflect major historical aspects. The Appendix lists all the responses in abbreviated form, enabling the reader to get an impression of the breadth and diversity of the material.

3 What Do They Know?

A summary of the results appears in Table 1. In the following, I present and discuss the three most noteworthy trends.

The numbers are absolute because of the almost equal number of responses in the four groups. Note that I scored the two last rows independently of the rows above.

Table 1. Responses in categories listed alphabetically, blank cells denote no response

	The History of the Computer		The History of the User Interface	
Category	Researchers	Students	Researchers	Students
Applications	3		3	1
Games		3		
Evolution	6	7	3	3
Internet	1	3	1	2
Miscellaneous	4	1	2	1
Organizations	1	5		1
Personal computer	5	18	2	1
Pioneers	6	1	3	1
Research			7	
Society	2	2		
Software	8	3		6
Technology	11	5	4	2
Use & User	3	1	6	2
User Interface	4	11	27	30
Total	*54*	*60*	*58*	*50*
Nordic		2	1	1
Pre-pc	36	7	23	9

Firstly, the *Nordic touch* is modest, in fact only four responses out of 222 (1.8%), as seen in the second-to-last row. The responses were:

o The Danish PC Piccoline manufactured by Regnecentralen from 1984 to 1989
o The Danish Computer Fair in Copenhagen
o A user interface development method by the Danish researcher Søren Lauesen
o Jakob Nielsen's alertbox at www.useit.com

These examples do not lend support to a strong Nordic anchoring as the Computer Fair was probably much like computer fairs in other countries and Jakob Nielsen is indeed Danish but has been living in the United States for several decades[1]. The limited Nordic touch is in line with the decline of the Nordic IT industry in the last decades. Thus, in Denmark, the best-known IT-company Regnecentralen closed in 1992 after two decades of organizational and financial turbulence [6]. Hence, it seems that knowledge of computer and user interface history is strongly internationally grounded.

Secondly, there is a marked difference in the responses in the two groups regarding the *user interface*. Consider first the following student response: Machintosh[2], Xerox Parc, GUI, Window metaphor, Desktop metaphor, Microsoft, DOS. Note that the first five of these seven items are canonical user interface concepts. Is this a response to the history of *computers* or to the history of *user interfaces*? It is the former, in fact. This student was extreme, but student responses on user interfaces to the question on

---

[1] In fact, students often ask me if he is Danish or American.
[2] Spelling error in original response.

computer history were much more frequent than researcher responses (11 versus 4). Hence, students seem to associate computer history much more strongly to the user interface than researchers. This trend is in line with a recent terminological shift towards use of the term user interface at the expense of the term computer. An example from a recent Ph.D. thesis is, "We become part of the interface or rather we bring the interface with us everywhere, we create practices around the interface" [1, p. 88]. Contrasting this, it is interesting to note that the students have far fewer answers in the category use and user (3 versus 9), perhaps because students are brought up with computers and therefore consider user-trouble an inherent and inevitable part of the game?

Thirdly, there is a very marked difference between the researchers and the students regarding the emphasis on *personal computers* in the history of computers. Here the students' responses are almost four times more frequent than the researchers' (18 versus 5). This trend is supported by looking at pre-PC responses in the bottom row. Only 7 and 9 of the students' responses are pre-PC, while the corresponding figures for the researchers are 36 and 23. Hence, there is strong evidence that the students seem to associate computer history with the PC era. Given that in the last two decades or so with client-server architecture, access to mainframe computers happens through PCs and not through "dumb" terminals, it is not surprising that students have little clues about large computers, let alone about their origin. Nevertheless, modern computer users are using more computers and more powerful computers than ever before. Surfing on the internet means using myriads of small and large computers, networks, and protocols – yet the computers are largely invisible. The interface appears to connect the user to other users and the vast amount of information and services. The technology itself has become hidden while the interface has come to the fore [4]. Hence, one of the key focal points in the area of human-computer interaction: to make *invisible* the *computer as such* seems to come closer to realization.

4 Conclusion

First, the Nordic touch was extremely limited as only four of 222 responses addressed the Nordic aspects. Secondly, the knowledge of both students and researchers seems heavily based on personal experience so that the researchers know much more about the earlier days of computing and interfaces. Hence, this study suggests that historical knowledge on computers and user interfaces is relative and associated with generation-specific personal experiences. Thirdly, there is a tendency amongst the students to conceptualize the history of computers in interface features and concepts. Hence, the interface seems to become the designation or even icon for the computer. We should interpret these conclusions with considerable caution due to the very small sample of IT-people recruited in my work context and the open-ended data collection method. The study is an indication of the lie of the land and may serve as a point of departure for future work.

After the study, an interesting twist emerged. It turned out that three of the four researchers did not know about the changing meaning of the term *computer* in the 1940s—from denoting a *person* doing calculations manually to denoting a *digital calculation device* [2] nor did several of them know that many of the first programmers were *women*. Indeed, this is a strong illustration of the above-mentioned generation-specific and experience-based knowledge of computer and user interface history.

References

[1] Christensen, M.S.: As We May Feel - Interpreting the Culture of Emerging Personal Affective Mobile Media. Ph.D. Thesis, IT University of Copenhagen (2006)

[2] Grier, D.A.: When computers were human. Princeton University Press, Princeton (2005)

[3] Jørgensen, A.H.: Exploring the History of User Interfaces: The Myth of Xerox Parc and Other Oddities. In: Proc. 6th Danish HCI Research Symposium, Aarhus, November 15, pp. 29–30 (2006)

[4] Jørgensen, A.H., Udsen, L.E.: From calculation to culture – A brief history of the computer as interface. In: Jensen, K.B. (ed.) Interface://Culture – the World Wide Web as a political resource and aesthetic form, Samfundslitteratur, pp. 39–64 (2005)

[5] Jørgensen, A.H., Myers, B.A.: User Interface History. In: Proc. CHI 2008 extended abstracts on Human factors in computing systems, pp. 2415–2418. ACM, New York (2008)

[6] Thorhauge, C.: Tidslinie over RC's historie [Timeline on the History of RC]. In: Isaksson, H., Pedersen, O. (eds.) Regnecentralen – Dansk Institut for Matematikmaskiner, Festskrift ved 50 året for oprettelsen, 12. oktober 1955. Dansk Datahistorisk Forening (2005)

Appendix

The 222 responses appear below in alphabetical order. They are organized according to Computer History Researchers, Computer History Students, Interface History Researchers, and Interface History Students. The original responses have been condensed in many cases while preserving the gist of the response.

Computer History
Researchers

2. 3. 4. and 5. generation
 programming languages
administrative systems
Alan Turing
Alan Turing
Alan Turing
Apple II
Basic
Citizens required to use IT
Compilers for high-level
 languages
DOS
Edsac/Eniac
Eniac
ferrite core
few and privilied users to
 everyone everywhere
Fortran
Hopeless operational
 procedures in embedded
 software, eg in DVD
 players
Hype and sales talk
IBM
IBM 3270
IBM pc
IBM/360
IBM OS/360
IBMs waterfall model
Internet
John von Neuman
John von Neuman
levels in systems and
 architectures
Macintosh
mainframe – mini – micro
 computers
mainframes
mainframes
microcomputers
Microsoft overtook IBM on
 the pc market
minicomputers
numerical calculations
operating systems
pc
pc
pc/Mac
pc-revolution
PDAs
process control
punched cards
punched cards
smaller and smaller

specialist to routine tasks
 for ordinary users
superstition and
 incompetent support
system development
the computer: an everyday
 appliance
ubiquitous comp.
Univac
user trouble
vacuum tubes to transistors
Vannevar Bush

Computer History Students

Alan Kay
Amiga 500
Apple
Arpanet
Atari, Commodore 64
Commodore 64 game
 console
Commodore 64 games
Commodore 64
 programming
Commodore 64 tv and
 casette tape
Computer Fair in Bella
 Center
Computer technology: IO
 to silicone chips etc.
Desktop-metaphor
Diskette development from
 8" til 3.5" to CD etc
Displays: from large and
 clumsy to flat, less bulky
DOS
DOS: this weird,
 impoverished place
Ethernet
Game consoles: Amiga,
 Sega, Nintendo
GUI
HTML – opened up with
 Flash etc – had not
 happened since LEGO
IBM
IBM
IBM
Internet – the computer
 becomes much more
 interesting
large computers
Machintosh
Macintosh: the first that my
 dad had in his office

matrix printer
Microsoft
Microsoft Bill Gates
miniaturization:
 mainframe, PC, PDA,
 portable, desktop
 computer etc.
miniaturize one computer
 for many users – one
 computer for one user
my first portable: an IBM
 Thinkpad
one user uses many
 computers: portable,
 PDA, cell phone, ...
operating systems like
 OS/2 and Windows'
pc
pc 286
pc 386
pc 486
pc 486 Windows 3.1
pc AT
pc IBM PC my mom used
 WordPerfect
pc Pentium
pc Pentium 2/3/4
pc XT
Piccoline
portable – a cool invention
portable in backpack, as
 you go
printer development:
 Matrix/9-24 til ink/laser
 printers
punch cards
the computer invented in
 the USA, applied in the
 military
the first computer was as
 large as a room
the first computers were as
 large as a room
the desktop computer becoming prevalent in a few
 years
time sharing
Unix
window metaphor
Xerox
Xerox PARC
Xerox PARC

User Interface History
Researchers

"terminal"
3-D animation
Adobe
Alan Kay
Apple II
Ben Shneiderman
CHI conferences,
  especially in 1984
Command dialogue
Command doialogue still
  thrives in Linux
Control panels with
  switches by the hundred
Convergence between
  word-processing and
  desk-top publishing
CUA standard
Direct Manipulation
Displays
Displays
Donald Norman
Donals Norman's book
  Psychology of Everyday
  Things
DOS on the microcomputer
Function keys in
  WordPerfect & Word
Gould & Lewis paper in
  Comm. ACM 1985
  "Designing for
  Usability…"
Graphics in process control
  applications
GUI
GUI
homepages still only made
  by freaks
HTML metafor differs
  from GUI metafor
IBM 3270
IBM 3270
Internettet
Jakob Nielsen's Alertbox
Jef Raskin's Apple II user
  manuals
Jef Raskin's work on the
  Macintosh
John Seeley Brown's
  keynote at CHI '83
Macintosh
Microsoft's Office-suite
Online access, not only
  specialists
Patricia Wright's FLUID
  model
Punch card/tape as input,
  print/batch as output
punch tape

scripts – a kind of
  command language
switches
teletype
teletypes
the Mouse
the mouse
the mouse
the user as factor
thinking aloud test
typewriter
user frustrations
walk-up-and-use need
web not applicable to GUI
  interfaces, but is being
  used anyway
websites: surf to another if
  it doesn't work
wide application of home
  computers because of the
  graphical user interface
WIMP: Windows, Icons,
  Menus and Pointing
  Devices
Windows, especially
  Windows'95
WYSIWYG: What You
  See Is What You Get
Xerox PARC
Xerox Star

User Interface History
Students

Accessibility
Apple
Apple II
Browsers: Netscape,
  Explorer
Cognitive load
Colour displays
Command dialogue to
  graphics
Desktop metaphor
Desktop metaphor
DOS
DOS
Double click: learning
  problems
Douglas Engelbart: As We
  ..
Graphics vs. codes, easier
  for ordinary users
GUI and not UI
HTML: decide appearance
  yourself

IBM PC used by my mom,
  blue-white, cursor block
Iconic user interfaces
Icons
Intuition: my two-year old
  nephew could swith
  Windows XP on and off
Joystick, not keyboard on
  C64 game console
LINUX
LINUX: various Linux
  distros
Macintosh
Microsoft
Microsoft made the use of
  computers increase –
  early 1980s
Mobile devices
Operating systems
OS X
Piccoline – graphic
  interface
Software on mobile devices
Text-based – DOS
  Piccolone
Text-based interaction
User Interface & usability
  focus today vs. 1980s
User Interface term -
  invented by tech people –
  hard, interface better
User Interface: engineering
  paradigm – before the
  human aspect
Virtual Windows by Søren
  Lauesen
WIMP: Windows, Icons,
  Menus, Pointing devices
Windows 2000
Windows 3.1 lack of
  consistency
Windows 3.11
Windows 95
Windows 98
Windows ME
Windows various versions
Windows various versions
Windows XP
Word
WordPerfect's commands
WWW

Increasing the Museum Value of Information Technology Objects

The Case of the Finnish Data Processing Museum Association

Emmi Tittonen

University of Jyväskylä
emtitton@jyu.fi

Abstract. In this article, we define the basic concepts of museum work, museum value, and contextual information with the help of a case study and literature. We base the case study on the empirical material of a project that aimed to gather knowledge of the collections of the Finnish Data Processing Museum Association. This article opens up the concepts and analyzes them in the context of museum work and information technology objects.

Keywords: Case study, Computer, Finland, Museology, Museum.

1 Introduction

Picture a big pink "tower" with black leather "benches" at its bottom, the Cray 1S supercomputer, standing in a computer exhibition.[1] By its side is the IBM Ramac 305: a big grey "box" with a "table". It is not easy to comprehend that both of these are computers. Looking at the Cray, a visitor gets little information. The poster by its side mentions the technical specifications. The case is better with the Ramac: a visitor can find some notions of where they used it and when. However, what does this tell to the visitor? To a person who does not know the history of IT, the available information does not tell anything. Only a guided tour held by an expert opens up the stories of the machines and the meaning they have on the history of IT and to the society in general.

I worked to increase the museum value and contextual information of the collections of the Finnish Data Processing Museum Association (Suomen Tietojenkäsittelymuseoyhdistys ry.) from autumn 2006 to the end of 2007. Two grants from the Ministry of Transport and Communications of Finland funded the project. The museum association is located in Jyväskylä, Central Finland, and it preserves and exhibits objects of IT. The association has about 250 objects of IT and related material in their collections and they work on converting old formats into contemporary formats, for example from punch cards to 3,5" floppy disks. [5]

---

[1] The Finnish Data Processing Museum Association has two permanent exhibitions in Jyväskylä, Central Finland. They are located on the premises of Jyväskylä University, the Agora building and on the premises of the Jyväskylä University of Applied Sciences, the IT-Dynamo building. [5]

J. Impagliazzo, T. Järvi, and P. Paju (Eds.): HiNC 2, IFIP AICT 303, pp. 45–54, 2009.
© IFIP International Federation for Information Processing 2009

The documentation project occurred in co-operation with Jyväskylä University Museum's Section of Cultural History. The project aimed to gather knowledge of 11 computers. With the help of this information, the museum association will improve their exhibitions, increase the general knowledge of their collections, and develop the listing of their collections. In this article, I present the museum association as a case study on how and why museological principles are important in IT museum work. Finally, in the epilogue I will tell the "real" stories of the IBM Ramac 305 and the Cray 1S.

2   The Museological Approach of the Project

2.1   The Museum Association's Story So Far

The beginning of the museum association is in a collection of computers of Mr. Ilari Taulio, a retired IBM maintenance engineer, who started the collection over thirty years ago. During the 1970s, he started to collect old computers, for example, from his employers and different institutions [9, 18]. During the 1980s, Mr. Taulio rented storages for the collection and called a committee to work on establishing a computer museum in Jyväskylä (1987). The committee had representatives from the Finnish State Computer Center, Jyväskylä University, and the Museum of Central Finland. The aim of the committee was to increase the collection and to exhibit the computers to the public. They also aimed to enhance the study of the history of IT by enabling researchers to have old computers at their disposal. Until the museum association was established in 1995, the museum committee tried to lay the foundation of computer museum work in Finland. The city of Jyväskylä, among others, supported the committee with monetary help on storage rents every year [1, 9, 18].

Since its establishment, the museum association has been working on the same goal of creating a national computer museum, as well as increasing and managing the collections. An essential part of their work has also been exhibiting computers to the public around Finland in various events and sites [5, 9, 18]. The work of the association is based on voluntary work of its members. The association also aims to preserve contemporary computers.[2]   During its existence, various institutes have donated money to help the association continue their work. They established the two permanent exhibitions at the beginning of the 2000s [5, 9, 18]. These present the history of IT in a context of change: a visitor can see how computers and components have changed in the course of time.

The beginning of the project lies in the events that took place in 2006. In the beginning of 2006, the city of Jyväskylä announced that it would not continue its monetary support to the association [6, 7]. From that day forward, the museum association was hanging on a thread. The situation was especially grim in April 2007: the association was served a notice of termination of rent agreement. The collections were facing the destiny of demolition when there was no money or no storages. Fortunately, with the help of the University of Jyväskylä, the collection was saved. The University of

---

[2] One part of the museum work is the documentation of the present. A voluntary association in Sweden SAMDOK (Samtids Dokumentation) created the basis of international contemporary documentation in the 1970's. Documenting the present brings today's culture closer. It also makes it possible to use more efficient methods in documentation [8, 12, 35].

Jyväskylä helped the association to rent a new, smaller storage space (250 m²). This meant that the collections had to be screened, but on which basis? Fortunately, the documentation project was already in progress and they used the preliminary results to help the screening. With less space, they reduced the collections from about 600 to about 250 items during the move in June 2007. Now the association can continue their work, since they have got further funding from several sources to maintain the new storages and develop further projects [5].

2.2 Museum Value and the Collections of the Museum Association

When we started to plan the project, the museum association had compiled a list of their "most valuable computers". The list consists of major developments from the history of IT: from punched-card machines to personal computers. It is their perspective on what are the most valuable computers in their collections. It was also the first step in valuing the collection.³ In museums, valuing means the evaluation of material and mental value of the objects. They can base the value of an object on aesthetic, intellectual, or sentimental basis [24]. The list also defined the basis of the diminished collection when we decided to build the new collection around it.

To the documentation project, I chose eleven computers or mainframes from the list. They include:

o Wegematic 1000 (University of Helsinki the 1960s; Jyväskylä technical Institution 1965–1986);
o Elliot 803 A, (Helsinki University of Technology the 1960s);
o IBM 1620 (Valmet Jyväskylä or Summa paper mill the 1960s);
o EAI Analogue Computer model 640/680 (Technical research Centre of Finland the 1960s / the 1970's);
o IBM punched-card machines: from card punch to tabulator etc. (various);
o IBM Ramac 305 (OTK the 1960s);
o MIR-2 (Helsinki University of Technology the 1970s / the 1980s);
o Cray 1S (CSC 1990's);
o Zuse Z23 (Maansähkö Oy 1962–1970; Riihimäki technical institution, 1970–);
o Digital Inc.'s PDP computers: especially PDP-11 and PDP-15 (various);
o Spear Inc.'s µ-Linc a.k.a. Mikro-Linc (University of Helsinki 1966–1978).

So what does the concept of museum value have to do with computers? Museology is a discipline that has been a part of museum work since the 18th century. As a theoretical discipline, it has been evolving all the time. It deals with the daily functions of museums and related "memory" organizations, as well as the theoretical aspects of all museum work. It is theoretically divided into two approaches. Museography or applied museology asks "how"; for example, which are the best-used practices of museum work. On the other hand, theoretical museology asks "why": for example, why we maintain museums. The (museum) object is a part of museological work and the methodology is based on the information value of the objects [16, 21].

---

³ The original list of "the most valuable computers" contains also these: Almex Optical Reader, IBM Mainframes (System 3 and 7, 3032), Data General Nova, SM-4 (CM-4; Soviet PDP-11 clone), PC and minicomputers (e.g. IBM, Nokia, HP) [1, 2].

From the beginning, the concepts museum value and context were the guidelines of the project. Museum value is a resource for managing the collections as well as a resource for defining the value of an object or the collections as a whole. Peter van Mensch, a Dutch museologist, has defined the concepts through a theory of life of a museum object [21]. They base the theory on the concept of an object's lifespan. The lifespan includes the original value of the object and the changes in its value during time. The information value of the object can diminish, disappear, or rise. In museology, museum objects are seen as objects that are separated from their original context and given a new context by moving them into a museum. The context changes also if an object is preserved as a museum object in its place in the environment. In a museum, the object is a representative of its original context and a resource for museum work. [21, 32]

As primary documents, museum objects are seen as direct witnesses of cultural and natural phenomena. We can also see the phenomena indirectly through secondary documentation such as literature and archival material. The secondary documents are not always seen as a part of museum work, even among museologists. [21] Archival material and literature are vital sources in historical research, but in museological research the object tells the information through its story. In my opinion, by combining these two disciplines' methods, we may complete the stories of the objects and the information value rises.

We define the museum value of an object mainly by its information; but in art museums, they also define the value by aesthetic values. Sometimes even other museums value their objects on aesthetic basis. This means that a museum might choose to save a presentable object. We also discussed aesthetic values when we started to define the salvageable computers: whether to take a computer which was presentable or which had a story to tell. In the end, we chose to emphasize the story of the machines.

We base the contextual information of an object on its lifespan. According to van Mensch's theory, the information value has three levels: The structural identity of the object contains the physical properties of the object. This means how it is built. Functional identity contains the functional properties and the significance of the object and its use. This means why they used a computer in a specific way. The contextual identity contains the object's relationship to its context. This means the relationship between the object and its environment: how the users of a computer reacted to it. [21, also 32]

This model is completed with the historical process that results in the final information value of the object [21]. This means the life history of the object and its effect on the information value. The final value is the basis on which we build our understanding of the past. The lifespan and the process of information are based on three stages of context. The conceptual identity means the beginning of an object's life: the idea that started its process of making. [21, 23, 32] This means the invention of a computer, for example, the idea that started the process of making the Wegematic 1000. The factual identity means all the characteristics of the object as it was intended and not-intended by the maker. It means the finished object with regard to its structure, function, and idea. [21, 32] The factual identity of the Wegematic is the finished product after the assembly line. The actual identity of an object is the result of its life [21, 32]. This means the story of the Wegematic to this day with all the marks its life has left on it: who made it, what it is, who used it and why, etc. Finally, it tells us the story of how it became a museum object.[4]

This way the museum value of an object is based on its information. We see the object as a data carrier: it carries all the information its life left on it [21]. This means that we see the information hidden in the lifespan of the object and that it can be found through research. The object might have changed during its life in its functions and appearance. In museology, we consider these changes through the object's identity: is it still the same as its inventor meant? The context varies in an object's lifespan, and again when the object is "muzealised". The primary context of the object is the initial context in which it functioned. We achieve the secondary context when the object has a documentary value: usually this means that the object has become a museum object. [21]

The information value changes for the last time when an object becomes a museum object. It gains a new context, a museological one. In a museum, we introduce the object to a new environment that changes its identity. As a document of the past, the object is a source of knowledge. It also becomes a witness or a testimony of the past. Unfortunately, the muzealisation of an object affects its data. The information levels are damaged through the acquisition process and preservation. In the end, the documentary value of the object determines the place of the object, whether or not it belongs to a museum. [21]

3 Ways to Increase the Museum Value of Information Technology Objects

During the 30 years of their existence, the museum association had hardly written down the life stories of the computers. Furthermore, they had written few donation forms of the studied computers. Although the catalogues were insufficient from a museological point of view, the museum association worked regularly in order to improve this situation. Catalogues are vital in regard to the museum value and the justification of an object's belonging to a museum. Proper cataloguing enhances the museum value of the collection as a whole, as well as enables researchers to distinguish scientific knowledge from non-scientific. Even one properly catalogued object enhances the museum value of a collection as a whole, instead of hundreds of insufficiently catalogued objects [33, 34, 35].

The documentary value of the objects was hidden in the lifespan. My work started with an investigation. First I had to figure out who had donated the computers and when using information provided by the members of the association. Concerning the lifespan, I had to begin from the muzealisation. After figuring out the story so far, I started to look for information on who had used these computers and where. I interviewed thirty-seven people and gathered archival material in order to collect the stories of the computers.

---

[4] The Wegematic 1000 came to the University of Helsinki in 1960 as a donation from the Swedish Wenner-Gren Institute. It became operational in 1961. In 1965, the computer was moved to be used at Jyväskylä Technical School. It was never used in Jyväskylä, because they could not make it work. It was donated to the museum association in 1986 [1, 2]. See also [14, 15, 30].

Interviewing is one of the most important methods of gathering contextual information. Memories tell a different story than facts do. Every person has individual experiences on how to use or program a computer, what difficulties they had while using it and what the world of computers felt like. Through interviews, we see the human experience. In museological context, the experiences of the users are vital to the museum value: they vitalize the object. Every object should have a story that tells to its viewer what it felt like to use it, touch it or look at it. Through the interviews I gathered first-hand and second-hand information of the computers. The second-hand information is important because the human experience can be used as an example of another similar object.

But what about the success of this project? All the information I gathered gave something new to the computers and to the history of Finnish IT. A few of the computers gained contextual information. Unfortunately, some computers (which should be the evidence of information technology) seem to stay uninformative. For a thorough investigation, the computers should be studied one by one. However, on the other hand, the project improved the knowledge and the museum value of the collections as a whole. Along the project, I helped the museum association to move and select the computers that were to be saved. I represented the museological expertise, and gave advice on what to consider as the basis of the selection: museum value of the objects. During this, the outlines of "the collection policy" were also created: the basis of the decision what computers to preserve. With it the association will be able to advance the collection they already have.

We improved the contextual knowledge of the machines with the interviews and the archival material. The information tells about the values and the conceptions of the past society and the culture. Combined with the human experience the facts tell the whole story of how and why the computers were used. Via these stories, we can begin to understand the impact computers had on our society. Although the gathered information was not very informative in the case of some computers, they all justified their place in the collections. This way "the list of the most valuable" is not the only justification. By being some of the oldest and most important computers in Finnish IT history, the justification is valid.

In the end, it is difficult to determine to whom this kind of collecting and documenting belongs. According to Finnish laws, there is only one very general ordinance about what museums must preserve: prehistoric or historic monuments (immovable artifacts) and movable artifacts and protected dead animals [4]. Museum workers have to decide themselves on what other material to preserve. There isn't any ordinance to save old computers. The museum association has done their work voluntarily with the help of professional museums. The members have decided on their own what computers or related material they collect. With a collection of this magnitude all the needed work cannot be done in a short period of time. Even with the help of professionals, museum work is comprehensive in nature.

4 Epilogue

Therefore, what are the stories of the IBM Ramac 305 and the Cray 1S? The museum value of the Ramac stayed the same. The Ramac is the world's first computer to use a hard disk drive. It celebrated its 50th birthday on 13 September 2006 [13]. The machine that stands in Agora is actually a part of the IBM Ramac 305 mainframe. In the exhibition, you will find the hard disk drive and the control board. The machine is an exhibition loan from the Technology Museum of Finland [1].

However, there is not much to tell about the machine. They possibly used it in the 1960s in a retail cooperative OTK (Osuustukkukauppa). At the same time, an IBM Ramac 305 was in use in a similar cooperative, Elanto, in Helsinki. This machine was famous: it even had a nickname, "Äly-Elo" [20, 28, 29]. The information of Elanto's machine represents second-hand information: it increases the value of the Ramac on display.

The story of the Cray 1S supercomputer is different. Its museum value was increased, and the justification of its existence in a museum is valid. Actually, that pink tower is a central processing unit (CPU) [3] that was never in use in Finland. The Ministry of Education of Finland set up a committee in 1977 to plan the obtaining of a new mainframe in joint use. After years of hard work, Finland got its first supercomputer. Cray X-MP EA/416 supercomputer was activated on the premises of CSC – the Finnish IT Centre for Science in January 1989. [11, 17, 19, and 27]

According to a story told by one of the association's active members, there was great interest about the supercomputer. People wanted to see what the supercomputer was that caused so much work and cost a lot of money. When the Cray X-MP had arrived, the public interest was so large, that CSC started to inquire if they could get a computer to exhibit, because only authorized personnel were allowed in the machine room of the Cray X-MP. After negotiations, a representative from Cray Corporation suggested a Cray 1S that was out of use. The computer had been in Netherlands in the use of Shell Corporation and they used it in calculations of oil search. [9, see also 11] However, there is also another story. According to the personnel of CSC, the Cray came from England, from a meteorological institute [11]. They stripped the CPU of all essential parts that makes it a functional computer before it came to Finland. There have been speculations that it happened because of the Iron Curtain era; that is, so the Soviets could not copy the technology [9]. This is the problem and the enrichment of memories. On one hand, this complicates the understanding of the machine and it can compromise the museum value when the contextual information is based on assumptions. On the other hand, this difference enriches the story. It shows the variety of human experience and the personal truth as one source of information.

Finally they brought the CPU of the Cray 1S to Finland in 1990s. The Cray stood in the hall of CSC's premises. Everyone who came to the building could see "Finland's first supercomputer". Some people even wanted to take their picture while sitting on the benches of the Cray [10]. It stood in the hall until 1999. That year they were to receive a new supercomputer so they donated the Cray to the association [9]. Later the Cray 1S went on display in the computer exhibition and it has represented the beginning of Finnish supercomputing ever since.

How does the Cray tell its story from now on? It tells us in the end about the beginning of the supercomputer era in Finland. Through the knowledge gathered in the project we can see the life story of the machine. It is not just this big, pink computer CPU in a computer exhibition. It is a document of the work done in CSC, but also a document of how and why supercomputing began in Finland. It is also document of the importance of computer museum work: by saving it, the association has preserved an important part of Finnish IT history. The stripped CPU also tells of past conceptions of the western society: how the technology should be protected. In the end, when this knowledge is added to the information in the exhibition, also the visitors of the exhibition will find the story behind the machine. The Cray 1S is truly a museum object with museum value.

References

Archival Material

[1] The Finnish Data Processing Museum Associations archival material
[2] The collections of the Jyväskylä University Museum, Section of Cultural History. JYU/KHO DUO 3781: Material gathered in the documentation project

Internet References

[3] The CRAY 1S – advertisement from the 1970s; Computer History Museum homepage. Marketing Brochures Collections, Digitized,
http://archive.computerhistory.org/resources/text/Cray/
Cray.CRAY1S.1979.102646188.pdf (23.10.2007)
[4] Finlex® Up-to-date legislation on the internet. The Antiquities act (in Finnish),
http://www.finlex.fi/fi/laki/alkup/1963/19630295 (23.10.2007)
[5] The Finnish Data Processing Museum Association (in English),
http://www.tietokonemuseo.saunalahti.fi/index_eng.htm
(23.10.2007)
[6] The decisions of the cultural board of Jyväskylä (in Finnish),
http://www3.jkl.fi/paatos/kulk/2006/14031700.0/frmtxt32.htm
(23.10.2007)
[7] The decision of the city council of Jyväskylä (in Finnish),
http://www3.jkl.fi/paatos/kh/2006/10041400.0/frmtxt153.htm
(23.10.2007)
[8] Information about the SAMDOK (in Swedish),
http://www.nordiskamuseet.se/makeframeset.asp?sUrl=http%3A//
www.nordiskamuseet.se/category.asp%3Fcat%3D305%26catname%3Dom_
samdok&Cat=305&catName=om_samdok&publicationid=23.10.2007

Interviews

[9] JYU/KHO Duo N3781:35 7.12. 2006. In the collections of the Jyväskylä University Museum, JYU/KHO DUO 3781
[10] JYU/KHO Duo N3781:48 26.3.2007. In the collections of the Jyväskylä University Museum, JYU/KHO DUO 3781
[11] JYU/KHO Duo N3781:50 26.3.2007. In the collections of the Jyväskylä University Museum, JYU/KHO DUO 3781

Journals

[12] Vilkuna, J.: Maailman tihein museoverkko (World's thickest museum network) (in Finnish) Helsingin sanomat (28.12.1996)

Literature

[13] Bashe, C.J., Johnson, L.R., Palmer, J.H., Pugh, E.W.: IBM's Early Computers. MIT Press, Cambridge (1986)
[14] Boman, R., Dahlberg, I.: Dansen kring guldkalven (Dancing around the Golden Calf. in Swedish). Askild & Kärnekull, Stockholm (1975)
[15] Hallberg, T.-J.: IT gryning. Svenskt datahistoria från 1840- till 1960-talet (The IT-dawn. Swedish computer history from 1840s to 1960s. in Swedish), Studentlitteratur, Lund, pp. 191–220 (2007)
[16] Heinonen, J., Lahti, M.: Museologian perusteet (The Basics of Museology in Finnish) Kolmas uudistettu laitos, pp. 14–24. Suomen Museoliitto, Helsinki (2001)
[17] Kauranne, T.: Maamme matkalla maineeseen eli kuinka tullaan supertietokoneen omistajaksi (Our country on its way to fame, how to become the owner of a supercomputer. in Finnish) Korkeakoulujen atk-uutiset. Supernumero 3-4/88, pp. 4–9. VTKK, Helsinki (1998)
[18] Ketky ry:n hallitus (toim.). Ketky ry 25 vuotta, Juhlajulkaisu (Ketky registered foundation 25 years. in Finnish). Ketky, Jyväskylä, pp. 54–57 (1997)
[19] Käpyaho, J.: Tieteen tietokoneet ja tietoyhteydet. CSC – Tieteellinen laskenta 25 vuotta (Computers and information connections of Science. CSC – Finnish Information Technology Centre for Science 25 years. in Finnish) CSC – tieteellinen laskenta, Espoo (1996)
[20] Manninen, A.T.: Näin tehtiin Suomesta tietoyhteiskunta (This is how Finland became an information society. in Finnish) Talentum, Helsinki (2003)
[21] van Mensch, P.: Towards a methodology of museology. University of Zagreb. Internet-published PhD.-thesis (1992),
http://web.archive.org/web/20000422030557/www.xs4all.nl/~rwa/contents.htm (23.10.2007)
[22] Paju, P.: Ensimmäinen suomalainen tietokone ESKO ja 1950-luvun suunnitelma kansallisesta laskentakeskuksesta (First Finnish computer ESKO and the plan for national computing centre in 1950s. in Finnish) Lisensiaatintutkimus, Turun yliopisto kulttuurihistoria. Turku (2002)
[23] Pearce, S.M.: Museums, Objects and Collections: a cultural study, pp. 192–193. Leicester University Press, Leicester (1992)
[24] Pearce, S.M.: On collecting. An investigation into collecting in the European tradition, pp. 353–357. Routledge, London (1995)
[25] Saarikoski, P.: Koneen lumo. Mikrotietokoneharrastus Suomessa 1970-luvulta 1990-luvun puoliväliin (The Lure of the Machine. The Personal Computer Interest in Finland from the 1970s to the mid-1990s. in Finnish) Nykykulttuurin tutkimuskeskuksen julkaisuja 83. Jyväskylän yliopisto, Jyväskylä (2004)
[26] Salmi, H., Paju, P., Parikka, J., Saarikoski, P., Sihvonen, T., Suominen, J.: Välimuistiin kirjoitetut. Lukuja Suomen tietoteknistymisen historiaan (Written in Cache. Chapters of history of Finnish IT. in Finnish) k&h, Turun yliopisto, kulttuurihistoria, Turku (2006)
[27] Serimaa, O.: Supertietokone (Supercomputer. in Finnish) Korkeakoulujen atk-uutiset. Supernumero 3-4/88, pp. 15–24. VTKK, Helsinki (1998)
[28] Suominen, J.: Sähköaivo sinuiksi, tietokone tutuksi. Tietotekniikan kulttuurihistoriaa (Getting familiar with the electric brain, getting to know the computer. in Finnish) Nykykulttuurin tutkimuskeskuksen julkaisuja 67. Jyväskylän yliopisto, Jyväskylä (2000)
[29] Suominen, J.: Koneen kokemus. Tietoteknistyvä kulttuuri modernisoituvassa Suomessa 1920-luvulta 1970-luvulle (Experiences with machines. Computerised culture in the process of Finnish Modernisation from the 1920s to the 1970s. in Finnish), Vastapaino, Tampere (2003)

[30] Suominen, J., Paju, P., Törn, A.: The Wegematic 1000 Computing Centre, 1959–1964. Translocal Co-operation. In: Bubenko Jr., J., Impagliazzo, J., Sølvberg, A. (eds.) History of Nordic Computing. IFIP WG9.7 First Working Conference on the History of Nordic Computing (HiNC1), pp. 463–485. Springer, New York (2005)

[31] Tienari, M. (toim.).: Tietotekniikan alkuvuodet Suomessa (The early years of Finnish IT. in Finnish) Suomen atk-kustannus, Espoo (1993)

[32] Valtonen, H.: Tavallisesta kuriositeetiksi. Kahden Keski-Suomen Ilmailumuseon Messerschmitt Bf 109-lentokoneen museoarvo (From Commonplace to Curiosity-The Museum Value of two Messerschmitt Bf 109 – Aircraft at the Central Finland Aviation Museum. in Finnish) Jyväskylä Studies in Humanities 49. Jyväskylän yliopisto, Jyväskylä, pp. 20–24 (2006)

[33] Vilkuna, J.: Museot ja tutkimus (Museums and Research. in Finnish) Osma. Suomen museoliiton juhlakirja. Vallisaari, H.(toim.). Suomen museoliitto, Helsinki, pp. 3–19 (1993)

[34] Vilkuna, J.: Ottaa vaiko jättää (To take or to leave. In Finnish) Museo 3/1993, Suomen museoliitto, Helsinki, pp. 2–7 (1993)

[35] Vilkuna, J.: Kestämätön kehitys (Unsustainable development. in Finnish) Näkökulmia museoihin ja museologiaan (Views to museums and museology. in Finnish) Vilkuna, J.(toim). Ethnos toimite 10. Ethnos, Helsinki, p. 92 (2000)

[36] Vilkuna, J.: Kulttuuriperintö ja kulttuuriympäristöt (Cultural Heritage and Cultural environment. in Finnish) Taiteen ja kulttuurin kentät. Heiskanen, I., Kangas, A., Mitchell, R.(toim.). Tietosanoma, Helsinki, pp. 274–275 (2002)

Preserving Our Digital Heritage: Experiences from the Pelikonepeijoonit Project

Mikko Heinonen[1] and Markku Reunanen[2]

[1] University of Tampere
mikko.heinonen@iki.fi
[2] University of Art and Design Helsinki
markku.reunanen@iki.fi

Abstract. Pelikonepeijoonit is a private Finnish computer and games console museum. Similar to most hobbyist collections, the first items were acquired out of personal reasons. During its eight years, the collection has grown significantly and started to shift towards a digital heritage preservation project. In this paper, we present the history of Pelikonepeijoonit, coupled with observations made throughout the years. A supporting study was also conducted among the Finnish game/computer collector community to gain additional points of view and validate the personal observations. The results of this study are presented in relation to digital heritage to link the two practices, the collector circles and the cultural heritage. Finally, we present some suggestions for further work based on the current and future challenges of the field.

Keywords: Digital heritage, computer hobbyists, museum.

1 Introduction

Pelikonepeijoonit ("Game Machine Rascals") is a private Finnish computer and games console museum project run by three collectors. During its eight years, the project has evolved from a small personal collection to a digital heritage preservation project, also bringing together other individuals with shared interests. The Pelikonepeijoonit museum currently hosts around 250 different devices, thousands of games and several hundred related items. The collection can be viewed online at *http://www.pelikonepeijoonit.net/*

In this paper, we shall discuss the overall goals of the Pelikonepeijoonit project, its current status, and draw conclusions on the meaning and challenges of such work. Connections to home computer and game console history as well as digital heritage are made in order to rise above the grassroots level of a personally motivated hobby. The apparent gap between official digital heritage initiatives and hobbyists is not easily bridged, so we shall also propose some approaches on how the two communities could better be brought together for the benefit of both.

1.1 Time Span of the Collection

The museum-owned devices mostly range from the 1970's to the 1990's, which obviously coincides with the domestication of the microprocessor and related appliances.

J. Impagliazzo, T. Järvi, and P. Paju (Eds.): HiNC 2, IFIP AICT 303, pp. 55–64, 2009.
© IFIP International Federation for Information Processing 2009

Suominen [19] and Saarikoski [14, 15] provide an overview of the period from a Finnish point of view. The work of Suominen mainly deals with the early mechanisms of technology domestication in Finland, whereas Saarikoski focuses especially on hobbyist use such as computer games. The compact overview by Haddon [7] provides an international perspective to the same period. For more in-depth discussion, we direct the reader to Kent [9], Forster [4] and Bagnall [1]. From these sources alone, the vast number of different collectibles becomes apparent, setting a challenging goal for museums wishing to obtain a comprehensive collection. As an example, according to Bagnall [1], over 1200 games were released for the Commodore 64 in both 1987 and 1988.

1.2 Digital Heritage Preservation

We can view digital heritage as a specific part of our cultural heritage. So far, the major focus has been on archeological artifacts, and while modern technology is widely used in these projects (often called *digital cultural heritage*), the technology itself has not been viewed as something in urgent need of preservation. When compared to tangible artifacts, the digital artifacts have two notable properties: we can reproduce them infinitely, and they are easily lost for good. The thirty-year old home computer history is already in threat of becoming lost heritage because of aging hardware and software, inaccessible media, lack of expertise and supportive legislation [20].

Books and other written material are one way of preserving the heritage, but even more important is the preservation of artifacts in order to facilitate future research. As of late, this need has started to gain official recognition, which has lead to initiatives such as the UNESCO charter [20] and the EU-funded DigiCULT [3]. In Finland, *Suomen Peliautomaattihistoriallinen Seura* is a society of coin-operated arcade machine collectors [18]. Personal collections and community websites such as *old-computers.com* with archives are two common ground-level approaches to the preservation. From the point of view of a wider audience, such approaches are static and communicative by nature, in contrast to so-called emulators running old software, which provide users with an interactive experience. From the heritage and accessibility perspectives, it is unfortunate that emulation is inherently illegal because of copyright legislation.

2   History of Pelikonepeijoonit

The Pelikonepeijoonit project stems from the individual collections of three Finnish hobbyists. Mikko and Ville Heinonen had started collecting different home computers and items related to gaming in the early 1990s, and were joined by Manu Pärssinen around 1998. After a period of searching for information on their items on the Internet, they noticed that in fact, they should start a website based on their collection to assist other like-minded hobbyists. The first version of the site was launched on 2 May of 1999 at the somewhat non-intuitive address *http://gamma.nic.fi/~mikkohoo/peijoonit*. The group did some small-scale dissemination of the site in Internet newsgroups and among friends. However, as the interests were purely non-commercial, they did not carry out any large-scale marketing effort. The site consisted of simple HTML pages for each computer or video game system in the Pelikonepeijoonit collection, presenting an image of the item and a basic technical description. Manu Pärssinen completely made the web design, while Mikko Heinonen supplied the core of the written material. From the beginning, the site was aimed at an international audience and was therefore written in English.

Judging by the response the site received, the initial estimate of the group was correct. The site received a number of mentions on other websites, in industry magazines and newspapers [18, 21] and the Pelikonepeijoonit group were interviewed for several different media. Manu Pärssinen received numerous web awards for his design work on the site. The collection also increased rapidly during the months following the launch of the site, mainly through trades from other parts of the world, trips to different countries, and through donations. Looking at the list of updates from 1999 [10], we see that updates on the website took place nearly every day, with new items being added weekly. The same pace continued well into the year 2000 [11] and beyond. During this time, the collection expanded from containing around 70 computers and video game systems to around 160.

2.1 Site Visitors

It is hard to estimate the actual number of people visiting the site, since reliable visitor counters were unavailable in 1999. By the time the site turned 2 years old in 2001, it had accumulated 28 000 visitors. The *IPstat* counter on the main page, started 21 August of 2000, lists 157199 real views and 70592 reloads up to 10 April of 2007 [8]. As site updates have been significantly slower in the past year due to time issues with the maintainers, the bulk of these visitors were accumulated before 2006.

In addition to containing information on the items owned by the group, the Pelikonepeijoonit website has hosted pages related to general information for computer and video game collectors. The first one of these, the PAL-NTSC compatibility page, was added in August of 1999. E-cards and similar entertainment items were included from the beginning. Visitors to the site were active in submitting additions and changes to the information pages, increasing their usefulness and popularity.

2.2 Co-operation with Businesses and Hobbyists

As the site grew in popularity, the Pelikonepeijoonit group received requests for co-operation from different fields of the gaming business. In 2000, Mikko Heinonen became a game reviewer at the website *Sooda.com*, later on at *Peliplaneetta.net*, partly due to merits and expertise from the Pelikonepeijoonit project. Manu Pärssinen has gained reputation as a game news journalist and reviewer on a number of websites. These positions were both partly due to the reputation received while working on Pelikonepeijoonit, and very helpful in terms of adding items to the collection. Press copies of games and promotional material were added to the archive after review.

In 2002, Pelikonepeijoonit were present at the *GameWorld* trade fair with their own exhibition [12], sponsored by Sanoma Magazines. This tradition has continued with smaller stands in 2003 (GameWorld), 2005 (Assembly) and 2006 (DigiExpo). In early 2003, the Tyrvää museum in Vammala, Finland, held an exhibition on "Digital Archeology" based on selected items from the Pelikonepeijoonit collection [13].

One of the key goals of the Pelikonepeijoonit project has been to bring hobbyists together both online and offline. The group arranged their first collector meeting, *Pelikonepeijaiset*, in July 2001. With the exception of 2002, similar events occurred each summer. The amount of visitors to these events has been between 20 and 30 people. The meetings have featured thematic exhibitions such as the collection of Sega items in 2006, shown in Figure 1. In February 2007, the first "Pelikonepeijaiset Winter" had taken place with around 10 attendants. The website also features a message board, which has some 20 active users (over 2000 registered), 1700 topics, and 9000 posts.

Fig. 1. Sega collectibles (image provided by Manu Pärssinen)

2.3 Future

Currently, the Pelikonepeijoonit group is extending collaboration with their visitors by rebuilding the site in Wiki format. The site will still include the information on the computers and videogames, but much more will be available for site visitors to edit. The idea is to manage better the wealth of material accumulated on the website, and to enable visitors who 'know better' to complement the information more easily than has previously been possible. The group hopes to encourage visitors to participate more in the development of the website, keeping the information more up-to-date, as well as simplifying updates for the site maintainers.

With the large number of artifacts, it is not feasible for individual collectors to maintain exhaustive collections of digital heritage items. During the course of the Pelikonepeijoonit project, the group has had to limit their collection on several fronts—such as leaving out most PC standard hardware, *Game & Watch* type digital games, systems with only a single built-in game, and so on. While most of the 'unwanted' items have so far found new homes with other collectors of differing interests, having to limit collections due to space restraints necessarily leads to material being discarded.

As years have passed and the Pelikonepeijoonit collection has grown, more emphasis has been laid on improving the general awareness on digital heritage issues—this article, indeed, forms part of these efforts. In the future, the Pelikonepeijoonit group hopes to work further to promote the preservation of home computing and digital gaming artifacts.

3 Supporting Study

A small-scale supporting study, based on a questionnaire, was conducted to understand better the hobbyist culture and to validate the experiences gained in the Pelikonepeijoonit project. While limited in scope, the results gained still reveal relevant trends and provide for a better generalization of the personal observations. The study addressed active Finnish computer, console, and game collectors and was implemented as a structured questionnaire.

3.1 Questionnaire

There were sixteen, mostly qualitative, questions altogether in the questionnaire. The number of questions was few to avoid frustrating the respondents. The themes addressed were roughly as follows:

o Demographic issues such as age, sex and occupation
o Personal motivation
o Methods of obtaining collectibles
o Problems and challenges of the hobby
o Methods of information retrieval
o Personal views on the hobby

The questionnaire was distributed electronically and advertised in various relevant forums such as IRC channels and the Pelikonepeijoonit discussion board, which reaches a large portion of the Finnish collectors. The answers were collected via email and analyzed thereafter. The respondents were asked not to reply onto the board itself, so that the previous answers would not skew the results. Before the launch, a pilot test was run to ensure the questions were understandable and to the point.

3.2 Results

We received fifteen responses in all, considered a representative sample of the Finnish collectors since the hobbyist circles are small. Such a sample does not allow for realistic quantitative analysis, so the material obtained was used to build a profile of a typical Finnish collector, to understand different points of view, and to discover trends.

According to our study, a typical Finnish collector is a male in his late twenties or early thirties, working in an information technology related field. The personal motivation for collecting often relates to machines owned in childhood, for example, Commodore computers or Sega consoles. We can explain this nostalgia by the fact that the persons have been in their late childhood or early teens in the eighties, which coincides with the home computer and microprocessor revolution—one could say that they represent the first generation that grew up with electronic toys and computers. Game playing has always been a popular use for the machines [15] and every single informant reported it as an important use for their collection.

Flea markets, Internet auction sites such as *eBay*, recycling centers and social networks are the most popular sources for collectibles. Out of these four, especially the social networks are held in high regard. The biggest problem in the acquisition process is the high price of items, partly due to postal fees and partly due to increasing prices in auctions. The acquisitions have been funded by savings from a daily job and, to a lesser extent, by the trading of duplicate items, or even a study grant. A representative collection of items requires considerable space for storage, a problem reported by half of the collectors. Another typical problem was the breakage of old hardware, coupled with the difficulty of obtaining spare parts.

The wide use of the internet as a communication channel and source of information is hardly a surprise, considering the technical nature of the hobby. Every single informant had used the Internet in some form for these purposes. The most popular sources of information mentioned were hobbyist web sites, search engines (usually *Google*) and discussion forums. Usenet news and modem-based bulletin board systems (BBS) had been of importance previously, but gradually lost their significance. The use of e-mail was almost completely omitted in the answers, which notably conflicts with the aforementioned importance of social networks. Most likely, this conflict has more to do with e-mail not being regarded as "Internet use" instead of hobbyists not using it.

4   Digital Heritage and Hobbyists

While museum authorities and official bodies are slowly starting to catch up with the need for digital heritage preservation, significant efforts have taken place among the individual hobbyists for quite some time already. Bridging the gap between the personal aspirations of individual collectors and the needs for a large-scale history preservation project will pose a challenge for any organization aiming to approach digital heritage preservation on a larger, better-coordinated scale. In addition to this, the scene is continuously changing, requiring any parties operating in the field to be able to assess future implications.

4.1   The Value of Personal Collections

As we stand, the responsibility for the systematic preservation of digital culture rests strongly on the shoulders of individual hobbyists. While public organizations are now starting to show limited interest towards the hobby, many collectors have already worked on their personal collections for well over ten years, preserving remarkable amounts of material that would otherwise most likely have been destroyed. Their motives for collecting are largely personal, with less focus on abstract goals such as digital heritage preservation. Regardless of the aims, collectors possess skills essential for the preservation efforts: they are networked (these days, mainly through the internet), they know the distribution channels, and they are used to dealing with aging hardware.

4.2 Current Trends

Looking at current developments within the media, we can see that the popularity of 'retro' is increasing. As a sign of this, the popular game player and game industry magazine *Edge* has published several special issues on the topic: *Edge presents Retro* [5] and three issues called *Edge presents File* [6]. These publications concentrate on historical computers and games machines, their collectability, and old product reviews from the beginning of the 1990s, when they started *Edge*. Combined with similar, albeit shorter accounts in other media, we can see that the topic is starting to gain increasing mainstream press interest as well. Well-known game characters such as Mario have already turned into pop culture icons, used by contemporary artists. The "I am 8-bit" exhibition in 2005 featured works from over 100 authors [16].

The *Game On* exhibition has been touring different museums of the world during the past few years, visiting Finland in 2003. The exhibition consists of display exhibits of the most popular arcade games, home computers and video game systems, as well as over 100 playable games for the visitor audience to try, ranging from the world's first computer game, *Space War*, to the latest offerings on the PlayStation 3 and Nintendo Wii consoles [17].

As current computers, game consoles and even handheld devices, such as mobile phones, are hundreds of times more powerful than vintage computer and gaming hardware, software emulation is becoming more and more feasible. While it started out as single projects to emulate popular hardware like the Commodore 64, emulation is now widespread and they attempt to emulate nearly every system in existence. Indeed, in the *Game On* exhibition the oldest games featured actually ran emulated on modern hardware.

New games machines, such as the Nintendo Wii, the Sony PlayStation 3 and the Microsoft Xbox 360, both emulate their predecessor hardware to be able to provide backwards compatibility and offer users downloads of older software for purchase. The Nintendo *Wii Virtual Console* is entirely based around the concept of emulating older Nintendo, Sega, and NEC game consoles. The user may purchase digitally distributed copies of these games to play on their system through an emulation layer.

While game manufacturers have embraced emulation for their purposes, hobbyist projects are generally not approved of. The owners of copyrights have systematically shut down websites containing ROM images (i.e. digital copies of the early game cartridges). Hobbyist groups have worked together with owners of copyrights to bring, say, hundreds of Commodore 64 and Amiga titles legally available for download on the Internet, but there are still countless systems which are inherently illegal to emulate.

4.3 Future Directions

As the popularity of 'retro' is on the increase, vintage games, machines and computers, and their software are continuously increasing in value. We can see this on auction sites such as *eBay*, and it was clearly brought up in the results of our study. At the same time, however, emulation is becoming more effective and allowing more and more people to access past software without the need to purchase or preserve special hardware. It is difficult to say how this will affect pricing in the end—emulator users may settle for seeing the product running on their system, or may want to acquire the actual hardware to be able to experience it better.

While the preservation of software in ROM dump files and disk images for emulation purposes has contributed vastly to preserving the software and program code of these titles, the original boxes, brochures, and promotional items are very much in danger of becoming 'extinct'. Cardboard and styrofoam boxes used to store systems and games, as well as instructions, background stories and such printed material, are more difficult to preserve due to space constraints—and may have often been thrown away entirely or in part soon after the item was purchased. Meanwhile, these items have greatly contributed to the entire experience of the product, and remain testament to the way digital culture has been seen in that day and age. Their value is unquestionable.

More than in most preservation projects, time is of the essence when preserving digital heritage items. The original storage media, such as ROM cartridges or magnetic tapes and disks, and even early CD-ROM discs, have a limited lifespan, a problem recognized also in the UNESCO brochure [20]. For example, there are dozens of prototype cartridges that we know to exist but have not been stored in ROM images. Acquiring these items before they disappear is the goal of a number of collectors, and active collaboration is taking place. To name an example, the Pelikonepeijoonit group sent a copy of the extremely rare Sega Master System game Smurfs 2 to Omar Cornut, a French specialist on the preservation of Sega Master System and compatible games, to be transferred from a cartridge to an ordinary file and archived [2].

This period also implies that the definition of 'antique' needs to be updated for the purposes of digital culture. Computers and game systems become obsolete and are replaced and recycled in a much quicker cycle than, say, automobiles or other consumer goods. With their in-built low life expectancy, computer and video games and other software run a risk of becoming partially or completely destroyed within 20 years of their introduction.

In terms of arranging exhibitions and joint efforts to preserve digital culture, cooperation with businesses has already been rather rich, as can be seen in the history of the Pelikonepeijoonit project. Companies have sensed public interest in old hardware and software and their attraction value for presenting new products. Meanwhile, offers and contacts from the public sector have been much scarcer, with the Digital Archaeology exhibition [13] being the only significant materialized product of this cooperation.

5 Conclusion

The history of Pelikonepeijoonit connects with the history of Finnish digital heritage preservation, and one is necessarily part of the other. The website started out as a single hobbyist project arising out of the need to experiment and publish content on the internet. It has since gained significant attention and coverage outside the collector circles. All the while, collecting and archiving artifacts related to our digital heritage has gained more and more mainstream appeal.

From a preservation point of view, some important issues stand out from our study. The collectors have been able to build noteworthy collections with modest sums of money: ten thousand Euros—the maximum reported in the results—is a relatively large sum for an individual, but in the scale of a museum or a foundation, it is not. The key to the collectors' success is the devotion of time coupled with knowledge of the domain. Similarly, the storage of items is clearly a problem for an individual, but less so for a museum. Finally, the reported rise of collectible prices such as in internet auctions suggests that the preservation efforts will become increasingly expensive over time.

In conclusion, the present time would be favorable for setting up national bodies to represent digital gaming and collectors, and starting a widespread project to preserve the history of home computing and digital gaming in general, and that of Finnish computing and gaming in particular. The prices of items are on the rise, but still seldom beyond the reach of well-coordinated public efforts to collect such items. We may also fairly and confidently state that many collectors are willing to participate in a jointly coordinated project by donating extraneous items from their collections. As an example, the Pelikonepeijoonit group helped *Game On* exhibition coordinator Barry Higgins by donating several *Pong*-type machines to be used by visitors in the exhibition.

Copyright legislation needs to take a clearer stand towards digital software products, taking into account their shorter life span when compared to other items. We argue that the publisher of a fifteen-year-old software product is no longer losing money since people are emulating it on modern computers. Meanwhile, the systematic, legal archiving of these items, both offline and online, would greatly benefit the preservation of the artifacts. Already, there is a large gray area known as 'abandonware' on the internet. It consists of software for which nobody is claiming copyright. The current legal point-of-view to archiving is counter-intuitive and may discourage people from sharing information on the products in question.

References

[1] Bagnall, B.: On the edge: the spectacular rise and fall of Commodore. Variant Press (2005)
[2] Cornut, O.: The Smurfs Travel the World (2000),
    http://www.smspower.org/db/smurfs2.shtml (Accessed 16/4/2007)
[3] DigiCULT: The DigiCULT Report. Technological Landscapes for Tomorrow's Cultural Economy. Unlocking the Value of Cultural Heritage. European Commission, Directorate-general Information Society (2002)
[4] Forster, W.: The Encyclopedia of Game. Machines—consoles, handhelds & home computers, 1972-2005. Gameplan (2005)
[5] Edge: Edge presents Retro. Future Publishing (2002)
[6] Edge: Edge presents FILE, vol. 1, 2, 3. Future Publishing (2006, 2007)
[7] Haddon, L.: Elektronisten pelien oppivuodet (The early years of the electronic games). In: Huhtamo, E., Kangas, S. (eds.) Mariosofia, pp. 47–69. Oy Yliopistokustannus University Press, Finland (2002)
[8] IPstat: Statistics for counter: The Arctic Computer & Console Museum (2007),
    http://www.ipstat.com/cgi-bin/stats?name=pkpipstat
    (Accessed 15/4/2007)
[9] Kent, S.L.: The ultimate history of video games: from Pong to Pokemon—the story behind the craze that touched our lives and changed the worldq. Prima Publishing (2001)
[10] Pelikonepeijoonit: Pelikonepeijoonit site updates in 1999 (1999),
    http://www.pelikonepeijoonit.net/olds1999.txt (Accessed 15/4/2007)

[11] Pelikonepeijoonit: Pelikonepeijoonit site updates in 2000 (2000),
     http://www.pelikonepeijoonit.net/olds2000.txt (Accessed 15/4/2007)
[12] Pelikonepeijoonit: Gameworld 2002. Finland's biggest gaming event (2002),
     http://www.pelikonepeijoonit.net/articles/gw2k2.html
     (Accessed 15/4/2007)
[13] Pelikonepeijoonit: Digital Archaeology, Exhibition at Tyrvää Museum, Vammala,
     Finland (2003),
     http://www.pelikonepeijoonit.net/articles/vlamuseum.html
     (Accessed 10/4/2007)
[14] Saarikoski, P.: Pioneerien leluista kulutuselektroniikaksi. Suomalainen kotimikroharras-
     tus tietotekniikan murroksessa 1980-luvun alusta 1990-luvun puoliväliin (From pioneer
     toys to consumer electronics. The Finnish computer hobbyists during the computer revo-
     lution from early1980s to the mid-1990s). Turun yliopisto (University of Turku) (2001)
[15] Saarikoski, P.: Koneen lumo. Mikrotietokoneharrastus Suomessa 1970-luvulta 1990-
     luvun puoliväliin (The Lure of the Machine. The Personal Computer Interest in Finland
     from the 1970s to the mid-1990s). Nykykulttuurin tutkimuskeskuksen julkaisuja 83. Jy-
     väskylä (2004)
[16] Scholz, A.: I am 8-bit. Sceen, Issue 01, pp. 60–65. CSW Verlag (2005)
[17] Science Museum: Game On (2006),
     http://www.sciencemuseum.org.uk/visitmuseum/galleries/
     game_on.aspx (Accessed 16/4/2007)
[18] Suominen, J.: Jassot, jukeboksit ja videopelit intohimon kohteena—peliautomaattien
     keräily Internetissä (Pajazzos, jukeboxes and video games as a passion–game machine
     colledtions on the Internet). Agricolan tietosanomat, 2/1999 (1999),
     http://agricola.utu.fi/tietosanomat/
     numero2-99/pelihistoriat.html (Accessed 28/11/2008)
[19] Suominen, J.: Koneen kokemus. Tietoteknistyvä kulttuuri modernisoituvassa Suomessa
     1920-luvulta 1970-luvulle (Experiences with machines. Computerised culture in the
     process of Finnish Modernisation from the 1920s to the 1970s). Osuuskunta Vastapaino
     (2003)
[20] UNESCO: Charter on the Preservation of the Digital Heritage (2003)
[21] Yli-Parkas, H.: Keräilijöille kelpaa kaikki Tex Willereistä Pokémoneihin (The collectors
     are interested in everything from Tex Willer to Pokémon). Keskipohjanmaa 17/4/2000
     (2000)

From Computing Machines to IT
Collecting, Documenting, and Preserving Source Material on Swedish IT-History

Per Lundin

Division of History of Science and Technology, Royal Institute of Technology (KTH), Sweden
plundin@kth.se

Abstract. This paper presents a large-scale project on collecting, documenting, and preserving source material on Swedish IT-history between 1950 and 1980. The project created new source material using methods of contemporary history such as interviews, witness seminars, and autobiographies. The paper describes the project's organization, its methods, and its results.

Keywords: Autobiography, documentation, history of computing, history of technology, interview, IT-history, oral history, Sweden, witness seminar.

1 Introduction

The intensity and speed of the development of computer technology imply new challenges for historians. The course of events is in many cases not documented. In other cases, source material exists only in the form of published reports or articles, often complicated and technical in content, and, therefore, difficult to penetrate and understand. Neither is it certain that this type of material is *representative* of the mental activity and the work that characterize technical and scientific activities. Different historical phenomena show different degrees of *visibility* in the existing sources. But how shall we be able to reach an understanding about phenomena that lack or have left insufficient source material? One approach is to *create* new source material by using different methods of contemporary history like interviews, witness seminars, and autobiographies.

In this paper, I will present a large-scale project on collecting, documenting, and preserving source material on Swedish IT-history between 1950 and 1980. The project entitled "From Computing Machines to IT" was finished by the end of 2008.

The starting point for the project was the difficulty getting a relevant and representative picture of the social phenomenon of IT as it has developed over the last fifty to sixty years from written sources only. IT-history may somewhat simplified be characterized by a development from the computing machines of the 1950s, narrowly concentrated on scientific computation, to IT, which, to an increasing extent, has become a *generic* technology. Today, it permeates a large number of the sectors of society as well as professional and cultural contexts. A fragmentation of the technical forms, the expertise, and the meanings of IT characterize this expansion. IT in society thus forms a terrain that is hard to grasp. We believe that the key to mapping it is through the actors in

J. Impagliazzo, T. Järvi, and P. Paju (Eds.): HiNC 2, IFIP AICT 303, pp. 65–73, 2009.
© IFIP International Federation for Information Processing 2009

the history of IT. That the first generation of Swedish IT-actors, with their unique memories, are passing away, accentuated, therefore, the urgency of the project.

The *main objective* of the project was to create, collect, preserve, and make source material on Swedish IT-history available in the form of knowledge outlines, interviews, witness seminars, and autobiographies (collected either "traditionally" or virtually). This material was administered and made available by registration in existing databases and through the publication of processed material in print and on the web. The work was done in accordance with scholarly methods and criteria, so that the results of the project can be used in future historical research in different disciplines. The project had four main tasks:

o   Organize and realize the collection of memories and material;
o   Make the results available in the form of databases and in edited publications; present the project and its results;
o   Compile knowledge outlines covering national and international research and existing empirical material and records;
o   Develop further and adapt methods of contemporary history to the study of technology and technology-related professional environments.

At the start of 2004, the Swedish Computer Society contacted the Division of History of Science and Technology at KTH and the National Museum of Science and Technology that promoted the project. The general organization of the project and the choice of methods are the product of a four-year collaboration between these three parties.

2   The Organization of the Project

A steering group led and organized the project. The documentation work was mainly carried out in a number of *focus groups*, a *research group*, and a *group for the administration of the material*. Therefore, I will describe these bodies in more detail below.

The project identified sixteen so-called *focus areas* in IT-history. These were early computers, healthcare, financial industry, industry, IT-industry, systems development, user organizations and user participation, transports, defense, public administration, telecommunications, higher education, archives, libraries and museums, media, schools, and commerce. A focus group, composed of a *research secretary* and a number of practitioners from the area in question, was in turn established for each area. The focus group identified to begin with important events, processes, and (still living) actors. Thereafter, it carried out interviews and held witness seminars with the actors whose memories needed collection. The research secretary acted as the link between the focus group and the research group. A *project secretary* supported the research secretaries in their work by coordinating the flow of material from the focus groups and the research group to the group for the administration of the material, which, in turn, classified the material and delivered it to the National Museum of Science and Technology.

The research group had two assignments. Firstly, it had an overarching responsibility for developing and evaluating the methods used, for keeping the project updated with the state of the research, and for establishing contacts with national and international research environments in the field. Secondly, in every focus group there was a research secretary with the responsibility of compiling a knowledge outline for the focus area and in consultation with the focus group, deciding which events and processes required documentation. Additionally, the research secretary had to decide to which extent and for which type of methods one should use and eventually give a final account of the work carried out. His or her task was to create and collect source material as well as to edit and publish it. I led the research group, which consisted of sixteen researchers. The Division of History of Science and Technology at KTH was the home of the project.

The group for the administration of material had responsibility for taking care of the created and collected source material and preserving it at the National Museum of Science and Technology. It also oversaw that individuals performed documentation efforts along the lines a long-term preservation practice requires.

3   Methods for Documenting IT-History

A way to document events and processes taking place in our recent past is to create and collect new sources about them with the help of methods such as interviews, witness seminars, and autobiographies. These have gained increasing popularity during the last decades because historians have turned their attention to our recent past. The purpose of using them is to get a more comprehensive picture of historical phenomena. Because of the proximity in time it is easier for us to put ourselves in the historical situation—not seldom have we ourselves experienced the period, albeit from a different perspective— and this gives us a chance to reach a deeper understanding of historical phenomena, which is not possible to get for times long past. Above all, historians have paid attention to the "hidden" history, i.e., to groups whose activities are not very well documented or not documented at all. Three categories of historical approaches can be distinguished. The first one deals with social groups that traditionally have had difficulty making their voices heard such as immigrants, workers, and women [13]. The second one pays attention to so-called "elite" persons, whose activities have had considerable influence on societal change. In this case, it is interesting to get a picture of events and processes that never were recorded such as lobbying [10]. The third category aims to grasp and understand scientific and technical expertise and practice, tacit knowledge, professional cultures, and user participation—different phenomena that have influenced, and influence, technological and societal change [3].

3.1   Knowledge Outlines

Knowledge outlines are a part of the work that consists of drawing a course map over the landscape of the past. The purpose of knowledge outlines is to give a guide for the principal task of creating and collecting source material. Which parts of the past should be documented and why? If there, for instance, are abundant written sources on the events and processes in a certain part of the past, it becomes less important to create and collect complementary oral sources. If, on the other hand, the events and processes have left no traces, or few, in the existing archives, it becomes more important to create and collect new sources about precisely these events and processes. However, an unexplored area in the landscape of the past is, at the same time, not a sufficient reason to start documenting. Such a project will easily become insurmountable. There are many unexplored areas. The documentation efforts should, therefore, ideally be linked to those problems that have been observed by earlier historical research on the given part of the past, and also, the role of the knowledge outline is to identify these. Thus, the compilation of knowledge outlines consists of two stages. In the first place, to get a picture of the existing historical research dealing with a focus area, and, in the second, to identify existing sources by compiling bibliographies and listing relevant archives. If carried out as described, the knowledge outlines will become an important preparatory work for the documentation efforts to follow.

3.2 Oral History Interviews

Interviews are a method for creating oral sources that have been used extensively for decades, and we drew particularly upon the experiences of the Charles Babbage Institute (CBI) in Minneapolis and the IEEE History Center in New Brunswick, since they have interviewed IT-actors since the beginning of the 1980s [2, 9]. One should emphasize that in many aspects oral history interviews differ from, for instance, job interviews or newspaper interviews. One aspect is the "best-before date". While a job interview has a best-before date of, say, three weeks, an oral history interview is required to last for at least fifty years. Another is the amount of preparation. The value of the oral history interview depends very much on the preparations, the purpose, and the questions, how the interviewer carries it out, and how it is documented. The interview can be more or less formalized regarding the questions posed, how careful the interviewer follows a questionnaire, which has been devised beforehand and how the interviewee's answers are dealt with and are followed up.

I would like to underscore that a crucial difference between oral and written source material is that the former is *created* in the meeting between the interviewer and the interviewee, which means that the conduct and questions of the interviewer affect the outcome of the interview. This so-called interviewer effect makes it important to take a critical stance vis-à-vis the problems that occur when researchers and actors actively create source material together [11]. A way to facilitate source criticism is to preserve the different steps in the processing of oral sources (recording of sound and images, transcript, and edited transcript). In the project "From Computing Machines to IT", we preserved material from all these steps in our work with oral sources at the National Museum of Science and Technology.

In the project, we conducted around 150 oral history interviews and we recorded them with sound in digital format and then transcribed them. The research secretaries then edited the transcript regarding readability and comprehension. At the same time, they aimed at keeping the transcript's oral character. Before making the edited transcripts available on the web, the interviewees had the chance to clarify, correct, or comment on their contributions. Minor changes such as corrections of names, dates, and technical concepts were inserted in the transcript without comments. In individual cases, the research secretaries added sentences or subordinate clauses, as suggested by the interviewee, to make lines of thought or conversations more complete.

Furthermore, we included extensive comments from the interviewee using addenda. The interviews are typically between one to three hours long and the edited transcripts roughly between fifteen and forty-five pages. They are available at the National Museum of Science and Technology's web page: www.tekniskamuseet.se/it-intervjuer.

3.3 Witness Seminars

The Centre for Contemporary British History (CCBH) has since 1986 been developing and using witness seminars as a documentation method in its research [1]. Witness seminars are a category of oral history methods where a number of individuals, who have participated in, and/or witnessed, a certain series of historical events, gather to discuss and debate their often different interpretations of the past events. Thus, we can consider them as group interviews. The witness seminars designed by the CCBH have become the model for similar documentation projects at a number of centers and institutes around the world. The Institute of Contemporary History at Södertörn University in Sweden, for instance, has carried out witness seminars patterned after the CCBH's. These seminars have dealt mostly with political history such as the women's liberation movement during the 1960s and the 1970s or the debate on industrial democracy during the 1970s and the 1980s [4, 5]. However, the questions and themes addressed by historians of science and technology are in many cases distinct from the ones studied by political historians. We were thus confronted with somewhat different methodological questions and aspects, and we, therefore, chose to model our witness seminars on the meetings that the Wellcome Trust Centre for the History of Medicine has been arranging since the 1990s, because they have been concerned with similar methodological questions and problems that we were faced with: How does one get hold of scientific and technical practice and the tacit knowledge embedded in it? How does one deal with sources that contain complex scientific and technical reasoning?

In the experience of both the CCBH and the Wellcome Trust, witness seminars, when compared to particular interviews, stimulate an entirely different interaction between the participants. The meeting becomes a sort of collective recollection. But they also point out that the method has some obvious disadvantages. The lineup of participants is critical to the outcome of the seminar. If potential witnesses are unable or unwilling to participate, there is not much one could do. There is also an inherent risk that conflicts may be suppressed and that dissentients are not able to make their voices heard, with too "streamlined" recollections as a result. Another danger is that the reminiscences may be too anecdotal; a feature witness seminars, of course, share with other forms of oral history [12]. Overall, a witness seminar can serve to highlight different interpretations of an event and thereby contribute to a deeper understanding of the complexity of historical processes.

In our project, we held almost fifty witness seminars. We processed them roughly in the same way as the oral history interviews with three important exceptions. Firstly, we recorded them with both sound and images. Secondly, we added explanatory footnotes to the edited transcripts. The footnotes contain biographical information about persons as well as descriptions of subjects mentioned during the seminar. The research secretary worked on the footnotes in close cooperation with the participants, and they, therefore, function as complementary source material. Thirdly, the edited transcripts were published both in print and electronic versions. Our witness seminars normally span over three to four hours and the edited transcripts are about forty to fifty-five pages long. The electronic versions are available in KTH's working paper series TRITA-HST at the Academic Archive On-line (DiVA): www.diva-portal.org.

Fig. 1. The project "From Computing Machines to IT" held its first witness seminar in September 2005. The theme for the seminar was "Working with the Computing Machines of the 1950s" and it was moderated by Lars Arosenius (not in the picture). From left to right: Carl-Ivar Bergman, Bengt Beckman, Hans Riesel, Elsa-Karin Boestad-Nilsson, Erik Stemme, Gunnar Stenudd, Bert Bolin and Gunnar Wahlström.

3.4 Autobiographies

Autobiographies are an effective and laborsaving way to collect the actors' experiences. A model for us was the collections of autobiographies that ethnologists at Nordiska Museet (the Nordic Museum) in Sweden have carried out since 1945. They did them with the help of detailed questionnaires and aimed at occupational groups of various kinds. The questionnaires were sent out *en masse* by mail or announced in the media. The result is a rich documentation of different work cultures in twentieth-century Sweden. For instance, the museum has published a selection of the collected life stories of engineers in the volume *Framtiden var vår* (The Future Was Ours). The autobiographical material gives a comprehensive and nuanced picture of the engineering profession and its role in Swedish society [14]. The method has several advantages. It is effective and timesaving. Furthermore, it makes it possible to collect large amounts of material. There are no direct intermediaries such as in interviews, and the material, therefore, becomes autobiographical in a unique sense. Nevertheless, it is also important to be aware of the drawbacks. These include certain individuals who had difficulty expressing themselves in writing; some choose not to participate; the collected written material may appear too carefully prepared and revised [6].

We collected about 250 autobiographies through different notices that featured between April and June 2007 in the daily press, specialist press, trade union press, and on the television. We wrote some of these notices for the genera public; we aimed others toward specific occupational groups such as metalworkers, nurses, and doctors. Roughly, 120 of these autobiographies are available at the National Museum of Science and Technology's web page www.tekniskamuseet.se/it-minnen. While the oral history interviews and witness seminars we have carried out paid attention to "qualified" users, the collection of autobiographies provides a more representative picture of IT-users in Sweden between 1950 and 1980. Among the collected stories, we also find those by secretaries and operators. A measure of diversity is the number of participating women. In the interviews and seminars we carried out, the share of women was only 7 percent while it was 21 percent in the collection of autobiographies.

3.5 Writers' Web

In the project "From Computing Machines to IT", we also developed tools for collecting autobiographies over the internet as an alternative to the "traditional" way described above. At least one similar attempt occurred internationally, although the outcome of this pioneering work was rather poor. One explanation is that the virtual platform developed was too complicated [8]. We considered this experience when developing our Writers' Web—a simple virtual platform based on the questionnaires we used for the collection of traditional autobiographies. At the Writers' Web, which has the URL http://ithistoria.se, the visitors are invited to write down their memories in the form of autobiographies. It is also possible for them to upload files of different kinds, for instance pictures. We, furthermore, provided the Writers' Web with a function that allows the visitors to comment on earlier uploaded contributions, and thus makes an interaction between the platform's visitors possible.

However, the Writers' Web was not as successful as our traditional collection of autobiographies. As of 2008 October, about forty life stories and comments appear at the Writers' Web. One explanation is that we did not combine the launching of the Writers' Web with nationwide notices. Another is that there are large variations in the familiarity with the internet among people with memories from the period between 1950 and 1980, depending on the professional, social, and cultural background. It is simply not possible to reach everybody with this kind of method.

Fig. 2. The project launched its Writers' Web in June 2007. The picture shows the homepage for the Writers' Web.

3.6 The Necessity of Reflecting over the Choice of Methods

The presentation and discussion of methods so far show that each of them has its pros and cons. A routine-like application of any method entails a risk of collecting material of less value for scholars. I would like to emphasize the necessity of reflecting over which method is most suitable in relation to the events and the processes documented. The relation between the methodological approach and the stories one wants to collect is crucial. Depending on what is required, this relation may be more or less formalized, structured, or guided. Is it the actors themselves or the historical events and processes of which the actors only constitute a small part that are the focus of the documentation efforts? For us, it was important to find a balance between the isolated autobiography and the "technobiography", i.e. the biography of the technology in question [7].

4 Conclusion

The work carried out in the project "From Computing Machines to IT" has led me to the conclusion that the interaction between the practitioners and the research secretaries in the focus groups was decisive for shaping the outcome of the documentation efforts. The practitioners taking part in the focus groups had, on the one hand, a comprehensive and profound *understanding* of the historical events because they had been *close* to them, while they, at the same time, had difficulty contextualizing and valuing the events precisely because of their involvement in them. The research secretaries, on the other hand, had as trained historians an ability to see the events as a part of *a greater whole*, precisely because of their *distance* to the past events. This interaction was also important in order to avoid so-called Whig history, that is, a history of the winners, since the networks that the focus groups emanated from in many cases represented the established actors.

References

[1] Centre for Contemporary British History's Witness Seminars,
    http://icbh.ac.uk/icbh/witness/welcome.html
    (accessed October 21, 2008)
[2] Charles Babbage Institute's Collections, http://www.cbi.umn.edu/oh/ (accessed October 21, 2008)
[3] Doel, R.E., Söderqvist, T.: The Historiography of Contemporary Science, Technology, and Medicine: Writing Recent Science. Routledge, New York (2006)
[4] Ekdahl, L. (ed.): Löntagarfondsfrågan: En missad möjlighet? [The Question of Employee Funds: A Missed Opportunity?]. Samtidshistoriska institutet, Huddinge (2002)
[5] Elgán, E. (ed.): Kvinnorörelsen och '68: Aspekter och vittnesbörd [The Women's Liberation Movement and '68: Aspects and Testimony]. Samtidshistoriska institutet, Huddinge (2001)
[6] Hagström, C., Marander-Eklund, L. (eds.): Frågelistan som källa och metod [The Questionnaire as Source and Method]. Studentlitteratur AB, Lund (2005)

[7] Henwood, F., Kennedy, H., Miller, N. (eds.): Cyborg Lives?: Women's Techno-biographies. Raw Nerve Books, New York (2001)

[8] Hessenbruch, A.: 'The Mutt Historian': The Perils and Opportunities of Doing History of Science On-Line. In: Doel, R.E., Söderqvist, T. (eds.) The Historiography of Contemporary Science, Technology, and Medicine: Writing Recent Science. Routledge, New York (2006)

[9] IEEE Oral Histories, http://www.ieee.org/web/aboutus/history_center/oral_history/oral_history.html (accessed October 21, 2008)

[10] McMahan, E.: Elite Oral History Discourse: A Study of Cooperation and Coherence. University of Alabama Press, Tuscaloosa (1989)

[11] Perks, R., Thomson, A. (eds.): The Oral History Reader, 2nd edn. Routledge, New York (2006)

[12] Tansey, E.M.: Witnessing the Witnesses: Potentials and Pitfalls of the Witness Seminar in the History of Twentieth-Century Medicine. In: Doel, R.E., Söderqvist, T. (eds.) The Historiography of Contemporary Science, Technology, and Medicine: Writing Recent Science. Routledge, New York (2006)

[13] Thompson, P.: The Voice of the Past: Oral History. Oxford University Press, Oxford (1978)

[14] Waldetoft, D. (ed.): Framtiden var vår: Civilingenjörer skriver om sitt liv och arbete [The Future Was Ours: Engineers Writes about the Their Lifes and Work]. Nordiska museet, Stockholm (1993)

Agentization in Computing: How to Ameliorate the Consequences of the History Today?

Kai K. Kimppa, Janne Lahtiranta, and Markku I. Nurminen

Turku Centre for Computer Science (TUCS), University of Turku
kai.kimppa@it.utu.fi,
janne.lahtiranta@it.utu.fi,
markku.nurminen@it.utu.fi

Abstract. In this article, we proceed by pointing out some significant events in the history of information systems that have contributed to the phenomenon which causes users to experience computerized systems as agents. Some issues discussed in relation to the phenomenon are the creation of master files (all data of one object class was collected together) and the use of integrated databases (multiple master files were integrated to an integrated conceptual schema). The increasingly intertwined functions of storing, processing, and transmission confused the picture further. Finally, we try to trace the reason to this tendency to animate or anthropomorphize information systems. A review of textbooks through historic periods is used to get support or counter-arguments to this hypothesis. We will also look into agentization and unintended subjectification of computer artifacts, and consider whether they have an impact on today's concept of the computer as an agent.

Keywords: Agentization, history of computing, information systems design, software agents.

1 Introduction

A consistent look into the history of agentization in computing is missing and people do not understand its effects on the use of computer artifacts. One reason for this is that the concept itself is a rather vague one; it applies notions such as autonomy, reactivity, and social ability to animate or inanimate objects alike. Throughout the history of humanity, people considered living beings and even natural phenomena as agents of one sort or another. Agentization in computing is a more modern phenomena and it is present, amongst others, in popular media and research (e.g. when computers were referred to using terms like 'electronic brains'), and in unintended subjectification of information systems (e.g. when the user perceives that the computer has a will of its own).

Were it so that we could create life into inanimate objects, would they become agents? The stories such as that of a Golem built by Rabbi Judah Loew (a.k.a. Löw) from the mud of the Vltava River [7, pp. 119-121 and 10, pp. 205-206] and Mary Shelley's Frankenstein [10, p. 206] depict a situation in which a humanoid construct

J. Impagliazzo, T. Järvi, and P. Paju (Eds.): HiNC 2, IFIP AICT 303, pp. 74–83, 2009.
© IFIP International Federation for Information Processing 2009

is brought to life as a mocking figure of a human. Stories like this lay a basis for later stories of robots, such as those written by Isaac Asimov (1920-1992) where he describes a very human-like robots and the three Laws of Robotics or Philip K. Dick's famous novel 'Do Androids Dream of Electric Sheep?' (1968), which was later filmed as 'Blade Runner' (1982). Similar stories have been written of artificial intelligences (AIs) becoming sentient, e.g. by Arthur C. Clarke '2001: A Space Odyssey' (1968) in which the computer 'HAL' becomes sentient.

Mainstream media has also built this image (e.g. 'electronic brains') as the popular press anthropomorphized the computer already in the 1940s [7, p. 121]. As presented in the Figure 1, there has also been an anthropomorphized image of a computer wearing a navy captain's hat on the cover of the Time Magazine in January 1950 and choosing a PC as the "Man of the Year" (or Machine in this particular case instead of a traditional Man of the Year) in January 1983 [2, p. 1]. This raised questions such as '[c]ould a computer be smarter than Man?' [7, p. 121]. Partly this kind of popular publicity can be explained as efforts of marketing or gaining acceptance. It is, however an expression of a deeper cultural meaning assigned to computers [11].

Fig. 1. Time Magazine covers from January 23, 1950 and January 3, 1983

The vision in the field of AI was at the time, that it 'would soon rival the human intellect in many areas' [2, p. 213]. Although there were critics, such as J.C.R. Licklider, who thought that the view was utopian (ibid.), programs such as the famous Eliza [13] were created. In anticipation of actual AIs, Alan Turing proposed the Turing's test: if a person cannot tell whether they are talking with a machine or not, then the machine is intelligent [7, p. 122]. As Levinson [10, p. 209] pointed out, Eliza could only fool humans for a limited amount of time that it was another human (as many of us have undoubtedly experienced).

2 Nordic Information Systems Research and Agentization

The Nordic information systems (IS) research and development has throughout its history called for critical and user centered approach for IS development [1]. When we look into the agentization of computer artifacts, we should consider whether the users have been sufficiently involved in the design of the artifacts they use. It can be argued, that had they been involved in the design process, the inner workings or at least the fundamental operation principles of the artifacts would be evident to the homogenous majority of the users (i.e. to users who come from similar background and do similar work under similar circumstances). Since this is not the case, the users start to experience the software 'doing things on its own' instead of responding to their needs and wants.

The fundamental problem with this kind of view to agentization as a design flaw (of a sort) is that considering the modern computer artifacts, such as operating systems and office applications, it is nearly impossible to identify any kind of homogenous user groups or majorities. Furthermore, complexity and user interface techniques of the artifacts create additional layer of complexity into the mix. It may be extremely difficult to unearth the operating principles of an artifact; they are buried below complex, and sometimes even extremely anthropomorphic, or human-like, user interfaces. However, it is in the spirit of the Nordic IS research to questions whether this needs to be and what could one do to ameliorate the situation – if it needs to be ameliorated.

3   Control and Computer Artifacts

People employ computers when they perform their work tasks by means of information systems. The better control they have over the systems, the less need they have to regard them as agents rather than tools. For an individual user, such control eroded not only by the seemingly 'intelligent' behavior of the computer. The loss of control is further amplified by the complicated structure of the IS, and its semantics and pragmatics. These factors have supported the tendencies to regard the IS as a subject; such tendencies go back to the beginning of the computer era, or even to the Hollerith technology.

Our presumption in this article is that agentization moves the control of the system from the human to a third party. This move can be the information system itself (although in this case the 'control' is illusory), or the complex system can be used (either intentionally or unawares) to lessen the feel of security and control of the workers over their working situation. One good test to find this phenomenon is to ask the users to check whether the dubious information they received from the system is correct. If they can identify the other users that are responsible for it, the IS remains as a tool, but if they ask help from the system operators (who cannot have a semantic and pragmatic touch to the information), the system has grown to a 'subject'.

These cases hint towards a more profound problem where end users even today consider the computer as an active agent, which they do not feel in control of in their activities either at work or at home. This is something that needs consideration in the design of information systems even today. One possible explanation could be that information systems have properties that have resemblance with actors simply because it has been the dominant paradigmatic notion among designers.

One of the reasons why agentization of computer artifacts is a particularly present problem in Nordic countries is the early adaptation of information technology in these countries. The situation is becoming even more relevant now in the advent of ubiquitous and pervasive computing. As by its definition, ubiquitous computing is always present without being directly visible. Ubiquitous computing can take away control from the user without the user even noticing the shift of power from the user to the system. Pervasive systems, again, as per the definition, pervades the living and working environments of the users making the world 'easier to handle' and 'easier to access'. At the same time, pervasive systems and embedding computing into the environment leave less and less room for the control of the system to the user, e.g. by making the system invisible to the user – what you do not know is there, you cannot control.

In the European Union (EU) at large and in Finland, policies regarding information and communication technologies (ICT) emphasize that quick adoption of ICT technologies is valuable per se, and to shorten the 'gap' between the EU countries and leading ICT provider countries it is paramount to 'be at the leading edge'. Unfortunately, this reasoning is problematic. Firstly, it promotes an idea that technologies in themselves would be valuable (which they are not) and secondly, it gives an impression that it does not matter how they close the 'gap' between the leading countries. Issues such as having a technology that is transparent to the user are forgotten and information systems are given an ever-greater access to control in our (private) lives.

As explained by von Neuman, what makes software so efficient is that we can leave it to complete automatically a given sequence of commands. For example, if in a web store we program a software 'agent' to execute buy and sell commands upon meeting certain conditions, we know for whom the system and the agent are working. However, when the software applications or 'agents' become more complex and ubiquitous, the actual human actor can disappear. For example, an anthropomorphic robot designed for home care of the elderly people such as the Pearl [6], can replace some of the functions of home care personnel and it 'does' different automated tasks, but for whom? If software 'agents' become extremely complex and they are left to execute series of orders, similar effects arise as those described in the following case from Sherry Turkle's book "The Second Self: Computers and the Human Spirit" (1984). In the first part of the book (Chapter 1): "Child Philosophers: Are Smart Machines Alive?" where the children ponder whether the computer 'dies' when it is turned off and especially why does the computer 'do' the things it 'does' – because 'it wants to' or because 'it is told to', and especially by whom is it told to 'do' these things. [12]

The question whether the computers are beyond our control is also a relevant problem. Even their programmers do not understand the complex programs of today. The reasons for this can be numerous such as lack of time available for familiarizing with the source code and the number of programmers working with the application. Some of the systems today are so complex that even though one has sufficient time to study the inner workings of the system, no one can really understand the big picture. Ironically, Langefors [9] already used the concept "imperceivable system" as a cornerstone of his theoretical analysis. The complexity of the systems, however, does not need to be a major reason behind agentization of the software. As long as the user feels to be in control of the system, the operation logic of the system is visible, the user can at least understand the causality behind the operation logic. The user can anticipate certain results and fulfill one's expectations – or at least the user understands why they are not fulfilled (if that is the case).

Computer programs can be complex and we cannot understand them for other reasons as well. One such reason is that all programs must go through a compiler transition and they end up as binary, as a collection of zeroes and ones. The compiler itself is a program that translates programs – and depending on how we implement the program and the compiler, the results may wary. A more relevant problem however is the learning programs. Who can be responsible of the results of the 'actions' a learning program does. Transparency is one solution for this dilemma; even though 'actions' of the program are difficult to predict, we can explain the logic behind the operation.

The agent metaphor itself, and uncritical use of it, are problematic. We often see 'agents' doing searches without giving a second thought to the activity. The use of the term might propel us into new and stimulating directions, but if we do not exit the metaphor from time to time and look into the usage critically, we may become its prisoners instead of it aiding us in the development of helpful software.

We humans seem to have a tendency to anthropomorphize different things such as software, animals, and even natural phenomena. In computing, this may lead to excess agentization of programs. Trying to simplify complex issue by using a metaphor may actually distort the concept itself to something else altogether, thus not explaining the actual phenomenon at all. Agentization, at least in part, may result from misunderstanding or it may be just a defense mechanism of a human mind. It seems natural to humans to do this. Starting from simple animism of things such as lightning being 'a spear from Zeus', the human mind finds within it a simple 'analogy' in real life as a parent or leader physically reprimanding a child or subordinate to today's agentization of complex software. The phenomenon of lightning must have been quite as complex to understand for the early man as the information systems of today are to a typical user. To avoid this, we might also want to consider actually trying to explain the working of software to the best of our ability instead of using analogies or agentizing it. Of course, the explanations can be too cumbersome for everyday use, but we must not forget them, lest we anthropomorphize unnecessarily.

What is a software agent? Is an actual software agent even possible? In AI research, it would seem that at least the aim is to create an actual agent. The current 'agents' however hardly qualify. Commonly demonstrated examples of 'AI' include autonomous consumer products such as the automated lawnmower (the Robomow[1]) or vacuum cleaner (the Trilobite[2]), which are rather similar in behavior. A real agent chooses; more specifically, it can choose differently. If element of choice does not exist, a real agency cannot either. Maybe we should talk about the anti-agentization of users. When the users do not question the 'decisions' the system 'makes' but rather attribute to a 'choice' to the system – "it did that" – both the 'end users' and the operators diminish in their capacity as decision makers and become unwitting objects for the system. The users actually degrade to the level of a machine themselves by doing things they are told to do even though they do not know the reason, only because the system told them. A similar situation holds for the operators of the system,

---

[1] http://www.friendlyrobotics.com/
[2] http://trilobite.electrolux.se/

where suddenly it is the system that 'needs' or 'wants' things instead of operators. The various issues introduced in this chapter have created a fertile ground for the development of information systems which made the actual agent disappear for the user.

4 The Invisible User

The argumentation around artificial 'intelligence' sometimes dominates the discussion around agentization. Therefore, the focus is in the behavior of the computer: Can the computer outperform human actors' abilities or capabilities? To play chess or to proofread a document can give an example of this. In most cases, the more or less 'intelligent' behavior is an outcome of deliberate purposeful objective and effort to create such an artifact. There is, however, another path to go towards ICT artifacts with agent-like properties. We seldom plan these paths consciously. What happens is that human actors gradually disappear from the sight and finally nobody seems to be in control of these artifacts.

This development is often due to the increasing complexity of information systems. The issue is not only in programs or in algorithms that may have characteristics with resemblance of intelligent behavior. We excessively use information technology for performing other functions as well. Most important functions on the side of processing are storing and communication. In what follows, we analyze the three main functions in the time perspective. We identify important events in the history of ICT and we highlight their possible contributions to making the human actor invisible.

During the batch-processing era, the agents and their roles were distinct. We delivered batch runs to the computer centers, where the operator performed activities in predetermined sequence. The operator could report about the status of different jobs, and no process executed unless the operator was in charge of it.

The situation changed slightly with the advent of multiprocessing and time-sharing. One processor could divide its capacity between different jobs by giving each of them a slice of time in their turns. First occurrences of this were background jobs such as pronging that occurred during such slices when the processor was less busy. In a time-sharing environment, a program could be loaded in the memory, ready for action but idle, like sleeping until it awoke by a particular trigger. Current graphical computer interfaces are essentially based in such waiting loops. When a program is running, in some way it has a life of its own, creating an illusion of an agent. Since the number of processors in our artifacts has increased dramatically since the first time-sharing operating systems, people are likely to expose themselves to this illusion more and more easily.

In storing, the illusion of agentization does not reflect intelligent behavior in such extent as in processing. Rather it highlights the role of the knowing agent. In the era of batch processing, the dominating sequential files did easily associate with a knowing subject. In fact, manual card files were better suited for such repository of a search date than the files on magnetic tapes or even on punched cards. Such a file was directly coupled to some application and the connection was pragmatically established. Gradually master-files replaced such application-specific files. The master-files collected all attributes of a certain object class to one collected file even if not all those data items were useful in any single application. We strengthen this change when the database concept integrated the conceptual schema between different object classes. Direct access and continuous availability of the database finally created a unit, which we could regard as a knowing subject for inquiry. On the other hand, it was difficult to identify and find human actors who stood and could take the responsibility for the semantics and pragmatics of various segments in the database. For some reason, this has not been a central design issue in information systems development.

Another problem that quite often confuses the users of a centralized information system is the dualistic nature of data storages. They are storages that document states and events from one point of time to another. This is the archiving function. However, in addition, they also use stored data. When one user writes a message and another user is reading it, it creates a communication link between them. Therefore, we can interpret an integrated information system as a communication network. However, such a network is nontransparent, due to three reasons:

o The volume and scope of a database are so large that the structure is unperceivable;
o The receiver often delays or triggers the message delivery, which mingles the archiving and communicating function within each other;
o The processing function is also involved. The receiver may get a message that was not entered by anyone. Hence, the message may be a report summarized by a piece of software.

All these three factors together indicate that it, indeed, is difficult to reconstruct the human agency structure embedded in an integrated information system. It is just natural that the users in most cases give explanations like "I received this information form the database" or "I have to enter this number because the system wants me to do it".

Many forms of electronic communication keep the user visible; in fact, they make the agentization concern even worse. For example, e-mail is rather visible and transparent form of communication. Even unwanted (junk mail) or anonymous senders of e-mail support the actor nature of the ICT artifact. On the other hand, most electronic services are based on the absence of the service provider. The service provider has made and started a program, an agent, which can respond meaningfully to the requests of the customer. However, electronic services must maintain the connection to human actors, because otherwise it would be very problematic to recover from errors and exceptional situations.

The concern for invisible user and disappearance of responsible human actors is not only a theoretical or conceptual exercise. It leaves the user without help, alone, when he runs to the problem of an unusual or exceptional situation, without practically any chance to check the origin of the problem or the consequences of alternative options to deal with it. Some authors have even argued that this nameless character of technology lends itself very well as a means of technical control. This is what happened with assembly lines during the first half of the 20th century.

"Struggle between workers and bosses over the transformation of labor power into labor was no longer a simple and direct *personal* confrontation; now the conflict was mediated by the production technology itself." [3, p. 118]

"Control becomes truly structural, embedded in that hoary old mystification, technology." [3, p. 125]

The increased use of computers as a means of control created strong resistance in Scandinavian countries. One slogan was: "We refuse to be detail-controlled", "Vi vägrar låta detaljstyra oss!" [4]. Furthermore, the defense of professional skills was important. Later, among many others, they established a Nordic Research project UTOPIA (1981-1985) to protect the maintaining and development of the skills of graphical workers. This time the frontline dealt with the whole profession, but the Scandinavian spirit was still clear: "To become masters of the machine", "At bli maskinens herrar" [5].

5 Classes of Agency

The real agency can disappear in various ways into the system. Below we list the ways we can transfer agency to the system, based on the previous analysis.

- o *Strong agency*: Makes genuine choices;
- o *Weak agency*: The actor executes a program but cannot check or correct the outcome;
- o *Lack of agency*: Everybody knows that the computer is not a real agent; no one is able to identify the real agent for different actions;
- o *Coordinative agency*: Coordinates actions, but does not perform them; another formulation of the invisible hand (or the boss):

    Edwards' Control policies
    Personal (by capitalist)
    Bureaucratic (by foremen by rules)
    Technical (nameless and "objective": we all have to obey the System)

- o *Replaced agency*: Imitation of the human actor's behaviour (e.g. modeling of their feelings);
- o *Agent without responsibility*: Expert systems; eroded responsibility.

In addition, the following constitutes a set of different relevant acts:

- o *Deliberate*: Not accidental;
- o *Causative*: Aiming at a goal that may be different from the present;
- o *Intentional*: Causation may be nondeterministic, not all shots hit;
- o *Competent*: Knowledgeable (Does not try to fly aircraft without adequate training);
- o *Motivation*: Purpose, benefit, duty (Why should the agent do it);
- o *Consequences*: Expected;
- o *Context*: Collaboration, coordination;
- o *Responsibility*: Accountability.

We combine these ideas in Table 1.

Table 1. Relationships between agency and action[3]

Agency

Act	Strong Agency	Weak Agency	Lack of Agency	Coordinative Agency	Replaced Agency	Agent without responsibility
Deliberate	Yes	Yes	Yes		No	No
Causative	Yes	Yes	Yes		No	Maybe
Intentional	Yes	No	No		No	Maybe
Competent	Yes	Maybe	Maybe	Maybe	Maybe	Maybe
Motivation	Yes	Maybe	Maybe	Yes	No	Maybe
Expected consequences	Yes	Yes	Maybe	Maybe	No	No
Context	Yes	Yes	Yes	Yes	Maybe	Maybe
Responsibility	Yes	No	No	Maybe	No	No

As can be seen, strong agent can perform any actions listed. At this time, a strong agent would be a human being, although it is – at least to a degree – imaginable that a system might eventually hold the same status. Whether that is desirable, is outside the scope of this paper. The typical situation is that of weak agency, e.g. in a web store where the software performs certain tasks instead of the actual human actor. The weak actor is never responsible for its actions nor can it perform intentional choices – it cannot decide that it does not want to perform an order given to it by the actual actor. Lack of agency is the same situation as weak agency – except that the actor behind the agent is unknown. This causes problems in many situations that can lead to agents without responsibility or even to a replaced agency. We can use coordinative agency on purpose or it can 'just happen'; it moves the agency via a bureaucratic or technical group from the users or leaders of an organization to e.g. an ERP system. Thus, the coordinative agency can function as if there was a lack of agency when there in fact typically is not. The three empty slots in the table (table 1) may be non-sensical as questions for a coordinative agency.

The situation becomes truly problematic when there is an agent without responsibility or when one replaces the agency. When we cannot identify the entity (e.g. a medical expert system) as a system in the first place [see e.g. 8] or we cannot identify the agent behind the system, who – or what – is the responsible party? Is the question of 'what' being the responsible party even sensible? How could a system be accountable for something? Thus, the agent can – and does – function without anyone in charge. It is easy to give examples when this would be problematic (e.g. a ubiquitous system that transfers the 'responsibility' of the wellbeing of an elderly person). We now replace the agency, previously held by home care personnel, by the system; yet, the system is not responsible for anything.

---

[3] Please note: many of the agencies can overlap each other.

6   Conclusions

To counter phenomenon of agentization and anthropomorphism, we need to take a critical view towards the new, especially ubiquitous software. The user needs to make decisions and must be in control. The users must decide what the system does and what the users want to do themselves. This, however, is becoming ever more difficult. A typical example is a ubiquitous home care system. The system collects information and 'acts' in the every day environment, but where do the commands come from? Who collects the information supplied by the system? For what purpose does one use that information? Presumably, the commands come from the home care or health care personnel and the information is used by them for the benefit of the user. Nevertheless, if the users are unaware of the usage they cannot control the 'actions' of the system or the use of the information. The system has become a semi-invisible tool for power over the user—a system 'out of control'.

References

[1] Bjerknes, G., Ehn, P., Kyng, M. (eds.): Computers and Democracy, a Scandinavian Challenge. Avebury, Aldershot (1987)

[2] Campbell, M., Aspray, K., Aspray, W.: Computer: A History of the Information Machine. Basic Books, New York (1996)

[3] Edwards, R.: Contested Terrain: The Transformation of the Workplace in the Twentieth Century. Basic, New York (1979)

[4] Ehn, P., Erlander, B., Karlsson, R.: Vi vägrar låta detaljstyra oss! (We refuse to be detail-controlled.) Rapport från samarbetet mellan Statsanställdas Förbund, avdelning 1050 och DEMOS - projektet, Stockholm, Arbetslivscentrum (1978)

[5] Ekdahl, L.: At bli maskinens herrar [To become masters of the machine]. UTOPIA report no. 19. Arbetslivscentrum, Stockholm (1984)

[6] Jajeh, P.: Robot nurse escorts and schmoozes the elderly (August 24, 2004), http://www.thematuremarket.com/SeniorStrategic/Robot_nurse_escorts_schmoozesthe_elderly-5260-5.html (accessed 13.04.2007)

[7] Kennedy, N.: The Industrialization of Intelligence: Mind and Machine in the Modern Age. Unwin Hyman Limited, London (1989)

[8] Lahtiranta, J., Kimppa, K.: Telemedicine and responsibility: why anthropomorphism and consent issues muddle the picture. In: 5th International WE-B (Working for e-Business) Conference, Fremantle, Australia (2004)

[9] Langefors, B.: Theoretical Analysis of Information Systems. Student Litteratur, Lund (1970)

[10] Levinson, P.: The soft edge: a natural history and future of the information revolution. Routledge, London (1997)

[11] Suominen, J.: Sähköaivo sinuiksi, tietokone tutuksi, [Getting familiar with the electric brain, getting to know the computer]. Jyväskylä (2000)

[12] Turkle, S.: The Second Self: Computers and the Human Spirit. Granada Publishing Limited, London (1984)

[13] Weizenbaum, J.: Computer Power and Human Reason. Freeman, San Francisco (1976)

Computer Fiction: "A Logic Named Joe"

Towards Investigating the Importance of Science Fiction in the Historical Development of Computing

David Ferro and Eric Swedin

Weber State University
dferro@weber.edu, eswedin@weber.edu

Abstract. The bulk of Science Fiction (SF) has not predicted the most influential computer technologies of the late 20th century. This paper begins with an exception entitled "A Logic Named Joe" and its accurate description of the contemporary environment of PCs and the World Wide Web. It then proposes the possible historical and cultural value of SF in techno-scientific development - more specifically computer development - in both the U.S. and Finland, and argues that social science approaches to understanding technoscience should take SF into account when describing those communities of practice.

Keywords: Science Fiction, SF, engineering, science, culture, "Murray Leinster", "A Logic Named Joe".

1 Introduction

With notable exceptions, the bulk of science fiction (SF) missed the possibilities of some of the most innovative and influential technologies of the 20th century. These innovations include personal computers, networks, the internet and world wide web, and online resources. This paper surveys some of that literature, especially a noteworthy exception – "A Logic Named Joe" – to kick-off the discussion of just how important understanding SF might be to understanding the culture of techno-scientific development and, more specifically, computer development.

2 A Logic Named Joe

Despite the stereotype that 'Science Fiction imagines and science makes it so', for a long time SF was thought to not have predicted the rise of technologies like the internet, world wide web, and personal computers. SF published and filmed in the first 2/3 of the twentieth century continually had larger machines and/or more powerful robots that acted as intelligent agents. It was the Frankenstein story told repeatedly, man recreating him or her self in mind or robotic form to reap the 'reward'. The 'Frankenstein' became larger and larger. E.M Forster's 1909 story "The Machine Stops" had humanity living in a worldwide city run by computer and the 1970 film *Colossus: The Forbin Project* had a massive computer taking over the world's nuclear weapons for examples. This continued up to the introduction of real personal computers where the emphasis moved to the dangers of virtual presence and hacking. The

J. Impagliazzo, T. Järvi, and P. Paju (Eds.): HiNC 2, IFIP AICT 303, pp. 84–94, 2009.
© IFIP International Federation for Information Processing 2009

'villain' (or potential problem) in these newer stories became the empowered individual – a theme, interestingly, that is found in "A Logic Named Joe" as well.

A short story by the author Murray Leinster (the frequently used pen name of Will F. Jenkins), "A Logic Named Joe," published in March 1946, in many ways predicted the rise of the internet, personal computers, and the convergence of interactive computing, television, and telephony. Like many stories, it plays with the idea of a 'naturally occurring' sentient mechanism - in other words, the machine just somehow 'woke up a bit more' when it was created. The difference is the almost prosaic presentation of the machine as a networked appliance. The protagonist himself is portrayed as an 'average Joe' computer technician who has a first-person style that evokes a 1940s plumber.

The story is concerned with a "logic" (a personal computer) sitting on a desk in the home of the protagonist. This logic is linked with other centralized and home logics that have become commonplace. In the story, logics have become knowledge resources, entertainment devices, and communication devices in the home. The logic named "Joe" develops a certain level of artificial intellect and then wrecks a bit of well-meaning havoc on society by helping people do exactly what they want – including some less than savory things. The protagonist saves society in the end by unplugging Joe from the network.

The creativity and prescience displayed in the creation of this story is astounding. In 1946, the public might have known of one electronic computer: the ENIAC. It was the size of a room. An army of women who flipped thousands of switches handled the input to the machine. Its output was the hundreds of blinking lights on its front panels. Among many other things, Leinster saw instead an easy-to-use keyboard and screen interface on a machine the size of a breadbox linked to millions of other similar machines. A computer of that size would not exist until the 1970s. The internet would not exist until 1969, the world wide web, not until the 1980s, and the combination would not become commonplace until the 1990s.

Here is some of the text of the story:

> *Say you punch "Station SNAFU" on your logic. Relays in the tank take over an' whatever vision-program SNAFU is telecastin' comes on your logic's screen. Or you punch "Sally Hancock's Phone" an' the screen blinks an' sputters an' you're hooked up with the logic in her house an' if somebody answers you got a vision-phone connection. But besides that, if you punch for the weather forecast or who won today's race at Hialeah or who was mistress of the White House durin' Garfield's administration or what is PDQ and R sellin' for today, that comes on the screen too. The relays in the tank do it. The tank is a big buildin' full of all the facts in creation an' all the recorded telecasts that ever was made— an' it's hooked in with all the other tanks all over the country...[16].*

Our question is: Did such a forward-looking story actually affect those developments? The story has a far more accurate description of our current state of PC and WWW development than Vannevar Bush's "As We May Think" Atlantic Monthly, July 1945 article. Bush's article has been mentioned by both Douglas Engelbart and J.C.R. Licklidder for their work in creating the origins of personal computing that includes hypertext and the internet [17, 27].

The story of this paper begins at Syracuse University Special Collections Research Center where the William S. Jenkins' papers are deposited, a collection of records that take up 68 linear feet (72 boxes) of documents and there are at least three boxes strictly of letters [22]. Under his pen name of Murray Leinster he is often called the "dean of science fiction" and he wrote hundreds of stories and books between 1919 and 1975.

We could find no direct correspondence that linked those creating the computing technologies of the twentieth century with "Joe" or any other Leinster story. However, what was found was a continual effort on the part of Jenkins and other authors to maintain science and scientific veracity and uphold those ideals in the fictional form they termed SF. In addition, we found evidence of the interaction and mutual support between scientific and SF worlds. The work established his network of correspondence and pointed the way to further investigation.

3 Why Look at Science Fiction?

To those of us in the computer world, the possibility of science fiction's impact on science and technology – and specifically computing development - seems obvious. We name servers for characters and locations from SF novels and movies. The language of SF seems frequently used in technical conversations. A 2006 Discovery Channel television program entitled "How William Shatner Changed the Universe" had the stories of a number of technologists and scientists crediting the 1960s television show *Star Trek* as influencing their career choices. The special has Marty Cooper inspired by the "communicator" to create a mobile phone with voice recognition and a flip top; Dr. Mae C. Jenison inspired to become an astronaut, and John Adler inventing the cyber knife inspired by the "tricorder". Authors such as Ben Bova (himself a retired aeronautical engineer) have been heard to say that "everyone who landed on the moon liked science fiction" [5]. A conversation between Astrophysicist Kip Thorne and Carl Sagan influenced both the science and science fiction of Worm Holes [38].

Although not an academic work, a James Frenkel book of essays looked historically at the 1979 SF work *True Names* by Vernor Vinge [12]. Vinge's book was another prophetic story about identity and security on the world wide web. In it, a highly capable web hacker is able to utilize resources on the web and then finds himself in a U.S. government led effort to capture an unknown hacker that threatens the security of the country. It pre-dated the web yet captured two important things. One was some of the critical issues of internet access we are faced with today where free access must be balanced against security and the possibilities of stolen identities. The other was one of the interesting characteristics of humans to create a "second self" or virtual identity through the computer; an idea that was studied extensively in the 1980s by Sherry Turkle [39]. Her book came out the same year (1984) that the very popular-fiction-influencing *Neuromancer* [13] came out that began the 'cyber punk' genre in SF.

Frenkel's volume contained essays from some of the seminal figures in the development of computing (including Vernor Vinge). Some of the authors not only complemented the story's predictive qualities but wrote about how influential the story was in their development efforts of the speculated but (at the time) still-not-created computer technologies that are so prevalent today. They included Danny Hillis (founder of Thinking Machines), Timothy C. May (former chief scientist at Intel), Marvin Minsky (cofounder of MIT AI Lab), and Richard Stallman (developer of GNU Emacs, founder of Free Software movement, and the GNU General Public License CopyLeft scheme).

Other examples of the influence of SF abound.   J.C.R. Licklidder (nicknamed "Lick") proposed the origins of the internet in his 1960 paper "Man-Computer Symbiosis".   He called it the Intergalactic Network.   In 1963, Lick wrote a lengthy memo to the prospective members of the Intergalactic Network in which he expressed his frustration over the proliferation of disparate programming languages, debugging systems, time-sharing system control languages, and documentation schemes.

"Is it not desirable or even necessary for all centers to agree upon some language or, at least, upon some conventions for asking such questions as 'What language do you speak?' At this extreme, the problem is essentially the one discussed by science-fiction writers: How do you get communications started among totally uncorrelated sapient beings?" [27].

There seems to be many SF references in the open source/free software community. In the 2001 documentary *Revolution OS* Richard Stallman receives an award from Linus Torvalds and he makes a somewhat obscure analogy between the history of open source and some characters in the original *Star Wars* movie. The audience of 3000+ laughs in a way that shows they obviously get the reference. Eric S. Raymond in his *The Cathedral and the Bazaar* argues that becoming a good hacker requires enjoying science fiction [30]. Between 2005 and 2006 a conference called *Linucon* attempted to combine open source hacking and SF [28]. The search for examples is an ongoing effort.

4 Theoretical Background

Fiction and literature that deals with science and technology in some way is critical for understanding the culture that creates that literature, and, reflexively, the science and technology that is created by that literature. There is a circularity of influences whether we are describing the technological culture at large or the specific ones of technological development. If we accept computer development as community, culture, or social process then there are cultural requirements. There are decisions by members of that culture as to who is in and out of that culture, language that informs and creates it, networks of relations woven, organization that is created and evolved.

For our purposes we can trace some of the academics generally investigating scientific and technological communities. For example, Robert K. Merton's 1942 "The Normative Structure of Science", created the Sociology of Science. Seminal works followed such as Thomas Kuhn's *The Structure of Scientific Revolutions* in 1962 [23] and Bruno Latour and Steve Woolgar's 1979 *Laboratory Life* ethnography [25] which started Actor-Network Theory (ANT). Applying similar approaches to history of technology led to Thomas P. Hughes' 1983 Networks of Power [21], who along with Wiebe E. Bijker and Trevor J. Pinch created The Social Construction of Technology (SCOT) field. Louis L. Bucciarelli's 1994 *Designing Engineers*, a participatory ethnography came out of this [8]. The various historical, sociological, anthropological, and, to a lesser extent, managerial and economic approaches have been consolidated into the field known as Science and Technology Studies (STS) – a multidisciplinary approach to understanding the social aspects of science and technology. Effective journalistic ethnographies of technological communities have proven informative as well, such as Tracy Kidder's 1981 *The*

Soul of a New Machine [24] and Scott Rosenberg's 2007 *Dreaming in Code* [31]. Donna Haraway's "A Cyborg Manifesto" has initiated a great deal of examining women in computing and computing culture [19].

Obviously, given the list above, techno-scientific culture has been given considerable academic attention. There has been far less examining of Science Fiction as a component of anthropological, sociological , philosophical, and historical studies of science and technology, but the exceptions and possibilities are interesting.

The bulk of study on SF that has occurred has taken place in Literary Studies and multi-disciplinary "Digital Culture" programs. For those interested in these approaches there are two journals: *Extrapolation* (which uses the term Speculative Fiction rather than Science Fiction) [11] and *Science-Fiction Studies* [33] that take theoretical approaches to examining science fiction. In addition, many of the SF authors themselves, such as Brian Aldiss [2], Ursula K. LeGuin [26], and Bruce Sterling [36], have taken a number of interesting theoretical approaches.

SF has been examined in anthropological and sociological ways in Finland somewhat. A sample includes Jaakko Suominen who wrote a monograph that examines the role of popular culture (including Science Fiction) on preparing the Finnish public for computers even before the first personal computer arrived [37]. Petri Saarikoski wrote about personal computer interest in Finland from the 1970s to the mid-1990s that touched on some literary influences [32]. Marja Vehvilainen has touched on literature and its effects on women in technical fields in her writings [40]. Suominen and Saarikoski are both writing from Digital Culture Studies perspectives. Vehvilainen is writing from a Women Studies/Feminist perspective.

There are interesting convergences occurring via many of the above noted disciplines that might benefit from some focus on SF. The history of technology and science has been moving in the direction of the lesser-known actors for more than two decades. For example, Shapin and Schaffer's *Leviathan and the Air Pump* [34] partially looks at the role of media for promoting/enrolling the public and, to some extent, removing the separation between those inside and outside of science. Examining the intersection of the user and technology, various approaches – SCOT, ANT, Feminist theory, Media Studies, Consumer Studies – came together in an edited volume, by Nelly Oudshoorn and Trevor Pinch, entitled *How Users Matter: The Co-Construction of Users and Technologies* [29]. In that book they conclude with the co-creation (adaption, adoption, and non-adoption) that occurs between consumers and producers of the technology. They credit feminist approaches for bringing this forward, rely on SCOT for its focus on the creative forces and the culture of invention in technological creation, and credit Media Studies as examining how media has influenced consumer choices. According to the historian Kimmo Ahonen "Thanks to the influential studies of Robert Brent Toplin and Robert Rosenstone, fiction film is [controversially] considered to be a useful source for various research questions [in historical research]" [1]. Finally, while admittedly little studied at this writing, some computer-human interface scholars have even begun to borrow from literary studies by creating "pastiche scenarios" that use literary resources. These resources are characters from fiction (including potentially science fiction but, interestingly, the authors were somewhat dismissive of the weak characterizations in the genre) – to create use cases that resonate more with designers and their customers [4].

Lastly, returning to history for a potential exemplar, there is *Doomsday Men: The Real Dr Strangelove and the Dream of the Superweapon* by P.D. Smith [35]. Smith focuses not only on the history of physics and military technology but the literature of apocalypse begun in the nineteenth century and specifically, H.G. Well's *The World Set Free*. According to Smith astrophysicist Szilard read Well's work in 1932, "the year before he came up with the idea that a nuclear chain reaction could be used to power a bomb, and said that Wells should be credited as 'father of the atom bomb' ". *Different Engines: How Science Drives Fiction and Fiction Drives Science* by Mark Brake and Neil Hook [6] also looks at the historical influence of fiction on the scientific enterprise from its inception. They note the importance of fictional works such as Francis Godwin's *The Man in the Moone* and Francis Bacon's *New Atlantis* as spurring, even preceding, scientific discovery and discussion.

5 Surveying Technologists on the Importance of Science Fiction

The authors conducted a survey to attempt to add primary research results to the questions related to the importance of SF as an aspect of those engaged in technoscientific endevours, The authors wanted to document the type of literature and media important to students who chose technoscientic fields of study, compared to those who had not, and how it influenced their views of society. In addition, we wondered how that might translate across national borders. That we can find no similar study points to the hole in our understanding of engineering culture as well as our stereotypical assumptions. Indeed, regarding assumptions, a student in one of the questionnaires noted "News Flash: Geeks like Sci Fi!" However, what is the evidence that they do and, much more importantly, what does it mean?

A survey was created that compared university students in three classes. These are four of the questions that were asked: "Had the survey taker:

o Played Science Fiction oriented video games
o Watched Science Fiction movies or shows
o Read Science Fiction for pleasure
o Thought that Science Fiction had influenced their views of the future?"

All three samples are small at this preliminary stage. In all, 67 students in three locations were given a survey: 13 in a general history class and 25 in a computer science class, both at an American university, and 28 in a computer science class in Finland. The history class consisted of students of many disciplines, including some technical/scientific fields.

The results show that the computer science classes in Finland and the U.S. track pretty well together, with both groups of CS students showing high levels of participation in all three activities of playing, watching, and reading SF oriented entertainment. The general history class in the U.S. was lower in games and much lower in reading. Most interestingly, the majority of students (54%) in the history class felt that SF had not influenced their perception of the future. The vast majority of the CS classes in both Finland and the U.S. felt that it had.

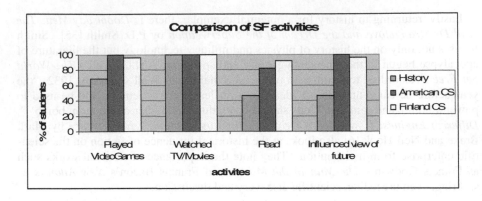

6 The Evolution of Science Fiction and Its Scientific Literacy

The results of this survey should not surprise us. Isaac Asimov, after a long break from writing fiction notes in 1967 "We are living in 'science fictional' world" – a world of increasingly realized scientific and technological advances [14]. If SF plays a large role in the 'science fictional' culture at large, one could speculate that it might play a larger role in the engineering and scientific communities that are closer to the creation of the 'science fictional' creations. The origins of SF included the idea of popularizing science and technology all along. It spoke to and was written by members of scientific and technological communities. As a result, SF became part of the Lingua Franca of those communities.

In the nineteenth century, the British originally used the term "scientific romance". Americans used "invention stories". Other terms included "off-trail stories, impossible stories, different stories, highly imaginative stories, weird-scientific stories, pseudo-scientific stories, scientific fiction, and scientific novels". Hugo Gernsback, editor of Modern Electronics and other magazine that often combined electrical hobbies with fiction, coined "scientific fiction", then "scientifiction", and finally "science fiction" in June of 1929 and since universally adopted [41]. Arguably, the most important award for a SF author is the Hugo Award, named for Hugo Gernsback. Finland appears to have followed the English terminology.

Science Fiction has been termed the literature with a sense of wonder with the Universe. From an interview with James Gunn:

> *"Yes. Generally speaking, people who are close to science, or people who are close to the science element in science fiction, maintain their hope and maintain their faith in science. The... you find them going around and explaining that while there are bad effects, most of the good effects are yet to come."* [15].

The trust in techno-scientific advance and adherence – within limits – to techno-scientific veracity has been critical to the core of SF. This was termed "Hard Science Fiction" by P. Schuyler Miller (a not very well-known science fiction author and regular book reviewer for *Astounding Science-Fiction* and *Analog* for 24 years) in a November 1957 editorial while he was discussing the re-publication of Campbell's

Islands of Space [42]. With changes in society such as the 1950s view of "better life through chemicals" brought to an end by books like Rachel Carson's *Silent Spring* [9], reactionary, less positivistic, and less optimistic "new wave" SF came about. This activity influenced the economic necessity of consolidation of SF with fantasy to create SF&F in the 1960s and made the term "hard" SF more important to those interested in the 'hard science' viewpoint.

The negotiation of what SF would be, however, had been a constant component of interactions between authors, editors, and fans. Gernsback often editorialized on the stories he published in his magazines as to their potential scientific veracity. He noted:

> *"In time to come, our authors will make a marked distinction between science fiction and science faction...By this term I mean science fiction in which there are so many scientific facts that the story, as far as the scientific part is concerned, is no longer fiction but becomes more or less a recounting of the fact"* [43].

He took one of the fathers of SF, Jules Verne, to task in Verne's "Off on a Comet" story:

> *"[T]he author here abandons his usual scrupulously scientific attitude and gives his fancy freer rein... Verne asks us to accept a situation which is in a sense self-contradictory..."* [43].

John Wood Campbell, Jr. took the post of editor of *Astounding Science Fiction* in 1937 and would introduce in a serious way what C.S. Lewis would term "engineers' stories". Now the veracity not only would run to the science, but to the scientists and engineers that were creating the science and technology. He encouraged a number of authors, including Isaac Asimov and Robert Heinlein, who had scientific or engineering backgrounds. In an interview in 1971 Asimov spoke of Campbell wanting realism, not that they "couldn't go out into the blue yonder" but that in the stories "scientists acted the way scientists do; that engineers acted the way engineers do; and in short that the scientific culture be represented accurately" [14].

The audience and authors may have evolved as well according to Asimov. There already existed a high percentage of technically oriented Americans reading and writing for the magazines. According to Everett F. Bleiler in *Science-Fiction: The Early Years*, almost half the writers had (or went into) technical, scientific, or medical backgrounds. Moreover, college education (93 of 510) and advanced degrees are in a higher percentage than the general American population of the time [3]. However, "While a subclass of mature readers persisted . . . this class diminished proportionately" [3]. Potentially as a reaction, in 1936 the market did change when *Wonder Stories* died and, the next year, when John W. Campbell Jr. took over *Astounding Stories*. He not only continued the attempt begun to add more scientific and technological accuracy but to raise the literary level as well. "[O]nly Raymond Z. Gullun, John Beynon Harris, Murray Leinster, Frank Belknap Long, C.L.Moore, Ross Rocklynne, Clifford Simak, E.E. Smith, and Jack Williamson continued as significant authors," continues Bleiler. Other writers continued with lesser effect and new authors sprang up such as Isaac Asimov, L. Sprague de Camp, Robert A. Heinlein, L. Ron Hubbard, Henry Kuttner, Fritz Leiber, Theodore Sturgeon, and A.E. Van Vogt [3]. The SF authors themselves argued for what SF would be. In an August 1951 letter to Truman Talley, Robert Heinlein writes, "I did not know that a Ray-Bradbury story was still under consideration. . . Ray is a prime example of the writer of pseudo-scientific fantasy...I have yet to read under his name any science fiction. He is ignorant of science, doesn't even know what the word means..." [20].

7   The Role of Predictions and a Conclusion

While Hard SF continues to play a role in SF, SF's adherence to realism and, thus, an adherence to accurate technical predictions, may or not be as critical to the traditional needs of storytelling such as theme, characterization, and plot. Futurology is a field fraught with difficulties. The accuracy of predictions by experts in their fields was found to be "at best weakly related to general technical expertise and unrelated to specific expertise" by George Wise in 1976 [44].

I would argue that predictive aspects of Leinster's "A Logic Named Joe" in describing our current networked society should be appreciated. However, its importance to our contemporary situation is more complex than technical accuracy. Thomas Haigh has noted, "Nothing tells us more about a society than its assumptions about its future" [18]. Indeed, the Leinster story tells us much of the society of 1946 post-war America, especially with regard to its assumptions of censorship. What stands in as the 'World Wide Web' of the story is far more restrictive concerning nudity, personal information, and potentially dangerous technical knowledge than the Web we know today – at least in most of the Western World However, it tells us as much about our current situation that it has been rediscovered and celebrated through the very mechanism that Leinster predicted – the world wide web. Moreover, I propose, that no matter how many technical predictions in SF go awry, the value is in the predicting itself. Author David Brin called them "thought experiments" where "tomorrow remains a popular playground" [7]. In many ways, they are like the thought experiments that engineers and scientists utilize everyday when imagining a future augmented by continued invention and discovery.

With further research, we will hope to discover more about how important a role SF plays in the communities where the future is created. How well does it conscript/retain and, in contrast, exclude membership to those communities? How big a part of the language is it in those communities? How much have the creations of those communities been shaped by it? In addition, does society depend on its assumptions? Perhaps, one might argue, democracy depends on it. In increasingly techno-scientific democracies like Finland and the U.S., a technically informed citizenship may thus depend, to some degree, on the literature of choice of the creators of that technology and science.

References

[1] Ahonen, K.: Interview with author David Ferro (November 2008)
[2] Aldiss, B.: Billion Year Spree: The History of Science Fiction. Transworld Publishers Ltd. (1973)
[3] Bleiler, E.F.: Science-Fiction: The Early Years, p. xxiv. Kent State University Press (January 1991)

[4] Blythe, M.A., Wright, P.C.: Pastiche scenarios: Fiction as a resource for user centred design. Interacting with Computers 18(5), 1139–1164 (2006)
[5] Bova, B.: Interview with author David Ferro. In: NSS Conference, Ogden, Utah, October 6 (2006)
[6] Brake, M., Hook, N.: Different Engines: How Science Drives Fiction and Fiction Drives Science. Macmillan, Basingstoke (2007)
[7] Brin, D.: The Life Eaters. Wildstorm Productions, La Jolla (2003) (Afterward)
[8] Bucciarelli, L.L.: Designing Engineers. The MIT Press, Cambridge (1994)
[9] Carson, R.: Silent Spring. Houghton Mifflin Company (1962)
[10] Engelbart, D.: Augmenting Human Intellect (1962),
     http://www.bootstrap.org/augdocs/friedewald030402/augmenting
     humanintellect/ahi62index.html
[11] Extrapolation (published quarterly by University of Texas, Brownsville, TX),
     http://fp.dl.kent.edu/extrap/
[12] Frenkel, J. (ed.): True Names: And the Opening of the Cyberspace Frontier, Tor Books (2001)
[13] Gibson, W.: Neuromancer. Ace Books, New York (1984)
[14] Gunn, J.: James Gunn's The Literature of Science Fiction Film Series (The History of Science Fiction after 1938 interview with Isaac Asimov (1971)) Center for The Study of Science Fiction Film Series 51, DMZ productions (2002)
[15] Gunn, J.: James Gunn's The Literature of Science Fiction Film Series (Theme In Science Fiction: A Discussion Between Gordon Dickson & James Gunn (1975)) Center for The Study of Science Fiction Film Series 51, DMZ productions (2002)
[16] Jenkins, W.F.: (published under actual name), A Logic Named Joe, Astounding Science Fiction (March 1946),
     http://www.baen.com/chapters/W200506/0743499107___2.htm
[17] Hafner, K., Lyon, M.: Where Wizards Stay Up Late, p. 38. Simon and Schuster, NY (1996)
[18] Haigh, T.: History of the Future (course), http://www.tomandmaria.com/st197
[19] Haraway, D.: A Cyborg Manifesto: Science, Technology, and Socialist-Feminism in the Late Twentieth Century. In: Simians, Cyborgs and Women: The Reinvention of Nature, pp. 149–181. Routledge, New York (1991)
[20] Heinlein, R.: Letter from Robert Heinlein to Truman Talley, August 1951, Syracuse University Library Archives (1951)
[21] Hughes, T.P.: Networks of Power: Electrification in Western Society, pp. 1880–1930. The Johns Hopkins University Press, Baltimore (1983)
[22] Jenkins, W.S.: (penn-name Murray Leinster) papers. Syracuse University Special Collections Research Center
[23] Kuhn, T.: The Structure of Scientific Revolutions. University of Chicago, Chicago (1962)
[24] Kidder, T.: The Soul of a New Machine. Little Brown and Company, Boston (1981)
[25] Latour, B., Woolgar, S.: Laboratory Life. Princeton University Press, Princeton (1979)
[26] LeGuin, U.K.: The Language of the Night: Essays on Fantasy and Science Fiction. Perigee, New York (1980)
[27] Licklidder, J.C.R.: Man-Computer Symbiosis (1960),
     http://groups.csail.mit.edu/medg/people/psz/Licklider.html
[28] Linucon, http://www.linux.org/event/2004/10/08/0001.html
[29] Pinch, T.: How Users Matter: The Co-Construction of Users and Technologies (edited with Nelly Oudshoorn). MIT Press, Cambridge (2003)

[30] Raymond, E.S.: The Cathedral and the Bazaar Musings on Linux and open source by an accidental revolutionary. O'Reilly Publishers, Sebastopol (1999)

[31] Rosenberg, S.: Dreaming in Code. Crown Publishers (2007)

[32] Saarikoski, P.: Koneen Lumo: Mikrotietokoneharrastus Suomessa 1970-luvulta 1990-luvun puoliväliin (The Lure of the Machine: The Personal Computer Interest in Finland from the 1970s to the mid-1990s - title translated from Finnish). Nykykulttuurin tutkimuskeskuksen julkaisuja 83, Jyväskylä (2004)

[33] Science-Fiction Studies (published three times a year (March, July, November) by DePauw University Greencastle IN), http://www.depauw.edu/sfs/

[34] Shapin, S., Schaffer, S.: Leviathan and the Air Pump. Princeton University Press, Princeton (1985)

[35] Smith, P.D.: Doomsday Men: The Real Dr Strangelove and the Dream of the Superweapon, Allen Lane (2007)

[36] Sterling, B.: "Preface" in Mirrorshades: The Cyberpunk Anthology. Arbor, New York (1986)

[37] Suominen, J.: Koneen Kokemus: Tietoteknistyvä kulttuuri modernisoituvassa Suomessa 1920-luvulta 1970-luvulle (Experiences with machines. Computerised culture in the process of Finnish Modernisation from the 1920s to the 1970s - title translated from Finnish), Osuuskunta Vastapaino, Tampere (2003)

[38] Toomey, D.: The New Time Travelers: A Journey to the Frontiers of Physics. W.W. Norton (2007)

[39] Turkle, S.: The Second Self: Computers and the Human Spirit. Simon And Schuster (1984)

[40] Vehviläinen, M.: Gender and Computing in Retrospect - The Case of Finland. IEEE Annals of the History of Computing 21(2), 44–51 (1999)

[41] Westfahl, G.: Cosmic Engineers: A Study of Hard Science Fiction (Contributions to the Study of Science Fiction and Fantasy), p. 5. Greenwood Press, Westport (1996)

[42] Westfahl, G.: Cosmic Engineers, p. 17

[43] Westfahl, G.: Cosmic Engineers, pp. 6–7

[44] Wise, G.: The accuracy of technological forecasts, 1890-1940. Futures 8(5), 411–419 (1976)

Annotations of First Generation Systems Development in Sweden

Janis Bubenko Jr.

Department of Computer and Systems Science, Royal Institute of Technology and Stockholm University, Forum 100, SE-16440, Kista, Sweden
janis@dsv.su.se

Abstract. This work presents episodes of first generation information systems development in Sweden using two particular computers, ALWAC IIIE, during the period 1957–1961, and Univac III during 1963–1964. The ALWAC IIIE at ADB Institute, Gothenburg, was used for technical as well as for administrative applications. Another episode concerns re-engineering of an inventory management application; it used the ALWAC IIIE for the Swedish Defence Material Administration in 1960. The next episode concerns the computer Univac III. A sales contract between Götaverken AB and Univac included a guarantee by Univac to transfer one of Götaverken's punched card routines to a magnetic tape oriented routine on Univac III. The development work was carried out on a Univac III at Kantonalbank in Bern, Switzerland. They did the work in night shifts during a period of five months. Only one Univac III was installed in Sweden.

Keywords: First generation, information system development, Alwac IIIE, Univac III, Gothenburg.

1 Introduction

Information systems development is today a complex activity encompassing many types of activities and involving different kinds of stakeholders. It uses many different methods, techniques, and supporting tools. The development process deals with issues of many kinds such as organisational, economic, administrative, technical, social, as well as political. During the 1950-1960 decade, called the *first generation of systems development*, the development process was much simpler.

In the 1950s, heavy emphasis was on primarily two types of activities: programming and testing. Very little effort was allocated to business analysis, requirements gathering, and other "early activities" of the systems life-cycle (for a good survey see [7]). Normally, they programmed in a low-level "machine language" corresponding to the computer at hand. Therefore, systems development related closely to a particular brand of a computer. The problem- and system-analysis phases of the life cycle were not well developed. They did not use structured and formal system description techniques. These first started to appear in Sweden around the mid-to-late 1960s, when methods and techniques for this were developed in Sweden's first university department of information systems [6]. On the other hand, this did perhaps not matter so much as the routines processed by these early systems often were limited and well

J. Impagliazzo, T. Järvi, and P. Paju (Eds.): HiNC 2, IFIP AICT 303, pp. 95–105, 2009.
© IFIP International Federation for Information Processing 2009

defined (by input-process-output descriptions and by flowcharts). Another, not often mentioned, trait of the first generation systems work was that it often implied "physically heavy" work. Input and output data as well as magnetic tapes required transportation to/from the computer centre; these media had a considerable weight, sometimes as much as 30-50 kilograms or more.

This article deals with first generation information systems development in Sweden using two particular computers, the ALWAC IIIE during the period 1957–1961 and the Univac III during 1963–1964. The author was closely involved with both these computers. Historically, this paper also gives an account of efforts to introduce and market two new computer brand names, ALWAC and UNIVAC, in Sweden in the late 1950s and in the early 1960s, respectively. Memories of ALWAC, presented here, complement well the history of ALWAC in Turku [9].

2 The ALWAC IIIE Computer

The industrialist Axel Wenner-Gren imported the ALWAC III E from the USA[1] in 1957. His idea was to use the ALWAC IIIE as a basis for further developing computing know how in Sweden and eventually to start Sweden's own manufacturing of computers. The Swedish production of the ALWAC III E was renamed to Wegematic 1000. Later, they were to produce an enhanced ALWAC IIIE, named Wegematic 8000, in the Nyman Factories in Bollmora in the southern part of Stockholm. The Wegematic 8000 never materialised. Incidentally, the name ALWAC is an acronym from "Axel Leonard Wenner-Gren Automatic Computer"[2]. The letter E stands for a special feature of ALWAC representing the E-register, an index register. An image of the ALWAC appears in Figure 1.

ALWAC III E was a drum-oriented computer. The drum had four "high-speed" 32-word channels with four read-write heads and 256 "slower" channels of 32 words each. A word consisted of 32 bits of data or two 16-bit instructions. An instruction had an operation code of 8 bits and an address field of 8 bits. The computer was not as fast as the Swedish BESK, or its follower the FACIT EDB, but it was slightly more "modern"; it had an index register suited for repeating operations, e.g. in matrix calculations. The input output capacity was low. For input, it used paper tape at a speed of a few hundred characters per minute or punched cards at a rate of about 100 cards per minute. Output operations, except tape, were very slow; written text appeared on a flexo-writer having a speed of less than an IBM electric typewriter, about 10 characters per second. The ALWAC III E in Sweden had no secondary storage such as tape stations or disks.

Electronically, the ALWAC IIIE had a vacuum tube design. The speed was about 200 instructions per second. Physically, the ALWAC IIIE was not as large as one remembers the Univac I or similar computers. It easily fit into a room of, say, 50 square meters. Of course, being a vacuum tube computer it needed cooling, normally through a double floor. Programming of the ALWAC IIIE was in pure machine code (see also Figure 3). They wrote programs in blocks of 32 words, or twice as many

---

[1] ALWAC Corporation, 13040 South Cerise Avenue, Hawthorne, California.
[2] Thanks to Tord-Jöran Hallberg for this information.

instructions. A block constituted a drum channel. An executing program entered one of the four "high-speed" channels and execution started at some specified location. A typical instruction word could look like 8707573b, which contained two instructions

Fig. 1. The ALWAC IIIE installation at Chalmers

    8707   : Copy the contents of drum channel 07 into high-speed channel 4
    573b   : Bring the contents of cell 3b into the index (E) register

The repertoire consisted of some 64 instruction types, including instructions for indexing, arithmetic, and reading and writing contents of drum channels into or out from the high speed channels. Our programs really looked like lists of eight hexadecimal digit phone numbers.

In the period from 1957 to 1961 about ten ALWAC IIIE or Wegematic 1000 computers were installed in Sweden, primarily in universities. See also appendixes in [9].

2.1 ALWAC at Chalmers in Gothenburg

The ALWAC IIIE was delivered to Chalmers in the summer of 1957 and gave the university a real "kick" in many topic areas. Personally, after the first programming course, the author started, together with Andrejs Grivans, to work on their master thesis topic, which concerned the buckling strength of arch bridges. Professor S.O. Asplund (head, Department of Structural Mechanics, School of Civil Engineering), who was a pioneer of computer usage at Chalmers, supervised us. A few years earlier, he had been using the BESK, the first Swedish computer located in Stockholm, for various stress calculations in structural mechanics. Other users of ALWAC IIIE were primarily researchers from departments belonging to the school of chemical engineering and researchers from departments within the school of electrical engineering. In addition, one frequently saw a few numerical analysts in the computer room.

An independent institute, the ADB-Institutet, initially led by Bertil Greko[3], administered the ALWAC IIIE at Chalmers. Until its "death" in the early 1970s, the ALWAC IIIE resided on the Chalmers campus. The institute had initially a staff of about five to six persons, including two or three engineers. Later it developed into a self-supporting organisation, by selling computer time to Chalmers and by doing consulting jobs and selling computer time over the western part of Sweden. The computer time "sold" to Chalmers was, I believe, extremely cheap as part of a deal between Chalmers and the ADB-Institute.

2.2 Technical Systems Applications

After 1958, I worked part time for a year in professor Asplund's consulting company (Autostatik AB). We developed programs for a wide range of calculations within the realm of structural mechanics [8]. Our efforts [1] in trying to sell these programs and services to engineering companies were not successful. The "market" was suspicious of "modern electronic gadgets" and preferred traditional, slide-rule calculations. The Swedish "market" was not yet ready to do business with us. However, only ten to fifteen years later the situation changed drastically. Many consulting companies in the field of engineering became heavy users of different kinds of software packages for engineering calculations, using their own computers or larger service centres. However, during the late 1950s it was not easy to do business by selling computational power to consulting companies.

2.3 Administrative Systems Applications

In 1958, the ADB-Institutet was, in fact, the major data consulting and service company in western Sweden[4]. It recruited young staff primarily from Chalmers, taught them programming, and gave them part-time, or hourly salaried jobs in developing programs and systems for business and industry in the western part of Sweden. Around 1957 the ADB-Institute also engaged in a managerial position Ingemar Dahlstrand, one of Sweden's first programming language scientists; he came from SAAB (Langefors' group) and in 1959 eventually moved to FACIT Electronics AB, EDB-centralen in Gothenburg, where he developed Sweden's first Algol compiler.

An active sales and marketing manager of the ADB-Institute was Sidney Werngren. Among other things he involved me in developing a program for inventory control and management of operations in a forestry industry, Forsviks Skogar, located some 250 kilometres north of Gothenburg [3]. This was a practically complicated system, primarily because data was "born" (captured) in the forest and the results of the computer run had to be delivered back 250 km away. We could not use ordinary

---

[3] Bertil Greko had a MBA from Stockholm School of Economics.
[4] Also FACIT started a computing center in Gothenburg at about 1959, using the FACIT EDB computer, a derivative of BESK.

pencil and paper in the forest because of rain and wetness. Instead, we used plastic sheets and permanent ink pens to register data about the work performed. There was no telecommunication solution at that time. For some reason we did not use the "tele-printer" in this application, probably because the forestry had no staff that could punch a teleprinter tape and transmit the information to Gothenburg. As all adminis-trative applications at this time, this one was also "batch-processing" oriented. It ran periodically, in this case once a month.

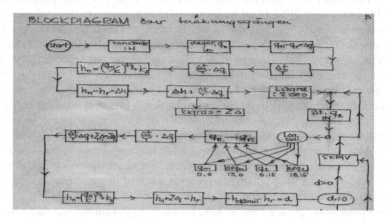

Fig. 2. A fragment of an original "problem-oriented" specification in 1957, a flowchart, show-ing the execution logic of a program

In its peak period, around 1960, the ADB institute's ALWAC IIIE computer was used both for numerical engineering calculations and for administrative applications, notwithstanding the computer's limited input/output speed and the lack of magnetic tape units. Companies such as Volvo, SKF, Ericsson, and the shipbuilding and ship-ping companies were the main customers. In this way, the ALWAC IIIE pawed the ground in western Sweden for more modern computers to come. It is interesting to note that six scientific paper presentations at NordSAM 61 in Oslo came from work-ers of the ADB institute.

2.4 "Re-engineering" at KATF

Today, Kungliga Armétygförvaltningen (KATF) has the name Försvarets Ma-terielverk, (FMV), in English the Swedish Defence Material Administration. It deals with material and supplies for the Swedish defence. My association with KATF in 1959 was due to my military service of 13 months. One of the ALWAC machines was donated (or sold) to the consulting company, Lundins Revisionsfirma in Vallentuna, north of Stockholm. The Lundin Company received a commission from KATF to develop a large program for inventory management and control of the equipment and material (e.g. including tanks, vehicles of all types) for the Swedish Army. This con-sultancy job was from KATF's side managed by Nils Enquist. The program was almost completed when the Lundin Company went bankrupt. KATF had now an "al-most completed" program (about 5000 instructions), no computer, and no one who knew about the program (except its creators Bengt-Åke Krantz and some other people then hired in at Lundins). No one at KATF knew anything about ALWAC programming. My luck was to be a young military aspirant who knew the ALWAC and ALWAC programming, and who could help them out of this situation. In 1959, KATF somehow managed to obtain the Lundin ALWAC and physically relocated it to a cellar of KATF at Gärdet in Stockholm.

My job was to "re-engineer" the 5000 instruction programme for KATF, and to make it work. What I had was machine code as shown in Figure 3. The program was not annotated in any sense. What I had to do was to reverse-program this code into a more problem-oriented description, like the flowchart in Figure 2. It was a considerable and complex re-engineering task. No other documentation existed. However, I did receive considerable help from Nils Enquist at KATF, a real enthusiast who had good knowledge about the expected logic of the inventory system ordered at Lundins. However, the way the program was developed and structured was a mystery I alone had to solve. It had taken me three months to do. In hindsight, this is probably the best way to teach somebody programming. Bengt-Åke Krantz, one of Sweden's pioneers in computers (and a mathematician) and the author of the program, was indeed a very skilful programmer. At this time all programming was a battle for space and time—you had not much of any of them. Therefore, some of Krantz's elegant, space-saving, algorithmic solutions, where a program gradually wrote over some of its own instructions, took me some time to understand and to appreciate.

The computer was "great news" at KATF. Many high-ranking military officers often visited the computer in the cellar. The computer's ability to play one or two simple games really impressed them.

The author's work at KATF also resulted in a generally usable "standard program" MIKE for matrix calculations [1]. The interpretative matrix calculation program began to appear at some of the other ALWAC installations in Sweden, mainly at the Uppsala installation. The author used it himself in doing numerical calculations (using a finite difference method for iteratively solving a system of partial differential equations) in his Licentiate Thesis [2]. They also used MIKE for stress calculations in the shipbuilding industry of Gothenburg [4].

```
2004
20 8707573b a0 21 f1410800 a1
24 5b3f1160 a4 25 2000eb37 a5
28 484a1724 a8 29 a104c558 a9
2c 2800f102 ac 2d f3017958 ad
30 a70e493b b0 31 6746495a b1
34 f3012800 b4 35 79464959 b5
38 f1433000 b8 39 4140e73b b9
3c f1013000 bc 3d eb41c55b bd
```

Fig. 3. A fragment of an ALWAC IIIE program in hexadecimal machine code. Black figures are addresses, red figures show the representation of the contents of a 32-bit word.

3 Univac in Scandinavia

During 1960, Sperry Rand[5] decided to try to enter the Nordic computer market, which at that time IBM dominated mainly through its punched-card installations. These installations gave IBM a large and loyal customer base. Other players on the Swedish market were Saab, ICL, Ferranti (with its Pegasus and Orion computers), and the French Bull computers. At that time, Sperry Rand Univac did not have any equipment installed in Sweden. All it could offer for commercial applications was the Solid State 80/90, a drum-oriented computer and one of the first computers to use solid-state components. However, the Solid State 80/90 was not very powerful compared to the computers of its contemporary competitors such as the IBM 1401 and 7070 machines. Univac had, on the other hand, excellent experience with real-time computers used in United States defence, for instance the Univac 490, a commercial copy of a computer Univac Federal Systems developed for the U.S. Navy. On the positive side of Univac at this time was the pending launch of two new products: the Univac 1107 primarily for scientific applications[6] and the Univac III for commercial applications. The Univac III and 1107 together with the real-time oriented 419 and 490 computers were the products of a small group of people[7]; they started to market them in the Nordic markets at the end of 1961. The first sales success of the group was the 1107 sales to Norsk Regnesentral (NRS). This installation as well as NRS's famous Simula software is extensively described in the book of HiNC-1 [5].

3.1 Univac III to Götaverken

IBM totally dominated the business data processing market in Sweden. It had more than 70% of the market. Control Data Corporation, ICL, Bull, Siemens, and "the rest" shared the remaining 30%. We managed, however, to convince Götaverken[8] (a shipyard in Gothenburg) to buy a Univac III for its administrative applications. Univac III was the last in a line of well-known computers: the Univac I and the Univac II. The Univac I was the "famous" computer delivered to the U.S. Census Bureau[9], Washington D.C. in 1951. The Univac III was not compatible with its predecessor Univac II. This fact probably hindered a wider sale of it. A successor of Univac III never materialized. The only Univac III sold in Sweden was the one sold to Götaverken in 1963, delivered in the fall of 1964. It had a core memory of 16K 25 bit words, 8 Uniservo III tape drives (speed: 133.000 characters per second), an 80-column card reader (600 cards per minute), a card punch, and a printer (1200 lines per minute). No random-access disk was included in the configuration. It used the BOSS operating system and it permitted

---

[5] Sperry Rand Corporation was formed in 1955 by the merger of Remington Rand and Sperry Gyroscope. Remington Rand had tried to enter the Nordic computer market earlier, before 1955, but failed.

[6] Computers for scientific applications had built-in functionality for floating-point calculations, business oriented computers had better functionality for character and string manipulation.

[7] The general manager of Univac Scandinavia was Stig Wahlstam, the sales manager was Christer Svensson, and the systems and programming manager was the author.

[8] Actually we convinced Mr. Viklund, Götaverken's data processing manager, while some of his staff, being old IBM punched-card users, were in heavy opposition.

[9] Many people consider UNIVAC I the world's first commercially available computer.

parallel execution of one main program plus a number of "spooling" programs such as cards-to-tape and tape-to-printer. It used programs written in the assembly language called UTMOST.

At that time, a computer sales contract normally involved an offer from the vendor to convert some of the customer's applications to the delivered equipment. This was also the case here. We had promised Götaverken to convert a large IBM punched-card application to Univac III. We hoped this would not take more than a couple of months. The work was free of charge for Götaverken. This sale also led to the opening of a local Univac office in Gothenburg in 1963.

The Götaverken application was a straightforward accounting routine. It included more than twenty runs on punched card equipment including sorting and collating. We designed the Univac III application having a structure very similar to the punched-card application, including a set of tape-to-tape processes. This set included a fair number of sorting operations. Therefore, the *description* of our application was a set of processes with defined inputs (on tape or on cards) and outputs (on tape or on printer). We described the processes by ordinary flowcharts. Records and their fields described the inputs and outputs.

3.2 Programming Univac III in Bern

A programming team, lead by the author, was formed in the second half of 1963. It included new recruits[10] to Univac Scandinavia. Peter Häggström and Åke Persson came from Gothenburg. Pavo Kosuta and Ralf Timell came from Stockholm. The first thing we had to do was to train the new team. The programming training as well as the application development operation was a bit complicated as no Univac III computer was available in the Nordic countries. At Kantonalbank in Bern, Switzerland, we managed to contract computer time on a Univac III. The bank's computer would be at our disposition five nights a week, from 00:00 HRS to 06:00 HRS. There was no office space available to us so all work had to be done in our hotel rooms.

The programming effort started in the fall of 1963. The application was well defined, in terms of a number of "inputs-process-outputs". It was easy to allocate well-bounded programming tasks to different programmers and then work in parallel. However, the programming took its time. We were programming in a low-level assembly language (UTMOST), which was close to machine language. The high-level language Cobol was neither reliable nor efficient enough at that time. We had also to punch the program-instruction cards ourselves. Our application consisted of more than twenty file-to-file processing programs of about 2,500 assembly level instructions each. Each program had taken two to four weeks to program and test. The whole effort to implement Götaverken's accounting system had taken about six calendar months and about twenty-four people-months of work. My estimate is our "average programming speed" was about ten instructions per person per hour, a satisfactory figure at that time.

Life as a night-shift programmer living and working in a hotel room was, at least at start, challenging and interesting. Our daily rhythm turned upside down. We slept between 08.00 and 16.00 after having breakfast at 07.00. Some programming work happened between 17.00 and 21.00. Then we had dinner before making our way to the computer centre.

---

[10] They all had university level education and some programming experience.

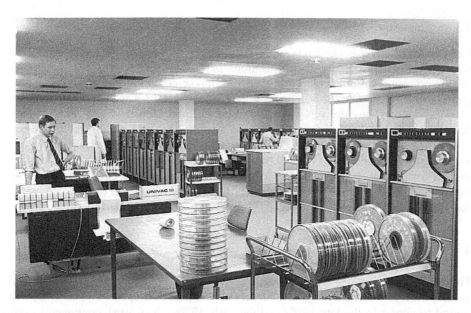

Fig. 4. A Univac III installation at Otto Group, Germany 1961 (with permission by the Otto Group). Magnetic tape reels shown in tin boxes in front.

One episode at the hotel is worth mentioning. All our data and programs were stored on large tape reels held in tin boxes. We had plenty of these tapes – more than two large suitcases. The suitcases rattled when we left the hotel shortly before midnight each night. One night the portiere could no longer refrain his curiosity about what we were doing at this time of day so he asked, "Wohin gehen Sie eigentlich meine Herren?"[11]. Our answer was truthfully, "Zur Kantonalbank, mein Herr".

We should mention another complication of this first generation era. The card equipment ordered by Götaverken was for 80-column cards (all IBM card machines operated on 80-column cards). The Univac III at Kantonalbank used 90-column cards. This was not a problem for our programming and testing work. A bigger problem was, however, to transfer all Götaverken's master cards to Uniservo III tapes. Götaverken had about 140.000 master cards – equalling seventy boxes of 2000 cards each, weighing about 10 kilos each. The whole batch thus weighed more than 700 kilograms! This batch was flown from Gothenburg to Düsseldorf, Germany, where we were permitted to use an 80-column card based Univac III to transfer the batch to two or three tape reels. They then transferred the tapes to our test-computer at Kantonalbank to complete the accounting application. When transferring the 140.000 cards to tape in Düsseldorf, we were relatively lucky. The whole operation took less than twelve hours. Only five to ten cards "jammed", where they had to be reconstructed and re-punched. When they delivered the Univac III to Götaverken in the fall of 1964, the promised accounting system was in operation and working according to specifications.

---

[11] "Where are you really heading gentlemen?".

3.3 Epilogue on Univac

The Univac III never became a big sales success. As far as I know, Univac contracted no other Univac III to a Nordic organisation. In total, Univac delivered about 95 Univac III computer installations worldwide. A Univac computer that made some progress on the Nordic market was the powerful Univac 1107 (or its derivatives 1106 or 1108) systems. They delivered these systems to Lund University and Stadsförbundet[12] in Sweden, to Finnish State Computer Centre in Helsinki, and to the Norwegian Computing Center in Trondheim. Other computers, delivered to Scandinavia include a Univac 494 to Danderyd's Hospital and a number of real-time computers (418, 494) to SAS for passenger and ticket management. Incidentally, Peter Häggström, one of the Univac III programming team members in Bern, became CEO of Unisys Sweden during the late 1980s.

4 Concluding Remarks

The above notes confirm that a structured "method" did not exist for description and development of information systems in the late 1950s and early 1960s. Such methods started to appear in the late 1960s and the early 1970s. Yet, work continued in systems development at that time occurred in a reasonably systematic and efficient way. This is probably because most "systems analysts and developers" at that time were engineers or mathematicians trained to work in a rational fashion. End-user participation in setting requirements was not common. Appendix A summarises some characteristics of systems development then and now.

References

[1] Bubenko Jr., J.A.: MIKE - ett interpretativt program för matrisräkning (MIKE - an interpretative program for matrix calculus (in Swedish)). Kungl Armetygförvaltningen, Stockholm (1960)
[2] Bubenko Jr., J.A.: Large Deflections of Rectangular Plates Solved by Finite Differences, Dept of Structural Mechanics. Chalmers Univ. of Technology, Gothenburg (1961)
[3] Bubenko Jr., J.A.: Ett system för lagerredovisning av virke. in NordSAM 61(A System for Inventory Control of Timber (in Swedish)), Oslo. preprints av sektionsföredrag (1961)
[4] Bubenko Jr., J.A., Jacobsson, Å. (eds.): Stödkrafter och Moment i Balk på Flera Stöd, Speciellt Tillämpbart på Propelleraxelledningar (Supporting Forces and Moments for Beams on Multiple Supports with a Particular Application to Propeller Axes (in Swedish)). Stiftelsen för Skeppsbyggnadsteknisk Forskning, Gothenburg (1961)
[5] Bubenko Jr., J.A., Impagliazzo, J., Sølvberg, A. (eds.): History of Nordic Computing (HiNC1). In: IFIP WG 9.7 First Working Conference on the History of Nordic Computing, Trondheim, Norway, June 16-18, 2003. Springer, New York (2005)
[6] Bubenko Jr., J.A., Jansson, C.-G., Kollerbaur, A., Ohlin, T., Yngström, L. (eds.): ICT for People. 40 Years of Academic Development in Stockholm, Department of Computer and Systems Sciences at Stockholm University and Royal Institute of Technology, Kista, Sweden, p. 426 (2006)

---

[12] The association of Swedish towns, today the association of Swedish communes.

[7] Couger, J.D., Knapp, R.W. (eds.): System Analysis Techniques, p. 509. John Wiley & Sons, Chichester (1974)

[8] Grivans, A., Bubenko Jr., J.A.: Snabblösning av byggnadsstatiska problem (High-speed Solving of Problems in Structural Mechanics (in Swedish)). Väg och Vattenbyggaren (3), 71–75 (1959)

[9] Suominen, J., Paju, P., Törn, A.: The Wegematic Computing Centre, 1959 - 1964. Translocal cooperation. In: Bubenko Jr., J.A., Impagliazzo, J., Sølvberg, A. (eds.) History of Nordic Computing (HiNC-1), pp. 463–486. Springer, New York (2005)

Appendix A

Some contrasting characteristics of systems development fifty years apart

Systems development in the fifties	Systems development now
The systems development problem was simple and mostly well defined.	The systems development problem is often complex and not well defined. Requirements are often unclear and frequently changing.
The development process contains only a few phases, programming and testing being the essential ones.	The systems development process contains many phases starting from business analysis, requirements elicitation, etc. to systems maintenance
Few types of "stakeholders"	Many types of stakeholders
The development time is long, sometimes more than a year	The development time is short thanks to the heavy use of standard software components
The developed system runs in batch mode and is used by experts only. User-friendly interfaces do not exist.	Systems are online, "real-time", and interactively used by non-experts. Interfaces are "user-friendly".
No data base access, no data base management systems in use	Users have through internet and advanced search engines access to a practically unlimited set of information sources
The computing hardware was expensive and not powerful. This generated a need to optimise the performance of a systems solution.	Hardware performance and cost is no longer a systems development problem. Additional processors and memory can be installed at low cost.
Computer based tools for systems development work did not exist.	There is an extensive market of various software tools that support systems design as well as collaborative systems development work.
Systems were developed in close physical proximity of the computer.	Systems development is not restricted by the distance to the computer(s) due to interactive development using high speed data links.

Centralized versus Decentralized Information Systems

A Historical Flashback

Mats-Åke Hugoson

Jönköping International Business School, Sweden
mats-ake.hugoson@ihh.hj.se

Abstract. This paper brings into question whether information systems should be centralized or decentralized in order to provide greater support for different business processes. During the last century companies and organizations have used different approaches for centralization and decentralization; a simple answer to the question does not exist. This paper provides a survey of the evolution of centralized and decentralized approaches, mainly in a Nordic perspective. Based on critical reflections on the situation in the end of the century we can discuss what we can learn from history to achieve alignment between centralized and decentralized systems and the business structure. The conclusion is that theories, management and practice for decisions on centralization or decentralization of information systems must be improved. A conscious management and control of centralization /decentralization of IT support is a vital question in the company or the organization, and this is not a task that can be handled only by IT-specialists. There is a need for business oriented IT management of centralization/decentralization.

Keywords: Structures of information systems, Systems interaction, Independence between systems, Centralization, Distributed systems, Decentralization.

1 Introduction

Should we centralize or decentralize information systems to create greater support to different business processes? Different approaches for centralization and decentralization have occurred during the last century; and there is not a simple answer to the question.

This paper gives a survey of the evolution of centralized and decentralized approaches, mainly in a Nordic perspective. The paper uses observations and episodes starting in 1965, which means that some of the conclusions reflect personal opinions. Other persons working in the field during this period may very well have reached other conclusions. As the topic centralization versus decentralization often causes debate, perhaps the paper can give additional fuel for discussions.

After a general analysis of what centralization and decentralization really means, starting from a business perspective, we follow and scrutinize the centralized track and the decentralized track for information systems.

A major difference between the two alternatives is the degree of independence between systems; therefore, we analyze the problem and principle of independence in detail. We relate the situation in the end of last century to the different views from some researchers. Finally, we address the aspects that we can learn from history, which leads to some conclusions.

J. Impagliazzo, T. Järvi, and P. Paju (Eds.): HiNC 2, IFIP AICT 303, pp. 106–115, 2009.
© IFIP International Federation for Information Processing 2009

2 The Concept of Centralization and Decentralization

In a business perspective, decentralization means that business can make decisions locally. A business unit can choose the way to use local resources to fulfill objectives for that unit. The unit must cooperate with other units in the company (perhaps also externally), and must report to management in a specified way. However, there is a freedom of action to perform *within* each business unit.

In addition, in a decentralized organization there must be a central coordination. Without management and control, the organization ends up in anarchy. Even if this central coordination such as standardization can set restrictions for each unit, the main criteria for decentralization is the right (and responsibility) to form an efficient *inner structure* in each business unit, using local resources to fulfill objectives and tasks that are set for the unit. Changes in this inner structure should not affect other units.

When applying the concept of centralization and decentralization to information systems, we must be more specific and analyze some different alternatives. To develop one common system for an organization is of course a centralized approach. To develop and implement a number of systems in the company is on the other hand not always a decentralized approach. If these systems are developed "wildly" without any coordination and have no computerized interaction, we must characterize it as anarchy. However, even if these systems have a computerized interaction the question remains: what is really a decentralized structure of systems? If the different systems have a common database, we must still consider it as a centralized approach, as each system is directly dependent of the common database, and a change in this database affects many systems. Also distributed systems with a centrally controlled data storage have a limited freedom of action in each local system.

A strict definition of decentralized systems could be that each system in the structure must fulfill specified demands on interaction with other systems, but it should be possible to develop (and change) the inner structure in each system, including data storage, without dependences to other systems, as long as the specified interaction stands. It must for instance be possible to insert systems of different origin into the structure. The main condition is that each system must interact with other systems as specified.

From this short analysis, it is evident that we must consider both the delineation of systems (central – local) and the principles for systems interaction when we discuss decentralized information systems. Independence between systems is a major criterion on decentralization, which we will discuss after a historical review.

3 The Centralized Track

According to a statement, which is said to come from IBM research and development in the early ages of computing, the estimation was that three or possibly four big mainframes would give enough computing capacity for the industrialized world, as long as could be foreseen. This really represents a centralized view, both on computers and on computing. Even if we cannot state the origin of this statement, it is easily verified that the start and evolution of computing in most companies followed a centralized track.

3.1   The MIS Concept in the 1960s

Between 1965 and 1970 industry initiated many large projects to support the total organization with *one* information system, generally referred to as the "management information system". For example, with Volvo, the project was named VIS; in SAAB it was the TIPS-project that had the same total scope.

There was a general opinion among people working with ADB (Automatisk Data-Behandling) – EDP (Electronic Data Processing) that this was the right approach, and the Nordic Data Union arranged conferences on the MIS concepts in Denmark, Norway, and Sweden.

However, there were people who did not fully agree to this 'one system approach'. At that time, I was a young systems manager and became secretary of the planning committee for these Nordic MIS-conferences. Professor Börje Langefors was an invited speaker to one MIS-conference in Kungälv, Sweden. I remember from the planning discussions that he hesitated, with the argument that total management systems are unperceivable and will fail. He had already in 1967 published a paper about "Directive Information for Systems Control" [7]. He pointed out the difference between directive and local information and he argued for a split between what we today refer to as executive systems and systems to support local operations. Furthermore, in the book System för företagsstyrning [8] he had presented Teorin för oöverblickbara system (The Theory for Imperceivable systems). He clarifies the necessity to handle complex systems through structures of perceivable subsystems instead of a total system approach. Anyhow, he accepted the invitation and gave at this conference a very humble presentation of his objections to MIS.

The outcome from the MIS-projects in different companies was generally not the expected. They gained experience, some results were achieved, and projects were perhaps not considered as failures. However, none of the projects mentioned ended up in a total management information system. Among the reasons given as explanation to the shortcomings, we often find technical limitations, lack of methodology, limited resources, or perhaps sometimes insufficient experience to run big projects, but the basic centralized approach was very seldom called into question. Also in the academia, the centralized approach has been dominating from the beginning. Some examples will be given.

3.2   VLDB in the 1970s

Development of database technology strengthened the centralized concept. The (implicit) basic assumption was that each company must have one total database, and therefore methods were developed to handle the large data base that was necessary to support the total organization. In the end of the decade conferences on very large databases (VLDB) were arranged all over the world.

3.3   The Search for a Total Integrated Conceptual Model in the 1980s

After the period with focus on technical databases, the data modeling and later the conceptual modeling became the dominant paradigms. Despite these changes, the aim was still to find a tool to make a total central model for the whole company. Thus, based on these theories they started new projects for total data models in many companies, even at Volvo.

People gradually understood that it was not possible or suitable to have all data processing in one system, but then this total conceptual model should serve as a blueprint to implement different information systems. The principle was that different systems should refer to a central data model implemented either as a central database or as a set of centrally controlled databases.

In the discussion about centralization versus decentralization, this view must still be considered as a centralized approach, even if the outcome is a number of systems. In this approach, there are strong dependencies between the different systems. There is not much freedom of action to implement systems of different origin in such a structure, which we took as a major criterion on decentralization. Attempts to split the central database into a number of distributed systems do not really change the picture as the inner structure in each system is still centrally controlled.

Another problem with total conceptual /data models was that a single project could generally not get an overview of the total conceptual model, in any case not in more complex organizations. The alternative was instead in practice to establish a number of projects within the company, each one using conceptual data modeling for the scope of their own system. The theoretical (and practical) problem was then to fit these models together.

In 1989, an IFIP conference on information system concepts took place in Namur, Belgium. One of the main themes was ways to integrate conceptual models, with presentations such as Integration of Information Submodels [6], and Levels of Abstraction as a Conceptual Framework for an Information System [5]. Attempts during the conference to discuss decentralization of these submodels, through other principles for interaction between systems, were directly rejected.

Again, we must view this as a centralized approach, limiting the freedom of action in each project. Before we sum up and state the results from the centralized approach during the last century, let us have a look at the decentralized track.

4 The Emergence of Decentralized Information Systems

As long as computing was performed as a 'closed shop' in the data hall, ideas of local systems were just ideas. At the end of the 1970s, when minicomputers and microcomputers began to be available at reasonable prices, the scene changed. At about the same time, new methods and tools for development of small systems were developed (prototyping, experimental design). In addition, system packages for local applications, for instance for production planning, appeared on the market. Suddenly, companies bought or developed and implemented local systems in different parts of their organization. One could view this movement as a protest against central systems (or at least as a way to fulfill local demands that could not be supported by centralized systems).

Professor Staffan Persson at Stockholm School of Economics used the programming language APL to develop local systems extremely fast. For example, within a day he could help a company find a solution to a planning problem, program the system, set it in operation on the computer he brought with him, and just leave a system in use on the table. This way to cut lead-time in systems development from several years to hours must be some kind of a record. These local systems evidently represent a high degree of independence, but according to earlier discussions, they do not fully meet the demands for decentralization, as they did not consider interaction with other systems. One could characterize this approach for systems development as anarchistic, and it very often caused conflicts with the IT-department.

A little more coordinated approach emanated from organizations with many units of the same kind. Healthcare is a good example. Extensive handling of local information, both for administration and for medical records, called for IT support. A local system was developed or bought, often based on local initiatives, sometimes as a part of an IT plan. When the system was tested and workable, it was implemented also in other units in the organization, but still as stand-alone systems. This represents a more long-term perspective that makes the structure of systems more unified and facilitates systems' maintenance; however, a decentralized structure of interacting systems was not achieved. The result is a set of information islands, as the systems have no computerized interaction. One might have to enter basic data for a certain patient several times, and there is no possibility for a doctor to get a total view of a patient's medical record.

Also, Professor Börje Langefors addressed the need for fast development of local systems. The tool he used, together with Ola Langefors, was Dataflex (a simple high level programming language) and he published a report [11] on Prototyping with Dataflex. In the work by Langefors we however find a more structured approach, than just to develop local systems. Already in 1982, he presented a report on Four Cases with Decentralized Management and Local Computers [9] and in another report [10] he discussed Integrated versus Decentralized Information Resource Management. The problem he addressed was to find a solution both to support users with local information from local systems, which exchange what Langefors calls translocal information, and at the same time maintain independence between these local systems. This gives us a reason to analyze independence between systems more in depth.

5   The Problem and Principle of Independence between Systems

Starting in the general principles for decentralization used in this paper, we define the basic demand for independence: Changes in one system (handling local information that is relevant for a certain business unit), should not cause changes in other systems that support other business units.

5.1   Systems Delineation

One condition for independence is that each local system is delineated to support only a specified business unit (an area of responsibility, for instance a business process). A simple example is given in Figure 1.

The system CRM (Customer Relationships Management) supports the Sales process from the very beginning of a customer relation and holds all necessary information for the sales process until the company invoices the deliveries. The LOGistics system contains modules for warehousing and delivery planning, and supports logistics until a delivery order is completed.

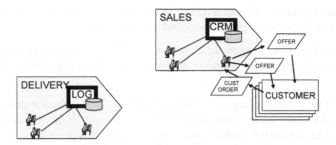

Fig. 1. Local Information Systems for the Sales process and for the Delivery process

5.2 Systems Interaction

These two systems CRM and LOG are independent of each other, but so far they do not interact, they are still two information islands. The challenge is to find the manner in which the systems can interact as two decentralized systems with maintained independence. To address this problem, we must answer two questions:

o What translocal information should be exchanged?
o How must translocal information be described and exchanged in order to maintain independence?

The general answer to the first question is that translocal information is the ordinary information exchanged between different business units to perform business. In the example, it is necessary for the Sales process to know what is available in the warehouse (including expected deliveries into the warehouse), called DISP QUANT in Figure 2, otherwise the company cannot give an offer with a delivery date to the customer. If the customer accepts the offer, the sales process must send a delivery order (DEL ORDER in Figure 2) to the Delivery process. When delivery is completed this must be reported back to the Sales process (DEL REP), as this information is the basis for the invoice to be sent from Sales to the customer. This translocal information constitutes three computerized messages as shown in Figure 2.

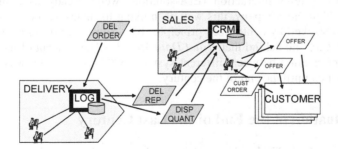

Fig. 2. Translocal Information to be exchanged as computerized messages between systems

We can describe these messages in detail through business analysis; the point is that we can do this without any knowledge about data storage or processing in each one of the two systems. This enterprise based systems interaction (discussed in [3] and [4]) takes us to the principle of independence that states:

Interaction between decentralized systems should be described independent of the inner structure in each system, in order to maintain independence between the systems.

We must then give the messages for interaction a technical format and transfer the data between systems with some message handling system in the company's IT-infrastructure. Standardized middleware is available for this process.

This approach represents a different way for interaction between systems, a change from access thinking to messaging. If we want to maintain independence, it is not enough to 'open the books' and show the data structures in each system. We must instead bridge the Interaction through messages based on business relations. It is not a question of understanding data in other systems; it is a question of understanding what translocal information to be transferred between the systems. The different data structures are local and they connect to the messages through mapping mechanisms, which must be developed and maintained for each system. If the inner structure in one system is changed, then we might have to change the mapping mechanism in that very system to maintain proper interaction. But, there will be no change in any other system as long as the business relation stands.

Message interaction ensures consistency in the structure. Customer information in the LOG system is, for instance, based on (derived from) computerized messages DEL ORDER, delivery orders. There is no manual updating of information on customers in the LOG system. Because of this, a certain customer in the CRM system may not yet be registered in the LOG system, as there has not been any delivery order so far. This is not inconsistency; it is just normal business interaction.

In the 1980s, the concept for decentralized systems using the principle of independence became part of business analysis [3] and later on presented as Verkssamhetsbaserad Systemstrukturering (Business Based Structures of Information Systems). In 1986, it was part of a presentation at the NordData Conference [4] and actually awarded the Nordic Prize that year.

The paradox is that this principle for systems interaction is quite natural in inter-organizational systems interaction (EDI-solutions were already used in the early 1980s) but within the company, this way of thinking for many years was (and sometimes still is) blocked by centralized principles like: *Store data once, General access to all stored data,* and behind that: *Total Data Models.* The concept of messaging for transfer of information between different systems within a company was not widely discussed or used until the end of the century.

6   The Situation at the End of the Last Century

The total result from IT development in the last century is not impressive from a structural point of view. Even if companies applied a centralized approach, in most cases it was not possible to use just one system in the company, or even to develop and maintain a total data model. When new systems came on board in the structure, they used principles for accessing and updating different databases, which in many companies and organizations ended up in complex structures of systems, often referred to as a "spaghetti structure". If one system changed, it affected many other systems. The structure gradually grew unstable.

The centralized approach often resulted in big systems and projects running for several years. Another problem had been the limited possibilities for users to have any real impact on the project. Researchers as Enid Mumford already addressed this problem in the 1970s and presented models for participative design [13], pointing out the value in the organization of user oriented development. However, this approach did not work so well in centralized projects.

On the other hand, in many cases the decentralized approach ended up in a number of separate systems, without any computerized interaction, with multiple updating, inconsistency, and unclear responsibilities for these different Information Islands.

Börje Langefors gave 1995 in the book Essays on Infology [12, p 159] a really good summary of the situation, which is here quoted:

Infology and Decentralization
Information systems theory has, since its beginning in the early 1960s, been facing a contradiction. One of its main visions was that data in the system had to be available to "everybody" (Langefors 1961,#29, 1963, # 37). But it was soon detected that a set of data does not inform everybody (the "infological equation." Langefors 1966, #1). It had to be concluded that efficiently designed information systems had to be structured as a network of communicating more or less separate subsystems based on local data systems. This insight took a surprisingly long time to gain recognition in the data profession, as well as, for instance, in accounting.

Even when, in the 1980s, small local systems came to be fairly common, this was in many cases due to the emergence of inexpensive micro-computers, rather than to an understanding of the often local character of data.

And, with the maturing of the technology of connecting small computers to form networks, one has begun again to talk about making all data accessible to everybody. We conclude that there is still lacking the understanding that some data are only intelligible to restricted groups of people. This suggests that there is need for case studies, in order to reach and disseminate a more concrete understanding of this aspect.

It is often stated, e.g. by data managers, that the popping up of isolated local systems will lead to chaos. Leaving aside the fact that some amount of chaos may be useful, we point out that keeping isolated such data as are in in any case unintelligible outside a limited context can't by itself generate chaos. Of course, such data as have to be used in several locations, but those only, must be subject to integrated management – but this should not be done indiscriminately.

From an international perspective during the last decade of the century, we can see that some researchers maintained the centralized approach while others questioned it. One example is Allen and Boynton who advocate a centralized structure, mainly from an IT point of view, and they argue that central structures are flexible since one can make changes centrally [1]. On the other hand, Bacon analyzes how systems decentralization can be derived from organizational principles [2].

7   What Can We Learn from History?

A rephrased question could be: When will we ever learn from history? Failures to implement real huge centralized systems in the last century such as the RAINBOW project, aiming at a total world wide system for the company TetraPak were followed by new failures like the SIRIUS project that tried to replace forty-two systems in the Swedish Defense organization with one big system. Worst of all, soon after the termination of this big project (which was closed down by the minister of defense) a proposal for a new total system, this time an ERP system, was given from the IT-specialists. It seems as if the fight between decentralization and centralization continues as with totally integrated ERP systems versus "best-of-breed" systems.

Another example on different competitive views on centralization /decentralization can be observed within the healthcare area. Many hundred separate systems containing medical records were implemented gradually over the last three to four decades in different medical clinics, healthcare centers, and medical support units. As a patient in Sweden is free to visit different healthcare units, there is a need to give the treating doctor a more complete view of a patient's different medical records. One alternative (the centralized alternative as proposed by some IT-architects) would be to gather all information from local treatments in a total centralized national database for medical records easily accessible by anyone with authorization. The other alternative is to create only an overview of patients´ visits in a coordinating system and then base systems interaction on transfer of requested medical records between existing local systems (the decentralized alternative). There is a huge difference in investments and in impact on the healthcare organization between the two alternatives.

The main problem is that the alternatives so seldom are evaluated. The focus for the IT specialist is generally on technical solutions for total access, not on the alignment between the organization and the structure of information systems, or on what centralization /decentralization ends up with in a long-term perspective.

In the connected society, we definitely have the technology to create suitable structures of systems, but there is no real interest to solve or even to discuss explicitly the balancing problem between centralization and decentralization. Centralists (often IT specialists) keep on proposing centralized solutions based on the basic believe that centralization is necessary to create order; while decentralized proposals, more aligned with objectives out in the organization, such as freedom of action to meet changes through step by step development of IT support, often come from local management. Sometimes a centralized alternative is chosen, sometimes a decentralized alternative is decided. A general observation is however that there is very seldom any real analysis of the alternatives behind the decision. What really must be centralized, what can more efficiently be handled locally, and how local systems can interact with maintained independence are questions seldom under discussion.

8   Conclusion

The conclusion is that theories, management, and practice for decisions on centralization or decentralization of information systems must be further developed. Langefors pointed out the "*lack of understanding that some data must be local, as these data are only intelligible to restricted groups of people"*. This is for sure true, but to my opinion *understanding* is not enough. A conscious management and control of centralization or decentralization in IT support is a vital question in the company or the organization, which is not a task that can be handled only by IT-specialists. The structure of information systems should be aligned with the business structure.

There is a need for business oriented IT management.

If the last century brought us extended knowledge about the outcomes from centralization and decentralization, including consequences and failures, then perhaps a main question for this century is how to use this knowledge to learn how to manage, balance, and control centralization and decentralization in a long-term perspective.

References

[1] Allen, B.R., Boynton, A.C.: Information Architecture. In: Search of Efficient Flexibility. MIS Quarterly/December (1991)

[2] Bacon, C.J.: Organizational Principles of Systems Decentralization. Journal of Information Technology 5 (1990)

[3] Hugoson, M.-Å., Hesselmark, O., Grubbström, A.: MBI-metoden, en metod för verksamhetsanalys. Studentlitteratur, Lund (1983)

[4] Hugoson, M.-Å.: Verksamhetsbaserad systemstrukturering. NordData, Stockholm (1986)

[5] Iivari, J.: Levels of Abstraction as a Conceptual Framework for an Information system. In: Proceedings on the IFIP TC 8 /WG 8.1 Working Conference on Information Systems Concept. Namur, Belgium (1989)

[6] Jardine, D.A., Yazid, S.: Integration of Information Submodels. In: Proceedings on the IFIP TC 8 /WG 8.1 Working Conference on Information Systems Concept. Namur, Belgium (1989)

[7] Langefors, B.: Directive Information for Systems Control. In: The analysis of Business Systems, Glerup, Lund (1967)

[8] Langefors, B.: System för företagsstyrning. Studentlitteratur, Lund (1968)

[9] Langefors, B.: Four Cases with Decentralized Management and Local Computers. Research report, Department of Computer Science, 82:09, Chalmers University of Technology & University of Gothenburg (1984)

[10] Langefors, B.: Integrated versus Decentralized Information Resource Management. Research report, Department of Computer Science, 83:09, Chalmers University of Technology & University of Gothenburg 1984 (1984)

[11] Langefors, B.: System development using Prototyping with Dataflex. Research report, Department of Computer Science, 84:03, Chalmers University of Technology & University of Gothenburg 1984 (1984)

[12] Langefors, B.: Essays on Infology. Studentlitteratur, Lund (1995)

[13] Mumford, E.: Systems design for people, Economic evaluation of computer based systems. Book 3, the National Computer Center (NCC), Manchester (1971)

Scientific Computers at the Helsinki University of Technology during the Post Pioneering Stage

Panu Nykänen and Hans Andersin

Helsinki University of Technology
panu.nykänen@tkk.fi, hans.andersin@tkk.fi

Abstract. The paper describes the process leading from the pioneering phase when the university was free to develop and build its own computers through the period when the university was dependent on cooperation with the local computer companies to the stage when a bureaucratic state organization took over the power to decide on acquiring computing equipment to the universities. This stage ended in the late 1970s when computing power gradually became a commodity that the individual laboratories and research projects could acquire just like any resource. This development paralleled the situation in many other countries and universities as well. We have chosen the Helsinki University of Technology (TKK) as a case to illustrate this development process, which for the researchers was very annoying and frustrating when it happened.

Keywords: Computing science, education, computing centre.

1 The Finnish State Computing Centre

The happy pioneering phase [3, 6] in the 1940s and 1950s when scientific university institutions used to design and build their scientific computers preceded the era of commercially produced scientific computers. The Committee for Mathematical Machines (Matermatiikkakonekomitea–Matematikmaskinkommit-tén) finished their task in the beginning of the 1960s. After a period of interregnum, the state responsibility for data processing matters transferred to the Finnish State Computing Centre (FSCC) that was founded in 1964. Actually, it had already started to operate earlier [4]. Before FSCC came into existence, an unsuccessful attempt was made in 1963 by the *Academy of Engineering Sciences* to form a national center for scientific and engineering computing [2].

Due to scarce financial resources available for acquiring computers, the university scientific staff lost their decision-making rights as to computer acquisition and resource allocation. The bureaucrats took over both within and outside the universities. In Finland, the Ministry of Finance on a yearly basis allocated funds for computer acquisition. When a university wanted to use the allocated funds for buying a new computer, it had to get the approval for its plans by the FSCC. In many cases, the situation deteriorated into open and bitter conflicts of interest. FSCC wanted to sell their services and computing capacity to the universities instead of letting them buy their own computers. FSCC also wanted to push certain computer brands instead of giving the universities free hands. One of the reasons was their belief in the blessings

J. Impagliazzo, T. Järvi, and P. Paju (Eds.): HiNC 2, IFIP AICT 303, pp. 116–120, 2009.
© IFIP International Federation for Information Processing 2009

of standardization. Another reason was that the bureaucrats generally mistrusted the competence of university professors to make rational decisions in selecting the best computer.

FSCC acquired its first large-scale scientific computer, an Elliott 503, in the mid-1960s. Interestingly enough, they physically placed it in the Helsinki University of Technology (HUT, in Finnish TKK) main building and TKK students and research workers heavily used it.

2 The Finnish Cable Works Becomes a Major Player

In December of 1958, Björn Westerlund was chair and CEO of the Finnish Cable Works (later Nokia). He suggested to the board of directors that one could add computers to the product program of the company. This resulted in giving the mathematician Olli Lehto (today a member of the Academy of Finland) the task of founding an electronic division within the Cable Works. In addition to Lehto the Cable Works' Electronic Division hired Tage Carlsson who then worked with the Committee for Mathematical Machines. They also added Lauri Saari from VTT (State Institute of Technical Research and Development) to the staff of the Electronic Division. When IBM – that already had Hans Andersin from the Committee of Mathematical Machines on board – hired Olli Varho (who later became the president of IBM Finland) from the Committee, this meant that all the key resources of the Committee were divided between the two major players in the computer market in Finland [3].

In the beginning, the Finnish markets alone were not big enough to attract other large international computer companies except IBM. During the cold war period, however, the Finnish foreign trade was heavily directed towards the Soviet Union and the big international computer companies apparently wanted to take advantage of this situation. In 1961, this led to agent agreements between the Cable Works and the French *Compagnie des Machines Bull* (CMB) with punched card machines and the computers Gamma 10 and Gamma 30 on one hand and the Swedish *Facit* with peripheral equipment on the other. Earlier the Cable Works already had agreements with the German *Siemens* and the British *Elliott Brothers* The agreements included sale to the Soviet Union [1].

The Finnish computer market was from now on for some time divided between IBM and the Cable Works (representing CMB, General Electric, Siemens, Facit, and Elliott). The Helsinki University of Technology (TKK) had to balance between these two major players. Cable Works was more technically and less commercially oriented than IBM and it attracted the engineers both at TKK and at VTT Technical Research Centre of Finland.

3 The First Scientific Computers at HUT/TKK

For users of scientific computers there were several possibilities to use computers outside TKK. Many scientists used the Postal Savings Bank IBM 650, the first operational computer in Finland, for their scientific and engineering computing needs already at the end of the 1950s. In 1960 TKK started to use the newly acquired Elliott computers (803 and later 503) of the *Finnish Cable Works.* When the *Northern*

Europe University Computing Centre (NEUCC) opened in Copenhagen in the mid-1960s, equipped with a world class scientific IBM 7090, many TKK users were among its clients. In addition, many of the companies having acquired computers suitable for scientific applications made their equipment available for TKK users.

Despite the abundance of computing power available outside TKK, the university appointed in September of 1960 a committee to investigate the need for computers inside TKK. The committee was chaired by Professor Erkki Laurila (Prof. of Technical Physics, later member of the Academy of Finland) with Professor Pentti Laasonen (Prof. of Strength of Materials) and assistant professor Olli Lokki (Prof. of Applied Mathematics) as members. The committee recommended that a scientific computer be acquired by TKK to avoid being too dependent on outside computers. Additionally, the computer education would require, according to the committee, that the students experience a possibility for "hands on" use of computers. The committee did not believe that the idea of the Finnish State providing a centralized computing resource would materialize for a long time to come. On the contrary, TKK could sell computer excess time to the State [7].

Because the computer would require local maintenance service and cooperation with the computer manufacturer, the feasible alternatives were only the IBM 1620 and the Elliott 803. The final decision was in favor of the Elliott computer due to the higher maintenance cost of the IBM machine and because the Computer Center of the Helsinki University had just decided in favor of the IBM 1620. IBM submitted a new proposal to TKK in March that in economic terms was almost identical to the Cable Work's proposal. This proposal was turned down but the IBM offer to give free computer time to TKK was gratefully accepted [8]. Consequently, the decision occurred by a wish to strike a balance between the two main players in the Finnish market. It was clearly also a gesture of friendship towards the Finnish Cable Works that had just begun its struggle for market shares in the Finnish Market.

The funds needed for the purchase were allocated in the State budget in January 1961 and in March, they made the decision to fund a computing Center at TKK. Rector Jaakko Rahola was to sign the agreement with the Cable Works. One of the motives for acting swiftly was the fact that computers got obsolete in no time at all. If TKK had not approved the delivery of the one-year-old Elliott 803, the delivery time of an updated version would have stretched out to be at least nine months. The Cable Work's Elliott 803 was free for delivery in April of 1961, which implied that the computer education would begin the same year. The university placed the TKK Computing Centre as a part of the Institution for Applied Mathematics. Later, they replaced the 803A with an 803B and simultaneously they added an IBM 1620 to the equipment of the TKK Computer Centre, probably in order to create a balance between the two main competitors IBM and the Cable Works.

When TKK Computer Centre moved 1968 from the old facilities of TKK in Helsinki City Centre to the Otaniemi Campus area, the laboratory got better possibilities for independent work.

4   The Bank of Finland Enters the University Computer Scene

A large step towards centralized university computing in Finland occurred during the end of the 1960s when the *Bank of Finland* allocated funds for acquiring large-scale scientific computing capacity to the universities in Finland. They purchased a Sperry Rand Univac 1108 and gave it to the FSCC to run. This caused a massive protest action among the universities that feared that the dictatorial FSCC would now put an end to all independent purchase of computers by the universities. As a compromise, they allowed the universities to buy terminal computers and equipment; they purchased 150 terminals and placed them at the universities all around the country.

TKK was very discontent with the situation but was finally able in 1970 to purchase a modern time sharing system, Hewlett Packard 2000, which served the basic courses of computer programming during some years to come [5]. The situation with regard to increasing the capacity of the TKK computing centre did not improve, however. The strategy of the bureaucrats was still to maximize the use of the centralized scientific computer capacity at the FSCC by allocating new computer money only to the peripheral universities. TKK was of the opinion that this strategy had stalled its development for nearly a decade. An interesting part of the history of computing at TKK, was the 1974 purchased MIR-2 computer that was manufactured by *Kievskij Zavod elektronnyh vytsislitelnyh i upravljajuštšihmašin* in USSR. They acquired the computer as a part of the bilateral export - import agreement between Finland and USSR, and as the payment for it was a huge amount of surplus eggs. Some of the bureaucrats could see MIR-2 as an addition to the computing capacity of TKK, but the director of the TKK computing center, Olli Lokki, warned of this point of view in his inauguration speech. Instead, TKK's own and several western researchers keenly familiarized themselves with MIR-2 as a rare example of a Soviet way to design computer architecture [9, 5].

A rebellious act by TKK was to save the money that had been allocated for other investments and expenses and use the resulting funds to buy a new computing system without asking anyone's permission. They installed a Digital Equipment Corporation's DEC System 20 during the first half of 1978 at the TKK Computer Centre and it served well for almost ten years.

Some of the research groups at TKK were able to obtain permission to buy their own computers. Most of these were minicomputers such as the PDP-8, PDP-11, and PDP-15 that started to appear in various laboratories in the beginning of the 1970s, mostly in dedicated applications such as process control tasks. The purchases of such small computers became deregulated and the discontent with FSCC among the university research staff diminished.

5 Concluding Remarks

The commercialization of computer and software design and manufacturing affected the universities in several ways. A positive result was the fact that most of the new commercial computers were more reliable and had more software capabilities than the ones built in the universities. At the same time, the need for scientific computing capacity grew beyond all limits at the universities and the government took the power to control the use and purchasing of the machinery. A negative result of the commercialization was that the innovative power and specialized know-how of university research workers was left untapped. This development was typical for most small countries.

One of the reasons for the State centralized computer policy was the wide spread belief in the blessings of standardization. It looked like that the bureaucrats generally mistrusted the competence of university professors to make rational decisions in selecting the best computer.

Despite of the limiting and often frustrating restrictions put on the universities, TKK was able to find the right shortcuts and ways to stay in the main stream of the development during the period of two decades covered by this report. We could observe five different strategic directions. These include: (a) Some TKK institutions continued to build special purpose computers for their own use, (b) some TKK institutions used outside computer resources for fulfilling their needs for computing power, (c) the establishment of a TKK computing center, (d) TKK took part in using FSCC computer resources, and (e) some TKK institutions bought computers for their own use.

References

[1] Aaltonen, A.: Nokian elektroniikkateollisuuden synty: nuorten kokeilijoiden ja keksijöiden pajasta huipputeollisuudeksi. In: Tienari, M. (ed.) [The birth of the electronics industry at the Nokia Corporation], pp. 118–119. Tietotekniikan alkuvuodet Suomessa. Gummerus Kirjapaino Oy, Jyväskylä (1993)

[2] Nykänen, P.: Tekniikan tiennäyttäjät. Teknillisten tieteiden akatemia 1957–2007. In: [The history of the Finnish Academy of Technology] Gummerus Kirjapaino Oy, Jyväskylä, pp. 47–48 (2007)

[3] Paju, P.: "Ilmarisen Suomi" ja sen tekijät. Matematiikkakonekomitea ja tietokoneen rakentaminen kansallisena kysymyksenä 1950-luvulla. English Summary [Building "Ilmarinen's Finland". The Committee for Mathematical Machines and computer contruction as a national project in the 1950s]. Turun yliopiston julkaisuja C 269, 440–457 (1950)

[4] Pietarinen, I.: Kun Suomen tietotekniikkaa ohjailtiin neuvottelemalla – Tietotekniikan neuvottelukunta 6.11.1975 – 31.12.1991. In: Tienari, M. (ed.) [The history of the committee of the information technology], pp. 273–274. Tietotekniikan alkuvuodet Suomessa, Gummerus Kirjapaino Oy, Jyväskylä (1993)

[5] Sarlin, K.: TeKoLan 30-vuotinen taival. In: [The history of the Helsinki University of technology Computer Centre]. Teknillinen korkeakoulu, Laskentakeskus, TKK OFFSET, pp. 4, 8, 9–12 (1991)

[6] Seppänen, J.: 30 vuotta tietokoneaikaa Teknillisessä korkeakoulussa. Historiaa ja muistikuvia Eskon ja Elliottin ajoilta. [30 years of computers at Helsinki University of Technology TKK] Teknillinen korkeakoulu, Laskentakeskus. Otaniemi (1991)

[7] TKKA The archives of Helsinki University of Technology TKK, Espoo that include the archives of the Executive Committee (Hallintokollegi, HK) and the archives of the Administrative Council (Opettajaneuvosto, ON). TKKA ON 15.12.1960, § 4 + liite muistio Erkki Laurila & Pentti Laasonen & Olli Lokki Osamietintö Teknillisen Korkeakoulun elektronikonetarpeesta 3.12.1960. TKKA HK 30.1.1961, § 10 + liite Erkki Laurila & Pentti Laasonen & Olli Lokki 20.1.1961 Teknillisen korkeakoulun elektronikonetarvetta käsittelemään asetetun komitean mietintö

[8] TKKA HK 20.3.1961, § 7 and § 8.

[9] Unpublished report Katsaus laskentakeskuksen toimintaan vuosina 1961–72 ja toiminnan kehittämisen lähitavoitteet. 9.4.1973. pp. 18–19. [A short history of TKK Computer Centre 1961 - 72]

Tool or Science? The History of Computing at the Norwegian University of Science and Technology

Ola Nordal

Department of Computer and Information Science, Norwegian University of Science and Technology (NTNU) N-7941 Trondheim, Norway
ola.nordal@hf.ntnu.no

Abstract. One may characterize the history of computing at the Norwegian University of Science and Technology by a tension between the computer as a tool in other disciplines and computer science as discipline in itself. This tension has been latent since the pioneering period of the 1950s until today. This paper shows how this have been expressed in the early attempts to take up computing at the University, and how it gave the Division of Computer Science a fairly rough start when it opened in 1972.

Keywords: Computer history, Computer science, History of computing in academia, Norwegian Institute of Technology (NTH), Trondheim, Norway.

1 Introduction[1]

The computer holds several identities – identities that have changed dramatically over a historically very short period. This means that the history of computing is not limited to a study of the technical development of computing machinery, but it also addresses the complex interaction between hardware devices, software devices, the computer as a communication device, and the computer as an information processing device. One of the driving forces in computer history has been the development of computer science in the universities. Despite this, sadly, the history of computing in higher education has received little attention in the historical literature, which is mainly concerned with hardware development or business history.[2] This omission is

---

[1] A few words on the background for this paper: In December 2005, the author started organizing a collection of old computers at the Department of Computer and Information Science at NTNU. The goal is to make the collection into a computer museum, and collect historical sources in connection with these machines. The collection is fairly extensive, counting approximately 1000 pieces of hardware, along with a good deal of software and documentation. The most notable objects are two Danish GIER computers (from 1962-1963), two Norwegian NORD-1 computers (from 1969-1970) and one PDP-8 (from 1965). While researching the history of the objects, the work gradually developed into a book project. This article presents some of the themes of this book, which will be due for release some time in 2009. I'm thankful to a number of people for kindly sharing their knowledge on the NTNU Computer history [21, 22, 23, 24, 25, 26, 27].

[2] A notable exception is [11]. In his thesis Campbell examines the rise of electronic computing at the University of Toronto, from the early attempts to obtain a computer in the after war years, to the creation of a Department of Computer Science in 1964.

J. Impagliazzo, T. Järvi, and P. Paju (Eds.): HiNC 2, IFIP AICT 303, pp. 121–129, 2009.
© IFIP International Federation for Information Processing 2009

especially notable in the few works on European computer history.[3] In my view, the academic institutions are a good place to study the multiple identities of the computer, and in this article, I will present some aspects of the history of computing at the Norwegian Institute of Technology (NTH) in Trondheim.[4] The main argument of the article is that the history of computing at NTH is characterized by a tension between the need for the computer as a tool, and the urge to study computing as science.

Computer science had a rather slow start in Trondheim. During the first ten years of the Division of Computer Science that opened in 1972, the teaching load was severe and time for research was limited. Many of the engineering departments at NTH wanted to keep the computer division solely as a service institution in connection with the already existing engineering programs, offering basic programming courses for their students, in the same way as mathematics and other auxiliary subjects. This was due to several reasons. One was that computer science was a relatively new branch of academia, still not regarded as a proper discipline by many.[5] Another explanation can be sought within the particular history and structure of NTH.

In this article, I will first give a brief overview of the history of NTH to suggest some possible explanations why computing had such a hard time finding its place at the institution. Then I will point to some early attempts to take up computing at NTH, and conclude with an overview of the way the *ACM Curriculum'68* inspired the computer science program in the Division of Computer Science.

2   The Norwegian Institute of Technology (NTH)

NTH was established in 1910 as the national institution for educating civil engineers in Norway [13][16][20]. Technological development was seen as the motor that should propel modernization, industrialization and prosperity, and in the Norwegian

---

[3] Another exception is the overview of curricula and research programs at the Nordic universities presented at the previous HiNC conference. See Kurki-Suinio, Reino, Birth of computer science education and research in Finland, Benediktsson, Oddur, Early curricula in computer science at the university of Iceland, and Espelid, Terje O. (et al.), Research and curricula development at Norwegian universities, in [9].

[4] Note on names, abbreviations and institutional development: The Norwegian University of Science and Technology (NTNU) in Trondheim was founded in 1996 as a merger between the Norwegian Institute of Technology (who also used its Norwegian abbreviation NTH in English), the College of Arts and Sciences (AVH), the Museum of Natural History and Archaeology (VM), the Faculty of Medicine, and the Trondheim Conservatory of Music. Since 1968 NTH, AVH and VM had been autonomous parts of a more loosely organized University of Trondheim. The industrial research institute SINTEF (Selskapet for Industriell og Teknisk Forskning, The Institute of Industrial and Technical Research) was founded in 1950, and cooperated closely with NTH. One of the two larger departments in SINTEF were ELAB, the Laboratory for Electrical Research, and RUNIT, the Computer Centre at the University of Trondheim. See [13, 14, 16, 20].

[5] The discipline of computer science emerged in USA during the 1950s and 1960s, and the American Association of Computing Machinerys (ACM) influential curriculum proposal *Curriculum '68* propelled the establishment of Computer Science programs in universities all over the world. For an overview on the development of Curriculum ´68 and early Computer Science, see [15].

context NTH should be spearheading this development. The structure of NTH reflects the Norwegian industry and political climate in that particular period and defined for a long time which disciplines and departments should be strong and influential. During the period 1905-1920, Norway experienced a great industrial rise, most notably in electrochemical and mining industry. The comparative advantages that Norway had were rich natural resources and cheap electricity from waterfalls and rivers. The modernization of the Norwegian ship industry occurred in this period, and the Norwegian merchant fleet was one of the largest in Europe. The strong departments at NTH were in electrical engineering (mainly focused towards hydropower), chemical engineering, ship and machine construction, and structural engineering.

During the interwar period, Norway and most other European countries went through a series of economical crises, and this halted plans for further development of NTH. This meant that NTH experienced problems due to lack of room and staff, and scarce funding for instrumentation and other necessary investments. They made several attempts and plans for a much-needed expansion of the engineering school, but they could not realize this until after the Second World War.

In the post World War II years, NTH had a slow start due to vacant professorships and an accumulated lack of teaching and laboratory space. During the 1950s and 1960s this gradually changed, and over a period of fifteen years NTH more than quadruplicated its size. Another significant event was the founding of the industry research institute SINTEF in 1950 [14]. SINTEF's main task was to establish a closer connection between NTH and the Norwegian industry. However, it also boosted the expansion and position of NTH, initiated research programs, raised new buildings, and helped with various administrative tasks. Although it was a separate organizational body, the SINTEF activity was always carefully coordinated with the different NTH professors.

3   The Birth of Computing at NTH/SINTEF

In the early 1950s, the most "natural" places to take up computing in an institution like NTH would have been either the divisions of mathematics or electrical engineering. However, due to the nature of NTH this proved difficult.

The mathematics department was in the relatively weak Department of General Sciences. The divisions of this department gave auxiliary courses to the engineering students, and, with a notable exception of the division of technical physics, the department did not have its own programs. Research was also limited, except for in the physics division. Werner Romberg, who started out as an associate professor (dosent) in physics in 1950 and was appointed Professor in Applied Mathematics in 1960, made the first attempts to take up digital electronic computing at NTH in the late 1950s. Romberg, being a distinguished mathematician, had previously worked on the differential analyzer at the University of Oslo. He had also been involved in the programming of the first Norwegian computer, NUSSE, which was built in Oslo in 1952-1954. For some time Romberg was a candidate for the position as director of the

Norwegian Computing Centre.[6] He also knew Konrad Zuse and his machines, and he had written vividly about them in the popular science journal *Fra fysikkens verden* [18, 19]. Nevertheless, Romberg lacked the political strength and skills needed to realize a pioneering project in Trondheim, and none of his attempts got any support from the founding authorities.

The division of electronics experienced severe problems regaining its strength after the Second World War. The only professor, Ragnar Skancke, had been a part of the national socialistic government during the German occupation, and in 1945 the field was virtually non-existent at NTH. Compared to heavy current technology, electronics had a weak position at the Department of Electrical Engineering until the end of the 1950s. This changed in 1960 when the department finally could move into new and improved buildings. The building plans had been generous, and to exploit the extra space, a SINTEF department for electronic research called ELAB was established [10]. ELAB gave work to many freshly graduated and enthusiastic engineers, and quickly turned out to be one of the most vigorous SINTEF departments.

One of these young engineers was Arne Lyse. After graduating as an engineer in radio technology, he had been working part time and studying computing at the University of Michigan from 1956 to 1959. He had a fascination for the potential of the capacitor, and even before they established ELAB, he had started a research group in digital technology. This group applied for the funding necessary to develop and build a computer, but failed – partly due to the plans being too ambitious, and that the Norwegian Council for Technical and Scientific research (NTNF) wanted to focus its recourses on the Computer Centre in Oslo [25].

These early attempts show that NTH lacked the right people in the right places, and did not enjoy the necessary support from the Norwegian research councils to take up a pioneering project like for instance the building of NUSSE. Pioneering activity followed another path at NTH. In 1952, NTNF supported Jens Glad Balchen and the Division of Engineering Cybernetics with enough funding to start the development of an analog computer. The first version of the computer DIANA (Differential Analysator) was finished in 1954. However, Balchen was not interested in computer development in itself. He only saw the computer as an important tool that he needed for his discipline. The background for *building* a computer instead of buying one was that the effort of constructing the machine would give valuable experience to the young engineering cybernetics milieu [17], p. 72. The view of the computer as merely a tool would persist for a long time at NTH.

4 The Computer Centre at NTH

In 1962 NTH bought its first digital computer [8]. The choice fell on the Danish GIER, a machine developed and manufactured by Danish Institute of Computer Machinery. To evade formal difficulties with the rigid NTH system and quarrels on who should administrate the machine, they arranged with SINTEF to establish a computer centre as a SINTEF division. Under the leadership of the energetic Norman Sanders,

---

[6] Letter from Werner Romberg to professor Johan Peter Holtsmark, University of Oslo, dated 31st of December 1950. Private archive *Tek. 62: Werner Romberg*, NTNU University Library Special Collections, box 1: Correspondence.

and later Nils Høeg and Karl Georg Schjetne, the Computer Centre at NTH developed into a dynamic service bureau for the Norwegian industry as well as providing computer resources for NTH.

An important aspect in the agreement between NTH and SINTEF was that the computer centre should provide courses for the NTH students. Although this method had been used in many other teaching institutions to handle the lack of academically trained expertise in computing, it was a unique arrangement in the history of NTH. Normally SINTEF research grew out of NTH activity, and it was previously unheard of that the teaching of a discipline solely could be handled by SINTEF. However, this also reflects the view that computing was not regarded as a proper discipline, and thus could be handled by non-academic personnel. During the first years people viewed the courses given more as training in necessary techniques rather than academic subjects.

To some surprise for both the academic staff at NTH and the people working in the computer centre, computing was an immediate hit with the students. Even before any formal course developed, several hundreds of students took voluntarily courses in ALGOL. Over the next decade, several thousand students took courses in programming and other aspects in the use of computers. They introduced approximately one new course each year until 1972 and gradually the courses gained more sophistication and complexity.

The first course in the NTH curriculum that took up digital computing was Rombergs *Numerical Methods I* and *II* from 1962-1963.[7] The courses were compulsory in the first year for students in construction engineering, electrical engineering, and chemistry. They were also elective for students taking a degree in technical physics. Among the topics discussed in *Numerical Methods I* were linear algebra and programming with "emphasis on methods that could be applied with electronic calculating machines" [2]. In *Numerical Methods II*, an introduction given to analog and digital computers, as well as elementary programming in ALGOL. However, the focus was on mathematical problems and the introduction to computing was only a limited part of the course.

The first course to focus explicitly on computing was *Course no 60: Structure and application of digital computing machines*, given by the Computer Centre at NTH in 1963-1964. The course seemed ambitious considering that there were only two lecture hours per week. The topics included history of computing, digital versus analog technology, logic, hardware, software systems on computers, application of computers, autocode, and the more cryptic theme entitled "technology and techniques of the future" [3]. The following year ALGOL was removed from the *Numerical Methods II* course, and instead a six-week course in ALGOL became compulsory before one could start [4]. *Course no 60* had this year changed the name to *ALGOL*, and were compulsory in the third year for chemists, and elective for the other students. Later the subject changed its name to *Elementary Programming*, taking up other languages as well, but always with an emphasis on ALGOL. Here it should be noted that at NTH, as in most other places, the debate on ALGOL versus FORTRAN as the preferred programming language was fierce and bitter.

---

[7] The course had from 1957 been a part of the auxiliary education in mathematics. Romberg had then given a short introduction to mechanical and electrical computers, without going in detail on how to program or utilize them. Private archive *Tek. 62: Werner Romberg*, NTNU University Library Special Collections, box 30: Lecture notes.

In the academic year 1970-1971, the computer centre offered a total number of twelve courses [7, p. 16]. These included:

Programming
Computers
Intermediate Programming
Programming Languages and Compiler Techniques
Data Structures
Information Systems
Project Work
SIMULA 67
Computer Systems Simulation
FORTRAN
COBOL
Machine code

The first attempt to formalize a curriculum in computing at NTH came in 1969-1970 with a specialization in information processing as one of five combinations leading up to a degree in technical physics. The combination had eighteen courses, of which twelve were courses in mathematics and physics and six were courses given by the computer centre. The Computer Centre developed four new courses especially for this combination [5]. Three associate professors (Terje Noodt, Tore Amble and Kjell Bratbergsengen) were also appointed to help the Computer Centre with the teaching. By this time, elementary programming had become mandatory for all engineering students, but apart from the information processing program there were few possibilities for those wanting to specialize in computing. The list of courses shows that there were some early attempts to take up a more theoretical approach to computing before they could establish a degree in computer science. In fact, at this point, the Computer Centre at NTH taught almost all the basic subjects recommended in the *ACM Curriculum'68*.

5   The Division of Computer Science

The discipline of computer science arose in some of the American universities during the late 1950s and early 1960s, often in strong connection with the departments of mathematics or electrical engineering. The key element of computer science was the study of computers "not as a static artifact, but as a system that carried out dynamic processes according to a set of rules" [7, p. 102]. This meant that the focus of computer science was on the study of algorithms, programs, and information, and not the study of computer hardware. Much of this line of thought was put down in the heavily influential curriculum proposal *Curriculum '68* – a document that it has been said was as important for the development of the computer as the EDVAC report of 1945. In *Curriculum'68* a strong emphasis was given to computer organization, system programming, compiler construction, discrete structures, system simulation, and information organization and retrieval [7, p. 106]. During the late 1960s, computer science gradually gained respectability finding a place in most higher education institutions [12, p. 103].

At NTH the Division of Computer Science[8] welcomed its first students in the academic year 1972-1973, and the combination of subjects had a heavy influenced from *Curriculum '68*.[9] As Espelid (et al.) points out, this did not fit well into the persisting view on what computing should be at NTH [9, p. 150]. Many had wanted to have computer technology only as a supplementary activity, supporting the already existing curricula in engineering. The reason for this was that many representatives of these communities wanted NTH to focus on the disciplines where the institution already had substantial activity, and not "waste resources" on starting up something completely new. According to this view, the computer department should focus on technical computing, and not on computer science. Nevertheless, it was also clear at the time that there was an emerging need in Norway for engineers holding a full degree in computing, especially since the demand for system developers had increased. In 1969 the socalled Barca-committee estimated that Norway needed another 530 engineers holding a degree in computing each year for the next sixteen years, and the Norwegian universities would not be able to fill this demand if they did not dramatically extend their education in computing [7, p. 12].

The solution at NTH began as a sort of compromise. From 1972 the Division of Computer Science annually admitted approximately twenty students in their third year, giving a specialization in computer systems, technical computing or information systems in the fourth year [7, pp. 26-28]. In addition to this, the division gave elementary programming training to all NTH civil engineering students; approximately 700 – 800 students attended each term. Therefore, even though the division only had 40 – 50 full-time computer students and an academic staff of only eight people as late as in 1980, they had to grade more than fifteen hundred examinations annually at the division [1].

One of the reasons for this rather slow start was that the division lacked financial and political support both from the NTH and from NTNF. Most of the funding from the research councils were given to the Computer Centre at NTH. The center had gladly given up its teaching activities, but kept the more profitable research activity. The administrative placement of the Division of Computer Science was another key factor. Before the division was founded, it had been a heated debate on which institutional unit it should be a part of. Suggestions to place it in connection with the existing divisions of mathematics or engineering cybernetics was turned down because both the Computer Centre and NTH feared this would have too much of an impact on the path computing would take at NTH. As a temporary solution, the division was placed at the Department of General Sciences. This secured freedom for the division to develop its own identity. However, it also meant that funding was scarce, since the Department of General Sciences politically and economically was one of the weakest at NTH. A heavy teaching load and almost no time or money for doing research characterized the first years of the Division of Computer Science. The need for a larger academic staff was clearly stated in every annual report from the division throughout

---

[8] The Norwegian name for the division was Institutt for Databehandling (abbreviated IDB). Sometimes the name is translated into English as the Division of Data Processing.

[9] This does not mean that all computer science influence came from this document. Much inspiration came from cooperating with the other Nordic institutions and especially Börje Langefors and his work on information systems was influential, and already in 1968 the Computing Centre offered a course in information systems [5].

the 1970s, but the university granted few new positions [1]. Substantially sized research programs were not granted before the early 1980s. Nevertheless, the field was extremely popular with the students, and the marks required for admission was for many years the highest at NTH. Sometimes this created envy in those departments that still had problems recognizing the need for a full curriculum in computer science at NTH.

From the late 1970s computer science at NTH grew at a steady rate. From 1978 the Division of Computer Science offered a full 4½-year program, immediately becoming the most popular degree at NTH. During the early 1980s, the financial situation got better and several research programs were initiated. The academic staff also increased dramatically. A closer connection to electronics and communication technology began in 1984 when the Division of Computer Science moved from the Department of General Sciences to a newly formed Department of Electrical Engineering and Computer Techniques. During the 1980s, this department grew to be the largest at NTH.

6 Concluding Remarks

It had taken almost twenty years from when they installed the first digital computer at NTH until the Division of Computer Science had reached a substantial size with its own research identity. We can trace much of this back to the division caught between the historically speaking strong engineering divisions at NTH. Moreover, even though the division grew strong and vigorous, the tension between the computer as a tool and the computer as a science has been latent ever since, and we can still see some debates between the computer department and other parts of NTNU.

References

Archives

Private archive *Tek. 62: Werner Romberg*, NTNU University Library Special Collections

Annual reports, reports etc.

[1] NTH annual reports from the departments and divisions, for the years 1972 to 1980, archive copy at the NTNU Technical Library, in Norwegian
[2] NTH Curriculum 1962-1963, archive copy at the NTNU Technical Library, in Norwegian
[3] NTH Curriculum 1963-1964, archive copy at the NTNU Technical Library, in Norwegian
[4] NTH Curriculum 1964-1965, archive copy at the NTNU Technical Library, in Norwegian
[5] NTH Curriculum 1968-1969, archive copy at the NTNU Technical Library, in Norwegian
[6] NTH Curriculum 1969-1970, archive copy at the NTNU Technical Library, in Norwegian
[7] Virksomhetskomiteen for Regnesenteret ved Norges tekniske høgskole, Utbyggingen av Regnesenteret NTH: Innstilling fra Virksomhetskomiteen for Regnesenteret ved Norges tekniske høgskole. NTH: Trondheim (1970) (The Further Expansion of the Computer Centre at NTH. Report from the Activity Committee for the Computer Centre at the Norwegian Institute of Technology, in Norwegian) (1970)

Literature

[8] Asphjell, A. (ed.): RUNIT 25 år, 1962-1987. RUNIT, Trondheim) (RUNIT 25 years, 1962–1987)

[9] Bubenko Jr., J., Impagliazzo, J., Sølvberg, A. (eds.): History of Nordic Computing IFIP Wg9.7 First Working Conference on the History of Nordic Computing (HiNC 1), Trondheim, Norway, June 16-18, 2003. Springer, New York (2005)

[10] Børresen, A.K.: Fra tegneøving til regneøving: Om undervisning og forskning innen elektronikk 1945-1970, STS-Rapport 12. Universitetet i Trondheim: Trondheim (1991) (From Drawing Assignments to Calculation Assignments. On Education and Research in Electronics 1945-1970, in Norwegian)

[11] Campbell, S.M.: The Premise of Computer Science: Establishing Modern Computing at the University of Toronto 1945-1965. PhD Thesis, University of Toronto (2006)

[12] Ceruzzi, P.E.: A History of Modern Computing. The MIT Press, Cambridge (2003)

[13] Devik, O.: N.T.H. femti år: Norges tekniske høgskoles virksomhet 1910-1960 (Teknisk Ukeblad: Oslo). (N.T.H. fifty years. Activities of the Norwegian Institute of Technology 1910-1960, in Norwegian) (1960)

[14] Gulowsen, J.: Bro mellom vitenskap og teknologi: SINTEF 1950-2000. Tapir, Trondheim (2000) (Bridge Between Science and Technology: SINTEF 1950-2000, in Norwegian)

[15] Gupta, G.K.: Computer Science Curriculum Developments in the 1960s. IEEE Annals of the History of Computing 29(2), 40–55 (2007)

[16] Hanisch, T.J., Lange, E.: Vitenskap for industrien: NTH - En høyskole i utvikling gjennom 75 år. Universitetsforlaget, Oslo (1985) (Science for the Industry: NTH – a University College in Development Through 75 years, in Norwegian)

[17] Kvaal, S.: Drømmen om det moderne Norge: Automasjon som visjon og virkelighet i etterkrigstiden, STS-Rapport 13. Universitetet i Trondheim, Trondheim (1992) (The Dream of the Modern Norway. Automation as Vision and Reality in the Post War Years, in Norwegian)

[18] Romberg, W.: Om utviklingen av relé- og elektroniske regnemaskiner. Fra fysikkens verden 11(2), 84–98 (1949); (On the Development of Relay and Electronic Calculating Machines, in From the World of Physics, in Norwegian)

[19] Romberg, W.: Zuses relé-regnemaskin. Fra fysikkens verden 11(3), 179–185 (1949); (The Relay Calculating Machines of Zuse, in From the World of Physics, in Norwegian)

[20] Wittje, R.: The foundation of N.T.H. in 1910 in International Context in Sørensen, Henrik Kragh and Reinhard Siegmund-Schultze. Perspectives on Scandinavian Science in the Early Twentieth Century, Novus forlag, Oslo, pp. 111–132 (2006)

Interviews (by the author)

[21] Jens Glad Balchen (26.04.2006)
[22] Kolbein Bell (11.07.2006)
[23] Kjell Bratbergsengen (29.06.2006) (17.08.2006)
[24] Aasmund Gjeitnes (31.08.2006)
[25] Johannes Moe (27.06.2006)
[26] Karl Georg Schjetne (10.02.2006)
[27] Arne Sølvberg (18.08.2006)

The Development of University Computing in Sweden 1965–1985

Ingemar Dahlstrand

Former affiliation of author:
Manager of Lund University Computing Center 1968–1980

Abstract. In 1965-70 the government agency, Statskontoret, set up five university computing centers, as service bureaux financed by grants earmarked for computer use. The centers were well equipped and staffed and caused a surge in computer use. When the yearly flow of grant money stagnated at 25 million Swedish crowns, the centers had to find external income to survive and acquire time-sharing. But the charging system led to the computers not being fully used. The computer scientists lacked equipment for laboratory use. The centers were decentralized and the earmarking abolished. Eventually they got new tasks like running computers owned by the departments, and serving the university administration.

Keywords: University, computing, center, earmarked grants.

1 University Computer Resources before 1965

In 1964, the Swedish government decided to organize computer resources for the universities. At that time, the universities' access to computing power varied a great deal and was insufficient in most places. Lund was best equipped with SMIL, a well-developed BESK copy of its own. Uppsala and Stockholm had access to state-owned BESK and Facit that were heavily loaded, however. Now those three machines were becoming obsolete. In Gothenburg Alwac III E minis were available, and a Datasaab D21, the latter however without supporting service, and the two universities there actually had to rely on Facit time donated by the service bureau Industridata for their computing science education.

2 The Proposed Organization

A scheme was set up which included fresh money earmarked for computer time. The universities shared out these grants to departments, which in turn passed them on to teachers and researchers. Universities used the money to pay for computer time from any of the computing centers being set up [1]. It was stressed that the money was intended for computer time. It could be used only to a limited extent for auxiliary services like programming and punching. Soon, Statskontoret interpreted "limited extent" as 8%, a rule that stayed in force as long as the grant existed.

The rules permitted the centers to earn money from external sources (the university administration was an external source) and this made it possible for us to acquire e.g.

J. Impagliazzo, T. Järvi, and P. Paju (Eds.): HiNC 2, IFIP AICT 303, pp. 130–137, 2009.
© IFIP International Federation for Information Processing 2009

extra equipment without going to Parliament. We will discuss various effects of this below.

The Government's Computer Fund owned the computers and they rented them by the hour. The rental covered amortization over five to six years and interest. Statskontoret (the state's agency for administrative development) managed the fund and had the final word on computer purchases for the whole government sector. Statskontoret was a powerful and competent computer customer, one of the largest in northern Europe, and had forced the vendors to accept a standard contract with strict rules for e.g. delivery tests. They were on the conservative side; that is, the vendor should be able to run a test batch on the equipment offered. They frowned upon selling equipment from blueprints.

3 The Computer Purchase Phase

During the first phase from 1965 to 1970, the centers were in turn equipped with large American computers, starting with Uppsala and ending with Lund, since Lund was reasonably well supplied to start with. The computer fund bought existing computers into the system and hired them out just as the new ones. Some of the purchases – Stockholm's in particular – were the subject of intense controversy. Statskontoret wished to create a common center for the universities there and for the FOA, a military research establishment. In those days, we thought that the capacity of a computer grew faster than its price tag, "Grosch's Law"[1]. There was therefore a temptation to pool resources in order to get something "really big". This marriage – like others of the same kind – proved less than happy, starting with disagreement on the choice of computer (IBM 360/75). There was also a permanent problem of separating the naturally secretive FOA users from the academics and students. Another quarrel broke out when Statskontoret tried to move Gothenburg's IBM 360/50 (which almost at once had to be exchanged for a larger 360/65) to Lund. Waiting at the end of the queue was one thing, but getting the leftovers from Gothenburg was taken as an open insult. Eventually Lund got a Univac 1108.

Users could spend the earmarked money at any of the centers. In fact, many researchers did use centers in other regions during this phase. In particular, Lund people ran a lot of remote batch on Uppsala's CD 3600 and got very good service and some Lund linguists carried on large concordance projects in Gothenburg.

Thus, the centers in some ways functioned as a consortium, though local boards ran them. In 1968, this became more pronounced with the creation of STUD (Styrelsen för Universitetens Datamaskincentraler, i.e. the Board of the University Computer Centers) [2]. STUD controlled budgeting and expenses, created job positions, and checked that the rules were followed. The three medium-size centers – Uppsala, Gothenburg and Lund – were expected to break even, whereas the larger Stockholm center had a surplus that covered the deficit of little Umeå. Though STUD rightfully belonged under the Chancellery of the universities, Statskontoret had permission to appoint its chairperson, giving Statskontoret a double control over our activity.

---

[1] Langefors has questioned whether Grosch's law ever held. It might have been an illusion, the effect of comparing old and slow computers with new and fast ones. Anyway, it played a role in our deliberations.

4 The Build-Up of a Complete Computing Service

The flow of money for computer time grew as the centers were equipped and by 1970 amounted to some 25 million Swedish kronor yearly (this was when gasoline was about one krona per liter). Including external income, our turnover surpassed 40 million and the centers together employed some 200 people. Financed by this flow we could build up full-scale centers with modern equipment including auxiliary units like paper tape readers and writers and curve plotters. Supporting services included programming, punching and a program library that brought home and put to use libraries like NAG (Numerical Algorithms Group) and IMSL (International Mathematical and Statistical Libraries). I can state flatly that we were quite a bit ahead of the private service bureaux like Industridata (where I came from in 1968 to take over the Lund center).

The centers themselves provided some interesting software like the GUTS time-sharing system of Gothenburg and the MIMER database system of Uppsala (named for the fount of wisdom in Nordic mythology). Lund's strong point was an early high quality, ink jet printer, designed by the Department of electrical measurements, and a package of pixel based graphics software. The Umeå center implemented automatic analysis of ECG measurements.

Our sites were on the whole Fortran sites. Algol remained in places and was for instance used a lot in Lund since Univac supplied an Algol compiler made in Norway as a part of Simula. Many other languages were available, but if they could not exchange files and subroutines with Fortran they did not make much of an impact.

5 The Customers

The customers were a very varied group. I take my examples mostly from Lund, but the picture was similar over the whole field. There were the number crunchers like the physicists and structure chemists. The medical faculty, including the special population research station of Dalby, made wide use of us for statistics. So did the social scientists. The linguists as mentioned had large concordance projects. Later the Slavics department in Uppsala made a parser for Russian. One could go on and on reciting project titles such as inventory of threatened Nordic landscape types, scintigram analysis of tumor location, allometry in the foot soles of eight sparrow species, disturbed eye movements in psychotic and alcoholic patients, and bilingualism in Yugoslav immigrant children.

The use of computing became broad. Hundreds of people passed through a center every day to submit runs before computing from terminals became a reality.

Many customers used our programming service. We must mention one unexpected benefit. For many customers it was a relief to discuss a project with an interested outsider who was trying to neither steal a good idea nor tear a poor one to pieces. However, the 8% rule held them back, since programming and punching cost a lot compared to computer time. The humanities had an extra hard time since programs and languages were mainly designed for technicians.

6 Economic Problems

About 1970 the computer fund decided to charge annual rates instead of hourly rates. This decision passed almost unnoticed but actually had a profound effect in that the centers were now saddled with large fixed costs. At about the same time the government seemingly lost interest in the supply of computer resources for the universities. Grants for computer time were frozen at the level achieved and from then on barely kept pace with inflation. Lund was particularly hit hard since it was the last to receive a computer; it received less money per student than the other regions and it did not achieve parity until 1977.

At the same time, it became imperative to upgrade our installations, first in order to achieve full-scale multiprogramming – we had only spooling of input/output to start with – and secondly to be able to offer computing from dialog terminals.

This meant we had to find external income. What was an extra bonus became a necessity, and it distracted us considerably from our main purpose—to introduce computing to researchers and students. In Lund, they were lucky to get many runs from the county's computing center, which was preparing programs for a coming Univac 1108 and later on from administrative runs and from external projects connected with the ink jet plotter. Eventually 25 to 50 percent of our income came from external sources, with great variations between the centers. Even so, we had to extend amortization time to make ends meet. In the case of Lund, it took us almost nine years to pay off the first computer and all its upgrading, by which time the main CPU was a bit outmoded.

The memory extensions needed for time-sharing were expensive, presumably because our computers were so fast. At one time, I suggested exchanging the Univac 1108 with one module of 64 K words for a somewhat slower Univac 1106 with three modules, which would have suited us better, at the same cost. The reaction was very negative. Speed still carried prestige, dating from the origin of computing, irrespective of whether we could sell it or not.

In this atmosphere, the right of researchers to run their projects in other regions was in practice suspended. Strong pressure for instance forced the Lund linguists to bring home their concordance projects from Gothenburg.

7 User Criticism of the System

The system worked as intended but users found it problematic in several ways. The money allotted was intended for one-shift operation of the centers. The idea was that the departments should find more money from other sources if the earmarked money was not enough. However, these other sources refused to grant computer money, referring to the existence of earmarked money. In Lund, which already operated SMIL more than one shift when the system started, grant money was used up before the term's end in the spring of 1966 so the students could not complete their test runs. Statskontoret had to admit free runs this once. It just would not have worked to stop the Lund people from using a machine they had built themselves. However, this did not solve the principal problem. The customers wanted the hourly rates reduced so the machines could have greater utility. This controversy raged for years until it was solved by introducing nightly low priority runs with low rates.

We had some other public relations problems with our academic customers. One was inherent in our charging money to build up our equipment. They felt that we, the computer people, should fight for more grant money, not push our begging onto our customers.

Another one was the way their applications for grants were processed. Researchers were used to having their applications judged and cut down, but usually that was done by peer review. In this case, the processing was seen as purely bureaucratic.

Researchers naturally found it hard to predict their need for computer time ahead of actual trial runs. This particular problem we solved in Lund by cancelling over-drafts against unused grants at year's end. Remaining overdrafts (usually 20%) had to be paid with fresh money. Only once did we actually stop a customer because of an overdraft. It was an extreme case of a researcher running a large graphics program interactively in prime time, in effect stopping everybody else.

A third cause of discontent was the new situation of the computer scientists. They had grown up with SMIL and were used to coming and going in the computer room, having the machine for themselves, seeing the lamps blink and actually hearing the flow of computation. Now they could only watch the computer from behind window glass, reinforced with metal wires. Looking back, it is curious that one did not realize from the start that computer scientists needed computers of their own, as laboratory equipment allowing them to experiment with languages and operating systems.

8 Decentralization

By 1977, the centers had fulfilled their first task of supplying powerful computing resources and making them widely used. At the same time, the first round of computers would soon be fully paid. A committee of academicians was formed to consider the future. Now the many controversies between the academics and Statskontoret took their toll. The committee decided that STUD should be disbanded, the centers decentralized, and the flow of grant money un-earmarked [3]. This was by no means an obvious outcome, e.g. the Danish universities' centers were consolidated at about the same time. Thus each of the five regions had a computing center dropped on them and started doing different things with them. We shall now follow the road that Lund travelled.

The immediate effects were not dramatic. The earmarking was relaxed in small steps and the faculties gained some control of the money. Now, the very basis for computing was changing. An investigation by lecturer Gustaf Olsson in 1980 pointed out some important facts [4]:

o The departments were buying mini-computers. From 1980 on the computing center would be supplying less than half of the computing power within the university, and that part would keep shrinking.
o These new computers were more cost-effective than those of the classical producers. They were also easier to run. Olsson therefore proposed a thorough investigation before buying another super computer.
o The computing center would be needed for other purposes. One was building a local network that would make it possible to reach any computer in the university from a terminal or another computer.
o Another task might be to run computers for the departments that owned them.
o A growing share of computing would be done with ready-made programs.
o Computing would be used by almost everybody in the university.

A paper from the mathematics and natural science (math-nat) faculty supported this analysis and went farther in some respects. In particular the faculty strongly opposed converting the center's new Univac 1100/80 from hire to purchase, lest our hands again be tied for several years.

Unfortunately, the center did not listen. It bought the 1100/80 with the support of the university administration but in stark opposition to the heaviest component of our regular customer base. This was just one example of how our dependence on external money had undermined the original purpose of supporting students and researchers. Another was the controversy over STUDOK, the system for documenting students' progress and grades. This, students felt, was inflicting on their integrity (and, we may suspect, made it too easy for parents to check on them). The administration had us take the job anyway and we were in no position to refuse, considering the amount of money paid. A third example was the re-wording of the center manager's profile and duties. The chief administrator deleted the sentence saying that the center manager might be performing research as part of the job. The administration wanted a businessperson to manage the center.

9 The Diverse Interests of the Faculties

In this situation, the faculties had somewhat different profiles. The math-nat people were already perfectly capable of buying and handling their own computers. The medical faculty could afford to buy all the service they needed from the center. The social sciences were well organized and already had a countrywide cooperation to acquire international databases and interesting program libraries. However, the humanities had not caught up with the rest. They were starved for money and had been held back by the lack of suitable languages and programs. In the scuffle over the grant money they lost out; the committee that divided the grant for good computed the shares according to computer time used over the years, not including programming and punching which would have been fair to the humanists. Thus, decentralization actually resulted in a bad setback to computing in the humanities.

I rather regret we did not use the temporary good economy when the Univac 1108 was paid for to make a strong drive within the university to find those many researchers who had not yet used us and give them a chance to try on the cheap. We should have abolished the 8% rule immediately when we were decentralized, to get a better picture of true customer needs.

The situation was further complicated by differences within the faculties about how to spend the money once they had received control over it. In each faculty there were people who wanted to use the money to buy their own computers, those who wanted to continue using the center, and finally those who were not interested in computing and wanted to spend the money on other things.

It is interesting to note that when the earmarking was dropped completely in 1980, the initial effect, lasting about a year, was a marked drop in usage of the center, followed by a bounce back and then a steady rise to ever-greater turnovers. No amount of bickering could stop computer use for long, if there was money available.

10 Marking Time

Things now rolled on for a few years with the center actually taking on all of the tasks proposed by Gustaf Olsson: building the network, running other peoples' computers, and even setting up an agency for distributing personal computers.

The basis for computing changed rapidly in these years. Punched cards were phased out as registration was done from terminals. Tape stations became less used as disk memories kept growing. Special printers and plotters were superseded by pixel-based laser printers. Thus, the need for a central computer to carry lots of extra equipment shrunk drastically. CPUs could be built cheaply and robustly, leading to a flow of minis and personal computers.

11 Reorganization

In late 1983, the university started a second investigation. This was a much bigger and more official affair than Gustaf Olsson's. It was headed by the dean of the natural science and technology college and included representatives from all faculties, the students, and the trade unions. Its purpose was to create an organization to assist the computerization of the whole university, including teaching and secretarial work. For the computing center, it turned out to be a rather nasty affair.

The driving force, lecturer Lars Philipson, wished to start a new computation unit, with fresh people, to take over user support and program library. The computing center, in his opinion, had shown it was not equal to the task ahead. Its service bureau function was to be liquidated as fast as possible and the external customers told good-bye, leaving the center with the network building and the running of department computers. The university administration ought to have computers of its own [5].

After intense debate through 1984, the final decision was taken in the university's board. The university administration refused to take over its own computing and in addition have one old and one new computing organization to deal with. The question of one or two organizations had to be put to a vote. The committee's two-organization proposal failed by one vote, the faculty representatives being voted down by a coalition of the administration, the trade unions, and the non-academic board members. The rector of the university very farsightedly came up with 4 million kronor to buy the existing computer off the computer fund, so the center could concentrate on its conversion to new tasks instead of earning external money.

Thus, the computing center changed into a computer center and went on with old and new tasks. The service bureau function withered away gradually and the 1100/80 was not replaced when it went out of production. Nevertheless, the center is still there today, running the network and many hundreds of computers and engaging in all kinds of projects for Lund University.

References

[1] Statskontoret, brev till K. Maj:t 14.10.1964, Dnr 1964:832, med bilaga Expertrådets utredning, Datamaskiner för utbildning och forskning vid universitet och högskolor (1964)
[2] Riksarkivet SE/RA/420483/420483.02/FV (UKÄs arkiv), Styrelsen för universitetens datacentraler, protokoll

[3] UKÄ-rapport 13 a, Datorservicegruppen, Datakraft för högre utbildning och forskning (1974)
[4] Lunds universitet, datorresursutredningen, Gustaf Olsson, Slutrapport (1980-04-10)
[5] Arbetsgruppen för utredning av inriktning och organisation av datorverksamheten vid Lunds universitet, Slutrapport (October 1984)
[6] Riksrevisionsverket, Datorcentralerna för högre utbildning och forskning – roll och styrning, Dnr 1985:100

A fuller account of the centers, with focus on the one in Lund, is given in my memoirs, which are deposited at the Technical museum (Tekniska museet) in Stockholm. There you will also find copies of the papers above, except for [2] which is only available at the Riksarvet. Here follows a translation of the references, along with their reference numbers within my deposited papers.

[1'] [XpR] Letter October 14, 1964 from Statskontoret to the government, and attached to it the expert group's proposal that founded the university computing centers, Computers for education and research at universities and colleges (1964)
[2'] Proceedings of the Board of the university computer centers (1968-1977)
[3'] [DSG] Report from the computer service group of the chancellery of universities: Computing power for higher education and research (1974)
[4'] [LTU 0:2] University of Lund, computer resources investigation, Gustaf Olsson: Final report, April 10 (1980)
[5'] [LTU 1:17] University of Lund, working group on direction and organization of computer activity, Final report (October 1984)
[6'] [LTU 2:26] Office of review and auditing, The computer centers for higher education and research (This paper is not cited above, but constitutes a comprehensive survey of the computing centers just before the local reorganizations started to have effect) (1985)

Information Processing – Administrative Data Processing

The First Courses at KTH and SU, 1966–67

Janis Bubenko Jr.

Department of Computer and Systems Science,
Royal Institute of Technology (KTH) and Stockholm University (SU),
Forum 100, 16440 Kista, Sweden
janis@dsv.su.se

Abstract. A three semester, 60-credit course package in the topic of Administrative Data Processing (ADP), offered in 1966 at Stockholm University (SU) and the Royal Institute of Technology (KTH) is described. The package had an information systems engineering orientation. The first semester focused on datalogical topics, while the second semester focused on the infological topics. The third semester aimed to deepen the students' knowledge in different parts of ADP and at writing a bachelor thesis. The concluding section of this paper discusses various aspects of the department's first course effort. The course package led to a concretisation of our discipline and gave our discipline an identity. Our education seemed modern, "just in time", and well adapted to practical needs. The course package formed the first concrete activity of a group of young teachers and researchers. In a forty-year perspective, these people have further developed the department and the topic to an internationally well-reputed body of knowledge and research. The department has produced more than thirty professors and more than one hundred doctoral degrees.

Keywords: Administrative data processing, information systems, university education, datalogy, infology.

1 Introduction

The situation in Sweden in mid 1960s regarding computers and education can be summarised as follows[1]. In total, more than 200 computers existed in the public sector and in business and industry. This corresponded to an investment of more than 500 million Swedish crowns. IBM, having a 70-75% market share, dominated the market. SAAB, CDC, ICL, Siemens, and other vendor companies shared the remaining 25-30%. Practically all computers were large[2], centralised, and operated in a "batch processing" mode. Communication of data using telephone lines was unusual (and slow, about 300 bps).

---

[1] This section is based primarily on the author's personal memories. Some information can also be found in [13].
[2] For instance IBM 7070, 1401, CDC 3200, Univac III, RCA 301, 501, Saab D21, ICL 1901, Burroughs B35600, etc.

J. Impagliazzo, T. Järvi, and P. Paju (Eds.): HiNC 2, IFIP AICT 303, pp. 138–148, 2009.
© IFIP International Federation for Information Processing 2009

The computing industry employed between 8,000 and 10,000 persons with jobs such as programmers, system analysts and designers, administrators, salespersons, and technicians. These professionals had no academic degrees in computer-oriented topics such as computer science or information processing. Such education at universities simply did not exist. Several of them had a basic university education as mathematicians, statisticians, engineers, or economists. They acquired their knowledge and skills in computers and programming by courses offered by the computer vendors. IBM, in particular, had a considerable activity in training of their customers' personnel in programming as well as in systems development and planning. People with an academic degree were often given a full year of full-time training at IBM before being placed to work as salespersons or system analysts.

Swedish university authorities became concerned with higher education in the field of computing. No university discipline in computing or in information systems existed at this time. What did exist were shorter programmes and courses in computer technology, programming, and systems planning and work, normally as part of other educational programmes. For instance, shorter courses in computer technology were normally part of electrical engineering programs, courses in programming part of programs in mathematics or statistics, and courses in systems planning and work were part of programs related to economics and business administration. Business schools at the university of Gothenburg and Lund were particularly active in integrating systems development knowledge in their MBA programs. However, there was no university degree in the disciplines computer science, information processing, or systems development. On the labour market, however, there was a definite need for specialists with these computer and systems development skills.

On April 3, 1963, the chancellor of Swedish universities appointed a commission[3] with a mission to investigate the issue of "Academic education on the topic of administrative data processing", and to come up with suggestions for action. The committee issued a report in November, 1964 [12]. The report observed the great need for increasing the number of qualified professionals in the administrative computing business, as well as the need for advanced research. It estimated the annual need of academically trained professionals in administrative data processing (economists as well as engineers) to about 400-500. The report recommended a new academic discipline named "Administrative Data Processing", including corresponding chairs, to be established from the academic year 1965-1966 at three universities (Gothenburg, Lund, and Stockholm). The report also suggested a preliminary course outline for the first three semesters.

The Swedish government decided to establish a joint chair at Stockholm University and the Royal Institute of Technology in 1965. We can best describe the focus of the discipline by the title of the professor's chair: "Information Processing with a specialisation towards methods for administrative data processing". This formal and very long name was later in everyday use replaced by the simpler "Administrativ Databehandling" (ADB), also called Administrative Data Processing (ADP). The content of the teaching in ADB resembled at that time to some extent what some universities in the USA and Europe taught in the discipline of "Information Systems".

---

[3] G. Hävermark (chair), O. Dopping (secr.), C-E Fröberg, B-G Andrén, C. Kihlstedt, B. Tell, C. Österberg, and W. Goldberg.

2 The First Courses

The first three-semester course structure at the department followed essentially the suggestions given in [12]. Primarily the author together with Börje Langefors designed the three-semester program. The first semester included topics such as computer systems and components, low-level programming languages, high-level programming languages, and performance analysis. The second semester focussed on methods for systems analysis and design, as well as issues related to administration, planning, and management in organisations. The second semester also included a substantial system design exercise; students had to develop and describe an information system for a business organisation according to requirements specified by the department. Students had to take a course on operating systems as well. In the third semester, students could take additional specialised courses; however, a large part of it was devoted to writing a bachelor-level thesis.

2.1 The B-Level Package

The first regular[4] course offered by the department was a 20-credit course for one semester starting in the fall of 1966. We called it a B-level course. The normal prerequisite for admission to the 20-credit B-course was a Swedish high-school degree including mathematics at least corresponding to the level taught in the high-school specialisation towards social sciences. Other backgrounds were permitted if accepted by the university authorities.

For a bachelor degree (Fil. Kand.) students had to complete 120 credits. A typical combination of courses would be 40 credits of information systems courses combined with 80 credits in other disciplines such as mathematics, statistics, business administration, languages, or arts. At that time, no particular 120-credit "study programs" such as "DSV-linjen" (the study program in Computer and Systems Sciences) or "Systemvetenskapliga linjen" (the study program in Applied Systems Sciences) existed.

Although the topic ADB was taught face-to-face at the Royal Institute of Technology (KTH), most students registered at Stockholm University. It frequently happened however, that students of KTH took some of our courses, as optional courses. Some of our early assistants, recruited in the spring of 1967, were actually KTH-graduates.

Students quite well appreciated the courses. The B-level courses offered during the late 1960s had an attendance of 400 to 500 students. I do not remember other limits of the number of attendees than lecture hall space. There were surprisingly many female students, perhaps more than 30%. Many students had already 60 to 80 credits in a number of other university disciplines. They were interested in doing the ADB-course as they, rightfully, expected to find jobs related to this new discipline. Many students had background studies in disciplines such as mathematics, statistics, and business administration. Information Systems was a topic for the future, they felt.

---

[4] A regular course is a course formally offered by the university such that it can be included in the study programme of a student for a degree. In this text we use a direct translation to English of various concepts then used by the department in order not to change the "flavour" of the computer "era" of the late sixties.

The B-level package included four parts, five credits each. It totalled 102 hours of lectures, and 62 class hours of exercises plus, of course, student's individual and/or group work and homework. This implied roughly 8-10 contact hours per week. Appendix A shows the four-course package[5] with the literature required for delivery of those courses and the examination summary students had to complete.

2.2 The AB-Level Course Package

The B-level course package of 20 credits was followed in the spring semester of 1967 by the next level package of 20 credits, the AB-level course package. However, not all B-level students continued on the next level – perhaps only about one hundred of them. As we will see, the AB-level courses focussed on information systems theory, IT in organisations, computing system analysis and design, and on a large case study.

This package of four parts consisted of 88 hours of lectures and 28 hours of guided exercises. It also included a large assignment (a case study) for group work. Appendix B shows the four-course package with the literature required for delivery of those courses and the examination summary students had to complete.

2.3 Higher Level Education

The AB-level package was followed in the fall of 1967 by a C-level package of 20 credits. The C package contained a number of courses on Information Systems Theory (advanced), IS and organisations, Real-Time systems, Databases and Database Management systems, Simulation and the Programming Language Simula, and the like. The main task for students of the C-level course was, however, to write a bachelors thesis that awarded them 10 credits. In the spring of 1968, D-level courses followed the C-level courses; doctoral (Ph.D.) candidates primarily studied D-level courses.

3 In Retrospect – Analysis and Discussion

I do not claim that the courses described above were the first courses, related to computing, taught at Swedish universities. However, I do claim that the course package described is the first comprehensive, academic "program" in Sweden for educating and training information systems analysts and designers. In our case, the package formed the basis for a new university topic "Information processing, specialising in methods for administrative data processing". We now offer additional comments on the course package, the topic, as well as on the department.

3.1 Our Discipline

The contents of the above three-semester course package included what was believed, at that time, to be a minimum of necessary, systematic knowledge for designing and building computer based information systems to support operative as well as directive

---

[5] The course descriptions of Appendices A and B are based on old, non-published administrative material at the department of ADB at KTH and SU in 1966 and 1967.

tasks in business and in organisations. The course structure was, therefore, rather like a *part* of an educational programme created for educating professionals for a particular job speciality – system analysts and designers. Clearly, it included topics which have to do with computer hardware, programming, management, and organisations, but which did not belong to the *core* of the discipline. Our experience tells that most of our students, majoring in our topic towards a bachelor degree, had complementary education in topics such as mathematics, statistics, or business administration.

What was the core of our topic, "Administrative Data Processing" (ADP)? At this stage, our topic was not exactly defined more than it had to do with essential knowledge needed for development and design of information systems. Furthermore, the persons responsible for designing the first course structure were themselves primarily "engineers" with experience of systems development, which gave the courses a practical and an engineering oriented flavour. Several years later Langefors wrote an article in the magazine of SSI [11] (the Swedish Society for Information Processing, then the representative of IFIP in Sweden) where he argued for considering our topic as consisting of two main parts. One part was concerned with analysis of organisations and their information needs. The other part was concerned with designing an information system, based on computers as well as on humans, who implemented those requirements. He called these parts the "infological" and the "datalogical" parts of ADP. Programming was not seen as a core part of the datalogical part. The core of the datalogical part was rather the technical design of a software system, similar to what we call "software engineering" today. On the other hand, every academic program to educate system developers should contain, of course, also knowledge of computer hardware and of programming. Every ADP student should be able to develop a computer program in a machine level language as well as in higher-level languages.

A substantial part of the early core of our discipline, was contained in the book "Theoretical Analysis of Information Systems" [9]. Students used this internationally well-reputed book mainly in second semester studies. During the seventies it became a "bible" for most academic "information system" courses and researchers in Sweden. Another book of substantial impact on the discipline was "System för Företagsstyrning (Systems for Enterprise Control)" [10]. Datalogical parts of the discipline Information Systems were to a large extent reflected in the textbook "Data Processing Techniques" [3], and to a certain extent also in the textbook "An Introduction to Operating Systems" [4]. Another textbook that had a impact on our department's first semester courses in 1966-67, and to some extent also on the technical parts of our discipline, was Olle Dopping's "Computers and Data Processing" [8].

3.2 Students' Reaction

Students' reaction to our course programme was very positive. After a few years, more then 400 students did annually register for the B-level package. The AB-level package attracted annually more than 100 students. About 25 of them continued to the C-level and the writing of a Bachelors thesis. Computer based information systems were now being introduced in practically all kinds of business. Our education seemed modern, "just in time", and well adapted to practical needs. Students, having passed the AB-level, had few problems to find a job as systems developers or programmers. Fortunately, also the business climate was very dynamic and favourable around the

1960s and the 1970s. Looking back at our first B and AB-level courses, I have no particular memories of many students quitting their education before completing a course. Perhaps this was the effect of our "quizzing approach[6]" to examination, which tended to "drag most students along" towards concrete results.

3.3   Was the Department's Education and Development Successful?

While we can answer this question, in the author's opinion, by a definite *yes*, the articulation of the answer can fill a whole book. Recently, the department celebrated its 40th anniversary. A book of more than 400 pages, presenting historical annotations of various kinds, was published [5]. It is difficult to evaluate the courses as such, but we can confirm that the education started in 1966 gave birth to an impressive development in Sweden. After a few years, a similar course structure was adopted at other universities, for instance in Lund, Gothenburg, and Uppsala. Many graduates of ADP were hired in qualified positions in business and industry. Luckily, some students also remained at the department as teachers and doctoral candidates. They later became deeply involved in developing the department as well as the topic and with helping other universities in starting up ADP education. They also became active in writing and publishing new textbooks for different parts of the topic. The department and its staff was also heavily engaged in supporting the public sector of Sweden, as well as Swedish business with vocational training based on parts of the course package above. Some of the department's staff later started companies, for instance ENEA[7], and research institutes such as V and SISU[8]. Many staff members became recognised professionals in the public as well as in the private sector. The department can proudly point to more than thirty persons that have had their basic education at the department and that have been appointed university professors in Sweden or elsewhere. The university awarded more than 100 doctoral (Ph.D.) degrees and about 100 Licentiate degrees. The current (2007) number of registered students per year is more than 1500.

The course structure has broadened considerably but it is fair to say that the first courses formed the basis for the first three-year academic programme in Sweden, the "Applied Systems Sciences" program (Systemvetenskapliga linjen) established in 1977. In 1993, the department started a four-year programme in "Computer and Systems Sciences". Other programmes started in the 2000s are, for instance, the four-year ICT and Communication Science Programme (2002). It is, however, beyond the scope of this paper to give a fuller account of the department's recent activities and course programmes. The interested reader is directed to the anniversary book [5]. In 1989, the department changed its name to Computer and Systems Science (Data och Systemvetenskap – DSV) in order to better characterise its essential orientation.

---

[6] See section Examination on the B-level in appendix A. The quizzing approach was regretfully discontinued in the early 70-ties, due to large manpower requirements for carrying it out when the student numbers grew larger.

[7] ENEA is a large Swedish software house.

[8] These institutes were foundations founded by a number of supporting Swedish organisations and companies. Institute V is oriented towards Business Administration and Development and SISU (the Swedish Institute of Systems Development) was oriented towards Information Systems Development.

3.4 International Outlook

In a Nordic perspective, the course package launched at KTH/SU in 1966-67 was one of the first, if not the first, in the Nordic countries. The situation in Denmark could be compared to what existed in Sweden 1965, data processing courses were integrated in business schools as parts of programs in management and administration.

On the European scene, some countries were moving fast ahead. Professor's chairs in business data processing had been established in Germany, in Switzerland, and in the Netherlands. The author has, however, no information about university programs developed at this time, similar to the one reported above. On the other hand, most western European countries were well ahead in scientific computing and in engineering computing as well.

As can be expected, the USA was the leading star in computing as well as in academic education in computing. Already in 1962, the Curriculum Committee on Computer Science (C^3S) was formed under the leadership of William F. Atchison. This committee presented preliminary recommendations for an undergraduate program in computer science in 1965 [1]. We should note that at this time already about twenty universities in the U.S. were offering bachelor programs in computer science or a similar topic, and about thirty were offering master programs. More than ten universities were offering doctoral programs.

What was the preliminary recommendation of C^3S compared to our course package above? Firstly, the topic was different. It had a mathematics oriented, theoretical content, designed primarily to educate future computer and software scientists and researchers. Secondly, it suggested a full three-year program with all courses defined to achieve a bachelor degree. The computer science program was designed by academics for the education of academics. The C^3S curriculum proposal became quickly disseminated to universities around the world. The well-known Curriculum 68 [2] followed it up.

What happened in the information systems area in the U.S.? We know little about the later part of the 1960s. In the early 1970s, ACM formed a subcommittee called the ACM Curriculum Committee on Computer Education for Management (C^3EM); J. Daniel Couger was its leader. Recommendations for a four-year undergraduate program aiming at the master level in information systems were published in 1973 [6]. This program has many similarities with the course package of this paper; it also permitted different orientations such as organisational or technological. These orientations are similar to the infological and datalogical realms discussed above. It is noteworthy that these recommendations did put a comparatively heavy emphasis also on knowledge in topics such as mathematics, logic, statistics, and operations research. These topics were not included in our course package. We could only hope that students did combine our ADP-courses with relevant courses in other formal topics. Unfortunately, courses in other disciplines were not, at that time, adopted for combined use together with ADP. The C^3EM recommendations were later, during the 1990s, refined in a collaborative curriculum effort of the ACM, AIS and AITP (formerly DPMA), called IS'97 [7].

3.5 How Did the Topic Develop in Sweden?

Langefors' associates and doctoral students, many of whom later became professors transferred the topic of information processing – ADP – to other universities in Sweden. It is beyond the ambitions of this paper to analyse the diffusion of the topic in Sweden.

This issue would need a paper, or even a book, itself. However, a very simplistic view of what has happened is that the topic has split in two parts. One part is mainly concerned with the "infological" part of the topic as described above. A majority of university departments in the former topic of ADP have this business and social science orientation. They call the topic "informatik". Another set of departments are concerned with both the infological and the datalogical realms but with a more pronounced engineering orientation. These departments call the topic "computer and systems science" or "information systems". What seems to differ between these two is not so much what courses are being offered but rather the basic valuations and attitudes of the staff. We can also say that the engineering oriented departments pay greater attention in their teaching to formal topics such as mathematics, logic, statistics, and formal methods in general.

4 Conclusions

The three-semester course package in information processing (administrative data processing) was at that time fully in par with, or even ahead of, other university programs elsewhere in the world. The course package supported the development of and gave identity to a university department that eventually has developed into a significant and influential educational and research entity in Sweden.

References

[1] ACM Curriculum Committee on Computer Science, A., An Undegraduate Program in Computer Science - Preliminary Recommendations. CACM 8(9), 543–552 (1965)
[2] ACM Curriculum Committee on Computer Science, A., Curriculum 68. CACM 11(3), 151–197 (1968)
[3] Bubenko Jr., J.A.: Databehandlingsteknik, 360 pages. Studentlitteratur, Lund (1967)
[4] Bubenko Jr., J.A., Ohlin, T.: Introduktion till Operativsystem, 520 pages. Studentlitteratur, Lund (1971)
[5] Bubenko Jr., J.A., et al. (eds.): ICT for People. 40 Years of Academic Development in Stockholm, Department of Computer and Systems Sciences at Stockholm University and Royal Institute of Technology, Kista, Sweden, 426 pages (2006)
[6] Couger, J.D.E.: Curriculum Recommendations for Undergraduate Programs in Information Systems. CACM 16(12), 727–749 (1973)
[7] Davis, G.B., et al.: Model Curriculum and Guidelines for Undergraduate Degree Programs in Information Systems. ACM Education Board, AIS, and AITP, DPMA (1997)
[8] Dopping, O.: Datamaskiner och Databehandling, 415 pages. Studentlitteratur, Lund (1966)
[9] Langefors, B.: Theoretical Analysis of Information Systems, 489 pages. Studentlitteratur, Lund (1967)
[10] Langefors, B.: System för Företagsstyrning (Systems for Enterprise Control, in Swedish), 178 pages. Studentlitteratur, Lund (1968)
[11] Langefors, B.: Behovet och framväxten av universitetsämnet Administrativ Databehandling (The need for and the progress of the university study program of Administrative Data Processing) SSI member bulletin (1979)
[12] UHÄ, Akademisk utbildning i automatisk databehandling. Betänkande avgivet av en av kanslern för rikets universitet tillsatt kommitté (Academic Education in Automatic Data Processing. A report authored by a committee appointed by the Chancellor of Swedish universities: Stockholm), Distribution: Nordiska Bokhandeln) (1964)

Appendix A

B-Level Package

B1 Introduction to automatic data processing (28 hours[9] lectures, 2 hours exercises)
It included topics such as

o Concepts of "information"; information needs and requirements in different organisations; formulation of problems, algorithms, flow-charts, programming.
o From algorithms in a problem-oriented language to (low-level) computer programs, including the binary number system, compiling, diagnostics, object code, components of a computer system.
o Data transports, secondary storage units, input/output, data communication.
o Operating systems, multiprogramming, multiple access; economical considerations of programming work.
o Technical and scientific applications (batch processing, multiple access processing).
o Administrative data processing applications (batch processing, real-time processing).
o Process control, industrial real-time systems.
o Information systems theory; data processing system development, stages of a systems development process (life-cycle).
o Study visit to a computer centre

B2 Introduction to programming (20 hours lectures, 10 hours exercises)
This part included lectures on topics

o Algorithms and flowcharts, including proof of algorithms.
o The syntax of the problem oriented language Algol 60.
o Data structures and their representation in a computer memory.
o Program structures, including procedures and blocks in Algol.
o Input/Output of data, including Knuth's proposal for input/output in Algol.
o Exercises involved algorithms, flowcharts, writing of programs in Algol, transformation of program to low-level code, etc. All students had also an individual assignment of completing a larger computer program including compiling and testing it (in batch mode) on a Control Data 3200 computer.

B3 Programming of a data processing problem and executing it on a computer (lectures 34 hours, exercises 40 hours)
This part included lectures on topics

o Programming in a low-level machine-oriented language (registers, instructions, interrupt management).
o An orientation of an assembly-level programming language.
o Programming in COBOL – a thorough treatment.
o Operating Systems – an introduction of the main principles.
o Orientation about other types of high-level languages such as PL/1, LISP, and TRAC.
o Exercises involved low-level languages as well as the high-level language COBOL. The operating system of the current computer CD 3200 was explained. Programming in COBOL of a larger assignment was carried out in two- to three-person groups under the guidance of assistants.

---

[9] A lecture was normally 45 minutes and it was presented to a large auditorium of all students. An exercise hour was 45 minutes given to a group of 15 – 25 students.

B4 Introduction to the theory of information systems and data processing system development work (lectures 20 hours, exercises 10 hours)
This part included lectures on topics

o Introduction to systems work (including the concept of precedence analysis, matrix representation of systems, etc.).
o Information Systems – an Orientation (including the economic quantity of information)
o Performance analysis of computing systems. Simulation.
o Practical aspects of system development work (including the systems life-cycle stages, choice of computer hardware, etc.).
o Exercises included systems algebra and computer system performance analysis.

Literature of the B-level study course
o Langefors B., "Problem, algoritm, datamaskin" (Problem, algorithm, computer), Studentlitteratur, Lund, 1966 (about 25 pages). (B1).
o Langefors, B., "Theoretical Analysis of Information Systems", Studentlitteratur, Lund. (sections 12.1 – 12.11 and 22.1 – 22.2) (B4).
o Gregory R.H. and van Horn R.L., "Automatic Data Processing Systems, Principles and Procedures", Wadsworth, 1965 (pages 1 – 125).(B1, B3, B4).
o T. Ekman and C-E Fröberg, "Lärobok I Algol", Studentlitteratur, Lund, 1964 (B2)
o Bubenko, Jr, J.A., "Databehandlingsteknik", Studentlitteratur, Lund. (about 70 pages) (B4).
o CD 3200 Computer System – Reference Manual (No. 60043800) (B3).
o CD 3200 Computer System COBOL (No. 60132000) (B3).
o An Algol manual for the CD 3200 computer (B2).
o Misc. material produced at the department (stencils).

Examination
Examination included written examinations as well as by "quizzing"[10] of the material presented at lectures and described in the literature studies above. The quiz questions are chosen among a large number of predefined questions distributed in advance to all students. Students could answer a quiz question orally or in writing depending on the nature of the question. If a student had passed all quizzes for a course module, then s/he could be excused for the larger written exam of the whole module.

Appendix B

AB-Level Package

AB1 System theory and control theory (20 hours lectures)
This module was based on books by Langefors (TAIS), Miller &Starr, and McKean. Its main topics were Decision theory, Analysis of Criteria, Systems Theory, and Control of Organisations.

AB2 Information Systems Theory and Data Processing Techniques (30 hours lectures)
This module was based on books by Langefors (TAIS), and Bubenko. Its main topics were System Algebra, File Maintenance techniques, Performance Analysis of computing systems, Evaluation of Information, and Design of Information Systems.

---

[10] My recollection of the quizzing system is extremely positive. Students were orally examined about four times during the course, three at a time. Face-to-face meetings between the examiner and the students made the students to work very hard from the very beginning of the course. Nobody wanted to show bad performance in front of their colleagues.

AB3 Systems Development Work for Administrative Applications (20 hours lectures)
This module was based on books such as "Dansk standardlön", case studies reported by Axelsson & Källhammar, and additional material handed out at lectures. It included a number of lectures regarding methods for systems work and a number of seminars of the different case studies.

AB4 Work on a practical case (18 hours lectures and seminars)
The students (in groups of two) were assigned a systems development task for a fictitious company called KOSAB. Requirements regarding information support in various parts of the company were formulated and given. The task was to develop and design an information system first at an abstract, infological level, and second, to transform this description to a datalogical level design. A seminar was the setting for presentation and discussion.

Literature of the AB-package
o   Langefors, B., "Theoretical Analysis of Information Systems", Studentlitteratur, Lund. (AB1, AB2).
o   Miller and Starr, Executive Decisions and Operations Research, Prentice Hall, Englewood Cliffs, 1965. (AB1)
o   McKean, R.N., Efficiency in Government through Systems Analysis, ORSA No 3, Wiley and Soons, 1964. (AB1)
o   Bubenko jr, J.A., "Databehandlingsteknik", Studentlitteratur, Lund. (AB2)
o   Dansk Standardlön, published by the Danish Federation of Employers. (AB3)
o   Axelsson and Källhammar, five case studies (AB3)

Examination
Modules AB1 and AB2 were examined by "quizzing". Modules AB3 and AB4 were examined by presentation in seminars. The whole AB package was, at the end, examined by a written exam as well as by an oral examination.

FORTRAN II – The First Computer Language Used at the University of Iceland

Oddur Benediktsson

Professor (Retired) University of Iceland
oddur@hi.is

Abstract. At the end of World War II, people considered Iceland an underdeveloped country. The use of IBM punched card systems started in 1949. The first computers appeared in 1964. Then the University of Iceland acquired an IBM 1620 "scientific" computer. The first computer language used to instruct engineers and scientists was FORTRAN II. The subsequent development gives an interesting picture of the advance of computer technology in Iceland.

Keywords: FORTRAN II, IBM 1620, programming education.

1 Introduction

The history of electronic data processing in Iceland extends back to 1949 when Hagstofa Íslands (Statistical Bureau of Iceland) obtained IBM unit record (punched card) equipment. By the early 1960s the Icelandic state, the municipalities, and the banks had developed a quite elaborate unit record data processing applications. The state and the town of Reykjavík established a joint data processing centre now called Skýrr. The first computers were installed in Iceland late in the year 1964; an IBM 1401 system at Skýrr and an IBM 1620 system to the University of Iceland [3, 8, 9].

With the acquisition of an IBM 1620 Model 2 computer in 1964, the University of Iceland entered the computer age. They introduced programming into the engineering curriculum the following year. The main programming language used was FORTRAN II. FORTRAN[1] remained the first computer language taught to both engineering and science students at the University of Iceland for the ensuing two decades. "Although the IBM 1620 computer was extremely modest by modern standards, it had a profound impact on the use of computers in science, engineering and other fields in Iceland. It played a decisive role in the introduction to the computer age in Iceland" [9].

2 Enters a Small Scientific Computer

In 1959, IBM announced the IBM 1620 Model 1 data processing system, a small, transistorized scientific computer. It released the enhanced 1620 Model 2 in 1962.

---

[1] The early spelling "FORTRAN" is used in this text except when quoting names of the resent standards that use "Fortran".

J. Impagliazzo, T. Järvi, and P. Paju (Eds.): HiNC 2, IFIP AICT 303, pp. 149–155, 2009.
© IFIP International Federation for Information Processing 2009

After a total production of about two thousand machines, the IBM 1620 was withdrawn late in 1970 [12]. Per Gerlöv, an engineer that started to work for IBM Denmark in 1960, states, "IBM 1620 was really the first personal computer. It was designed for computation intensive work and was normally programmed in FORTRAN. IBM Denmark ordered a "scientific" computer of the type IBM 1620 for demonstrations purposes. This machine had core memory of 20.000 decimals, and came with a FORTRAN compiler. The computer weighted ca. 600 kg and was sold for about 500.000 DKR or alternatively leased for 1.600 USD per month. This IBM 1620 demonstration machine was installed at IBM Denmark in 1961" [5].

Fig. 1. The purchasing contract for the IBM 1620 being signed by the Rector Ármann Snævarr. Seated opposite Ottó A. Michelsen, the IBM representative in Iceland. Behind from left Trausti Einarsson, professor in geophysics, Magnús Magnússon, the head of the University Computing Centre, and Jóhannes L. L. Helgason, the financial director of the university. *(From the Ottó A. Michelsen collection by the courtesy of University of Iceland Digital Library)*

The IBM 1311 disk storage drive with removable disk packs was released in 1962 – "one of the most important new products we have ever announced" [7]. The 1620 Model 2 could be enhanced with the 1311 disk storage drives and with an early version of a disk operating system called Monitor I. "Monitor I, a collective name for four distinct but independent programs – Supervisor, Disk Utility, SPS II-D, and FORTRAN II-D programs – is a powerful, combined operating and programming system. Systems of this type have previously been available only on other large-storage capacity computers. The 1311 Disk Storage Drive with two-million positions of storage makes possible the implementation of such a system on the 1620" [6].

University of Iceland acquired an IBM 1620 Model 2 computer late in the year 1964. The system was purchased as contrasted to being leased on monthly charges, as was the common practice in those days. As a result, the system was in use over a decade. Figure 1 shows the signing of the IBM 1620 contract.

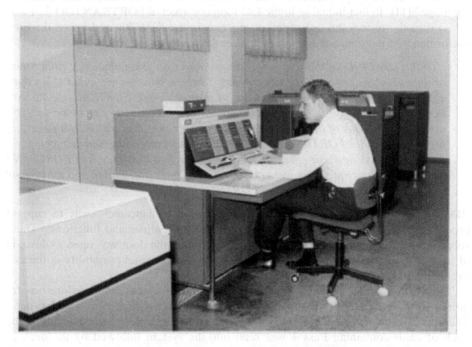

Fig. 2. The IBM 1620 configuration in 1967. Hördur S. Arinbjarnar is working at the console. A part of the IBM 1311 disk unite is to the left, IBM 1622 Card Read-Punch to the right and in the background the IBM 1625 Core Storage Unite housing the 40,000 digit magnetic core internal memory. *(Photo by Dr. Thorsteinn Sæmundsson who was a staunch user of the 1620 and employed it to compute the Almanac for Iceland)*

The acquired system had a magnetic core memory of 40 thousand "binary coded digits". The initial system was limited to input/output of programs via punched cards. The card reader/punch unit read cards at the speed of 250 cards per minute and punched cards at the rate of 125. The original configuration had merely punched cards as input/output. However two 1311 magnetic disk storage units were soon added and subsequently a line printer making the system into a full fledged stand alone scientific computer – although with minute capacity in computational speed, internal and external storage capacity when compared to the computers at the time of this writing. Figure 2 shows the 1620 configuration before the printer was acquired.

3   The Evolution of FORTRAN

The development of the FORTRAN language started in the fifties. In late 1953, John W. Backus submitted a proposal to his superiors at IBM to develop a more efficient alternative to assembly language for programming their IBM 704 mainframe computer. A draft specification for The IBM Mathematical Formula Translating System was completed by mid-1954. This was an optimizing compiler, because customers were reluctant to use a high-level programming language unless its compiler could generate code whose performance was comparable to that of hand-coded assembly language" [11]. In fact indexing in the DO loop construct in FORTRAN (DO 35 I = 1, 10...) directly mirrors the use of index registers in the IBM 704 and hence the high performance of the translated program [5]. In the words of John W. Backus,

"To this day I believe that our emphasis on object program efficiency rather than on language design was basically correct. I believe that had we failed to produce efficient programs, the widespread use of languages like FORTRAN would have been seriously delayed... Unfortunately, we were hopelessly optimistic in 1954 about the problems of debugging FORTRAN programs (thus we find on page 2 of the Report, "Since FORTRAN should virtually eliminate coding and debugging...") and hence syntactic error checking facilities in the first distribution of FORTRAN I were weak. Better facilities were added not long after distribution and fairly good syntactic checking was provided in FORTRAN II" [2].

IBM's FORTRAN II appeared in 1958. The main enhancement was to support procedural programming by allowing user written subroutines and functions. These subprograms were relocatable at load time. Therefore, the door was open to develop libraries of reusable subprograms. This together with program portability is the key to successful and durable software development.

The 1620 FORTRAN II was two-pass compiler. An elaborate procedure was required to translate a FORTRAN II program on a 1620 punched card based system: The source code was punched into cards on an IBM 29 card punch machine. The deck of cards containing Pass 1 was read into the system followed by the deck of source code. The results of Pass 1 - the intermediate code – got punched into a deck of cards that is if the source code had been free of syntax errors. The deck of cards containing Pass 2 followed by the intermediate output was read in and the object code for translated program got punched out. Several deck of cards were then read in: A deck of cards containing program loader and object code for built in functions (SIN, COS, SQRT...) followed by the object code, again followed by previously compiled subprograms if any, and finally followed by the input data to be read by the program. The output of the program were punched to cards then to be listed on a line printer elsewhere. If the output was limited it could be listed on the console typewriter. Gunnar Thorbergsson, a now retired surveyor, used the IBM 1620 extensively. He describes aptly all the shuffling of card decks needed to run a large computational application on a card based 1620 system [10]. A commonly cited source indicates

"By 1960, versions of FORTRAN were available for the IBM 709, 650, 1620, and 7090 computers. Significantly, the increasing popularity of FORTRAN spurred competing computer manufacturers to provide FORTRAN compilers for their machines, so that by 1963 over 40 FORTRAN compilers existed. For these reasons, FORTRAN is considered to be the first widely used programming language supported across a variety of computer architectures" [11].

Even in those early days of computing, the portability and compatibility of programs had been recognized as a major challenge to the emerging software industry.

Perhaps the most significant development in the early history of FORTRAN was the decision by the American Standards Association (now ANSI) to form a committee to develop an "American Standard FORTRAN". The resulting two standards, approved 1966, defined two languages, FORTRAN (based on FORTRAN IV, which had served as a de facto standard), and Basic FORTRAN (based on FORTRAN II). The FORTRAN defined by the first standard became FORTRAN 66 [1]. FORTRAN 66 effectively became the first "industry-standard" version of FORTRAN. Subsequent standards FORTRAN 77, Fortran 90, FORTRAN 95, and FORTRAN 2003 have striven to follow the evolution in programming languages. For example, FORTRAN 2003 has object-oriented programming support: type extension and inheritance, polymorphism, dynamic type allocation, and type-bound procedures. FORTRAN is presently in widespread use for computational intensive applications in engineering and science. Vast libraries of subprograms exist [11].

4 The First Programming Language at University of Iceland

The first computer to reach Iceland was an IBM 1620 Model 1 system. "In October 1963, the IBM representative in Iceland arranged for an IBM 1620 Model I computer to make a "stop-over" in Iceland en route from Canada to Finland. We taught courses

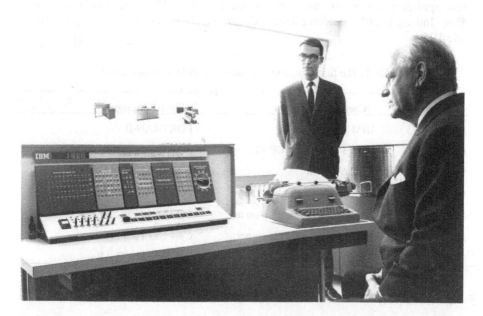

Fig. 3. IBM 1620 usage introduction held at IBM in Reykjavík in October 1963. The president of Iceland, Mr. Ásgeir Ásgeirsson (seated in foreground), showed deep interest in the first computer to reach Iceland. In the background is Mogens Hansen, Systems Engineer of IBM Århus, who came to Iceland to conduct FORTRAN courses. *(From the Ottó A. Michelsen collection by the courtesy of University of Iceland Digital Library)*

in FORTRAN programming with support from IBM in Denmark and people had the opportunity to use the computer. This aroused great interest, primarily among scientists and engineers" [9]. Figure 3 was taken at this occasion.

Programming became part of the engineering curriculum in 1965. The programming language used was the 1620 FORTRAN II. Two computer science programs were initiated at the University in the science faculty in the early years: a BS degree program in computational mathematics was introduced in 1972 and a BS degree program in computer science introduced in 1976 [4].

Table 1 shows the first computer language taught to engineering and science students at the University and the computer systems used. It should be noted that computer application topics were being taught in other lines of studies of the University such as business administration, economics, library science, linguistics, and sociology.

Table 1 shows the typical evolution of the computer technology for a small university in a non-industrial country. The evolution starts with the single user IBM 1620 computer in the 1960s and continues with the multi user VAX-11 systems with numerous ASCII terminals in the 1970s and early 1980s. At the time of this writing in the year 2007 most every student owns a PC that is networked in the classroom and at home with so to speak unlimited capacity for computation and storage. The machines have access to a host of local servers together with the seemingly unlimited resources of the web.

We can now easily program applications as in multimedia, network access, database management, and mobile technology in Java and other languages on a PC. These applications were unimaginable on the 1620 FORTRAN II environment in the 1960s. Indeed, people could not have even conceived most of the current applications in the 1950s.

Table 1. The first programming language and the computers used

Period	Computer System	First Language
1965 – 1975	IBM 1620	FORTRAN II
1976 – 1978	IBM 360/30 and PDP 11	FORTRAN IV
1979 – 1982	DEC VAX-11	FORTRAN 77
1983 – 1986	DEC VAX-11 and PCs on net	FORTRAN 77 and Modula-2
1987 – 1990	DEC VAX-11 and PCs on net	FORTRAN 77 and Turbo Pascal
1990 – 1996	Unix servers and PCs on net	C++ and Turbo Pascal
1997 – 2006	Unix servers and PCs on net	Java and MATLAB

5   Conclusion

At the end of World War II Iceland was an underdeveloped country. The economy was based mainly on fishing and farming. In contrast to its recent past, by many of the standard measures Iceland is now one of the most affluent countries in the world. Information technology has played a large part in this transformation. The society was able to shunt industrial revolution and enter into the modern day information age directly. This evolution is at least partly mirrored by Table 1 that reflects the development of scientific computer technology in the last four decades.

References

[1] ANSI X3.9-1966. USA Standard FORTRAN. American National Standards Institute. (Informally known as FORTRAN 66)

[2] Backus, J.: The History of FORTRAN I, II, and III. In: ACM SIGPLAN History of Programming Languages Conference, SIGPLAN Notices, vol. 13, pp. 165–180 (1978)

[3] Benediktsson, O., et al.: Computerisation of the Icelandic State and Municipalities: 1964 to 1985. In: Bubenko Jr., J., Impagliazzo, J., Sølvberg, A. (eds.) History of Nordic computing: IFIP WG9.7 first working conference on the history of Nordic computing (HiNC1), Trondheim, Norway, June 16-18, 2003. Springer, Heidelberg (2005)

[4] Benediktsson, O.: Early Curricula in Computer Science at the University of Iceland. In: Bubenko Jr., J., Impagliazzo, J., Sølvberg, A. (eds.) History of Nordic computing: IFIP WG9.7 first working conference on the history of nordic computing (HiNC1), Trondheim, Norway, June 16-18, 2003. Springer, Heidelberg (2005)

[5] Gerlöv, P.: Personal communication. Copenhagen 13 (October 2007)

[6] IBM 1620 Monitor I System Reference Manual. IBM System Reference Library. File No. 1620-36. Form C26-5793-4 (1965)

[7] IBM Data Processing Division chronology, http://www-03.ibm.com/ibm/history/exhibits/dpd50/dpd50_chronology.html (Accessed April 7, 2007)

[8] Kjartansson, O.: Data Processing with Unit Record Equipment in Iceland. Mentioned in this volume titled History of Nordic Computing 2, Turku (2007)

[9] Magnusson, M.: The Advent of the first General Purpose Computer in Iceland and its Impact on Science and Engineering. In: Bubenko Jr., J., Impagliazzo, J., Sølvberg, A. (eds.) History of Nordic computing: IFIP WG9.7 first working conference on the history of nordic computing (HiNC1), Trondheim, Norway, June 16-18, 2003. Springer, Heidelberg (2005)

[10] Thorbergsson, G.: Early use of computers for adjusting triangulation in Iceland. Mentioned in this volume titled History of Nordic Computing 2, Turku (2007)

[11] Wikipedia, FORTRAN, http://en.wikipedia.org/wiki/FORTRAN (Accessed April 6, 2007)

[12] Wikipedia, IBM 1620, http://en.wikipedia.org/wiki/IBM_1620 (Accessed April 6, 2007)

The Development of Computer Policies in Government, Political Parties, and Trade Unions in Norway 1961–1983

Knut Elgsaas[1] and Håvard Hegna[2]

[1] Researcher/Project director at the Norwegian Computing Center 1963–1973,
Head of Division at the Norwegian Telecommunication Administration, 1973–1980,
Managing director of Oslo Data, the Computing Center of City of Oslo, 1980–1991
elgsaas@c2i.net
[2] Senior Research Scientist (emeritus) at the Norwegian Computing Center 1962–2006
hegna@nr.no

Abstract. A "Council for Government Electronic Data Processing" was established in 1961. This was the start of development of a common policy for computers and data within the public administration. In 1969-70, computers got on the agenda of political parties and the trade unions. In the course of the seventies and the beginning of the eighties the government, the political parties, and the trade unions established a more comprehensive view of data political questions that we will designate by the term *data policy*. This paper puts some light on the causes and forces that drove the evolvement of a data policy within these central sectors in Norway. We will also show how various actors of research, trade and industry, and political life influenced the development of data policy and present links between the actors that indicate that they mutually influenced each other.

Keywords: Data policy, Norway, government, politics, trade union.

1 Introduction

A well-functioning public sector is a prerequisite for the continuation, development, and acceptance of the welfare state. Since the end of the 1950s, this has meant a growing and timely use of computers and data processing in public administration. Norway's Central Bureau of Statistics (Statistisk Sentralbyrå, SSB) started using punched card equipment, made by Hollerith, for the census as early as in 1894. Public electronic data processing began in 1958 when SSB installed its first electronic computer, an English Electric DEUCE MARK II that was run by the Norwegian Computing Center (NCC)[1]. That same year, an IBM 650 at Bergen University and

---

[1] NCC, Norsk Regnesentral, was established in 1952 by The Royal Norwegian Council for Technical and Scientific Research as a national coordinator of computing for pure and applied research. SSB had no experience with neither running a data processing facility nor do any programming in 1958, so NCC was offered the responsibility of running and administering the use of the SSB computer. In the 1960s, NCC was a combined computing facility and research institute in computer science and quantitative methods, see [9]. After 1970, while keeping the same, now somewhat confusing, name, NCC was re-focused and has since been a research foundation [18].

J. Impagliazzo, T. Järvi, and P. Paju (Eds.): HiNC 2, IFIP AICT 303, pp. 156–170, 2009.
© IFIP International Federation for Information Processing 2009

West Norway Punched Card Center (Holkortsentralen for Vestlandet) was used for the calculation of taxes for the the Ministry of Finance. Several public services were on the verge of replacing or complementing their punched card equipment with electronic computers in the next few years.

Computers were expensive and huge machines, costly to run and costly to program. The Government saw a need for coordinating public data processing and in 1961 established a "Council for Government Electronic Data Processing" (Rådet for elektronisk databehandling i staten, DB-rådet). This was the start of development of a common policy for computers and data within the public administration. During the sixties and seventies the Government, the political parties, and the organisations of employers and employees developed a more comprehensive view of data political questions that attempted to establish policies and tools to take advantage of the benefits and manage the threats that came with the new technology. It is these comprehensive policies which we will designate by the term *data policy*.

DB-rådet was to consider questions of importance concerning public data processing and was given a wide mandate. DB-rådet should lay down regulatory lines, advise about acquisitions, promote integration and coordinate the use of data processing equipment, and evaluate the results. In 1974, a specific point about promoting long-term integration and coordination was added to the mandate [15]. During the coming years, DB-rådet and its secretariat, which was led by Kåre Fløisand, had a strong influence on the computer situation in the public sector. Fløisand, who had a background as assistant at the previously mentioned IBM 650 installation in Bergen, was the head of the Data Processing Department of the Government Institution of Organization and Management (R-direktoratet). One particular result of the work of DB-rådet was the proposal in 1970 to establish a central public data facility, the State Computing Center (Statens Driftsentral, SDS). Leif Olaussen, the Head of Planning in R-direktoratet and former Director of the Norwegian Computing Center, led the work leading to the proposal. Fløisand was chosen as the leader of the project group that planned SDS, which was to be the common service facility for small and medium sized public services [12]. SDS was established in 1972.

DB-rådet did not stop there; it wanted to go further on the line of centralization of public computing. In the opinion of DB-rådet, a joint plan for system development and data processing for the whole public sector was needed. A government report advocating this view came in 1973 [19]. DB-rådet secretariat leader Fløisand and Arne-Erik Hilmen of R-direktoratet wrote the report.

However, several main public institutions (Post Office, Telecommunication Administration, and National Insurance Administration) opposed DB-rådet and their view came through both in the Government and in the Parliament. The Minister for Consumer Affairs and Administration, the administrative superior of R-direktoratet, stated that administrative routines and systems development was the responsibility of the particular institution. They considered data processing a support function that did not need any central planning [29][2]. The Parliament was of the same opinion as the Minister [14].

---

[2] In a private conversation with Elgsaas, a high executive of the Ministry for Consumer Affairs and Administration said that the DB-rådet secretariat leader was furious when he did not get the support of the Ministry.

2 The Public Sector I – Policy and Procurement

The Norwegian data industry, including Norsk Data, Kongsberg Våpenfabrikk, Tandberg, and Mycron, grew up in the 1970s. Both the political parties and the trade unions urged that this new industry should be supported, mainly by requiring that government administrations and institutions buy Norwegian hardware and software. This in many cases led to conflicts in connection with computer procurements.

At the root of the conflicts lay the Government's incompatible goals and instructions for public procurements. A perspective analysis for Norwegian electronic industry [23] recommended that Norwegian electronic products, including data products, should be chosen by public institutions when they were as good as or better than foreign products and when the product was of a significant public importance or was seen as a course in the establishment of a new industrial development[3]. At the same time, public services were required to follow a set of rules for tenders that would lead to the selection of goods based on a total evaluation of price, quality, and other features of importance for the tasks for which the equipment was intended.

Each public enterprise, such as the State Railway (Norges Statsbaner), the Telecommunication Administration (Televerket), Norway Mail (Postverket), or public service, such as the National Insurance Administration (Rikstrygdeverket) and others, were at the same time required to do their work as efficiently as possible. If one of these public works preferred foreign products, problems arose. Public services had instructions to report their procurement plans to DB-rådet. DB-rådet should then give their comments. The leader of DB-rådet was also the leader of the Government Institution of Organization and Management (R-direktoratet) which acted as the secretariat for DB-rådet. This gave R-direktoratet a possibility to have considerable power and influence on computer procurements in the public sector. By playing on the side of the Ministry of Industry (Industridepartementet) and the political wish to support Norwegian computer industry, R-direktoratet exploited this possibility. Kåre Fløisand played a central role in this. Cooperation with the Ministry of Industry gave him the influence on public data processing that his own Ministry had denied him.

The role of DB-rådet, as the name implies, was only advisory, while the Ministry of Industry could impose their policy only on its subsidiary activities. However, there was a way around this. If DB-rådet and R-direktoratet were dissatisfied with a decision of a public institution to buy a foreign computer, the institution would be asked to deliver further clarifications and deliberations. Such demands could be stretched to absurdity. As an example, in the mid-1970s one institution was asked to produce a detailed plan for its computer activities until the year 2010[4]. This kind of deliberate procrastination worked in some cases. In the end, many institutions understood that if they should get any new computer equipment at all, they would have to buy a Norwegian computer.

---

[3] One member of the committee that did the analysis was Jan Balstad, representing The Norwegian Iron and Metal Workers Union, who had been a member of the steering committee for the Iron and Metal Project (see below).

[4] One of the authors referred to this incident and gave the name of the institution in a public speech in The Norwegian Computer Society on October 20, 1977 [10]. He was not corrected by R-direktoratet representatives in the audience, but he has not been able to reconfirm the information for the HINC2 conference.

Regarding computer procurement, the most well known of these conflicts occurred in the National Insurance Administration (Rikstrygdeverket, RTV). RTV wanted a new computer solution based on a central IBM computer with communication to local insurance offices through a system of regional computer facilities already established for data processing to Norwegian local communities. R-direktoratet wanted a solution based on Norwegian computers and systems. The role of Kåre Fløisand shows through clearly in document from Ruth Drolsum and Arne-Erik Hilmen of the RTV Systems Department on June 23, 1977 [8]. They wrote:

> *"In September 1976 RTV forwarded a proposal for a test project for INFOTRYGD (the new information system for the National Insurance Administration). The case was taken up in DB-rådet. The DB-rådet secretariat under hand contacted Norsk Data and showed them the plans of RTV. Based on this information, and without first contacting RTV, Norsk Data put forward a sketch of a solution with a cost estimate. DB-rådet included this in its answer to the Ministry of Social Affairs and Health. RTV reaction to this procedure was strong. In a letter to the Ministry, RTV expressed that it considered this kind of practice principally unsound."*

Hilmen had worked on the side of Fløisand only three years earlier. He now saw for himself the consequences of the recommendations supported by R-direktoratet.

After a long decision process, they decided that RTV should establish two different solutions. The first 40% of the local offices would connect to an RTV-system at IBM-based regional computing centers. The other 60% of the offices would use Norsk Data facilities with a separate RTV-system. Consequently, RTV had to maintain a very comprehensive set of regulations and databases on two different computer systems. The result of the "compromise" decision was a very costly and unsuitable solution for RTV [12].

After some years, the industrial policy that gave preference to Norwegian computer products came into discredit. It was unwound after the demise of Norsk Data in 1990-92. One reason why a public committee in 1978 (see below and [24]) proposed that the DB-rådet should cease its activities was the experience with how it attended its advisory role with respect to public computer procurement.

3 The Trade Unions

3.1 The Iron- and Metal Project

The Norwegian Iron- and Metal Workers Union (NJMF) in 1971 decided to establish a research project, strongly inspired by Professor Kristen Nygaard who was then Research Director at The Norwegian Computing Center (NCC). The project would contribute to a strengthening of the influence of trade unions and employees on the introduction and use of data systems and data technology in the work place [11].

The project came because of cooperation that had evolved from 1967 between Nygaard, employees at NCC, The Trade Union School (LO-skolen) at Sørmarka outside of Oslo, and several central representatives of NJMF and The Norwegian Confederation of Trade Unions (LO). In 1967, Nygaard had been asked to lecture on modern technology in a course named "The labour movement looks to the future" at LO-skolen. This led to further lectures in local union shops as well as at LO-skolen.

Nygaard was concerned that operations research, the Simula language that he designed at NCC with Professor Ole-Johan Dahl [3], and other IT-tools should not be used for the sole benefit of the owners and the employers. It was important that the workers should acquire the knowledge and competence necessary to influence the design of the workplace and their own working conditions. At the end of the 1960s, many local unions in connection with the introduction of numerically controlled machines approached NJMF. Both the central and the local level of the unions were uncertain about the new technology and the possible consequences of its use. The NJMF national congress in 1970 [16] made the following resolution:

"In connection with the development and use of computers, the congress underlines that a deliberate effort should be put forward to counteract the tendency to establish systems where humans are treated as a mechanical and programmable production factor. Where management is not willing to cooperate, the union must by themselves carry out such studies as will be necessary to strengthen the work place under the objectives of the workers and demand that the proposals that are brought forth shall be considered by the business management."

The time was therefore ripe when Nygaard suggested that NJMF should apply for research funding from the Royal Norwegian Council for Technical and Scientific Research (NTNF). The purpose of the application was "to build a base of knowledge at least equal to that which is available to the employers", as is stated in one of the notes that lay at the foundation of the decision of NJMF to send the application in 1970.

This was the first time that a trade union had applied for funding for this kind of a project. The application was to be handled by the Research Committee for Mechanical Industry, a subcommittee of NTNF. The committee held its meetings in the premises of The National Mechanical Industry Organization (MVL), i.e. the employer organization for this sector of Norwegian industry. MVL did not want a project where NJMF co-operated with "the radical researchers of the Norwegian Computing Center"[5]. They tried to move the project over to The Norwegian Institute of Technology (Norges Tekniske Høyskole, NTH) in Trondheim, a research environment of which MVL felt more comfortable. The leadership of NJMF, with the full support of the leader Leif Skau, opposed this attempt by MVL to move the project. The project started at NCC in January of 1971.

Kristen Nygaard became the project leader. The project steering committee, led by Leif Skau, consisted of representatives from LO, Jan Balstad from NJMF, Knut Elgsaas from NCC, and representatives from several other research institutes (including Norwegian Productivity Institute (Norsk Produktivitetsinstitutt) and the Norwegian Work Research Institute (Arbeidsforskningsinstituttet)). Four local union shops, geographically spread over the southern part of Norway, were selected to take part in the project. These were located at Hydraulikk in Brattvåg, Kongsberg Våpenfabrikk in Kongsberg, Norwegian Electric Brown and Bovery (NEBB) in Oslo, and at Jonas Øglænd Bicycle Factory in Sandnes.

The original project plan included studies of one or more of the systems for planning and control that were set up for implementation in mechanical industries at the

---

[5] This NCC reputation was a result of the well publicized dispute between NCC and NTNF in 1969-70 [9].

time. Several documents along that line were produced in the spring of 1971. However, Nygaard noted that it was difficult for the union representatives from the shops to see any direct relevancy between this work plan and that which the representatives could use for concrete work at the various union levels. Nygaard saw that there was a danger that the reports would just end up in the shelves of the shop stewards, unused, maybe even unread.

It was important for NJMF and NCC that the project gave real and useful results. In a proposal from the project group suggesting a change of strategy and work focus that was adopted by the steering committee in the autumn of 1971, results were defined like this:

> "Results are all actions from NJMF, centrally or at the local level, that with support from the project aim to give the organization and its members a larger influence on data processing and control tools in their work place."

> "From this viewpoint, working papers and research reports from the project will be useful only to the extent that they lead to actions of the organization leadership, divisions, or local shops."

At first, the project group concentrated its work on establishing suitable educational material for shop stewards and industry employees. This resulted in the textbook "Planning, Control, and Data Processing, a basic textbook for trade unions". The book was available in May 1972 and was published by Tiden in 1974 [26].

The textbook formed the basis for the work started by the shops of the participating enterprises from the summer of 1972. The purpose was that the shops should test a way of working that the project group thought would be common in the future, "that shops themselves would study their important questions within their work place" with assistance from experts from outside and personnel from the business itself.

The shop at Hydraulikk made a business policy action program. The shop at Kongsberg evaluated a new control system, the shop at NEBB evaluated the organization, control systems, and working conditions, and the shop at Øglænd among other things made an evaluation of the planning of a new production building.

When the Iron- and Metal project ended in the spring of 1973, eight reports had been produced, including a final report and the four reports from the participating shops. About 120 people took part in the production of the reports. Among these were elected stewards and representatives of local shops and divisions as well as central people of NJMF, the project group and the steering committee [17].

The project was a very special one within Norwegian research at the time, both with respect to whom commissioned it and whose interests the project was to address. The definition of project results was also a special one. The results were not reports that gave academic merit to the researchers, but the actions that the research and studies triggered off at NJMF, at the local or central level.

The Iron- and Metal Project was later in the seventies followed by two similar three-year projects, first for The Norwegian Union of Commercial and Office Employees in 1976-78, later for The Norwegian Union of Chemical Industry Workers in 1977-79 [13].

The Iron- and Metal Project also had other important consequences for trade union involvement in the introduction and use of new technology in Norway. The Data Agreement established between The Norwegian Confederation of Trade Unions (LO) and The Norwegian Employers Organization (NAF) in 1975 and two important sections in §12 of the Working Environment Act of 1976 came as a direct result of the project and the engagement that it created in the trade unions.

3.2 Data Agreements

The set of agreements between employers and employees have always been a central means for the trade unions in their work to attend to the interests of their members. In 1974, the world's first data agreement was established between Viking-Askim AS and the local shop at the enterprise. The background was that the enterprise wanted to introduce a new data system for control of their car tire production. The trade union asked Kristen Nygaard for help in the discussions with the employer. The result was an agreement that gave the employees a right to information and participation in the design, introduction, and use of data systems in the enterprise. Less than a year later LO/NAF agreed on a "Framework for Systems based on Data Processing". A similar agreement was established between the government and trade unions in the public sector.

One presumption of the Data Agreements was that a local shop steward should have the opportunity to establish the competence necessary for evaluating the effect that the data systems would have on the working conditions. The workers had a long time negative experience with data experts brought in by the employers who lacked the ability to communicate with the workers and understand the problems connected with the introduction of new data systems.

3.3 The Working Environment Act

The new Working Environment Act was adopted in 1977. The act covered working hours, holidays, employment, etc. In §12 on *The Organization of Work* a new provision was introduced in section 3 stating

> *3. Concerning systems for control and planning.*
> *Workers and their elected representatives shall be kept continuously informed of systems used in planning and that are necessary to accomplish work, including planned changes to such systems. They shall be given the training necessary to familiarize themselves with the systems, and they shall take part in designing them* [1].

This provision has the LO/NAF framework as its background, but covers systems for planning and control in general, not just those that are based on data systems. The provision applies to all enterprises in Norway. The Norwegian Labour Party was in power when the new Working Environment Act was prepared. Considering the strong ties between the Labour Party and LO, it was not difficult for central actors within the trade union movement, as well as for engaged members of the Labour Party, to influence the Government to introduce a provision like this in the new law. Torbjørn Berntsen, MP for the Labour Party, led the handling of the law in the Norwegian Parliament. He had been a local trade union leader for the iron- and metal-workers at Aker Mechanical Workshop, a large ship building enterprise, and he had close ties to the environment around Jan Balstad and other NJMF representatives with links to the Iron- and Metal Project and their demand for participation and influence on systems for control and planning.

4 The Public Sector II

In 1975, the Ministry of Consumers Affairs and Government administration appointed a committee to conduct an inquiry into the problems involved in decentralizing public data processing and improving its efficiency. The committee's terms of reference were as follows:

o To report on the future requirements for data processing in municipal, county, and national administration;
o To evaluate the possibilities of decentralizing public data processing and making it an effective means in improving the efficiency in public institutions;
o To propose measures of an organizational, economic, system-analytical and technological nature to achieve the goals of decentralization and efficiency.

The leader of the committee was Knut Elgsaas, formerly Head of Projects at NCC and a member of the Iron- and Metal Project steering committee, now head of the Division for Rationalization in the Norwegian Telecommunication Administration. Among the committee members, one finds Ruth Drolsum, Head of Office in the Systems Department of RTV and Drude Berntsen, Director of NCC from 1970, and thus a former director for both Elgsaas and Kristen Nygaard, the leader of the Iron- and Metal Project. Director Drude Berntsen had been secretary to the Government appointed committee that reported on "Electronic Data Processing in the Health Service" one year earlier [21].

The committee, often referred to as the "Elgsaas committee" after the name of its leader, concluded its work in 1978 [24]. The Ministry, as is common procedure, sent the committee's report to a public hearing. In 1982 the Government presented a report on public data processing to the Parliament (Stortinget) based on the committee's report and the hearing [30].

The committee expected a strong growth in public data processing, especially in connection with economic systems, personal data systems and text processing systems. There would be more stringent quality requirements imposed on public data processing in the future. Decentralization of tasks to counties and municipalities would require new systems with better opportunities for interchange of data between public institutions. The committee emphasized the importance of developing common systems. Instead of the individual institution each developing its own data system for the same purpose, use of joint development of common systems would mean a reduction of cost for public administration. The committee expected that data terminals would be as common in public offices in the 1980s and 1990s as telephones and typewriters were around 1978. Computers of high processing and storage capacity would gradually become part of the ordinary office equipment.

To ensure an efficient use of new technology in public administration the committee proposed a series of practical means and measures concerning:

o Planning and budgeting of data processing;
o Systems development, maintenance and operation;
o Introduction of quality control, DP-auditing;

o Education;
o Research and development;
o Standards;
o Security and protection in public data processing;
o Statutes and regulations.

The committee pointed out that the number of candidates graduating annually with data processing as their main subject was far too low. There was an urgent need to increase the capacity of the educational system to meet the demand for skilled data professionals in public and private sector. It was proposed that the Ministry of Education prepared an educational plan concerning all aspects of data processing at the universities and colleges in Norway. The practical measures and proposals were generally welcomed in the hearing of the committee's report.

The committee also made proposals concerning the organization of public data processing. Norway had 435 municipalities at that time and 19 counties. Half of the municipalities had less than 5000 inhabitants. To build a base for decentralizing public data processing and use the scant resources in qualified data professionals most efficiently, the committee proposed the establishment and development of regional data centers offering services in public data processing. The seven existing municipal computing centers and the State Computer Center should be the pillars of support in the development of the new regional centers. The municipal data centers were located in different regions of Norway and were owned by municipalities and counties.

The committee was of the opinion that there was no longer a need for the Council for Government Electronic Data Processing. DB-rådet, against a minority of three who had been members of the above committee, fought for its continued existence in two reports in 1979 and 1980 [27]. Nevertheless, the Government agreed with the committee and the Council was abolished in 1980.

As might be expected, almost all counties and municipalities acclaimed the proposal of regional centers. Government Ministries were generally more reserved to the idea of regional centers while some were against it. That was quite natural; the establishment of regional centers would remove some influence and power from the Ministries. Privately owned data centers were of course against the introduction of public regional centers.

After the general election in 1981, a conservative government was formed replacing the Labour government that had appointed the committee. The new Government did not like the idea of regional centers. Since most of the proposals from the committee would cost money, the new Government was not very enthusiastic about those ideas either.

In a report on public data processing presented by the government to the Parliament in 1982, they actually made no concrete proposal. Nevertheless, the Parliament had a long debate about public data processing in 1983 based on the reports from the Government and the committee. Many members of the Parliament were happy for the opportunity to take part in a debate about data processing. The last speaker in the debate, Petter Thomassen from the Conservative Party, remarked:

> "I will at the end of the debate like to stress the fact that this has been a special data political day. This has been the first time in the history of the Parliament that we have had such a thorough debate about data processing."

Thomassen had some of his background from the position as Director of Nordlands-data, a private computing center in Bodø, and he had been central in the formulation of the Conservative Party data policy (see below and [6]).

Looking back, the greatest sin of omission by the government and the Parliament at that time was the reluctance to go for a vigorous increase in the capacity for education of data professionals. One of the main reasons for cost overruns and scandals in public and private data processing in the eighties and nineties was the lack of qualified data professionals at the decision-making levels. Consequently, the Parliament later got several opportunities for thorough debates about data processing and cost overruns.

The most important results of the committee's work and report was that it led to a stronger interest in and attention to data political questions. Following the presentation of the report in 1978, the political parties competed in establishing their own data policy. Trade unions that did not belong to the Trade Union Congress, also found it necessary to present their own data policy. The increased interest in data processing and data policy resulted in the years 1978-83 in the production of several Government reports and committee deliberations aimed at meeting data political challenges, for instance one on "Computers in school" in 1983 [31] and the start of commission work on "Data technology and societal vulnerability" [25][6].

5 The Political Parties

5.1 The Privacy Issue

The political parties had shown little interest in data political questions in the sixties and the first part of the seventies. A certain interest in the cost of computers and the possibilities for a better public service was of course present. However, there was little concern for the societal consequences of the use of this new technology. One exception was the question of privacy and data protection in the wake of the large computerized files that were a prerequisite for the new social benefit system that was introduced in 1967. But even this question had been brought up and discussed by data specialists long before the politicians showed any interest in it. As an example, a Central Personal Register and a unique personal identity number for all Norwegian citizens had been introduced in 1964 with very little real political debate [2]. However, in 1970 DB-rådet initiated a project at the Department of Civil Law at the Faculty of Law, University of Oslo with a request to study "privacy and governmental data banks". This led to a report [28] and later to the appointment of two government committees to report on problems related to data protection and privacy issues in the private and public sector respectively. The chair of the first committee was Tore Sandvik, a professor of law at the University of Bergen. The committee reported in 1974 [20]. The second committee chairperson was Helge Seip, a newspaper editor and politician (MP 1954-61 and 1965-73) with experience as a minister in a coalition Government (1965-70) as well as the leader of the liberal party (Venstre). His committee, whose secretary was Arne-Erik Hilmen, reported in 1975 [22]. The committees' work and the lawmakers' conclusions

---

[6] The committee responsible for this report was led by Helge Seip, head of the Data Inspectorate, who had earlier been the leader of the public committee reporting on data protection in the public sector, see next section.

were much inspired by the legislation that had already been introduced in Sweden in 1973. Norway's Data Protection Act was adopted in 1978 and came into use in 1980, after the Data Inspectorate that was a main provision of the law had been established [7]. Helge Seip became the first leader of the Data Inspectorate and Ruth Drolsum of RTV was part of its first board.

5.2   Each Party Appointed a Data Committee

Until the end of the seventies, two central data political questions concerned the political parties in Norway. These were *computer privacy* and the *fear of unemployment*. The parties on the left were particularly concerned about unemployment and the consequences of new technology in the work place. They also had a concern that private interests would create large databases of consumer profiles for marketing and other commercial purposes. The parties on the right were less concerned about the work place. However, on the question of computer privacy they sided with the left, although their concern would put more weight on the fear of governmental citizen control and Big Brother tendencies. The work leading to the two privacy reports of 1974-75, see above, took the question of privacy out of the political debate in Norway and with it, most other data political questions. For a while, they saw these as less important than the privacy issue.

The debate resulting from the inquiry on de-centralization and improvement of efficiency in public data processing in 1978 led several political parties to appoint committees to formulate proposals for data policies. The Labour Party (Arbeiderpartiet) started its work in 1978. The Christian Democratic Party (Kristelig Folkeparti) followed in 1979 and the Conservative Party (Høyre) in 1980.

Jan Balstad, who was then the leader of NJMF and had been a member of the steering committee of The Iron- and Metal Project, led the Labour Party Data Committee. The Committee members were representatives of the party and important trade unions. Professor Kristen Nygaard and Knut Elgsaas, an early member of the Iron- and Metal Project steering committee, were also members of the Data Committee.

The Data Committee report with recommendations was delivered in 1980 [4]. It had a distinctly positive attitude to the introduction and use of data processing in public service and in private business. Data technology was seen as an important tool for sustaining the competitive power of Norwegian economic life internationally. According to the report, improved data- and telecommunication could make it possible to improve the service level and at the same time free the workers from routine work and give them time for more direct service to clients and customers.

At the time, the fear that the new data- and communication technology would lead to an increase in the level of unemployment was strong. The report therefore stressed that:

> *"In spite of factors of uncertainty, the Committee will hold on to the conclusion that data technology in the short run may give considerable employment problems, unless the authorities and the trade union bring in countermoves to prevent such a development."*

In line with the ideological foundation of the Labour Party, the Committee held that a condition for exploiting the positive effects that may come from the new technology was that an active state intervened with measures that would reduce or even remove possible negative consequences of the technology.

The Data Committee proposed several measures that would provide efficient use of new technology, including more education on the use of computers in general, stronger efforts to educate computer specialists, a quality assurance for data systems, and more resources put into computer research.

The Christian Democratic Party Data Committee recommendations [5] were mainly in line with those of the Labour Party proposals. The committee also expressed fears that new technology could lead to unemployment. In the view of the Committee, a higher unemployment level should be met with a more even distribution of paid work. This was in direct discord with the view of the Labour Party Data Committee, which was clearly against using a reduction of working hours as a means to reduce unemployment. The Christian Democratic Party Data Committee also attached more importance to using new technology actively to increase economical and technological development in the Third World. The leader of this committee was Tor Brattvåg who had previously made a report on learning and education for the "Elgsaas committee".

The recommendations of the Conservative Party Data Committee did not differ much from those of the two other Committees. However, on two central points this committee had significantly different views. The Conservative Party Committee [6] did not fear a negative change in employment because of the introduction of new technology. This Committee expected that problems could show up in some branches of the economy, but this could best be met by giving trade and industry better operating conditions. The Committee also meant that competition and the use of tenders should be the normal situation for procurements of computer systems in the public sector. The Labour Party and Christian Democratic Party Committees wanted public acquisitions of computer hardware and software to contribute to the development of a Norwegian data industry.

The leader of the Conservative Party Data Committee was Petter Thomassen, an MP who in 1965, at the age of 24, had been part of the establishment of Nordlandsdata, the first private computer center in the north of Norway, and its first director. Thomassen had been much concerned over computer privacy and had written a book on the topic [32]. He was an outspoken opponent of the proposal of the "Elgsaas committee" to strengthen public data processing in Norway and was of the opinion that free competition was the best solution. In the last half of the eighties Thomassen was Minister of Industry (1985-86) and Minister of Trade and Industry (1989-90).

The data policy proposals from the three committees were already marked by the ideological base views of the respective parties. The result of the ensuing discussions within the parties therefore was mainly an increase in the interest for and attention to data policy questions.

6 Conclusion

The rapid development of data technology from 1960 to 1980 was challenging for the public administration, the political parties, and the trade unions. They had to develop a strategy and a policy that could exploit the new possibilities and solve the problems that appeared. Their data policy was a means for these three central sectors of society to reach their primary goals and interests. They formed the policies under mutual influence and inspiration. To some extent, the same people in varying roles, often with backgrounds from the same institutions, took part in the work to find an answer to the data political challenges in the three sectors.

That a small number of individuals were the driving forces behind many of the data policy decisions that were formulated during these years should not be seen as the result of some form of conspiracy. In the sixties and seventies, the number of computer experts were few, the number of experts interested in politics and the societal aspects of their special fields of expertise were even fewer. Often these would be colleagues who had been working together in the same institution or been members of the same committees over many years. Of course, they inspired each other and as time went by, they had a common experience that led them to see problems and solutions from the same angle. Add to this that Norway's population was, and still is, small. When forming a committee on the national level or within a political party, there just were not many interested and engaged experts from which to choose.

Finally, it is worth noting that for the most part, the introduction and use of data systems and technology in the public sector and economic life in Norway in the seventies and eighties went without conflicts and problems between employers and employees. This was largely a result of the involvement in data policy by the trade unions and the ensuing introduction of §12 in the Working Environment Act.

References

[1] Arbeids- og sosialdepartementet: Lov om arbeidervern og arbeidsmiljø m.v. (Lov 4.2.1977 nr. 4) (Ministry of Labour and Social Affairs: The Working Environment Act), http://www.lovdata.no/oll/nl-19770204-004.html (Last checked September 24, 2007) (ISBN 82-504-1271-0)

[2] Bing, J.: Data Protection in Norway, Norwegian Research Center for Computers and Law (1996), http://www.jus.uio.no/iri/forskning/lib/papers/dp_norway/dp_norway.html (Last checked July 20, 2007)

[3] Dahl, O.-J., Nygaard, K.: The Development of the Simula Languages. In: Wexelblat, R.L. (ed.) History of Programming Languages. Academic Press, New York (1981)

[4] Datapolitikk. En innstilling og et debattopplegg fra DNA's datapolitiske utvalg (1980) (Data policy. A report and a plan for discussion from the Labour Party Data Committee)

[5] Datateknologien og samfunnet. En innstilling fra datapolitisk utvalg i Kristelig Folkeparti (1980) (DataTechnology and Society. A report from the Christian Democrats Data Committee)

[6] En fremtid med datateknologi. En innstilling fra et utvalg nedsatt av Høyres stortingsgruppe. (A Future with Data Technology. A report from a committee appointed by the Parliament Representatives of the Conservative Party) (1980)

[7] Djønne, E., Grønn, T., Hafli, T.: Personregisterloven med kommentarer (The Data Protection Law, with Comments), Tano, Oslo (1987)

[8] Drolsum, R., Hilmen, A.-E.: Note from Systems Departement, RTV. June 23 (1977)

[9] Elgsaas, K., Hegna, H.: The Norwegian Computing Center and the Univac 1107 (1963-1970). In: Bubenko Jr., J., Impagliazzo, J., Sølvberg, A. (eds.) History of Nordic Computing: IFIP WG9.7 First Working Conference on the History of Nordic Computing (HiNC1), Trondheim, Norway, June 16-18, 2003. Springer, New York (2005)

[10] Elgsaas, K.: Myndighetenes forhold til norsk EDB-industri: Foredrag på møte i Den Norske Dataforening 20.10.1977. (The relations between the Government and the Norwegian data industry) A speech at a members meeting in The Norwegian Computer Society October 20 (1977)

[11] Espeli, T. and Elgsaas, K : Datateknologi i et samfunnsmessig perspektiv; (Data Technology from a Social Perspective) in NR 1952-2002, pp. 200–207. Oslo (2002) (see [19] below)

[12] Haraldsen, A.: Den forunderlige reisen gjennom datahistorien (The amazing journey through computer history), Tano-Aschehoug, Oslo, page 87, 130 (1999)

[13] Haraldsen, A.: "The Scandinavian school" i systemutvikling (The Scandinavian School in System Development). In: 50 år og bare begynnelsen, Cappelen, Oslo, ch. 5 (2003)

[14] Innst. S.nr.256 (1974-75). Innstilling fra administrasjonskomiteen om planlegging av databehandling i forvaltningen. (Report on Planning of Goverment Data Processing from the Parliament Administration Committee) (1974-1975)

[15] Kgl. Res. 3.5.1974: Mandat til rådet for databehandling. (Royal Order May 3, 1974: Mandate for "Council for Government Electronic Data Processing")

[16] Norsk Jern- og Metallarbeiderforbund: Referat fra Landsmøtet til NJMF 1970 (Minutes of the Norwegian Iron- and Metal Workers Union National Congress 1970)

[17] Norsk Jern- og Metallarbeiderforbund: Styringskomiteens sluttrapport for forskningsprosjektet B1201, 3143: Planleggingsmetodikk for fagbevegelsen (Final Report from the Steering Committee of Research Project B1201, 3143: Planning Methodology for the Trade Unions), June 29 (1973)

[18] Norsk Regnesentral 1952–2002 (The History of the Norwegian Computing Center 1952-2002); Norsk Regnesentral, Oslo, September 2002 (in Norwegian)

[19] NOU 1973:43 Planlegging av databehandling i forvaltningen. (The planning of data processing in the government). A report to the Ministry of Consumers Affairs and Government Administration (1973)

[20] NOU 1974:22. Persondata og personvern (Data on Individuals and Protection of Privacy) Report to the Ministry of Justice (1974)

[21] NOU 1974:54:"Elektronisk databehandling i helsevesenet" (Electronic Data Processing in the Health Service). Report to the Ministry of Health (1974)

[22] NOU 1975:10 Offentlige persondatasystem og personvern (Public Databases on Individuals and Protection of Privacy) Report to the Ministry of Justice (1975)

[23] NOU 1976:30 Perspektivanalyse for norsk elektronikkindustri (A perspective analysis for Norwegian electronic industry), A report to the Ministry of Industry (1976)

[24] NOU 1978:48: Offentlig databehandling. Desentralisering og effektivisering. (Public Data Processing. Decentralization and increased efficiency). Report to the Ministry of Consumers Affairs and Government Administration 1978.

[25] NOU 1986:12 Data-teknologi og samfunnets sårbarhet (Data Technology and Societal Vulnerability) (1986)

[26] Nygaard, K., Bergo, O.: Planlegging, styring og databehandling. Grunnbok for fagbevegelsen (Planning, Control, and Data Processing, A basic textbook for the Trade Unions) Tiden forlag, Oslo (1974)

[27] Rådet for elektronisk databehandling i Staten (Council for Government Electronic Data Processing): Organisering av databehandlingsvirksomheten i forvaltningen (Organization of data processing within the government) (June 1980)

[28] Samuelsen, E.: Statlige databanker og personlighetsvern (Public Databases and Protection of Privacy) Norwegian University Press, Oslo (1972)

[29] St. melding nr. 37 (1974-1975): Om planlegging av databehandlingen i forvaltningen (Planning of data processing in Government) Statement to the Parliament from the Ministry of Consumers Affairs and Government Administration (1974)

[30] St. melding nr.12 (1982-1983): Desentralisering og effektivisering i den offentlige databehandlingen (Decentralization and increased efficiency in public data processing). Statement to the Norwegian Parliament from the Ministry of Consumers Affairs and Government Administration (1982)

[31] St. meld. nr. 39 (1983-84) Datateknologi i skolen (Computers in School). Statement to the Norwegian Parliament from the Ministry of Education and Church Affairs (1983)

[32] Thomassen, P.: Privatliv og EDB: hvordan kan vi beskytte oss? (The private sphere and computer processing: How can we protect ourselves?) Cappelen, Oslo (1977)

Computer Industry as a National Task

The Finnish Computer Project and the Question of State Involvement in the 1970s

Petri Paju

University of Turku, Department of Cultural History, FI-20014 Turku, Finland
petpaju@utu.fi

Abstract. This article studies a forgotten research project of recent Finnish history of information technology by the name of "Suomalainen tietokoneprojekti", in English "The Finnish Computer Project" (FICO). The FICO project was a government-sponsored research project initially aimed at producing a Finnish (mini) computer for international markets, especially in socialist countries. Researchers carried out the project in 1975-1976. However, after the researchers had produced their preliminary study report in six months time, the project was not continued. I argue that historians have misrepresented the FICO project in recent research and when properly studied, the project can offer new perspectives to an early development phase of present-like science and technology policy in Finland. Notwithstanding FICO's topicality, this article focuses on examining what the involved people meant by the "national task" of the project. I further argue that we can best understand FICO as a continuation of earlier ideas on building high technology, in this case electronics and computers, capabilities and expertise as a Finnish national project. Moreover, focusing on these distinct national projections in action might offer one key to understanding similar attempts at "national projects" in other countries as well.

Keywords: Computer industry, survey, national project, state-ownership, The Finnish Computer Project, Hans Andersin.

1 Introduction to a Forgotten Project[1]

One of the most forgotten, yet also most misrepresented projects of recent Finnish history of information technology has been "Suomalainen tietokoneprojekti" or "SUTI-projekti", in English "The Finnish Computer Project", with an abbreviation FICO project. This paper presents and examines that arguably unsuccessful project from the 1970s Finland for the first time.

Generally, the FICO project is virtually forgotten. However, existing literature references it ambivalently. On the one hand, two data processing history outlines list it in a neutral manner. People who were familiar with the project compiled those outlines [30, 24]. On the other hand, two books by historians offer a much more negative, even

---

[1] I thank Bruce Johnson for valuable comments on the content of this article and on my English.

J. Impagliazzo, T. Järvi, and P. Paju (Eds.): HiNC 2, IFIP AICT 303, pp. 171–184, 2009.
© IFIP International Federation for Information Processing 2009

shadowy image of the FICO. Surprisingly these historians have not studied the project; however, based on other contemporary or later hostile sources, they mention it briefly and deem it potentially harmful to Nokia or the field of computer technology in general and in addition, one of the writers claims the FICO was doomed to failure. This interpretation arises from connecting the FICO with ideas of full-scale state-ownership and even nationalization [19, 23, and even 17], which I think is a mistake.

Surprisingly, none of the above writers has used the public report that the FICO project produced; for an exception, see [22]. I suggest that their detailed report is a valuable source of information not only for studying the project itself but for studying this field in general, for instance as the account reveals some of the researcher's thoughts in this emergent phase of the microcomputer technology [13].

It is well known that history of technology, and history of information technology in particular, tend to be written from the perspective of "winners" [15]. That view runs the risk of making historical knowledge biased in a way that might have serious effects on our understanding about history and subsequent conclusions. Even a while after beginning this study, it was unclear if this mostly forgotten project had resulted in more than the published report of the IT production sector in Finland – it turned out some of its thoughts were actually carried out in successive projects. Moreover, what could make the FICO project relevant today is that it was executed right before from what have been seen as formative years of the later Finnish information technology policy and related research and business decisions. At the end of the 1970s and especially in the early 1980s, with the FICO project fresh in memory, they made important decisions regarding science and technology policy in Finland. I argue the FICO can inform us about this Finnish process of national information technology development from an unusual, 'loser perspective'.

In an international context, the FICO was far from being unique. In fact, the FICO project had taken on many influences from abroad as well as from, at that time, current developments in Finland. Starting in the middle 1960s several governments in both west and east had begun developing national capabilities in computer industry to respond to the "American challenge" by the market leader International Business Machines (IBM) and other U.S.-based companies [16]. Of course, these attempts occurred in Finland too, another country where IBM was a market leader in data processing. From domestic influences to the FICO, we can discuss only its relation to the Social Democratic Party in this article, although we will highlight other avenues of research.

Firstly, this article begins by raising basic questions regarding the FICO project, particularly its project's background and its objectives. The article draws primarily on interviews with some of the people involved, published sources such as the report of the project, and to a lesser extent, archive records. Secondly, this paper studies the meanings attached to the projects' national character, evident already by the naming of the project; see also [18, 27, 28]. Despite all its topical features, I argue that we can best understand the FICO project as a continuation of earlier ideas of a Finnish national project in computers and electronics where national ambitions were first established and tested in the 1950s. By analyzing aspects of this nationally minded project, the paper might offer insight not only for understanding Finnish development but for parallel ones in other Nordic countries such as those related to Regnecentralen, DataSAAB, Norsk Data, and Luxor Ab [see 20, 17].

2 Influence of Economic Pressures and Ongoing Discussions

As elsewhere in the industrial countries, the computer and the electronics industries in general had been a hot discussion topic for some years in Finland during the late 1960s and early 1970s [see 11, 31, 36, and 23]. Discussions were partly fueled by the fact that since the middle of the 1960s governments in countries such as Britain, France, West Germany, and the Soviet Union had begun developing national capabilities or national champions in computer industry [16]. From 1972 onwards, there was an attempt for a European joint effort, a company named Unidata, which lasted until the end of the year 1975. The Finnish experts knew also of a Danish-Swedish industry plan that however had been abandoned [14].

The contemporary, global, and societal context included the oil crisis and consequent economic depression in Finland too [37, 29], which increased interest toward concurrent advancements in computer technology such as minicomputers, recent microprocessors and their anticipated growing uses in various walks of life. Visions of information networks combined with the future of television added to these expectations [see 33]. In Finland, industrialization had been a central issue that brought many changes following the Second World War. Furthermore, they actively contemplated and planned for new industrial sectors in many groups of industrial, economic, and political nature. In the 1960s, several Finnish companies had entered electronics and were building their expertise with their first products [22].

In society, the 1970s was a decade of heated political activism, debate, and controversy in Finland. Politically, the extreme left was working in a highly visibly manner for a socialist revolution – posing a threat that could be overemphasized by, and for the benefit of, those in politically right-wing parties. In the political turmoil and economic difficulties, governments were rather short-lived. Nevertheless, leading political parties were the Social Democrats and the Centre Party, former agrarians, working in cooperation to build the welfare state. Both had their own industrial political program. The SDP's program strongly favored statist industrial politics that would empower the worker and have his/her voice heard in economic decision making [35, 7].

Discussions that eventually lead to the FICO began in 1972, when the Ministry of Finance's co-ordination department, responsible for controlling and guiding data processing in state departments and their installations, appointed a Committee for Computer Policy (or Politics even) (Tietokonepolitiikkakomitea 1972-1974) [30]. This committee forecast an immense growth in computerization. Similar to most industrial countries, the committee wanted to promote domestic production. Among other things, it suggested the state to increase its role as a coordinator in the field, and of computer production too. However, the committee did not make definitions of industrial policy (and politics) [23] in its final report of 1974 but called for further research on the subject [7]. Based on the report of the Committee for Computer Policy, an interim government of non-party ministers appointed both an advisory board (ATK-alan neuvottelukunta) to create a national meeting place for the fast growing field, and some weeks later in November 1975, the interim government established the Finnish Computer Project, with the abbreviation FICO. (Suomalainen tietokoneprojekti or SUTI, in Finnish.) From where did the initiative come?

3   The Finnish Computer Project Brings Actors Together

According to the archive records, it was Hans Andersin who developed the basic ideas for the new project in the spring of 1975 [1]. Andersin was the first professor of data processing technology in Helsinki University of Technology (HUT) since 1970, and acting professor since the chair was established in 1968.[2] In the spring of 1975, Professor Andersin gave a presentation where he basically outlined the future project [11]. The conference was "Data Processing Day", an annual meeting organized by a registered association Otadata. Otadata was an association that had been established in the late 1960s by Andersin and his colleagues and students to support and foster data processing expertise by organizing seminars and by funding publications. Interestingly enough, the idea of forming an association to advance the computing field and its domestic knowledge occurred in the Finnish Committee for Mathematical Machines in 1955. Hans Andersin had had his first experiences of the new computing field working for that committee [27, 28]. By 1975, the Otadata association had extended its social influence by spreading information on electronic data processing in school-TV and other channels [cf. 32; see also 21].

The Data Processing Day also attracted participants from state organizations and companies [9]. Professor Andersin was familiar with the recent Committee for Computer Policy report, and in addition, he had been working on the Committee for Machine Independence in State Data processing that studied how to reduce Finnish dependency on multinational companies [38], such as the market leader IBM. Actually, Andersin had sent his preliminary plan for the new project to the co-ordination department of the Ministry of Finance prior to his presentation at the Data Processing Day [1, 2].

In his 1975 talk, Hans Andersin examined the possibilities of Finnish computer industry. To this end, he discussed the history of the field. Surveying past experience, Andersin said that planning Finnish computer industry had not been thought of when the ESKO, the first electronic computer to be constructed in Finland [see 26], was build in the latter half of the 1950s. The audience already knew at that time that he had been involved. Referring to a project that dated back to the 1960s, he mentioned a Finnish-made Strömberg [Selco] 1000 computer, which became a computer for process control and not a general-purpose computer. In all, he discussed several efforts at building up Finnish computer industry and weighed arguments for and against increased coordination in this sector. In conclusion he suggested a new project "Suomalainen tietokone", in English "A Finnish Computer", be started in some university which would collaborate with other universities and interest groups. Research and development could take place in the universities but a new, strong, and independent company would take responsibility of manufacturing and marketing. This outline was indicative to the later project [11].

Professor Andersin's ideas could not have resonated much better with those in the topical discussions and reports regarding the need to promote domestic production and increase coordination in Finnish computer-related activities. In November 1975, the Helsinki University of Technology and the Ministry of Finance initiated the FICO-project collaboratively. The project was financed by the Ministry of Trade and

---

[2] See also Enlund and Andersin, in this volume.

Industry. The project became known as the Finnish Computer Project. Kauko Pursiainen from the Ministry of Finance headed the FICO management group and Hans Andersin became leader of the project group. They had both worked in the Committee for Machine Independence in State Data Processing [38].

Hans Andersin recalled that the FICO project aimed "at getting the Finnish computer industry to accept one standard computer for everybody's use. I was very much involved in this (in retrospect naive) project." [5]. From the published final report produced by the FICO-team in HUT, we can conclude that the FICO-project was driven by ideas of re-organizing and gathering up information technology (computer-related) industrial and other activities (education, research) under a national objective. They argued this as a necessity to develop effectively this industry sector in Finland [13].

How was this "national project" visible or performed in practice – or did it stay on paper?

The FICO-project seems to have been national first of all so that it involved participants and support from many actors or organizations, both public and private. The management group of the project consisted of state officials (like Pursiainen), researchers (Andersin, Sulonen), and a company representative (from Enso-Gutzeit). The project organized two wide-ranging panels with business and client representatives and visited companies to create discussion and ask comments. The project's discussion meetings were attended by representatives from companies like Datasaab-Valmet, Digelius Electronics, Nokia Electronics, Outokumpu, Sponsor, Strömberg, Televa, Tietotehdas, TYPLAN,[3] the state's computer centre VTKK and state-funded research institutions like VTT. (By contrast, the project involved only one university, HUT.) In addition, the project received three expert reports, one of them from IBM Finland (Olli Varho, CEO). They did all this outreach activity to develop a shared understanding of and support for the project's objective of developing this industry sector in Finland in a nationally coherent and efficient way [13]. In other words, in practice the "national project" meant a partly public and to some extent open process and debate. Similar openness and outreaching had already taken place in the project with the ESKO computer in the 1950s [27].

According to interviewees, the FICO was generally well accepted. For example, Nokia welcomed the new project and the idea of cooperation. They wanted to offer their products for other Finnish companies to use. On the other hand, IBM discouraged the project from trying to build a new Finnish production company [5, 7; see also 9].

What was the FICO's relation to politics and especially to the Social Democratic Party? The interviewees agreed that the FICO was not regarded as a political project. The FICO management group was however well aware of the industrial political programs of the Social Democratic Party and the Centre Party. Andersin called the project "inspired" by the ideas of SDP [5, 7, 8, and 9]. It could also be relevant that soon after the FICO was established, a new government began work. Both of the FICO's responsible government departments were taken over by social democratic ministers. Eero Rantala, age 34, became a minister for trade and industry. Early in 1976, they created Valco, a new state-run technology company with strong support by the SDP [31]. The study of Valco Company's possible influence to the FICO is not part of this work.

---

[3] See Enlund and Andersin, in this volume.

4 Public Report 1976 Revealed Contents: FICO's Thorough Analysis and Discussion

The FICO research project produced a report of about 85 pages, of which some 70 pages were analysis, followed by 15 pages of proposals. This final report drew on information from the panels organized by the project, company visits in Finland and abroad and several international market forecasting analyses, to scrutinize various activities, including their strengths as well as weaknesses, of the industry in Finland. In all, the report gathered and published information on the field to an extent probably unprecedented.

The report explored different avenues of possible future development. In general, the computer business was to grow rapidly and towards smaller computers, using microprocessors in distributed systems, close to end users. It also mentioned computers at home although mostly the users that were talked about in detail would be situated in offices and companies – presumably, as these were more imminent growth areas [13]. In fact, most of these anticipated developments had already been on the table from early seventies in for example the Otadata association's events and magazine [see 10], but the report offered updated information on the latest market changes and calculated estimates of the future.

In order to promote the Finnish computer industry, the FICO group came up with suggestions to increase coordination and cooperation among the actors of the field. These options were built on products that the group foresaw as promising. The report presented four product areas that the project team considered suitable for a developed Finnish computer industry.

Firstly, microprocessor services would centralize some of the companies' activities at the time. This unit could manufacture microprocessors for Finnish companies to use in their various other products.

Secondly, manufacturing minicomputers (in Finnish pientietokoneet, based or constructed on computers such as Nokia MIKKO 2 or Selco 1000 by Strömberg) developed in Finland or elsewhere and their related appliances.

Thirdly, producing application oriented systems (as for example in health care, teaching and office sectors).

And fourthly, producing software (knowledge management systems and commercial and administrative systems).

Kauko Pursiainen recalled that the focus of the FICO changed in more than one way as it proceeded. Software grew increasingly important during the research process, which began with hardware orientation. In addition, the project leader Hans Andersin seemed to lose his interest in the FICO; however, when asked about it, he denied such a change, Pursiainen continued [7].

By this time, it is most likely that Hans Andersin had learned that other interested parties or groups had their competing views of nationally preferred development in the future Finnish IT industry. Looking back, Andersin wrote, "At that time Nokia claimed to have a computer suitable to be that "standard Finnish computer" and also some other Finnish companies had developed computers that would fit the goal of the project. This resulted in a conflict that made the project work difficult if not impossible to carry out" [5]. For example, the state-owned Televa had built a minicomputer of its own. One could hardly expect coherent and prompt action in this environment, which the FICO report also described as somewhat lacking in trust among stake-holders. Nonetheless, the project kept writing for its publication. In addition, in the course of the process the FICO team abandoned its originally central idea of a distinct Finnish computer as a principal goal, in favor of broader ambitions to building up the industry [14].

In all manufacture and marketing, the report stated, the goal needed to be exporting the products, since Finnish markets were too small. Concerning international market-ing, the research team noted that Finland was well situated, since the country was on good terms with both the West and East - that is the Comecon or socialist countries. In fact, this position could make the Finnish IT firm an interesting partner to foreign companies [13; see also 34]. Interestingly, and again consistent with the events of the 1950s [27, 28], this national project had adopted a fundamentally international view on future markets. However, seeing commercial potential in the socialist countries was not an unusual vision in Finland at that time. In fact, other Western European national champions had targeted those markets too [31, 16].

The FICO report was unusual in not only being thorough but also in making the project's aims, and indirectly its values, explicit in public. The report listed a set of goals and criteria for the future enterprise. These goals included particularly benefit-ing national economy, increasing preparedness for crises (national security, including military interests, went unmentioned elsewhere) and achieving a "distinctive identity" for this activity and probably its products. The last one did not mean national identity but a Finnish brand name or trademark [13].

Based on these criteria and the product focus, the FICO-project formulated alterna-tives for supporting the growth and coordination of the field in Finland through exist-ing companies or a new company. Options for a new firm included a company focused on marketing, a company solely devoted to research and development work, and a new full-scale company with its own marketing, R&D and production. The report stated that in principle, the new full-scale company could be created by strongly supporting the growth of either Nokia or Strömberg among the existing com-panies. Either of those two was large enough to take on this "major national task" ("kansallinen suurtehtävä"). The state was another option for ownership of the new company. Other ownership options were a small or a large group of state and private companies joining forces [13].

5 The FICO Publicly Suggests a New Company with Likely State Involvement

The last chapter of the report elaborated the alternative of a new full-scale company, which was project's suggestion for action. The suggested company would preferably have a broad ownership structure, including the state, and leaving open the possibility of a joint stock company with the state as the majority share holder (as in the case of Valco, 60% state). Its main activity would be producing application-oriented sys-tems. The suggestion included projections for the first five years of the company. To fulfill the plan it would take 25.6 million Finnish marks (circa 15.8 million EUR (year 2007)) over five years and by that time employ 476 persons (in Helsinki, capital area). According to the plan, the company could start in 1977-1978, but only after more detailed planning and research. The report envisioned a relatively low-risk quick start, with a small group of actors, choosing a safe product (preferably something already commissioned), buying an already working company, and using mostly subcontractors in manufacturing [13].

Regardless of which option would be chosen in the future, the project team emphasized that education and research on information technology should be developed and advanced in Finnish universities. Furthermore, the report suggested building a very close relationship between universities and the new company. Those relations were not seen as problematic – a stand (of industry funding endangering the impartiality of research) taken in the Ministry of Education at the time. Here it was a professor, Hans Andersin, who promoted close cooperation between university research and the imagined company. Tellingly of close relations, he had colleagues in University of Tampere who were not included in the FICO process and had they been, they would have been partly influenced by viewpoints inside Nokia with which they cooperated closely in software development [6]. Again, it is worth mentioning that these ideas were not new. In fact both Andersin's interest in applying research in society and his consequent interest in the commercial sphere had surfaced earlier while he was working for the ESKO project in the 1950s [27, 28].

The major issue dividing the parties involved was the role of the state. The FICO report claimed the state had a responsibility in diversifying the production structure of the economy, which would legitimize state actions. According to Eero Rantala, the SDP regarded current technological change as a parallel with the foundation of the state-owned oil company Neste in the late 1940s. In their program, the SDP explicitly invoked economic sovereignty as a national goal [35, 8]. In the industry, a new company with state-involvement was not desirable – at least not in Nokia. According to Martti Häikiö, political radicalism had created fears among Nokia management of planned nationalization. Lauri Saari, a key figure of Valco Company, wrote that the plans for a state electronics concern appeared in the press and were misreported as paving the way for nationalization [31, 19, see also 3].

Whatever the current beliefs of Nokia and other stakeholders, it is evident that there existed widely different interpretations of what was best for the nation, or of the preferred solutions for a "national project" in this new field. For this particular industry in Finland, a connection to a political party and a clear interest by the SDP was quite new, certainly as compared with the 1950s. However, this does not mean that the SDP was not working for a national mission of its own. Nevertheless, its interest added a party political dimension to the conflicting views among which the FICO sought a unified national project. The FICO had no single solution or preference regarding the state's role in its proposed national project; in these circumstances, it could not have had one. Overall, the parties were far from unanimous in this respect, which we can see as one of the "national questions" of the FICO: coping with conflicting views regarding the state's role.

When assessing the national arguments, qualities and possible impact of the report, one should remember that all this information generated by FICO was publicly available. This is especially important since Martti Häikiö and Ari Manninen in their research seem to indicate that the FICO project was not public but somewhat shadowy and had potentially dangerous objectives (cf. [19, 23]). Significantly in regard to FICO's open and public national interests and wish to contribute socially, Hans

Andersin and Reijo Sulonen published a detailed article presenting the FICO's work titled "Data Processing Industry Seeks Cooperation" in a respected thrice-monthly economic journal *Talouselämä* [14, 9; see also 4].

6 FICO – Continuing in a National Tradition

Even though the FICO at first looks like a response to current challenges in line with the Committee for Computer Policy (1974) and the co-ordination department of the Ministry of Finance, to acquire deeper understanding of the FICO's national ideas it is necessary to examine the early Finnish history of IT development. After all, Hans Andersin, the FICO's key planner, had been one of the central figures already when electronic computing began in Finland in the 1950s [26].

According to my recent research, a tradition of considering computers from a national perspective had been created in Finland in the 1950s. In fact, this tradition preceded the first operational mainframe computer (from IBM) in Finland, which had been taken into use in a state-owned bank in 1958. Meanwhile in another project commenced in 1954 a computer called ESKO was under construction. Materially the ESKO was based on a German G1a computer from Göttingen [see 26]. Besides developing that machine, a national board of scientists called *Matematiikkakonekomitea*, the Committee for Mathematical Machines, acted strongly for organizing a nationwide cooperation in a national-minded spirit. Building the ESKO took until 1960, finally resulting in an outdated computer. Nevertheless, the project had, by design, given important stimulus to business also, including the Finnish Cable Factory company that in the mid-1960s became a high-tech part of the Nokia [26-28].[4]

This early project by patriotic scientists with its national impetus was in no small part executed by the civil engineer Hans Andersin who in 1956, that is simultaneously with his work for the scientist's committee, had also began to work for the IBM in Finland [27, 28]. Since the end of the Committee for Mathematical Machines, Hans Andersin had in the 1960s continued to labor for IBM, followed by a change to the new state's computer centre VTKK (est. 1964), which operated under the co-ordination department of the Ministry of Finance. These actors (with the possible exception of IBM), I suggest, maintained the tradition of national duties created by the Finnish Committee for Mathematical Machines.

This is because the Committee for Mathematical Machines had, on a self-appointed mission, strived to control and to guide the nascent Finnish computer field. This task of controlling and guiding was taken over by the subsequent State Data processing committee (1960-1961) and officially passed on to the co-ordination department of the Ministry of Finance, although reduced to controlling and guiding data processing in state departments and their installations. The co-ordination department had continued in this (centralized) tradition, when it nominated the Committee for Computer Policy in 1972, mentioned above [27, 30]. Therefore, in addition to being based on the report of the Committee for Computer Policy, the new Finnish Computer Project, FICO, inherited ideas for its national project and its goals from the 1950s both

---

[4] This influence was most evident in the Finnish Committee for Mathematical Machines' attempt to establish a national computing centre in the 1950s. The Finnish Cable Factory company (later Nokia) turned this idea into a business unit [27, 28; Cf. 19].

through its official founder, the co-ordination department of the Ministry of Finance, and through its initiator and project leader Hans Andersin.

7 Consequences of the Project

It is worth asking – although probably difficult to answer in detail – what were the possible consequences of the FICO project. Despite the FICO's brief existence, the project had several repercussions. Consequently, another project called KESTI (Keski-Suomen tietojenkäsittelyteollisuus, Data Processing Industry of Central Finland) was established in central Finland. Hans Andersin changed his job (in 1978) to a state-owned company Valmet after he had met Valmet's CEO during the FICO process and discovered that they were seeking new product areas in automation (currently, Valmet's successor company is called Metso). Perhaps more importantly, the FICO and its public report sparked new discussions among the information technology professionals [see 25] who also mobilized the political parties to begin formulating programs regarding this new technology and its social impact. As previously noted, the Otadata association and its Data Processing Day were used to foster discussion [4, 12, 29; see also [23]. This debate about technology and politics could in turn have had its impact on the prospective Technology Committee (1979-1980) and the many reforms in the early 1980s.

According to economics researcher Raimo Lovio, despite the fact that the state companies in electronics (Valco and Televa) did not continue as independent companies after the late 1970s they acted as generators of new business units. In the 1980s, Lovio continues, the state assumed a new role in developing the industry: no longer an entrepreneur but playing the role of venture capitalist (including funding research) [22]. Rather than generating new business units, the FICO project was a different kind of catalyst, the impact of which is likely to remain blurred. Moreover, studying the FICO – a path not taken – does throw light on ideological underpinnings in technology policy decisions of the early 1980s that today seem value-neutral but in fact, they were highly debated at the time.

On the one hand, then, the FICO's proposals for increasing direct state-involvement in the industry failed to draw support at the time. Later, those ideas would be forgotten altogether. One could say it was probably the first and the last (official) effort at establishing a state-owned or state-run company for the computer industry in Finland. Yet this would be too narrow and one-sided an interpretation of the ideas of the project team, since they also made alternative suggestions. These ideas, on the other hand, point to future developments in Finnish information technologies, which actually took place later, such as focusing on supporting the growth of private companies or a company.

When interviewed, Reijo Sulonen, at the time a recent PhD and currently a HUT Professor since the 1980s, contemplated that in retrospect the FICO was most important in providing a forum for discussion among the stakeholders in computer-related production. It is difficult to study these interactions in detail, and to prove direct causal relations to what happened afterwards. Nonetheless, it probably encouraged common understanding, continued exchange, and indirectly, led to actions that outlasted the FICO by years [9]. Re-organisations of the industry and related changes in industry and technology politics in the late 1970s and early 1980s tend to confirm this, although the role of the FICO can only be accurately assessed after further research.

8 Conclusion

As we have seen, the FICO research project was very much at the cutting edge, sensitive to both technological and political developments in Finland and abroad, particularly the Eastern bloc markets. However, I hope to have shown that even more interesting and revealing than the at that time topical features of the FICO were the continuities it incorporated. In several respects the FICO project built on earlier ideas of what a Finnish national, technological project should be like, since similar features were present in building the ESKO computer and a national computing centre in the 1950s. These features of a national high-tech research-intensive project included wide participation, half-open debate of experts, commercial interests also towards markets abroad, cooperation between the state and private sector and even idealistic national aspirations for unity. Compared with earlier projects and attempts, the FICO was more politically inspired nationally minded endeavor than before although its suggestions probably got most of their political load in the heated debate of the day. FICO's alleged or current inclination to the SDP should not prevent from realizing that the project, along with the SDP, was on a mission to fulfill much older that is nationally deep-rooted and postwar generated ideas of a Finnish high-tech know-how and industry [27, 28].

In broad terms, the FICO project exemplifies the complex interaction of culture (especially national aspirations), politics, and technology that shape technological and national developments in all the Nordic countries. Furthermore, focusing on the distinctive national ideas and projections in play might offer one key to understanding similar attempts at "national projects" in other countries as well. It remains to be seen if and what these stories could tell of the Nordic experience of computer industry in general. The FICO further demonstrates that the national ambitions connected to information technology were not abandoned or forgotten in the immediate postwar years or the 1950s, as is the common understanding. Rather, those ideas and practices were molded into the structures and ideologies of the new field. They became axiomatic and they would continue to contribute until at least the 1970s and perhaps beyond. Finally, these national ambitions require further study to acquire deeper understanding about the developments in the computer industry.

References

Archives
Government Archives, Prime Minister's Office, Helsinki (Valtioneuvoston arkisto); Ministry of Finance, co-ordination department archives (Valtiovarainministeriö, järjestelyosasto, kansio Hc 60, Suomalainen tietokone.) Since 2008, the Government Archives is part of the National Archives Service (Kansallisarkisto).

[1] Andersin, Hans/TKK: "Suomalainen tietokone." Aloite valtiovarainministeriön järjestelyosaston atk-jaostolle 15.4.1975. Liite pöytäkirjaan neuvottelusta 14.5.1975 valtiovarainministeriön järjestelyosastolla. Siht. Juhani Pöyhönen. (A Finnish computer. Initiative to the ADP-section of the co-ordination department, the Ministry of Finance, in Finnish)

182   P. Paju

[2] Pöytäkirja neuvottelusta 14.5.1975 valtiovarainministeriön järjestelyosastolla. Siht. Juhani Pöyhönen. (Minutes of a meeting in the co-ordination department of the Ministry of Finance, in Finnish) Ministry of Finance, co-ordination department Archives Collections of Kauko Pursiainen

Ministry of Finance, co-ordination department Archives

Collections of Kauko Pursiainen
[3] Presentation handouts concerning Nokia's development, 1975-1980. No author, from c. 1976 (In Finnish) (1976)

Helsinki University of Technology Library, Espoo
Collections of Jouko Seppänen, OtaDATA Newsletters.

Personal Archives of Veikko Jormo
[4] Presentation handout Hans Andersin: "Suomalainen tietokone," (A Finnish computer, in Finnish.) (length five pages) attached to a letter from Hans Andersin to Veikko Jormo, Espoo 26.4.1976. In: Presented with identical name and mentioned (distribution as a handout) in proceedings of Tietojenkäsittelypäivä 1976 (Data Processing Day), Espoo, Otadata ry (1976)

Interviews and correspondence (by the author)

[5] Hans Andersin, communications during 2006 and 2007, incl. discussions and email letters
[6] Reino Kurki-Suonio, email letter 19.10.2007
[7] Kauko Pursiainen, phone interview 24.10.2007
[8] Eero Rantala, email letters 29.10.2007 and 1.11.2007
[9] Reijo (Shosta) Sulonen, interview 26.10.2007

Literature

[10] Andersin, H.E.: "Anti-data-ideologia". (Anti-data ideology, in Finnish.) (OtaDATA Association's Newsletter) OtaDATA 2/1972, 1
[11] Andersin, H.: Suomalaisen tietokoneteollisuuden mahdollisuudet (Possibilities of Finnish computer industry, in Finnish). In: Proceedings of Tietojenkäsittelypäivä 1975 (Data Processing Day). Espoo, Otadata ry (1975)
[12] Andersin, H.: "ATK – haaste puolueille" (ADP – a Challenge for political parties, in Finnish). In: Proceedings of Tietojenkäsittelypäivä 1977 (Data Processing Day). Espoo, Otadata ry (1977)
[13] Andersin, H.E., Parkkinen, M., Sulonen, R.: Esitutkimus suomalaisen tietojenkäsittelyteollisuuden kehittämismahdollisuuksista. (Preliminary study of development possibilities in Finnish data processing industry, in Finnish) Helsinki University of Technology, Information Processing Laboratory, Sarja A, 7/76. Espoo (1976)
[14] Andersin, H., Sulonen, R.: Tietojenkäsittelyteollisuus tavoittelee yhteistyötä (Data Processing Industry Seeks Cooperation, in Finnish) Talouselämä 17/1976 39, 20–22, 57–58 (1976)
[15] Bijker, W.: Of Bicycles, Bakelites and Bulbs – Towards a theory of sosiotechnical change. The MIT Press, London (1995)
[16] Coopey, R.: Information Technology Policy: Competing for the Future. In: Coopey, R. (ed.) Information Technology Policy. An International History, pp. 1–23. Oxford University Press, New York (2004)

[17] Gram, C., Laaksonen, T., Ohlin, T., Lawson, H (Bud.), Skår, R., Stangegaard, O.: History of the Nordic computer industry. In: Bubenko Jr., J., Impagliazzo, J., Sølvberg, A. (eds.) History of Nordic Computing. IFIP WG9.7 First Working Conference on the History of Nordic Computing (HiNC1), Trondheim, Norway, June 16-18, 2003, pp. 179–190. Springer, New York (2005)

[18] Hecht, G.: The Radiance of France. In: Nuclear Power and National Identity after World War II. MIT Press, Cambridge (1998)

[19] Häikiö, M.: Nokia Oyj:n historia. 1. Fuusio. Yhdistymisten kautta suomalaiseksi monialayritykseksi 1865-1982 (History of the Nokia Corporation, part I, in Finnish) Helsinki (2001)

[20] Johansson, M.: Smart, Fast and Beautiful. On Rhetoric of Technology and Computing Discourse in Sweden 1955-1995. CD-ROM. Thesis for the Ph.D. degree. Linköping Studies in Arts and Science 164. Linköping University, Linköping (1997)

[21] Jotuni, P.: Teknillisessä korkeakoulussa atk 'läpäisee' kaikki oppiaineet (ADP permeates through all subjects in Helsinki University of Technology, in Finnish) IBM-katsaus 4/1991, 10–17 (1991)

[22] Lovio, R.: Evolution of Firm Communities in New Industries - The Case of the Finnish Electronics Industry. Acta Universitatis Oeconomicae Helsingiensis Series A:92. The Helsinki School of Economics and Business Administration, Helsinki (1993)

[23] Manninen, A.T.: Näin tehtiin Suomesta tietoyhteiskunta (How Finland was made into an information society, in Finnish). Helsinki, Talentum (2003)

[24] Nevalainen, R.: Suomi tietoyhteiskunnaksi – eespäin tiedon poluilla ja valtateillä. Tietoyhteiskuntatoiminnan lyhyt historia (Finland into an information society – forwards on the paths and roads of information. A Short history of information society activities, in Finnish) SITRA, Helsinki (1999)

[25] Otala, M.: "Suomalainen ja tietokone," (A Finn and the Computer, in Finnish). In: Proceedings of Tietojenkäsittelypäivä 1977 (Data Processing Day). Espoo, Otadata ry (1977)

[26] Paju, P.: A Failure Revisited: The First Finnish Computer Construction Project. The Establishing of a National Computing Center in Finland. In: Bubenko Jr., J., Impagliazzo, J., Sølvberg, A. (eds.) History of Nordic Computing. IFIP WG9.7 First Working Conference on the History of Nordic Computing (HiNC1), Trondheim, Norway, June 16-18, 2003, pp. 79–94. Springer, New York (2005)

[27] Paju, P.: "Ilmarisen Suomi" ja sen tekijät. Matematiikkakonekomitea ja tietokoneen rakentaminen kansallisena kysymyksenä 1950-luvulla. Doctoral dissertation with English Summary (The Finnish Committee for Mathematical Machines and computer construction as a national project in the 1950s, in Finnish.) University of Turku publications C 269, Turku (2008)

[28] Paju, P.: National Projects and International Users: Finland and Early European computerization. IEEE Annals of the History of Computing 30, 77–91 (2008)

[29] Proceedings of Tietojenkäsittelypäivä 1977 (Data Processing Day, in Finnish). Espoo, Otadata ry (1977)

[30] Pursiainen, K.: "Valtionhallinnon tietojenkäsittelyn alkuvaiheita." (Early Phases of Data Processing in State Administration, in Finnish). In: Tienari, M. (ed.) Tietotekniikan alkuvuodet Suomessa (The First Years of Information Technology in Finland, in Finnish), Suomen Atk-kustannus Oy, Jyväskylä, pp. 205–242 (1993)

[31] Saari, L.: Valcoinen kirja (A book on Valco, in Finnish). Tammi, Helsinki (1981)

[32] Saarikoski, P.: Koneen lumo. Mikrotietokoneharrastus Suomessa 1970-luvulta 1990-luvun puoliväliin (The Lure of the Machine. The Personal Computer Interest in Finland from the 1970s to the mid-1990s, in Finnish) Nykykulttuurin tutkimuskeskuksen julkaisuja 83. Jyväskylä (2004)

[33] Salmi, H.: Televisio, tietokone ja tietämisen politiikka. Tietämisen teknologiat vuoden 1975 tv-dokumentissa Maailmantelevisio (Television, computer and the politics of information. Information technologies in a 1975 TV documentary World Vision, in Finnish). In: Salmi, H., Paju, P., Parikka, J., Saarikoski, P. (eds.) Tanja Sihvonen ja Jaakko Suominen: Välimuistiin kirjoitetut. Lukuja Suomen tietoteknistymisen kulttuurihistoriaan (Written in the Cache. Contributions to the cultural history of Finnish computerization, in Finnish) k & h. Turku, pp. 55–79 (2006)

[34] Seppänen, J.: SEV-yhteistyön mahdollisuudet suomalaiselle tietokoneteollisuudelle. In: Proceedings of Tietojenkäsittelypäivä 1976 (Data Processing Day). (Comecon-cooperation possibilities for Finnish computer industry, in Finnish). Espoo, Otadata ry (1976)

[35] SDP: n teollisuuspoliittinen ohjelma. Hyväksytty SDP:n puoluekokouksessa Jyväskylässä 5.—8.6.1975. (Social Democratic Party's program for industrial policy 1975, in Finnish) (1975)

[36] Suominen, J.: Koneen kokemus. Tietoteknistyvä kulttuuri modernisoituvassa Suomessa 1920-luvulta 1970-luvulle. (Experiences with machines. Computerised culture in the process of Finnish Modernisation from the 1920s to the 1970s, in Finnish). Vastapaino, Tampere (2003)

[37] Wallenius, J.: Irti lamasta – tietokoneet tuottamaan (Breaking free from the recession – computers to increase production, in Finnish). In: Proceedings of Tietojenkäsittelypäivä 1976 (Data Processing Day), Espoo, Otadata ry (1976)

[38] Valtion Atk:n koneriippumattomuustoimikunnan mietintö. Komiteanmietintö 1973: 116. Helsinki 1973. (Report of the Committee for Machine Independence in State Data Processing, in Finnish) (1973)

Information Systems and Software Engineering Research and Education in Oulu until the 1990s

Henry Oinas-Kukkonen[1], Pentti Kerola[2], Harri Oinas-Kukkonen[2],
Jouni Similä[2], and Petri Pulli[2]

[1] Faculty of Humanities, History, Centre of Excellence in Research,
P.O. Box 1000, FIN-90014 University of Oulu, Finland
Henry.Oinas-Kukkonen@oulu.fi
[2] Department of Information Processing Science, P.O. Box 3000,
FIN-90014 University of Oulu, Finland
Pentti.Kerola@oulu.fi, Harri.Oinas-Kukkonen@oulu.fi,
Jouni.Simila@oulu.fi, Petri.Pulli@oulu.fi

Abstract. This paper discusses the internationalization of software business in the Oulu region. Despite its small size, the region grew rapidly and very successfully into a global information and communication technology business center. The University of Oulu, which was the northern most university in the world at the time of its establishment (1958) had a strong emphasis on engineering since its very beginning. Research on electronics was carried out since the early 1960s. Later, when the Department of Information Processing Science was founded in 1969, research on information systems and later also on software engineering was carried out. This paper discusses the role of the information systems and software engineering research for the business growth of the region. Special emphasis is put on understanding the role of system-theoretical and software development expertise for transferring research knowledge into practice.

Keywords: Information systems, software engineering, information processing science, Oulu, Finland, history.

1 Introduction

The University of Oulu came into existence in 1958, at the time as the northernmost university in the world. The Department of Information Processing Science came into being in 1969 [17, 32]. The University of Oulu is a multidisciplinary university, which was successful in creating a base of innovations for local production and economy [30]. The yearly student intake at the department slowly rose from the first ten in 1972 to the level of twenty-five in 1985 [31]. This paper focuses on the role of system-theoretical and software-oriented research expertise behind the rapid and successful development of the business in the region. We describe the developments of information systems (IS) and software engineering (SE) research and study educational efforts in these areas.

Some of the authors of this paper are senior scholars at the Department of Information Processing Science at the University of Oulu with different scientific backgrounds

J. Impagliazzo, T. Järvi, and P. Paju (Eds.): HiNC 2, IFIP AICT 303, pp. 185–194, 2009.
© IFIP International Federation for Information Processing 2009

and paradigms of the field. They also have professional careers in the practice, being involved in many of the development steps under investigation.

2 Scientific Research Reaches International Level

During the period of 1985 till 1990 there were relatively little international business activities going on with the software companies at the Oulu area. Company image building, venture funding as well as European R&D projects were still lying ahead. CCC Software Professionals, however, was an exception. Its international operations were started right after its founding in 1985 through delivering large software projects to Soviet Union and some also to Saudi Arabia. CCC was also to become the first Finnish partner in a Eureka R&D project. The Riskman[1] project was prepared from 1989 onwards through one of its sister companies in Athens.

Whereas the software business activities were still a few, the main thread of becoming more international in the region had taken place through scientific activities, which was quite natural as science by definition is international. The information systems research entered a new era during this time through producing high quality scientific publications. Studying these mature scientific publications, i.e. established journals and very high-quality conferences, during as well as before the period under investigation, is a key method to study the internationalization process in this article. Admittedly, the effect of scientific publications on practice sometimes occurs hand in hand with the scientific progress in the information and communication technology (ICT) field, but most often the progress follows several years.

Professor Pentti Kerola had previously studied information systems development with major emphasis on systems design and modeling, introducing the 'PSC systemeering model' [18, 20].[2] The motivation for this research had stemmed from practice, but it was, however, theoretically oriented. During 1979-1980 Kerola was a Visiting Researcher at three universities at the U.S., namely University of Michigan at Ann Arbor, Florida International University, and University of California at Irvine.

At the Department of Industrial Engineering at the University of Michigan, Kerola was involved with a pioneering research effort on software engineering, known as the ISDOS project[3] led by professor Daniel Teichrow. This project focused on defining the problem statement language (PSL) and its automated tool support. This research was mainly computer science oriented.

Research collaboration with Professor William Taggart at Florida International University had started a little bit earlier. Taggart was interested in the information systems architects' roles and the PSC systemeering model [36]. The joint work with Florida International University involved a softer theme, namely human information processing styles. Kerola's interest and enthusiasm on the human side of technology already had become evident ever since he started working at the Oulu area. In their joint work, Kerola and Taggart discussed the importance and challenges of self-evaluation for human information processing styles, the gathering and interpreting of data related to such styles, as well as the implications of this for human resource

---

[1] http://www.eureka.be/inaction/AcShowProject.do?id=530
[2] PSC is an acronym for Pragmatic-Semantic-Constructive systems development approach.
[3] ISDOS is an acronym for Information System Design and Optimization System.

planning in systems development projects [22, 27].[4] Kerola became a recognized scholar in this field, appearing as a keynote speaker at key conferences [24].

Professor Peter Freeman, a software guru at the University of California at Irvine, invited Kerola to visit him. This visit had a strong influence in the future developments of information processing science (IPS) in the Oulu area. The collaboration with UC Irvine deepened the research interest on software engineering environments and processes. Kerola and Freeman jointly introduced the PSC systemeering model into the software engineering community and analyzed software life cycles in conjunction with this [21]. Later Freeman published a textbook on approaching software engineering holistically as a system and treating it as an organizational function carried out by humans [2]. This research collaboration also led to other researchers from Oulu visiting UC Irvine. The works of Freeman boosted the birth of two important scientific fields, namely systems analysis and software engineering, which led to multiple research efforts in systems analysis and design methodologies in the Oulu region.

Much of the original research work with software engineering environments and processes, end-users and ease of use occurred at the multidisciplinary and humanistic SYKE research project[5] during 1982 to 1985. The majority of the researchers from this project entered into business. On the other hand, based upon this line of research, Risto Nuutinen, Erkki Koskela, Juhani Iivari and Pentti Kerola analyzed and described the role of information systems architect in the information systems curricula [28].[6]

Building on top of the systemeering research, Juhani Iivari and Erkki Koskela published their research on systems and process modeling and software quality in *MIS Quarterly* in 1987 [9]. This landmark paper emphasized the levels of abstraction as a key construct for systems design and introduced the PIOCO model[7] for systems modeling and design. This model was later applied on the development of embedded systems at Technical Research Centre of Finland (VTT, *Valtion teknillinen tutkimuskeskus*) [7].[8] Juhani Iivari carried out with this line of research [8,11], analyzing and conceptualizing in parallel with Barry Boehm a new way of approaching software and systems development instead of the traditional waterfall model, namely the hierarchical spiral model [1, 13, 14]. This work has contributed to the birth and advances in object-oriented and agile systems development approaches.

During the academic year of 1988-1989, Juhani Iivari visited Professor Heinz Klein at the State University of New York Binghamton as well as Professor Rudy Hirschheim who had just moved into the University of Houston. Iivari worked with Klein and Hirschheim on analyzing different information systems development approaches and methodologies. These research collaborations later evolved into multiple articles in top scientific journals.

The major information systems research topics that were tackled at Oulu, but which were still to grow in international cooperation included the role of activity

---

[4] Myllykangas provides a deep and first-rate analysis of the IPS research carried out at the University of Oulu in 1973—2004.

[5] SYKE is an acronym for the Finnish words "Ihmiskeskeisen Systemointimetodiikan Kehittäminen".

[6] See also [27], pp. 51-52.

[7] PIOCO is an acronym for Pragmatic-Input/Output-Constructive/Operational systems development approach.

[8] Also see [27], pp.49-50.

theory and its applications to information systems research and development [25], organizational implementation [3, 4, 5, 6, 33], end-user satisfaction [10, 12, 34], as well as computer-aided software/systems engineering. The main international contacts within these took place through the Nordic IS community, in particular through the annual working seminar for researchers and doctoral students, known as Information systems Research seminar In Scandinavia. Pentti Kerola, Pertti Järvinen, and Eero Peltola had founded this IRIS conference series in 1978.

In sum, information systems research at the Oulu area had entered into a new era in the late 1970s or early 1980s via getting international. During the period of 1985 to 1990, the level of publications reached the level of high quality and stabilized. The main research activities in this research tradition were information systems development and software engineering environments and processes. Most of the research projects were funded by Tekes, nowadays known as Finnish Funding Agency for Technology and Innovation, or by Academy of Finland[9]. We should also note that teaching and education activities were built directly on top of the core competences produced through scientific research in the information system and software engineering fields, providing a textbook example from a successful university key function, i.e. transfer of knowledge from the academia into practice. Companies such as Mobira and CCC Software Professionals benefited greatly from the accumulated software and systems development competence, in particular related to conceptual modeling and software process modeling.

3   Curriculums and Knowledge Transfer in Higher Education

Veli-Pekka Leivo's M. A. thesis in general history [26] gives an excellent description and analysis about the educational activities at the IPS institute. In this section we focus on the most fundamental educational sub-areas of the institute: master (undergraduate) [19, 29] and doctoral (postgraduate) education [23] from the viewpoints of different interest groups in their activities of knowledge transfer. *Informatics* is by its nature a methodological discipline, bearing connections with many other sciences [15].

technological disciplines, primarily electronics and digital signal processing, on which research and development in information processing and communication technology relies

structural and cross-sectional disciplines, including mathematics, statistics, general systems science and logic, which generate the formal general means, methods and theories required

behavioral sciences and humanities, including philosophy, psychology, neuroscience, history, social psychology and work science, which study individual and group behavior and knowledge, information and data on human activities

economics, administration and the social sciences, which are concerned with behavior and management of business and social organizations with the role and significance of information processing, including knowledge transfer, in these.

Organizationally the Department of Information Processing Science was a faculty-independent unit, directly under the board of Oulu University from the very beginning

---

[9] http://www.tekes.fi/eng/; http://www.aka.fi/en-gb/A/

up to 1985. Then the board decided to separate computing services from the research and educational activities of informatics, with the purpose to clarify the organization of computing services. At the same time, they raised a sensitive problem: Which faculty would be the optimal place for IPS in the technologically modern university? The final decision and organizational selection was the Faculty of Science because of the traditional position in the other universities. It also was contradictory with the recommendation of the IPS Institute — preferring the Faculty of Technology.

During the years of late 1970s and early 1980s the Department of Information Processing Science, following the reform of the university degrees, designed and developed the master level degree program in information systems architect (ISA). The metaphorical title of the holistic working role was based on the information systems research. An ISA is a professional, who can design the strategies of information systems development in organizations together with different interest groups and manage the development using those strategies.

In the middle of 1980s, software engineering (SE) supplemented the master program. A SE is a professional, who can produce interactive and end-user-oriented (applicational) software and manage development projects.

The sub-areas and levels in which these professionals expected to operate appear in Figure 1; the total field partitions into three levels from the point of view of the utilization of information and data systems, with the inclusion of software systems.

ORGANIZATIONAL	LEVEL	" ISA--ISA--ISA "	"SE "
USER	LEVEL	" ISA--ISA "	" SE--SE "
TECHNICAL	LEVEL	" ISA "	" SE--SE--SE "

Fig. 1. Levels in which ISA and SE were expected to operate

Both of the professional roles cover all three levels, but with a different focus and weight. The task of a professional at the organizational level is to define how information systems and computer/communication technology in general can be exploited to achieve the aims of particular organizations, while the task at the user level is to define information systems in such a way that those will serve day-to-day interests of the user optimally. One may see the task at the technical level as constructing software of high technical quality that conforms to the definitions and aims specified at the other levels.

The content of education and teaching in those curriculums fall into the following ten themes:

o professional orientation
o preparation for participation in the working community
o development of problem solving abilities
o introduction to scientific paradigms, different kinds of work and methods
o introduction to organizations, their main functions utilizing data systems, and industrial software production

o data management and organizational principles of data generation
o introduction to human behavior and informational activities
o computer hardware and software systems
o software systems, programming and programming technologies
o data systems, their life cycles, systems development methods and technologies.

The most fundamental core of education is in the themes 4 through 7. From the viewpoint of successful knowledge transfer between researchers and practitioners the special weight and focus occurs in the studies during the project work courses [35]. The total obligatory educational effort appears in the three stages:

Foundations: principles of project work and programming project in 'labs'
'Real life' effort: practical teamwork and project seminar
Research effort: research teamwork and M.Sc. thesis seminar

Those stages began in 1972 and the same principal of implementation has continued into these days. Up to 1990s, over one hundred real-life projects were implemented at the department.

The programming project was a five study-week course implemented during the third study year in the fall and spring semesters. The aim was to integrate the knowledge from the preceding courses, especially courses on the principles of project work, software design, and programming. Usually in one semester five projects on the average were carried out. There was no charge for these projects. The estimated amount for student work was 200 hours/student with three to five students in a project. The younger students worked under the management of older students who were receiving extra credit from optional participation. Nearly all the projects were delivered to real customers in the surrounding community. Basically the requirement was that the specifications for the project should be "ready" when the projects began. This did not hold true in all cases and many times the students had to work with developing or at least refining the specifications together with the customers.

The real-life project work was a six study-week course implemented during the fourth study year in the spring semester. The aim of the course was to integrate the knowledge from the preceding courses of the second stage. Usually eight to ten projects were carried out during one semester. The students worked about 250 hours/student and the staff from the department acted as project managers. The department charged the customers at the delivery of the project and compensated the students for their work.

In project seminars each group wrote a report where own selected experiences were compared to and evaluated with results reported in scientific publications. Each had to select one or two topics where to concentrate. The structure and style of the report was to follow that required in scientific papers.

The group presentations tried to be as effective as possible with the sharing of the experience. The seminars were moderated by the use of an opponent group, whose task was to support the dissemination by various ways, catalyzing discussions, and criticism. The students were encouraged to use innovative forms of interaction.

The diversified IS and SE research produced the feasible base to develop a holistic and highly interactive educational system at the institute. On the one hand, the ICT practice directed the different kinds of research interests, which on the other hand positively influenced on the selection of higher educational aims and contents. As the international review committee evaluated in 1990:

> "... the ideas emanating from the comparative research of IS Curriculums have been utilized in the design of the own curriculum... the teaching programme seemed to be a comprehensive, well-balanced IS Curriculum, covering theoretical as well as applied subjects." (our condensation) [16]

In nation-wide doctoral education, the institute actively participated in the Finnish Doctoral Programs of Information Systems Research and Information Technology. Professor Pentti Kerola was the first coordinating professor in 1985-1986 for ISR doctoral education. Later during early 1990s, Professor Juhani Iivari had the same position.

The institute has been especially active and collaborative in the development of the IRIS conferences where the special focus has been in supporting higher studies of doctoral students. The same aim, but more local, has been in the KISS-effort, Kilpis-järvi IS symposiums. There, in the most creative natural environment, in the north-ernmost region of Finnish Lapland near the Norwegian border, young doctoral students and their international and Finnish mentors have since 1989 interacted especially with the purpose of refining the doctoral research plans.

The association of information processing students at the Department of Informa-tion Processing Science, Blanko, has existed since 1973 in order to create a social spirit among the students by offering recreational opportunities and organizing vari-ous educational events outside the degree program. Officially, Blanko had regular student positions in the committee of educational development in the institute.

The most significant annual event has been the Blanko conference series, where re-searchers as well as practioneers have presented newest information in the form of a general interest seminar about the research and educational experiences as well as practical industrial experiences of the field. The Association of Electronics Engineers and the Data Processing Association of the Northern Finland have been the contribut-ing partners. During the 1980s, the Blanko conference series grew radically from the viewpoint of media exhibitions. Regrettably, the whole process of Blanko conference declined radically in the years of early 1990s during the severe economic recession and has only during the last five years reclaimed some of its former status. Still, the active student interaction with different business, communal and other organizations positively influenced on the good balance between the demand and supply of univer-sity level work force at the Oulu ICT area.

4 Conclusion

The level of publications by the researchers of the Department of Information Proc-essing Science reached the level of high quality and stabilized by the 1990s. The main topics were information systems development and software engineering proc-esses and environments.

Teaching and education activities were built directly on top of the core compe-tences produced through scientific research in the information system and software engineering fields. The diversified IS and SE research tracks produced a feasible base for developing a holistic and highly interactive educational system in the department. During this period, the ICT practice directed research interests and educational contents providing a textbook example from a successful university key function: *Transfer of knowledge from the academia into practice*. In the future work, the original contracts and project reports between the department and companies should be studied. It would also be worthwhile to take a closer look at the active student involvement with business, community and other organizations, which, in a positive way, greatly influenced the balance between the demand and supply of university degree work force at the Oulu ICT area.

Acknowledgements

We wish to thank Juhani Iivari and Mikko Myllykangas for their constructive comments on earlier versions of this paper.

References

[1] Boehm, B.: Improving software productivity. IEEE Computer 20(9), 43–57 (1987)

[2] Freeman, P.: Software perspectives – The system is the message. Addison-Wesley, Boston (1987)

[3] Iivari, J.: A planning theory perspective on information system implementation. In: Gallegos, L., Welke, R., Wetherbe, J. (eds.) Proceedings of the Sixth International Conference on Information Systems, Indianapolis, Indiana (1985)

[4] Iivari, J.: Implementability of in-house developed vs. application package based information systems. In: Maggi, L., Zmud, R., Wetherbe, J. (eds.) Proceedings of the Seventh International Conference on Information Systems, San Diego (1986)

[5] Iivari, J.: An innovation research perspective on information system implementation. International Journal of Information Management 6(3), 123–144 (1986)

[6] Iivari, J.: Implementability of in-house developed vs. application package based information systems. Data Base 21(1), 1–10 (1990)

[7] Iivari, J., Koskela, E., Ihme, M., Tervonen, I.: A hierarchical metamodel for embedded software. In: Barnes, D., Brown, P. (eds.) Software Engineering 1986. Peter Peregrinus, London (1986)

[8] Iivari, J.: Dimensions of information systems design: A framework for a long-range research program. Information Systems 11(2), 185–197 (1986)

[9] Iivari, J., Koskela, E.: The PIOCO Model for Information Systems Design. MIS Quarterly 11(3), 401–419 (1987)

[10] Iivari, J.: User Information Satisfaction (UIS) Reconsidered: An information system as the antecedent of UIS. In: DeGross, J.I., Kriebel, C.H. (eds.) Proceedings of the Eighth International Conference on Information Systems, Pittsburgh, Pennsylvania (1987)

[11] Iivari, J.: Levels of abstraction as a conceptual Framework for an Information System. In: Falkenberg, E.D., Lindgren, P. (eds.) Information System Concepts: An In-depth Analysis, pp. 323–352. North Holland, Amsterdam (1989)

[12] Iivari, J., Karjalainen, M.: Impact of prototyping on user information satisfaction during the IS specification phase. Information & Management 17(1), 31–45 (1989)

[13] Iivari, J.: Hierarchical spiral model for information system and software development, Part 1: theoretical background. Information and Software Technology 32(6), 386–399 (1990)

[14] Iivari, J.: Hierarchical spiral model for information system and software development. Part 2: design process. Information and Software Technology 32(7), 450–458 (1990)

[15] Kaakinen, Iivari, J. (eds.): Institute of Information Processing Science, Yearbook 1987. University of Oulu (1987)

[16] International Committee, Evaluation of Research and Teaching in Computer Science, Computer Engineering and Information Systems, pp. 31–33. Publications of the Academy of Finland, Helsinki (1990)

[17] Julku, L., Kyösti.: Oulun yliopiston perustamisen historia (History of the Founding of the University of Oulu), (Rovaniemi: Pohjois-Suomen Historiallinen Yhdistys, 1983), pp. 274-294 (1983) (Summary in English)

[18] Kerola, P., Järvinen, P.: Systemointi, II, Tietosysteemin rakentamisen ja käytön systeemiteoreettinen malli (Systemeering II, A system-theoretical model for the building and use of an information system), Helsinki, Gaudeamus (1975)

[19] Kerola, P., Koskela, E., Nuutinen, R., Riekki, T.: Tietojenkäsittelyn perustutkinnon kehittämisestä Oulun Yliopistossa (On Development of Master Level Degree Programme), University of Oulu, Institute of Information Processing Sciences, A 10 (1979)

[20] Kerola, P.: On infological research into the systemeering process. In: Lucas Jr., H.C., et al. (eds.) The information systems environment: Proceedings of the IFIP TC 8.2 Working Conference on the Information Systems Environment, Bonn, West Germany, June 11-13, 1979, North-Holland, Amsterdam (1980)

[21] Pentti, K., Freeman, P.: A comparison of lifecycle models. In: Proceedings of the 5th international conference on Software engineering, San Diego, California, United States, pp. 90–99. IEEE Press, Piscataway (1981)

[22] Kerola, P., Taggart, W.: Human Information Processing Styles in the Information Systems Development Process. In: Hagwood, J. (ed.) Evolutionary Information Systems, pp. 63–86. North-Holland, Amsterdam (1983)

[23] Kerola, P.: Tietojenkäsittelytieteen ja tietotekniikan tutkijakoulutuksen kehittämisestä – valtakunnallista synergiaa etsimässä (On the development of researcher training for information processing science and information technology – searching for national synergy), Hallinnon tutkimus, Vuosikirja, osa 2 (1986)

[24] Kerola, P.: Knowledge about human information processing styles and learning styles in the education of systems architects. Education & Computing 6(1-2), 3–14 (1990)

[25] Kuutti, K.: Activity theory and its applications to information systems research and development. In: Proceedings of the IFIP WG 8.2. Working Conference, Copenhagen, Denmark, December 14-16, 1990, pp. 195–216 (1990)

[26] Leivo, V.-P.: Tavoitteena talouden ja yhteiskunnan tarpeiden tyydyttäminen. Tietojenkäsittelytieteiden laitoksen opetus vuosina 1969–2002 (Appeasing the Needs of the Economy and the Society. Teaching in the Department of the Information Processing Science, 1969 - 2002). M.A. Thesis. University of Oulu, Department of History, General History (2005)

[27] Myllykangas, M.: Tehtaista nettikauppaan ihmisen ehdoin. Tutkimustoiminta Oulun yliopiston tietojenkäsittelytieteiden laitoksella 1973–2004 (From Factories to eCommerce in Line with the Anthropocentrism. Research in the Department of the Information Processing Science, M.A. Thesis. University of Oulu, Department of History, General History, p. 48 (1973)

[28] Nuutinen, R., Koskela, E., Iivari, J., Kerola, P.: Design and implementation experience of a curriculum for the information systems architect (ISA) reflected on the IFIP/BCS curriculum. In: Information systems education: recommendations and implementation, pp. 179–203. Cambridge University Press, Cambridge (1986)

[29] Nuutinen, R., Koskela, E., Iivari, J., Kerola, P.: Design and implementation experience of a curriculum for the information systems architect (ISA) reflected on the IFIP/BCS curriculum. In: Buckingham, R.A., Hirschheim, R.A., Land, F.F., Tully, C.J. (eds.) Information systems education: recommendations and implementation. Cambridge University Press, New York (1986)

[30] Oinas-Kukkonen, H., Similä, J., Kerola, P., Pulli, P., Saukkonen, S.: Development in the Growth Base of the 'Oulu Phenomenon'. The role of systems/software methodologies. In: Bubenko, J., Impagliazzo, J., Sølvberg, A. (eds.) History of Nordic Computing. IFIP WG9.7 First Working Conference on the History of Nordic Computing (HiNC1), Trondheim, Norway, June 16-18, 2003. IFIP International Federation for Information Processing, vol. 174, p. 435, 436, 445. Springer, New York (2005)

[31] Oinas-Kukkonen, H., Similä, J., Pulli, P.: Main Threads of ICT Innovation in Oulu in 1960—1990. In: Proceedings of Session 90, IEHC 2006, XIV International Economic History Congress, Helsinki, Finland, August 21-25, p. 19 (2006),
http://www.helsinki.fi/iehc2006/sessions81_124.html

[32] Salo, M.: Pohjoinen Alma mater. Oulun yliopisto osana korkeakoululaitosta ja yhteiskuntaa perustamisvaiheista vuoteen 2000 (Alma Mater of the North. Role of the University of Oulu in higher education and in society). Pohjois-Suomen Historiallinen Yhdistys, Rovaniemi, pp. 15, 252 (2003)

[33] Similä, J., Nuutinen, R.: On the analysis of the user role in the context of adp systems implementation: theoretical, methodological and operational aspects and the first results of a case study. In: Proceedings of the Fourth International Conference on Information Systems (ICIS 1983), Houston, Texas, pp. 197–222 (1983)

[34] Similä, J., Nuutinen, R.: An operationalized model for success in the user role. In: Proceedings of the Human-Computer Interaction (INTERACT 1984), pp. 547–554. North-Holland, Amsterdam (1984)

[35] Similä, J., Saukkonen, S.: How to Teach Project Working Capabilities for Information Technology Students at the University Level. In: Proceedings of the ISSEU 1997 International Symposium on Software Engineering in Universities, Rovaniemi, Finland, March 6-8 (1997)

[36] Taggart, W.: Human information processing styles and the information systems architect in the PSC systemeering Model. In: Proceedings of the 17th Annual Computer Personnel Research Conference, Miami, Florida, United States, pp. 63–78. ACM Press, New York (1980)

The Impact of Computer Science on the Development of Oulu ICT during 1985–1990

Henry Oinas-Kukkonen[1], Jouni Similä[2], Petri Pulli[2], Harri Oinas-Kukkonen[2], and Pentti Kerola[2]

[1] Faculty of Humanities, History, Centre of Excellence in Research, P.O. Box 1000,
FIN-90014 University of Oulu, Finland
Henry.Oinas-Kukkonen@oulu.fi
[2] Department of Information Processing Science, P.O. Box 3000,
FIN-90014 University of Oulu, Finland
Jouni.Simila@oulu.fi, Petri.Pulli@oulu.fi,
Harri.Oinas-Kukkonen@oulu.fi, Pentti.Kerola@oulu.fi

Abstract. The region of Oulu has been emphasizing the importance of electronics industry for its business growth since the 1960s. After a pitch-dark recession, the region developed in the 1990s into a new, well-established hub of information and communication technology (ICT) in Finland. The city with its 100,000 inhabitants occupied nearly 10,000 ICT professionals in 1995. This article will contribute to the body of research knowledge through analyzing the role of computer science, in particular information systems and software engineering, for the development of the ICT industry in Oulu in the latter half of the 1980s. This analysis is based on a variety of both primary and secondary sources. This article suggests that the system-theoretical and software-oriented research expertise played a key role for the rapid and successful ICT business development of the Oulu region.

Keywords: ICT, Finland, Oulu, history, GSM, telecommunications, mobile, expertise, technology transfer.

1 Introduction

Due to a variety of reasons Oulu was in a serious period of recession and unemployment in the 1970s. However, the declining region was able to ride the big wave of electronics innovations. Much of this was a result from the local business networks that enabled an innovative way of working [19]. Moreover, this resulted in a wide interest towards the region of Oulu; for example, instead of seeing a well-known "must" for a Soviet leader, the Lenin Museum in Tampere, the Soviet president Mikhail Gorbachev chose to visit Oulu Technology Park (*Oulun teknologiakylä*) in his visit to Finland in October 1989 [6, 17].

In the 1980s, the population grew into 103,500 inhabitants. Oulu was the sixth largest city in Finland in 1990. Within the last fifteen years, Oulu has gained approximately 26,000 new inhabitants; however, at the same time for the first time in its history, the number of children under the school-age has dropped below 10%, and,

J. Impagliazzo, T. Järvi, and P. Paju (Eds.): HiNC 2, IFIP AICT 303, pp. 195–208, 2009.
© IFIP International Federation for Information Processing 2009

simultaneously the number of people over 65-years-old has risen above 10%. The inhabitants of the city were relatively young and Oulu became the fastest growing region in the country in the 1990s [12].

Students flocked to the university. The University of Oulu had been established as late as in 1958, at the time as the most northern university in the world. The Department of Information Processing Science was established in 1969 [7, 37]. Today, the University of Oulu is a multidisciplinary university, which is typically stated to have created the networks and an innovative basis for the promotion of local production and economy [18]. The yearly student intake of the Department of Information Processing Science gradually increased from the first 10 in 1972 to 25 in 1985. Companies in the region had close ties with it. For example, Timo Korhonen, a graduate from the department, managed Eurodata's system group. It subcontracted the software development for the embedded cash register system from Dataskill, which also had very strong ties with the department (Juhani Iivari, Seppo Koivumaa and Jouni Similä). During this period, the average number of master's graduates was only 5-10 annually [19]. Despite of its small beginnings, one of the pioneering efforts to give birth to the software industry in the Oulu region was the formation of Blanko conference series, which started in 1973 [18].

The founding of the first software companies took place in the late 1970s – among others, the first software house Dataskill in 1976 and Systepo in 1979. Later, Kari Pankkonen, a graduate from the Department of Information Processing Science, brought forth the software company Modera in 1982. Also computer manufacturers established offices in Oulu, for example Nixdorf in 1979 and HP in 1981 [19]. Yet, it seems that the slow pace of the early 1980s caused the Oulu region to reach out for new ways to support business. *Oulun teknologiakylä* or Oulu Technology Park[1] was established in 1982 [10, 57].

In an earlier paper, we discussed the impact of computer science on the development of the ICT field in Oulu region through the first half of the 1980s, and it was found out that the integration of technological, mathematical, and humanistic competence had been successful, a liberal and broadminded intellectualism had been relatively common in the area, and best practices had been actively sought. Moreover, the expertise produced through information systems and software engineering research had played a role in the 'industrial explosion' of the region, in particular via the development of embedded software. Three areas had special significance: 1) a high individual variety of educational knowledge, 2) an awareness of team/project/social cooperation, and 3) systems/software methodological knowledge diffusion and transfer through a value chain originating from the Department of Information Processing Science [18]. This paper maps the earlier results with the findings from the latter part of 1980s, i.e. before the blow of recession in the early 1990s.

The main research challenge in this paper is to understand the impact of information systems (IS) and software engineering (SE) research on the ICT development in Oulu the latter half of the 1980s. The paper focuses on the system-theoretical and software-oriented research expertise behind the rapid and successful business development of the region.

---

[1] An area for high-tech industry following the example of Silicon Valley; known for explosive growth of electronics industry there.

Some authors of this paper are senior scholars at the department; however, they represent different scientific backgrounds and paradigms of the field. They also possess impressive careers in practice, being involved in many of the historical development steps under investigation. Of course, one must carefully scrutinize the primary information provided by using source criticism in line with the scientific research methods of history science. Published literature on high technology in the Oulu region and memoirs of people involved in the events will aid in balancing the view taken to the development. The main newspaper in the region, *Kaleva*, has been used as a key source for material. This is highly relevant because the magazine participated very actively discussing the development.

In summary, based on a variety of both primary and secondary sources this paper analyses the ICT development in the Oulu region during the latter part of 1980s and the role of computer science in it.

2 Development of ICT Business Climate from 1985 to 1990

2.1 Infrastructure Development – From "Technology Village" towards Technopolis

The City of Oulu had been somewhat lacking in the activities of forming the technology policy of Oulu during the 1970s and the early 1980s as was noted in our earlier article about the "Oulu phenomenon" [18]. After the polemical public appearances of Antti Piippo in 1979 and the 1980s as executive director of Aspo Electronics, the City of Oulu also actively and massively started to promote the electronics industry and especially the establishment of an electronics park in Oulu, which was finally realized in 1982 [10]. In 1985, however, Technology Park Oulu Ltd (Oulun Teknologiakylä Oy[2]) still functioned in the old dairy near the center of the city notably lacking in space, services, and modern facilities for growing high-tech companies.

In early 1985, the City of Oulu ordered an action plan from the Hansacon consultancy company that came out with two projects. "Technology City of Oulu"[3] (*Teknologiakaupunki Oulu*) would concentrate on the possibilities of development in industry, research, and education. A major initiative was to be the building of the new Technology Park in Linnanmaa near the University of Oulu. "Computer Land of Oulu" (*Tietokonemaa Oulu*) on the other hand would concentrate on the development of tourism [4,43]. The plan was approved by the city administration and both projects were started during the spring of 1985 [8].

---

[2] Oulun Teknologiakylä translates directly as "Technology Village of Oulu". Metaphorically this is a very interesting connotation and describes quite well the village type culture and community of the park during the 1980s. However the term technology park is used subsequently following the convention adopted by the organization itself.

[3] "Technology City of Oulu" has ever since the early 1980's worked as a very powerful metaphor promoting and marketing the technological know-how from Oulu within the whole country as well as internationally. Later metaphors promoted by the City of Oulu e.g. "Quantum Leap to the Future" or the present "Oulu inspires" have at least so far managed not as well in this task.

Especially the "Computer Land of Oulu" project, which was later that year re-named as "*Tietomaa*" ("Data Land"), received much early publicity in the press as may be seen in the references to *Kaleva*. The Technology Park Oulu, however, came up as a close runner-up and proved to be in the end the required "spice" to transform the city into a real technology center of Finland especially through the decision of the Nokia owned Mobira company, to decentralize its software development in Oulu and in the technology park to be built in Linnanmaa. According to the interview of Heikki Huttunen, director in Mobira, the main reason to start software development activities in Oulu was the availability of qualified personnel provided by the local research and education units. In addition, the decision to start operations in the tech-nology park instead of the Nokia factories in Rusko (a suburb of Oulu) was deliberate. Mobira saw clear possibilities of cooperation with the companies already established in the park and it also considered the proximity of the university a great benefit [13].

2.2 Growth of Technology Park

In 1985 when the building of the new technology park in Linnanmaa was started there were 39 companies and about 200 employees registered within the park [44]. We must dismiss one "urban legend" right away. For decades, the rumor in the IT sector in Oulu has been that the Technology Park was built in the form of row houses so that the buildings could be sold to private citizens in case the project did not succeed. Private communication with the architect who designed the first row houses as well as a member of the board of Oulu Technology Park during that time clearly indicated that no such directions were given to the architectural firm and no such discussions were held in the board [2, 34]. Additionally, it would not have been economically feasible or rational to design the buildings in that manner according to the architect. The rumor is probably due to an interview in 1989 with the managing director Pertti Huuskonen of Oulu Technology Park in which he perhaps jokingly noted that in bad times the buildings could be converted to residential buildings [45]. However, Juhani Saukkonen, one of the employees of Tietomaatio Pasanen in the Technology Park remarked that the standing joke at those times was to refer to the possibility of reallo-cating the facilities for other purposes of usage, including residential purposes [33].

In the first phase, the technology park was to provide facilities for six companies and a similar size row house was to be started right after the first one was finished. Altogether, in the Linnanmaa area building rights were reserved for 30,000 square meters or for 100-150 companies. The growth of the park proceeded quite rapidly. In August 1985, there were 35 companies and more than 200 employees in the Technol-ogy Park [50]. By September 1985, at the start of the building of Linnanmaa area, the number of companies was 39 and the number of employees more than 250; in January 1986, there were 42 companies and about 250 employees [27]. Apparently due to limitations in offered space by April 1986 when Mobira, Outel, Noptel and Prometics occupied the first company row house in Linnanmaa, the number of companies in the park had grown to 44 but the number of employees was still reported as 250 [47]. By May of 1986, the second company row house to be built by November 1986 was al-ready fully reserved and the number of companies was 46 [26]. Plans were changed and instead of building one more company row house a decision was made to con-struct two company buildings during fall of 1986 and complete the Technology Park main building for services needed by companies; additionally, they started discussions regarding raising stock capital [28].

2.3 Within and Outside "Teknopolis Linnanmaa"

The growth of the Technology Park was parallel with similar development in companies outside the park in the electronics or other high technology companies. According to an estimate published in October 1986 by *Kaleva* more than 600 new jobs had altogether been created in the Oulu area compared to 2500 jobs at the time of the establishment of Technology Park [25]. About half of these 600 new jobs may have been created outside Technology Park. As a counterpart, the study reports a similar size loss in jobs in mass industry during the same period. A vigorous restructuring of industry had started.

The growth of the Technology Park continued in 1987. By the inaugural ceremony of the main building in March 1987 there were already 65 companies and about 350 employees listed within Technology Park, about half of them in the Linnanmaa area and half in the city center. In his inaugural ceremony speech the present rector of the University of Oulu Markku Mannerkoski coined the term "Teknopolis Linnanmaa" referring to the whole area comprising the University, Technology Park and Technical Research Centre of Finland (VTT, *Valtion teknillinen tutkimuskeskus*) [61].

In June 1987 the stock capital of Technology Park was doubled through open issue share from 8 million Finnish marks (FIM) to 16 million with the number of stock owners rising to more than two hundred and plans for listing in the over-the-counter (OTC) outside the stock exchange itself. The "Teknopolis Linnanmaa" term soon gained popularity first in marketing of the area as the original purpose was. In July 1987, the number of companies in Linnanmaa had grown to 50 and in the city center to 30 with altogether about 400 employees [48]. VTT later in August 1987 released its plans to build a sizable building right next to the Technology Park [60] and this truly earned the area the term "Technopolis". Later the term was adopted as a marketing term for the Technology Park using the term "Teknopolis Oulu" and even later in the 1990s, Technopolis Oulu became the official name of the company.

Telenokia announced in November 1987 its plans to construct what would become in 1989 the largest building in the Technology Park. The Telenokia facilities would house in the beginning 100 employees. In November 1987 the Technology Park comprised of 80 companies and 500 employees [49]. Telenokia's plans apparently replaced the earlier published plans by Nokia to build a sizable R&D center in Oulu; in any case, no such research center outside company production units has ever been built in Oulu [14].

Even though the Finnish Innovation Fund (Sitra, *Suomen itsenäisyyden juhlara-hasto*)[4] research report in August 1988 on the "Oulu phenomenon" stated that the Technology Park had gone through two strong development phases and was then settling on a development plateau, the number of companies and employees continued to grow [39]. In September, *Kaleva* reported that the Technology Park had 85 companies and 600 employees. Comparative figures in other Finnish technology parks were: Otaniemi 65 companies and 300 employees, Turku 35 companies and 500 employees, and Tampere 55 companies and 500 employees [40].

---

[4] Sitra. http://www.sitra.fi/en/

Technology Park had also acquired new major high tech companies [36] as well as major enhancements of present companies in the park [15, 16]. Oulu had begun to interest automatic data processing (adp) companies [20, 23, 41] and electronics industry [5] also generally and some had already made decisions to redistribute software development in Oulu [32]. Internationalization of the Oulu companies was also on the door in a major scale [9]. Major breakthroughs in international markets were published also by companies originating from Oulu [24]. In fact as also the *Kaleva* article reports, this deal by CCC Software Professionals was already the fourth such project delivered abroad. The labor ministry came to help as well with a special dedicated education program tailored for software houses [58]. In short, the economy was booming. This boom lasted until 1990 when first signs of the coming recession appeared in *Kaleva* [3].

2.4 Knowledge Transfer from Research and Education to Practice – Cases of Mobira and CCC

The economic conditions for growth of ICT companies in Oulu region were very stimulating during 1985-1990. There was plenty of capital and loan money available. The banks readily offered money for loans, so almost anybody could get a loan to buy an apartment or set up a company. We may form a general picture of the development of ICT companies based on Figure 1. The figure shows the number of new ICT companies established yearly from 1968 to 1990 as well as the cumulative number of companies.[5] In the figure, we see two growth periods: one starting from about the year 1981-1982 and one with an even steeper slope from about 1985-1986. It is noteworthy that the number of companies established during the five years between 1986 and 1990 is more than double the number of companies established during the seventeen years between 1968 and 1985. "Main Threads of ICT Innovation in Oulu in 1960—1990" provides a more detailed analysis [19].

Knowledge transfer from the Department of Information Processing Science to the practitioners acting in the industry has happened in several ways throughout the years. The major societal impact has of course been the number of students graduating from the department and seeking employment in industry and other organizations. The number of graduates has risen steadily with increased student intakes. During the years 1985 to 1990, the student intake rose from 25 to 40 and the number of graduates rose from a three-year cumulative average of 7 to about 20.

---

[5] Sources of the Figure 1: Kaupparekisteri (Trade Register of the National Board of Patents and Registration of Finland, in Finnish). CD-KATKA 1/03 (Helsinki: Patentti- ja rekisterihallitus, 2003); An email message from the Managing Director of Dataskill Oy Seppo Koivumaa, 25.5.2006; Ilkka Heikura, *Sähkötekniikan ensimmäiset vuosikymmenet Oulun yliopistossa* (Oulu: Avanti Management Oy, 2005); Mika Kulju, *Oulun ihmeen tekijät* (Helsinki: Ajatus, 2002), Mika Raunio, *Luova kaupunki, inhimilliset voimavarat ja kaupunkiseudun kehitys* (Tampere: Tampereen yliopisto, 2005); Eino Tunkelo, *Oulun teknologiakylä 1980—1988. Miten syntyi Oulu-ilmiö?* (Oulu: Suomen Itsenäisyyden Juhlavuoden 1967 rahasto, 1988);"CCC - Finding Solutions", http://www.ccc.fi/1.htm; "Insoft Oy - The visualizer of software development", http://www.insoft.fi/eng/pr2About.htm; "MCon Partners OY", http://www.mconpartners.com/tiki-index.php?page=Partnerit; "Meet Oulu Hightech – teknologiavierailut", http://www.congressoulu.fi/meetouluhitech/hitechyritykset.html

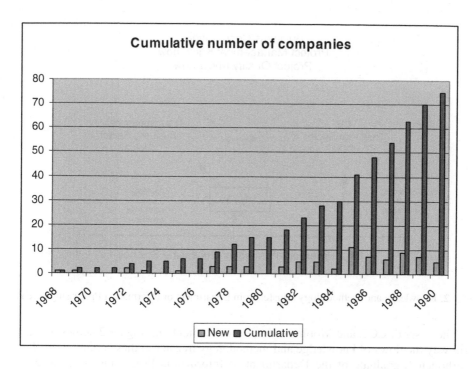

Fig. 1. ICT companies established in Oulu area between 1968 and 1990

Many of the graduates of the department had already started industrial IT companies in the 1980s. The impact of the department's research and education as part of the "Oulu phenomenon" has been analyzed, e.g. in "Development in the Growth Base of the 'Oulu Phenomenon'. The role of systems/software methodologies" [18] and in "Main Threads of ICT Innovation in Oulu in 1960—1990" [19].

We may trace in a natural way an important part of the societal impact of the activities of the Department of Information Processing Science to the start of student projects already in the 1970s. The student projects - Project 1 and Project 2 - were obligatory courses in the curriculum during the third and fourth year. Both projects were carried out in close cooperation with industry and produced tangible deliverables in a real-like project management situation. Currently, about 40 projects with 3-5 students in each project are carried out yearly with more than 30 industrial clients – some projects are reserved for internal departmental and university needs. The student projects have been described in more detail in "How to Teach Project Working Capabilities for Information Technology Students at the University Level" [38]. As one of the results of the student projects the department has had excellent relations with industry now already for more than three decades. These relations have been utilized to hold a steady flow of academy-industry R&D cooperation projects. It is our intention to investigate later more deeply the impact of the student projects in the knowledge and methodology transfer.

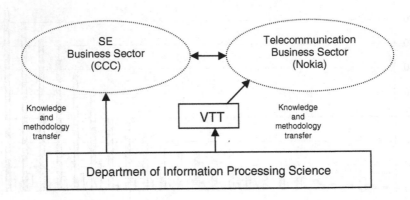

Fig. 2. Knowledge and methodology transfer from Department of Information Processing Science

The cases of CCC and Mobira warrant special attention. Figure 2 shows in a general way the flows of knowledge and methodology transfer to these companies. Timo Korhonen, a graduate of the Department of Information Processing Science, established CCC in 1985. One of the founders of the company, Jouni Similä, is also one of the authors of this paper. The development of the quality system of the company started utilizing a student project from the department in 1985 and led from the company side by Jyri Pyrrö, again a graduate of the department. A series of student projects followed during the coming years. The development of the quality system of the company was later directed by one of the staff and former director of the department, Erkki Koskela, who joined the company in 1988 and became its quality director and later vice executive director. The company eventually became the first software house in Finland to receive the ISO 9001 certificate in 1991.

A favorable development was the growth of Nokia operations in the Oulu region. In the 1980s Nokia had several business divisions in the Oulu region, mainly telecommunications equipment manufacturing (base stations, transmission links, modems, cabling) as well as research and development unit (Nokia Data point of sales terminals) and partial ownership in the Mobira company (later Nokia Mobile Phones). Mobira was finally taken over by Nokia by 1989. Besides pioneering of Nordic NMT cellular mobile phones, US AMPS and UK TACS mobile phone systems had become commercial successes.

GSM system history has been studied in detail in a Research Institute of the Finnish Economy (ETLA, *Elinkeinoelämän Tutkimuslaitos*)[6] report [30] . Basically Nokia had along the pioneering success of analog NMT, AMPS and TACS mobile phone systems become a key player in the development of the second generation digital mobile phone system (GSM) during late 1980s. The development of the GSM

---

[6] ETLA, The Research Institute of the Finnish Economy, http://www.etla.fi/eng/index.php

system was a huge European joint effort that involved hundreds of companies. Nokia was only one of the companies involved. However, through alliances, a focused approach, and commitment it managed to gain a strong position in the GSM development. As an example, in 1988 Nokia entered into an industrial alliance with AEG, Alcatel/SEL and Nokia (ECR consortium) to build, manufacture and sell the GSM base stations. It was a huge task even for Nokia at that time, so a joint effort seemed necessary [30]. However, what was not commonly known at that time, Nokia decided, in parallel to ECR alliance, to develop its own GSM base station. For the Oulu region, Nokia's GSM gamble meant big research and development projects involving several subcontractors.

On the GSM cellular phone development side, Mobira Oulu research and development unit had gained earlier respect for its successfully delivered software development projects. It obtained the required software design expertise from research and academic partners such as VTT and the Department of Information Processing Science. A more detailed report of the knowledge and methodology transfer appears in in "Development in the Growth Base of the 'Oulu Phenomenon'. The role of systems/software methodologies" [18]. After Nokia took over the Mobira company, the software engineering process knowledge was transferred to several other Nokia units. In Oulu, expertise from the Nokia Data point of sales terminal software was contributing to the mobile phone software expertise, for example operating system and input/output systems and user interface skills and expertise were gained from there. During the period from 1988 to 1990, first prototypes of GSM terminal were built by Nokia (electronics were a size to fill a van) and Nokia Oulu software team was heavily involved. They designed the software architecture of the first GSM phones following RTSA/SD (Real-Time Structured Analysis and Design) method [1].

In the late 1980s, Mobira started to expand its operations in Oulu especially through subcontracting [16]. This did not go unnoticed by CCC but it still took more than a year before people at CCC recognized Mobira as a potential customer. The main attention at CCC during late 1980s was spent on the huge international delivery projects to Soviet Union, which came to a sudden end when Soviet Union collapsed in 1991. The first mention of Mobira in the potential customer lists of CCC was in December 1988 and the first projects began over the next few years. The growth of subcontracting was however quite rapid. In less than five years CCC became one of the most important subcontractors of Mobira that had changed its name to Nokia Mobile Phones (NMP) by then and in 1995 about one fifth or fourth of CCCs total software development was directed towards NMP. By then, CCC had gained NMP's respect through its superior software project management and quality knowhow [31].

2.5 Development of Tietomaa and Medipolis

Tietomaa and Medipolis provide some sidetracks in the development of high tech in Oulu, so it is worth taking a brief look at them. The plans for Tietomaa were grand from the first beginning. The first capital stock was two million Finnish marks (about 330 000 euros) and the plan was to increase the capital stock to ten million Finnish marks very rapidly [29]. T total investment need was estimated as 30 million Finnish marks. The City of Oulu decided that it would hold at least 50% of the capital stock.

Eventually when the increase in capital stock was announced, it was undermarked so in 1988 the capital was raised to 8.4 million Finnish marks instead of ten million [51].

The idea was also to build the center in Linnanmaa near the University of Oulu; however, this never happened. Instead Tietomaa originally opened its activities in 1986 in an old garage [59] and finally and permanently in 1988 in an old leather factory[7] both near the center of the city. Descriptive of the high early publicity of the project was that the present managing director, Timo Patja of the Technology Village, gradually withdrew from his position and eventually became the managing director of Tietomaa. High tech companies like Nokia, Datagent, Valmet, FCI Data, Teknoinvest as well as Kunnallistieto and Pohto also joined the center already in 1985 [42].

Eventually, Tietomaa's plan was to build an ICT recreation center or a science center for which the required investment was needed. However, in the beginning Tietomaa concentrated in offering practical ICT courses to professionals working in the industry as well as to laymen interested in the field [21, 54]. The plans were grand in this as well; the ambitious goal was to raise the 3% share of the national education markets that the City of Oulu held at that time to a 6-7% share. Already in 1985 the city government sent the draft training proposal for a request of comment to all relevant parties, including the Department of Information Processing Science [22]. The response of the department was not overenthusiastic; instead the department became active in promoting its own education needs in the public [55]. Tietomaa organized also some ICT conferences from 1985 to 1987 [11, 35, 53, 56]. The education business disappeared from the *Kaleva* headlines quite rapidly, there is no mention of it in *Kaleva* from 1988 to 1990. Officially, the education business was finished in 1991 according to the Tietomaa history web pages[8]. There is no mention of conferences as well from 1988 to 1990 in *Kaleva* so apparently this part of the business disappeared at the same rate.

As a science center, Tietomaa has however been quite successful. In fact Tietomaa was the first science center established in Finland and presently markets Oulu and its know-how nation-wide quite efficiently. The main form of activity presently is the holding of exhibitions which was started already in 1986 [52] and has been continued regularly yearly since 1993 with changing themes.

The road towards Medipolis was started in August 1986 when two biotechnology companies started functioning in the Technology Park [46]. The University of Oulu had already in June 1986 made the decision to establish Oulu Biocenter. Hopes were high for repeating the success of information technology in biotechnology. However even by the present standards, these high hopes were not realized in any meaningful scale and during the late 1980s, progress was minimal.

3 Conclusion

The ICT business climate heated up in Oulu in the latter part of 1980s. The Technology Park grew alongside the electronics and other high technology businesses. About a half of the new jobs however were created outside the Technology Park so its effect

---

[7] Tietomaa. History, http://www.tietomaa.fi/eng/tiedekeskus/historia.html
[8] Ibidem.

in the growth of new business was not during this period as prominent as later in the 1990s. Companies such as Mobira and CCC Software Professionals benefited greatly from the accumulated software and systems development competence, in particular related to conceptual modeling and software process modeling. Knowhow on software engineering methodologies and environments transferred well from academia to companies. This was evident in the case of Nokia Mobile Phones and its early operations in Oulu. The ICT growth further accelerated in the 1990s and it had a remarkable impact on the story of Nokia GSM, when the markets really took off around 1995.

Acknowledgement

We wish to thank Mikko Myllykangas for constructive comments on earlier versions of this paper.

References

[1] Alanko, J.: Partitioning of layered mobile communication software. Licentiate Thesis, University of Oulu, Department of Electrical Engineering (1994)

[2] Architect Jarmo Similä, employee of Laation Arkkitehtitoimisto in the 1980's, communication on February 10 (2007)

[3] ATK-alan yritykset laman puristuksessa – Tilauskanta supistunut, yrityksiä lopetetaan (Companies in adp field pressed by recession – Volume of orders decreased, companies being closed down), Kaleva, 7.8.1991 p. 15 (1991)

[4] Edellytyksiä kyllä on, kunhan niitä käytetään tehokkaasti. Oulusta voidaan rakentaa Suomen teknologiakeskus (There surely are possibilities once they are utilized efficiently. Oulu can be built into technology center of Finland), Kaleva 30.1.1985, p. 16 (1985)

[5] Elektroniikka Oulun seudulla vauhdissa (Electronics going strong in Oulu area), Kaleva 9.7.1988, p. 16 (1988)

[6] Gorbatshovin yllätysvierailun syyt – Oulun teknologia kiinnostaa Tampereen museota enemmän (Reasons of Gorbatshov's surprise visit – Oulu's technology is more interesting than Tampere's museum), Kaleva 27.10.1989, p. 24 (1989)

[7] Julku, L., Julku, K.: Oulun yliopiston perustamisen historia (History of the Founding of the University of Oulu). Pohjois-Suomen Historiallinen Yhdistys, Rovaniemi, p. 274, 294 (1983)

[8] Kaupunki pääosakkaaksi Oulun tietokonemaahan" (City becomes the main shareholder of the Computer Land in Oulu), Kaleva 10.4.1985, p. 6 (1985)

[9] Kehitysyhtiö näkee vielä paljon tekemätöntä työtä: Oululaiset teknologiayritykset vasta kansainvälistymisen ovella (Development company sees a lot of work to be done: Oulu's technology companies only at the door of internationalization), Kaleva 16.6.1988, p. 19 (1988)

[10] Keskiviikkona perustettu Oulun Teknologiakylä Oy selvä osoitus: Oulun elinkeinopolitiikkaa kehitetään nyt tarmokkaasti (The Technology Park founded on Wednesday gives a clear sign: Oulu's industrial policy is now being developed vigorously), Kaleva, 1.4.1982, p. 18 (1982)

[11] Kotien tietokoneistus uuden askeleen edessä" (Home computerization faces with a new step), Kaleva 20.8.1987, p. 15 (1987)

206   H. Oinas-Kukkonen et al.

[12] Manninen, T.: "Kasvun aika: Oulu 1945 – 1990", Oulun vuosisadat 1605—2005 ("Period of growth: Oulu 1945 – 1990", Oulu's centuries 1605 – 2005). Pohjois-Suomen Historiallinen Yhdistys, Rovaniemi, p. 151, 152 (2005)

[13] Mobira hajasijoitti ohjelmistoryhmän Ouluun (Mobira decentralized its software group into Oulu), Kaleva 12.10.1985, p. 20 (1985)

[14] Nokia rakentaa mittavan tutkimuskeskuksen Ouluun (Nokia will build a large research center in Oulu), Kaleva 17.3.1987, p. 22 (1987)

[15] Nokia-Mobira laajentaa: Ouluun matkapuhelimien kokonaiskehittelyä (Nokia-Mobira is expanding: whole development of mobile phones into Oulu), Kaleva 13.8.1988, p. 18 (1988)

[16] Nokia-Mobiran Erkki Veikkolainen: Tieto-taidon myynnillä Oulussa nykyistä enemmän markkinoita (Nokia-Mobira's Erkki Veikkolainen: through selling the know-how more markets than presently in Oulu), Kaleva 26.5.1988, p. 22 (1988)

[17] Oinas-Kukkonen, H.: Moderni ja monipuolinen 'haitekkikaupunki'. Oulun vuosisadat 1605—2005 (Modern and versatile hightech city. Oulu's centuries 1605—2005). Pohjois-Suomen Historiallinen Yhdistys, Rovaniemi, pp. 179–181 (2005)

[18] Oinas-Kukkonen, H., Similä, J., Kerola, P., Pulli, P., Saukkonen, S.: Development in the Growth Base of the 'Oulu Phenomenon'. The role of systems/software methodologies. In: Bubenko, J., Impagliazzo, J., Sølvberg, A. (eds.) History of Nordic Computing. IFIP WG9.7 First Working Conference on the History of Nordic Computing (HiNC1), Trondheim, Norway, June 16-18, 2003. IFIP International Federation for Information Processing, vol. 174, pp. 425–447. Springer, New York (2005)

[19] Oinas-Kukkonen, H., Similä, J., Pulli, P.: Main Threads of ICT Innovation in Oulu in 1960—1990. In: Proceedings of Session 90, IEHC 2006, XIV International Economic History Congress, Helsinki, Finland, August 21-25, 2006, vol. 19, p. 2, 18, 19 (2006), http://www.helsinki.fi/iehc2006/sessions81_124.html

[20] Ohjelmistotuotantoa suunnataan ulos pääkaupunkiseudulta – Oulussa alan koulutusta laajennetaan ensi vuonna (Software production channeled out from capital city area – education in the field will be expanded in Oulu next year), Kaleva 13.10.1988, p. 22 (1988)

[21] Oulu aikoo merkittäväksi tietotekniikan kouluttajaksi (Oulu aims at becoming major information technology educator), Kaleva 9.4.1986, p. 24 (1986)

[22] Oulu selvittää tietotekniikan koulutusta (Oulu investigates information technology education), Kaleva 4.5.1985, p. 5 (1985)

[23] Oulu yhtenä vaihtoehtona – ATK-alan yritykset haluavat maakuntiin (Oulu as an alternative – Companies in ADP field aspire for provinces), Kaleva 8.6.1988, p. 5 (1988)

[24] Oululainen ohjelmistotalo teki miljoonakaupan Neuvostoliittoon (An Oulu-based software house made a million sale into Soviet Union), Kaleva 23.8.1988, p. 16 (1988)

[25] Oululaiset teknologiayritykset luoneet parissa vuodessa 600 uutta työpaikkaa (Technology companies in Oulu have created 600 new jobs in a couple of years), Kaleva 6.10.1986, p. 11 (1986)

[26] Oulun Teknologiakylä kasvaa huimaa vauhtia (Oulu Technology Park is growing with a wild pace), Kaleva 20.5.1986, p. 15 (1986)

[27] Oulun Teknologiakylä paisuu Linnanmaalle (Oulu Technology Park expands into Linnanmaa), Kaleva 25.1.1986, p. 19 (1986)

[28] Oulun Teknologiakylän on pysyttävä virkeänä – Etumatkan varmistaminen noussut haasteeksi (Oulu Technology Park has to stay alert – Securing the head start risen as a challenge), Kaleva 19.6.1986, p. 15 (1986)

[29] Oulun Tietokonemaa nytkähtää liikkeelle (Computer Land of Oulu is jerked in motion), Kaleva 11.4.1985, p. 15 (1985)

[30] Palmberg, C., Martikainen, O.: Overcoming a technological discontinuity: the case if the Finnish telecom industry and the GSM (Helsinki: Research Institute of the Finnish Economy, 2003), 55 pp. Discussion Papers no. 855 (2003)

[31] Personal archives of Jouni Similä, Technical Director of CCC from 1987 to 1997

[32] Philips hajauttaa Ouluun ohjelmistosuunnitteluaan (Philips decentralizes its software design into Oulu, Kaleva 23.6.1988, p. 19 (1988)

[33] Private communication on April 5 (2007)

[34] Professor Samuli Saukkonen, communication on February 10 (2007)

[35] Publicum -87 tuo Ouluun tietotekniikan uutuudet – Vastauksia käytännön ongelmiin (Publicum -87 brings the new information technology to Oulu – Answers for practical problems), Kaleva 24.7.1987, p. 14 (1987)

[36] Rautaruukille New Technology – yksikkö Oulun Teknologiakylään (A New Technology unit for Rautaruukki into Oulu Technology Park), Kaleva 27.5.1988, p. 16 (1988)

[37] Salo, M.: Pohjoinen Alma mater. Oulun yliopisto osana korkeakoululaitosta ja yhteiskuntaa perustamisvaiheista vuoteen 2000 (Alma Mater of the North. Role of the University of Oulu in higher education and in society). Pohjois-Suomen Historiallinen Yhdistys, Rovaniemi, p. 15, 252 (2000)

[38] Similä, J., Saukkonen, S.: How to Teach Project Working Capabilities for Information Technology Students at the University Level. In: Proceedings of the ISSEU 1997 International Symposium on Software Engineering in Universities, Rovaniemi, Finland, March 6-8 (1997)

[39] Sitran tutkimus etsii uudesta riskirahoitusmallista kiriherkkyyttä menestystarinaan: Ouluilmiön" jatkuvalle voimistumiselle löytyy yhä paikallista ja tehokasta potkuvoimaa (Sitra's research searches spurt responsiveness from a new risk financing model for the success story: Continuous enhancement of the "Oulu phenomenon" is still finding local and efficient sparking power), Kaleva 29.8.1988, p. 11 (1988)

[40] Suomen teknologiakeskukset kurkottavat – Oululaiset asettaneet tavoitteensa korkeimmalle (Finnish technology centers reach out – Oulu has set its goals the highest), Kaleva 7.9.1988, p. 22 (1988)

[41] Suuria ATK-taloja kiinnostaa toimintojen sijoittaminen Ouluun (Large ADP houses interested in relocating their activities in Oulu), Kaleva 27.5.1988, p. 16 (1988)

[42] Teknologiakaupunki Ouluun perustettiin Tietokonemaa (Computer Land has been established in the Technology City of Oulu), Kaleva 20.5.1985, p. 15 (1985)

[43] Teknologiakaupunkikuvaa vahvistetaan (The image of Technology City is strengthened), Kaleva 30.1.1985, p. 10 (1985)

[44] Teknologiakylä aloittaa rakentamisen Linnanmaalla (Technology Park will begin contruction work in Linnanmaa), Kaleva 26.9.1985, p. 18 (1985)

[45] Teknologiakylän anti alkamassa (Issuing of shares of Technology Park about to start), Kaleva 19.4.1989, p. 18 (1989)

[46] Teknologiakylässä aloittaa kaksi biotekniikan yritystä (Two biotech companies about to start operations in the Technology Park), Kaleva 14.8.1986, p. 15 (1986)

[47] Teknologiaprojektien vauhti ei laannu Oulussa (The pace of technology projects not slackening in Oulu), Kaleva 9.4.1986, p. 24 (1986)

[48] Teknopolis Linnanmaa rakentaa tietoverkkoa – Kaksi uutta yritystaloa rakenteilla (Technopolis Linnanmaa builds data network – Two new company buildings under construction), Kaleva 30.7.1987, p. 11 (1987)

208   H. Oinas-Kukkonen et al.

[49] Telenokiasta Teknologiakylän suurin yksikkö – Rakentaminen aloitetaan ensi kesänä (Telenokia to become largest unit in Technology Park – Construction will begin next summer), Kaleva 20.11.1987, p. 17 (1987)

[50] Tietokonemaasta tulee oululaisen osaamisen kaivattu käyntikortti (Computer Land will become the longed-for business card for Oulu's know-how), Kaleva 24.8.1985, p. 15 (1985)

[51] Tietomaa ei ole koskaan valmis (Tietomaa is never finished), Kaleva 11.6.1988, p. 7 (1988)

[52] Tietomaa haastaa elokuun näyttelyllä – Suomalainen tietotekniikan koulutus vielä lähtökuopissaan (Tietomaa challenges with the August exhibition – Finnish information technology education still in the starting pit), Kaleva 17.7.1986, p. 16 (1986)

[53] Tietomaa kokosi atk:n asiantuntijat Ouluun (Tietomaa gathered adp experts in Oulu), Kaleva 7.8.1986, p. 19 (1986)

[54] Tietomaa kouluttaa P-Suomea mikromaailmaan (Tietomaa training the Northern Finland into the microworld), Kaleva 21.4.1986, p. 17 (1986)

[55] Tietotekniikan koulutusmäärät eivät juuri nouse (The numbers of information technology education are not really rising), Kaleva, 14.5.1985, p. 7 (1985)

[56] Tietotekniikan soveltaminen meille sopiva toimintakenttä (Applying information technology a suitable field of action for us), Kaleva 21.8.1987, p. 16 (1987)

[57] Tunkelo, E.: Oulun teknologiakylä 1980—1988. Miten syntyi Oulu-ilmiö? (Oulu Technology Park 1980—1988. How was the Oulu phenomenon born?). Suomen Itsenäisyyden Juhlavuoden 1967 rahasto, 1988, Oulu, p. 1 (1988)

[58] Työvoimaministeriö auraa ATK-taloille tietä Ouluun (Ministry of Labour plows way for ADP houses in Oulu), Kaleva 28.6.1988, p. 15 (1988)

[59] Vanhasta autokorjaamosta Oulun Tietomaan lähtöalusta (An old garage becomes the foundation for Oulu's Tietomaa), Kaleva 4.11.1985, p. 5 (1985)

[60] VTT: n talo rakenteilla Oulun Linnanmaalla (VTT's building under construction in Oulu's Linnanmaa), Kaleva 26.8.1987, p. 1 (1987)

[61] VTT: n tuleva pääjohtaja Markku Mannerkoski – Suomi kaipaa huipputekniikkaa tuottavaa omaa teollisuutta (VTT's future general director Markku Mannerkoski – Finland needs its own industry that produces top technology), Kaleva 20.3.1987, p. 16 (1987)

Reflections of Computing Experiences in a Steel Factory in the Early 1960s

Pertti Järvinen

Department of Computer Sciences, FIN-33014 University of Tampere, Finland
pj@cs.uta.fi

Abstract. We can best see many things from a historical perspective. What were the first pioneers doing in the information technology departments of Finnish manufacturing companies? In early 1960s, I had a special chance to work in a steel industry that had long traditions to use rather advanced tools and methods to intensify their productivity. The first computer in our company had such novel properties as movable disk packs making a direct access of stored data possible. In this paper, we describe the following issues and innovations in some depth. These include (a) transitioning from the punched card machines to a new computer era, (b) using advanced programming language to intensify production of new computer software, (c) drawing pictures by using a line printer, (d) supporting steel making with mathematical software, (e) storing executable programs to the disk memory and calling and moving them from there to the core memory for running, and (f) building a simple report generator. I will also pay attention to the breakthrough in those innovations and in this way demonstrate how some computing solutions were growing at that time.

Keywords: Report generator, Virtual memory, Path dependency.

1 Introduction

Mason et al. [18] said that historical analyses broaden our understanding of those processes by which information technology is introduced into organizations and of the forces that shape its use. They use the expression "dominant design" to describe a new configuration of an organization's technology, strategy, and structure. A dominant design is manifested in several ways: a new organizational infrastructure, new functionality, new products, new services, new production functions, or new cost structures. By changing the basis of competition in the industry, a firm that institutes a dominant design secures an initial competitive edge. According to Mason et al. [18] the Information Systems (IS) research literature contains very few examples of historical analyses.

This paper describes some key issues and a few computing solutions to shed light on a pioneer manufacturing company and its first years to utilize a computer. According to Mason et al. [19] historical research offers perspectives on phenomena that are unavailable by any other methodological means. They reflect the cultural circumstances and ideological assumptions that underlie phenomena and the role played by key decision makers together with long-term economic, social, and political forces in

J. Impagliazzo, T. Järvi, and P. Paju (Eds.): HiNC 2, IFIP AICT 303, pp. 209–216, 2009.
© IFIP International Federation for Information Processing 2009

creating them. Based on my recent efforts at collecting various research methods [13], I can say that a historical method is a rarity in the methodological information systems literature.

The rest of the paper consists of the following topics: introduction to the computer usage, FORTRAN programs for administrative purposes, visualizing some reports, supporting the making of stainless steel by computer, towards a primitive operating system and the computer-aided development of reporting software.

2 Transitioning from the Punched Card Machines to the Computer Era

My description concerns the OVAKO steel factory at Imatra in Finland. In 1963, the company bought its first computer, an IBM 1401 with a punched card reader, line printer, operator console, and four discs units with movable disk packs. The latter were rather new. The IBM marketing men and consultants said that it was then the second newest computer with the same sort in Europe. To relate our hardware with some other installations at the same period, I refer to McKenney et al. [20] who mentioned IBM 1401 in their famous case of Bank of America, where they describe the way they used magnetic tapes for storing bank accounts at that bank. The Bank of America nicely describes both the path dependency [5] and the importance of the selection decision in transitions from the earlier hardware generation to the next generation.

In 1963, I began working with three other IT colleagues. I consider those colleagues as IT experts because they were the only people who could design and execute computer programs. My colleagues, because of their economic education, implemented such administrative applications as payroll, invoicing, order processing, bookkeeping, and budgeting. The company hired me because my scores in the IBM programmer test were acceptably high. My job concerned industrial applications, because as a mathematician, I also had some knowledge of physics and chemistry. My working period started June 1st, about three months before the installation of IBM 1401. I participated in the FORTRAN programming course organized by IBM.

An important observation was that the earlier punched card experts were not able to move easily to the computer time, although our computer used punched cards as input media. The stored program and especially disk memory were quite strange to punched card experts. For example, the chief of the earlier punched card department had designed a new payroll system for a computer, and he based his sketch of the new system upon seventeen sum-cards. The latter meant that the intermediate results in a particular phase of wage calculation process were stored to a new card (sum-card) which was thereafter punched as an intermediate output and later read as an intermediate input for the next phase of that calculation. This example demonstrates that "when novelty increases, the path-dependent nature of knowledge has negative effects because the common knowledge used in the past may not have the capacity to represent novelties now present" [5].

3 FORTRAN Programs for Administrative Purposes

In different places of the factory, there were certain people (more than thirty in continuous three-shift-work) for performing production inspection (PI). Those PI people recorded every event and state-transition considered important. Based on their data, they manually generated different kinds of production and deviation reports.

The new computer was very expensive. The local management wished to produce visible results as soon as possible. For programming, there were two compilers available, one for an assembly language (called Autocoder) and another one for the FORTRAN language, mainly intended for mathematical calculations. The expressions for input and output in FORTRAN were very restricted and simple, but the language itself was quite easy to learn. Although with Autocoder language it was possible to read all kinds of special markings punched on cards, and although in Autocoder there were especially a wide range of expressions for printed output, it demanded a rather long time to become familiar with all the features of Autocoder. Therefore, at the beginning of my job as a programmer I selected FORTRAN, which I used in my programming efforts. My first task was to develop the computer programs that would produce similar reports on production and exceptional events as was earlier done manually. About one year later, I changed those FORTRAN programs to the Autocoder programs with better output quality.

4 Drawing by Using a Line Printer

In a steel making process, they cast molten steel into moulds and after solidifying, they removed the ingots and set down to thermal ingot furnaces for two to four hours before lifting them up for rolling. The number of thermal ingot furnaces was about five. The company described their "used capacity" as a percent share for each hour each day as a figure, that earlier one worker drew manually. The production inspection people recorded all the processing phases of ingots and in this way produced the raw data for the drawing. They produced a figure for the used capacity of all the thermal ingot furnaces once a day.

To produce the same figure with computer was not a trivial task, although there were times by the clock of ingots both when set down and when lifted up. Some ingots were not immediately placed into the ingot heating furnaces but they were allowed to cool completely. Later, they would take them into the ingot heating furnace. Their heating would then require many hours and the heating period could continue from one calendar day to the next. They would have to reconstruct the development of the ingot heating furnace history of the previous day at the beginning of each day. The consideration of clock times required a special care in the program. The local manager, the main user of the figure, gave strong criticism based on bad appearance in the first versions of those figures.

I later saw how the Cascade project [1] built a graph production system. Its purpose was to produce a hardcopy version of information analysis documentation in a proper format. Documentation consisted of tables, matrices, and graphs.

5 Manufacturing Stainless Steel

The main part of steel production from the factory was for different construction steels and for railway building as rails and base plates. Although small, the relative portion of stainless steel was increasing. The main part of stainless steel had type 18/8 or 18/10; it means that percent of chromium (a rather expensive raw material) is 18% while the percent of nickel is 8% or 10%. In addition, the acid sustainable steel contained a small amount of molybdenum about 3%, a very expensive raw material. We now describe the way I utilized computer calculations in the manufacturing of stainless steel.

In the production of steel, the starting point is scrap. Occasionally, they use a small portion of iron ore. They first place the scrap into a furnace and with the use of electricity, the scrap melts. From the melted batch, they do a chemical analysis. In the factory, they built a very efficient arrangement with pneumatic mail for taking this analysis in the chemical laboratory. It took only two minutes. After knowing the content of the initial batch, they add suitable amounts of different additional materials (e.g. Ni, FeCr, FeMo, SiCr and CaSi for slack reduction [15]) to the initial batch. Before adding new materials, and if necessary, the company removes the harmful material.

In the process of making stainless steel, the company could obtain chromium and nickel from the initial batch or from different additional materials that might contain different contents of chromium and nickel. The experts of stainless steel knew that all the chromium and nickel that existed in the additional materials would transfer to the final stainless steel. This fact helped in the calculations because it influenced the amount of additional materials added into the initial batch. We could mathematically describe this problem as a system of seven equations.

After discussion with the technical supervisor of the smelting department, I had developed a computer program to solve the system of seven equations. In practice, after doing the chemical analysis of the initial batch and making the transfer to the furnace, the supervisor made a telephone call to the computer room to report the results of the analysis. The operator then entered those analysis data into my program by using the computer console. It took about thirty seconds to calculate and print the result back to the console. The message was something as, "Please add m kg of material A, n kg of material B, etc." They kept the telephone line open and after the results were ready, the operator told the result to the supervisor.

During the first series of stainless steel making, they produced about 25 smelting charges. The technical boss was at the smelting plant and I was in the computer room. Manufacturing of one batch took about 4 hours to make, so the first series took more than one week to make. Sometimes both the technical boss and I had to wake up in the middle of night for taking care of this calculation. Nevertheless, I was happy because all the batches made went inside of the very tight limits, i.e. no smelting batch was a scrap.

In steel industry Fabian [8, 9] rather early in the 1950s applied linear programming to all stages of steel making – from coal and ore through finished products. Some sub model is close to the one I had prepared. Fabian's largest process model covers the whole production. One expert in operations research, Bo Nyholm, encouraged me to consider a similar model, but the complexity of product assortment with many production paths on the one hand and the shortage of computer memory and suitable program package on the other hand prevented realization of our attempt.

6 Systems and Applications Programs: From Punched Cards to Disk Storage

The sorting program produced by IBM for our IBM 1401 computer filled two cases, about 4000 punched cards. It would take many minutes to load the cards from the card reader into the core memory. When I followed the reading process, I found that the card reader was reading about half of the cards at the steady rate. After a more careful study, I found that those cards belonged to a sub program intended for sorting data on magnetic tapes, but we did not have any tape unit. I removed those cards, and thereafter the sorting program functioned correctly in our context with four disc units.

The reduced set of the punched cards belonging to our sorting program was still rather large. Its input from the card reader took a long time. Therefore, I continued my studies to shorten the loading time. I had an idea to locate the sorting program to a disc unit. After recording it in the disc unit, the sorting program, I could move the sorting program to the core memory by a short and simple call from the console. The operators were happy, because they saved time in two respects. The loading time was then shorter than before, and the loading always succeeded which was not always true with punched cards. After many repeated usage times they got worse and created a jam in the card reader.

After my first successful trial to utilize disk memory for the sorting program, I applied the same idea to my application programs. I recorded them into the disk memory and I could call them by name from the operators' console. At the same time, I eliminated the so-called IOCS (Input Output Control System) cards from the front of the program cards. Later, I understood that those IOCS cards were the beginning of an operating system, and my arrangement was in fact a simple operating system.

The next step forward was to avoid the upper limit of the core memory of 12K. I compiled my large program as components and located every component to the disk memory. When executing the large program, I read, or my main program read, one component after another from the disk to the core memory. In this way, I could prepare about 100K program and execute it without any problem. Later, I understood that I had applied an idea of the virtual memory and its static (pre-planned) approach to storage allocation [6].

7 A Simple Report Generator

The first programming tasks were to read a set of punched cards and to write a report. Later, a major part of report requests concerned data in different files stored on disks. The structure of a reporting program was somewhat similar. This created a desire to automate my programming efforts. Hence, I developed a special program for reporting purposes. Later, I recognized that I in fact developed a simple report generator.

It was possible to give the name of a sorted file as a parameter for my report generator. In addition, a user would give the names of data items moved from the file into the report. The order of the data items determined the presentation order of the output form. One could compute a certain output item from stored data items. The way to perform those computations could have a representation as a "mathematical" formula allowing addition, subtraction, multiplication and division operations in addition to brackets. My report program interpreted and evaluated the expression in run time and produced an output to a certain location on the report. We could count the general or total sums and the intermediate sums. After leaving the steel factory 1967, I heard [21] that they used my report generator for many years to do various kinds of tasks; it also functioned as a simple spreadsheet.

The most demanding task in the development of the report generator was an evaluation of the mathematical expression. Later I understood that I in fact solved the problem of the way to transform recursions into iterations ([16], p. 37).

Our report generator differed from ordinary application programs in many ways because it had interpretive flexibility. Doherty et al. [7] define interpretive flexibility as the capacity of a specific technology to sustain divergent opinions. They have also found that

> *"… all technologies offer a range of functions and features that will facilitate some activities, while inhibiting others. Based upon the evidence from the empirical study, it became clear that there were upper and lower limits with respect to the functions that the system supported, and that these boundaries constrained the way in which the technology could be interpreted. More specifically, it was possible to discern, what we have termed, 'enforcing constraints' that make certain elements of the system's functionality mandatory. At the opposite end of the spectrum, it was also possible to identify 'proscribing constraints' that delineate the functions that do not exist, or for whatever reason cannot be used."*

Because our report generator was more flexible than any single report program, its interpretive flexibility was much larger than any report program, or it cannot be included into the domain of the interpretive flexibility concept at all.

My report generator was the first step in the sequence of my trials in computer-aided design of information systems. The next step in early 1980s was a simple file generator that demonstrated how it was easier to support human memory by computing systems than human data processing [12]. My group's last step in late 1980s was to develop an application generator, Genera [14]. It was similar to an interpreter capable of analyzing and executing Pascal-type specifications. We could quickly generate some twenty to thirty applications with Genera until the commercial application generators made it obsolete.

8   Discussion

In this work, we demonstrated that the transition from punched card machines to a computer made big changes in storing data. Computers can support people's memory with storage media allowing quick storing and retrieval properties. We also showed how the third generation programming language, even such one intended to mathematical calculations, could intensify software production compared with the traditional solution of that time, an assembly language. To eliminate manual work I used the computer to draw some figures. The only device for that purpose was the line printer, not very suitable for such a task.

In addition to those primitive and easy computer applications, we also used a computer for some demanding tasks. Firstly, to solve a set of seven equations is impossible with paper and pencil at the blast furnace with noise and heat. In this task, the computer is superior compared with a human being. We then also demonstrated networking in the germinal form. Secondly, we utilized the disk memory of our computer to improve operators' work by storing our programs to disk and calling them into running from there. Our advances are clearly steps towards modern operating systems. Thirdly, we developed a report generator with spreadsheet facilities. In our construction, we needed knowledge later theorized in connection with compilers.

Gaines and Shaw [10] were a few of the first researchers who performed a historical analysis of hardware/software, state of artificial intelligence and state of human-computer interaction. They structured their analysis into eight years periods based on new generations of IBM big computers. They especially studied consecutive phases of the development of human-computer interaction. They used the model of the six eras as follows:

> *"Each technology ... seems to follow a course in which a breakthrough leads to successive eras: first replications in which the breakthrough results are copied widely; second empiricism in which pragmatic rules for good design are generated from experience; third theory in which the increasing number of pragmatic rules leads to the development of deeper principles that generate them; fourth automation in design based on the theory; finally leading to an era of maturity and mass production based on the automation and resulting in a rapid cost decline."*

By referring to the model of six eras I can say that my innovations or breakthroughs can be found in the computer literature, but were not available at our company. Few people (if any) in Finland then knew those innovations and their design concepts [22]. Knowledge and algorithms concerning construction of compilers [2, 3] and operating systems [4] were already published in the scientific literature in the 1960s and early 1970s. But the March and Smith's seminal article of design research [17] was published as late as 1995. That article outlines what is design science in information systems, and what are the potential results. March and Smith first wrote that in addition to new design knowledge the new instantiations also can be accepted as research outcomes. Hevner et al. [11] later supported that claim.

I know that this paper has its specific limitation, i.e., it is based on personal memories. But I am happy that I could send the draft to two of my colleagues from that time (Managers Kostamo [15] and Ruotsi [21]) for verification. They both confirmed my text. Another limitation is that my contributions are based on one case only. But to my mind, it is not a very severe shortcoming, because my contributions belong to design research. Instead of providing mathematical or statistical evidence for my tentative contributions, which is normal in mathematics or social and natural sciences, I "proved" my contributions by demonstration. For example, it was possible to satisfy most of the report requests by my report generator.

References

[1] Aanstad, P., Skylstad, G., Sølvberg, A.: Cascade – a computer-based documentation system. In: Bubenko, J., Langefors, B., Sølvberg, A. (eds.) Computer-Aided Information Systems Analysis and Design, pp. 93–118. Studentlitteratur, Lund (1971)

[2] Aho, A.V., Ullman, J.D.: The Theory of Parsing, Translation and Compiling. Parsing, vol. I. Prentice-Hall, Englewood Cliffs (1972)

[3] Aho, A.V., Ullman, J.D.: The Theory of Parsing, Translation and Compiling. Compiling, vol. II. Prentice-Hall, Englewood Cliffs (1973)

[4] Brinch Hansen, P.: Operating System Principles. Prentice Hall, Englewood Cliffs (1973)

[5] Cohen, W.M., Levinthal, D.A.: Absorptive capacity: A new perspective on learning and innovation. Administrative Science Quarterly 35(1), 128–152 (1990)

[6] Denning, P.: Virtual memory. Computing Surveys 2(3), 153–189 (1970)

[7] Doherty, N.F., Coombs, C.R., Loan-Clarke, J.: A re-conceptualization of the interpretive flexibility of information technologies: Redressing the balance between the social and the technical. European Journal of Information Systems 15(6), 569–582 (2006)

[8] Fabian, T.: A linear programming model of integrated iron and steel production. Management Science 4(4), 415–449 (1958)

[9] Fabian, T.: Process analysis of the U.S. iron and steel industry. In: Manne, A.S., Markowitz, H.M. (eds.) Proceedings of a Conference sponsored by the Cowles Foundation for Research in Economics at Yale University, April 24-26, 1961, pp. 237–263. Wiley, New York (1963), http://cowles.econ.yale.edu/P/cm/m18/m18-09.pdf

[10] Gaines, B.R., Shaw, M.L.G.: From timesharing to the sixth generation: the development of human-computer interaction. Part I. International Journal of Man-Machine Studies 24(1), 1–24 (1986)

[11] Hevner, A.R., March, S.T., Park, J., Ram, S.: Design science in information systems research. MIS Quarterly 28(1), 75–105 (2004)

[12] Järvinen, P.: The ABC System – A Collection of Research Articles, Report A112. Department of Mathematical Sciences. University of Tampere, Tampere (1983)

[13] Järvinen, P.: On Research Methods. Opinpajan kirja, Tampere (2004)

[14] Järvinen, P., Kiukkonen, P., Koskivirta, M., Välimäki, H.: How flexible software could support learning? Presented in Social implications of home interactive telematics (HIT) conference, Amsterdam, June 24-27, p. 16 (1987)

[15] Kostamo, P.: Manager of Steel Department 2007, interview 19.2.2007 (2007)

[16] Kurki-Suonio, R.: Computability and Formal Languages. Studentlitteratur, Lund (1971)

[17] March, S.T., Smith, G.F.: Design and natural science research on information technology. Decision Support Systems 15(4), 251–266 (1995)

[18] Mason, R.O., McKenney, J.L., Copeland, D.G.: Developing an historical tradition in MIS research. MIS Quarterly 21(3), 257–278 (1997)

[19] Mason, R.O., McKenney, J.L., Copeland, D.G.: An historical method for MIS research: Steps and assumptions. MIS Quarterly 21(3), 307–320 (1997)

[20] McKenney, J.L., Mason, R.O., Copeland, D.G.: Bank of America: The crest and trough of technological leadership. MIS Quarterly 21(3), 321–353 (1997)

[21] Ruotsi, E.: Manager of Production Inspection Department, interview 13.11.2006 (2006)

[22] van Aken, J.E.: Management research based on the paradigm of the design sciences: The quest for field-tested and grounded technological rules. Journal of Management Studies 41(2), 219–246 (2004)

Early Use of the Computer for Adjusting Triangulation in Iceland

Gunnar Thorbergsson

Formerly surveyor at Orkustofnun, Iceland
g@os.is

Abstract. Triangulation for long has been the backbone of land surveying and mapping. This work outlines its history in Iceland and provides an example of observations and computation in a triangulation network before the computer era came of age. The work describes briefly a computer program written in 1965 for the adjustment of observations in triangulation networks and mentions later improvements of the program.

Keywords: Iceland, surveying, triangulation, adjustment.

1 Introduction

People believe that the ancient Egyptians practiced land surveying, but triangulation, theodolites, and least squares adjustments are more recent. Willebrord Snellius (1580–1626) measured a network of 33 triangles early in the 17th century and the theodolite, an optical instrument for observing horizontal and vertical angles, was developed later in that century. Carl Friedrich Gauss (1777–1855) did triangulation work and invented the method of least squares.

Danish authorities had the coastal areas in Iceland surveyed and mapped in the beginning of the 19th century. Björn Gunnlaugsson (1788–1876), an Icelandic mathematician, surveyed and mapped the interior in the years 1831–1843. The Danish general staff started a new triangulation and mapping of Iceland in scale 1:100,000 in the year 1900. Geodætisk Institut concluded this work in 1939, while Iceland was still part of Denmark [3]. The governments of the United States, Denmark, and Iceland financed a first order triangulation of Iceland in 1955–56 [2]. See Figure 1.

Orkustofnun (National Energy Authority) started land surveying shortly before the middle of the 20th century. Extensive leveling networks were established and new triangulation networks were connected to the first order network from 1955–56. The National Land Survey of Iceland started aerial photography in 1955 and from that time, Orkustofnun used aerial photographs in its mapping projects. We established ground control for mapping in scale 1:20,000 with 5m contour intervals of large areas, and for maps in larger scale of smaller areas. We did this work for the purpose of hydropower development. Before the end of the century, we had surveyed about one-third of the country, mainly in its interior, and mapped a quarter of the country in this way; however we subcontracted the photogrammetry work to various Icelandic and Scandinavian engineering firms.

J. Impagliazzo, T. Järvi, and P. Paju (Eds.): HiNC 2, IFIP AICT 303, pp. 217–224, 2009.
© IFIP International Federation for Information Processing 2009

2 Adjustment before the Computer Era

In the summer of 1962 surveyors at Orkustofnun did triangulation and leveling work at Búrfell where Landsvirkjun (The National Power Company) was going to build a hydro power plant. In the spring of 1963, the adjustment of the triangulation was not finished and the author worked long hours computing in order to finish a report and then get out in the field. His coworkers had already left for the northwest of Iceland where they would spend the summer and where he wanted to be, but engineers needed the results of the surveying at Búrfell during the summer.

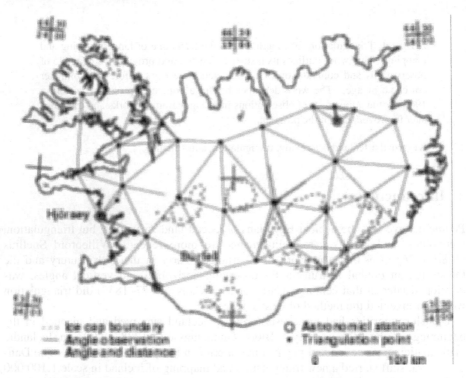

Fig. 1. Observations in the first order triangulation network in Iceland were made in 1955–56 by Geodætisk Institut of Denmark with the assistance of the National Land Survey of Iceland. The network adjustment took place in Denmark. The *Hjörsey geodetic datum of 1955*, named after an astronomical station in the network, was used by surveyors working in the latter half of the 20th century. Búrfell is the site of a hydro power plant built in 1966–69.

The author used an electromechanical calculator, pen, and paper for the calculations. The repetitive nature of the task, but especially the author's wish to be elsewhere, made him seriously consider its future automation by means of an electronic computer.

2.1 Background

The geoid is a property of the gravity field of the earth [9]. At sea, it roughly coincides with mean sea level. The Hayford reference ellipsoid used in the Hjörsey geodetic datum has a standard form, but its location and orientation were determined mainly by astronomical observations in 1955, to approximate the geoid locally in the region of Iceland. After Danish surveyors established the first order network, Icelandic surveyors, when computing in the Hjörsey geodetic datum, assumed that the local normal to the ellipsoid and the local vertical axis at a point coincide.

When observing at a triangulation point (the station), where a theodolite has been set up, centered and leveled, the observer can rotate the upper part of the theodolite with the telescope about the vertical axis, but the lower part contains the horizontal circle at rest in the *horizontal plane* of the station.

A triangulation network has triangulation points and lines of sight joining them in three dimensions. Each point of the network, a triangulation point or a point on a line of sight, is projected along the local normal onto the surface of the ellipsoid, where a second network is produced. The surface of the ellipsoid is projected by means of a mathematical formula, Lambert's conformal conical projection, onto the *projection plane*, where a third network is created. The images of the lines of sight are curves and the observed horizontal angles (in the first network) are reproduced unchanged as angles between (tangents to) these curves. Since this is complicated, geodesists preferred to replace the curves with straight lines and a fourth and final network is created. From the actual observations in the three-dimensional network and approximate coordinates in this fourth network, geodesists have deduced formulas for computing the so-called reduced observations which may be treated as if they were observations made in the two-dimensional space of the projection plane.

2.2 Field Work

The fieldwork culminated in observations of horizontal angles at the triangulation points. A simplified description of the observations at a station is to say that the field operator aimed the theodolite at the targets (the distant triangulation points) in clockwise order and

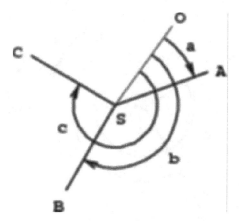

Fig. 2. The horizontal plane at triangulation point S: Triangulation points A, B, and C are observable targets. The lines of sight are projected vertically onto the horizontal plane where they meet the horizontal circle (at rest during observations) in graduations or numbers a, b, and c. The line SO passes through zero on the horizontal circle. The numbers a, b, and c are recorded in the field book. They are a set of direction readings. In this case, the number of targets, which must be less than eight, is three.

read the horizontal circle each time. (In fact, we repeated this twelve times and then computed the means). This gave one *set of direction readings* (see Figure 2). By this method of observation adjacent angles (b – a and c – b in Figure 2) are correlated but the direction readings are not. To observe the adjacent angles in an uncorrelated manner would require a more complicated procedure of observations in the field.

2.3 Office Work

The most time consuming part of the office work was adjustment of observations. In *adjustment of indirect observations* [8] in a triangulation network, the horizontal co-ordinates of the unknown points are to be determined in a way that minimizes the sum of squares of observation residues. We previously computed the heights above the reference ellipsoid of all points in the network and during the adjustment considered the heights known. The author used this variant of adjustment in the computation of the horizontal coordinates of triangulation points at Búrfell.

We computed the initial coordinates for the unknown points, usually by forward section from two known or already computed points. Denoting the initial coordinates of point P_i by (X_i, Y_i), they would later become $(X_i + x_i, Y_i + y_i)$, where x_i and y_i are coordinate changes to be found by adjustment. In this *initial network*, with some points with known coordinates and unknown points with initial coordinates, distances and directions were carefully computed.

We reduced each observation so that the *reduced observation* became as if we had made it in the straight-edged network in the plane. These reductions were made using precomputed tables and diagrams. The reductions take into account the curvature of the

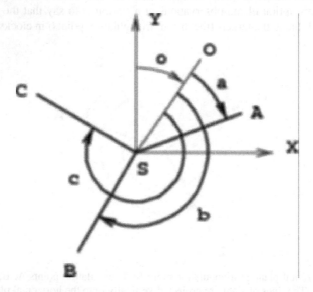

Fig. 3. The projection plane: S is the image of a station joined by straight lines to the images of targets A, B, and C. Line SO passes through zero on the image of the horizontal circle. Angles a, b, and c are *reduced observations*. The unknown angle o, clockwise from the Y-axis to the line SO, is named *orientation constant*. The observed direction angles or *directions* to the targets are o + a, o + b, and o + c.

earth and the distortion due to Lambert's conformal conical projection onto the plane and, in the case of distance between two points, the different heights of the points above the Hayford reference ellipsoid. (However, we observed no distance at Búrfell).

The expression $atan2(X_i + x_i - X_0 - x_0, Y_i + y_i - Y_0 - y_0)$ holds for the angle at station P_0 clockwise from the Y-axis to the line joining P_0 to target P_i. With the help of Figure 3 this direction angle for the line joining station to target can be expressed differently, resulting in an *observation equation*, loosely formulated as "observation constant + reduced direction reading + residue = arctangent function". The arctangent function has to be linearized by Taylor's expansion before being used in linear equations.

Each of the m observation equations in a set of m direction readings contains an unknown orientation constant and a residue, but the orientation constant does not occur in other equations. It is easy to prove by the method of least squares, that the sum of the m residues is zero, and an equation created by summing the m observation equations is free of residues. We could use this equation in at least two different ways for eliminating the orientation constant from the observation equations. In Method 1, the orientation constant is eliminated from the equations by subtracting the mean of the m equations from each of the equations, but the number of unknown variables in each observation equation is thereby increased. In Method 2, the orientation constant is deleted from each of the m observation equations and the truncated equations used with weight 1, provided the equation formed by summing the m truncated equations is used with weight $-1/m$ when the normal equations are formed. This gives the same normal equations as Method 1. See "Schreibersche Summengleichung" in [10].

The first stage of the adjustment at Búrfell involved six unknowns and four known triangulation points. We used a precision of eight decimal digits when computing distances, directions, and coordinates in the initial network, but four or five digits in the following matrix computations. We used Method 2 and a simulation shows that we needed 1440 multiplications and divisions for the matrix computations. For simplification, we show the use of Method 1 (requiring 2310 multiplications and divisions) in the following discussion.

We can write the observation equations for the whole network in matrix notation as $v = Bx - r$. Here v is a vector of unknown residues, r is a constant vector, x is an unknown vector of changes to the initial coordinates of unknown points, and B is a matrix of rows as many as there are observations; and columns as many as there are unknown coordinates. The vector r has a component in the column space of B and a component orthogonal to that space, hence v is least when it is equal to the latter component and its component in the column space of B is zero, which means that $B^T v = 0$. The normal equations $B^T B x = B^T r$ follow. We need to compute the upper triangular part of $B^T B v$ and the right hand side vector $B^T r$.

By its form the normal equation matrix is positive semidefinite and it will be positive definite if regular. We can infer some properties of the matrix from the network from which it is computed. The matrix may be singular if the surveyor forgets to make observations in some part of the network. It will be regular if no part of the network could move relative to the rest without contradicting observations. The normal equations were solved by Gaussian elimination [4].

3   A Computer Program for the Adjustment

In December 1964, an IBM 1620 Model II computer became available at the Computing Center of the University of Iceland [7] and in 1965, the author wrote a FORTRAN II program for adjustment of triangulation using adjustment of indirect observations. At first, the computer was without removable disk and without a printer. Input, output, and even external storage had to be on punched cards (named IBM cards) and FORTRAN II used statement numbers in its branching and looping statements that could easily have resulted in "spaghetti code".

We could do the adjustment in one or more stages in one computer run. The input to the program was on punched cards and consisted of a dictionary stack, one observations stack for each stage of adjustment, and a coordinates stack. The dictionary stack was used for translating point names into point numbers, an observations stack contained observations for one stage of adjustment and instructions for the initialization of coordinates of unknown points, and the coordinates stack contained a list of points with or without coordinates.

At each stage of adjustment, we could use a chain of triangles, specified on a punched card, to direct the computation of coordinates of unknown points. Each triangle contained at least two observed angles and each chain at least two points known initially or from the adjustment in a previous stage. Alternatively, we could use a card with a sequence of point names to direct a special routine to compute the coordinates of each of the points by resection. We used the formulation in *Handbuch der Vermessungskunde* for the reduction of observations to the plane [5].

The observation equations for each set of direction readings were formed as explained in the previous section. They were not stored but used to compute their contribution to the normal equations. If any residues were outside specified bounds, the program reported all such residues and the processing stopped.

We solved the normal equations by Cholesky factorization [4]. We computed the elements of the diagonal and super-diagonal of the inverse of the normal equation matrix (but not the entire inverse matrix) and they were used for computing mean errors of coordinates and the parameters of error ellipses and confidence ellipses for the unknown points [8].

The program consisted of a small main program and five subroutines running one after another, each invoking a number of other subroutines and using the COMMON declaration (i.e. global data) for data storage. We used this structure to maximize storage space for the normal equations and we implemented vectors and matrices as one-dimensional arrays. The first version of the program was about 2100 lines of code.

4   Adjustment Using the Computer

The use of the program changed the work of the surveyor by enabling him to plan larger networks or have larger parts (up to 23 unknown points) of a network adjusted as one whole, and he could spend more time in the field and less time in the office.

At Orkustofnun there was access to a card punch machine where the data was entered into white IBM cards. We then brought the cards to the Computing Center at the University where computer operators kept the program on differently colored cards. A stack of cards with the first part of the program was put in front of the input cards in the input card hopper, the program started, and cards with intermediate results appeared in the output card stacker. An operator then put these after the second part of the program in the input card hopper, and so forth. The juggling of card stacks became rather complicated if the adjustment was in many stages. We would then take the final output cards to the Skýrr computing center elsewhere in Reykjavík where an operator used an IBM 1401 computer to print their content [1].

5 Later Improvements

The first version of the program did not accept observations of distance, but subsequent versions did. By then the Computer Center had added removable data storage disks and a printer to its computer system; as a result, the juggling of card stacks or trips to the second computer were no longer necessary. Later versions of the program used heights above the reference ellipsoid and a three-dimensional model avoiding reductions to the plane, the normal equation matrix was stored as a variable-band matrix, and free adjustment [6] was possible.

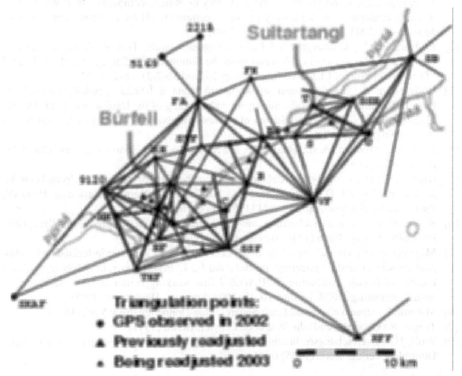

Fig. 4. In 2003, the 40-year-old triangulation in Búrfell area was readjusted with some of the triangulation points fixed by GPS observations. Of the five hydro power plants in the Þjórsá-Tungnaá river system, the 270 MW plant at Búrfell was built in the years 1966–1969 and the 130 MW plant at Sultartangi in 1997–2000.

We used this program as late as 2003 for re-computing old triangulation networks with some of their points positioned by GPS observations (see Figure 4). By then the computer era had revolutionized land surveying, partly by computers embedded in surveying instruments, and with new technologies such as the Global Positioning System. In the earlier years, triangulation had been greatly facilitated; finally, it became almost obsolete.

Acknowledgements

My thanks go to Oddur Benediktsson for his help and encouragement and to Bragi Thorbergsson and the editors for their careful reading of the English text.

References

[1] Benediktsson, O., Gunnarsson, J., Hreinsson, E.B., Jakobsson, J., Kaldalóns, Ö., Kjartansson, Ó., Rósmundsson, Ó., Sigvaldason, H., Stefánsson, G., Zophoniasson, J.: Computerisation of the Icelandic State and Municipalities: 1964 to 1985. In: Bubenko Jr., J., Impagliazzo, J., Sølvberg, A. (eds.) History of Nordic computing: IFIP WG9.7 first working conference on the history of nordic computing (HiNC1), Trondheim, Norway, June 16–18, 2005. Springer, Heidelberg (2005)

[2] Böðvarsson, Á.: Greinargerð frá Landmælingum Íslands. Tímarit Verkfræðingafélags Íslands 2.–3., 56. árg (1971); A report from the National Land Survey of Iceland. Journal of the Association of Chartered Engineers of Iceland 56(2-3), 18–21 (1971)

[3] Böðvarsson, Á.: Landmælingar og kortagerð Dana á Íslandi. Upphaf Landmælinga Íslands, Landmælingar Íslands, Surveying and mapping of the Danish in Iceland. The beginning of the National Land Survey of Iceland. The National Survey of Iceland. Reykjavík, 1996 (in Icelandic)

[4] Duff, I.S., Erisman, A.M., Reid, J.K.: Direct methods for sparse matrices. Clarendon press, Oxford (1989)

[5] Kneissl, M.: Die Längen- und Richtungsreduktion bei der konformen Kegelprojektion. In: Jordan, W., Eggert, O., Kneissl, M. (eds.) Handbuch der Vermessungskunde, Band IV, Zweite hälfte, Stuttgart, pp. 841–844 (1959) (in German)

[6] Koch, K.-R.: Parameterschätzung und Hypothesentests in linearen Modellen. Ferd. Dümmlers Verlag, Bonn (1980) (in German)

[7] Magnússon, M.: The Advent of the first General Purpose Computer in Iceland and its Impact on Science and Engineering. In: Bubenko Jr., J., Impagliazzo, J., Sølvberg, A. (eds.) History of Nordic computing: IFIP WG9.7 first working conference on the history of nordic computing (HiNC1), June 16–18, 2005. Springer, Heidelberg (2005)

[8] Mikhail, E.: Observations and Least Squares. Dun-Donnelley, New York (1976)

[9] Torge, W.: Geodesy, 2nd edn. Walter de Gruyter, Berlin (1991)

[10] Wolf, H.: Ausgleichsrechnung. Formeln zur praktischen Anvendungen, p. 143. Ferd. Dümmlers Verlag, Bonn (1975) (in German)

Data Processing with Unit Record Equipment in Iceland

Óttar Kjartansson

(Retired) Manager of Data Processing Department at Skýrr, Iceland
ottark@heima.is

Abstract. This paper presents an overview of the usage of unit record equipment and punched cards in Iceland and introduces some of the pioneers. The usage of punched cards as a media in file processing started 1949 and became the dominant machine readable media in Iceland until 1968. After that punched cards were still used as data entry media for a while but went completely out of use in 1982.

Keywords: Data processing, unit record, punched card, Iceland.

1 Hagstofa Íslands

Hagstofa Íslands (Statistical Bureau of Iceland) initiated the use of 80 column punched cards and unit record equipment in Iceland in the year 1949. The first machinery consisted of tabulating machine of the type IBM 285 (handled numbers only), the associated key punch machines, verifiers, and a card sorter. See Figures 1 and 2. This equipment was primarily used to account for the import and export for Iceland. Skýrr (Skýrsluvélar ríkisins og Reykjavíkurborgar - The Icelandic State and Municipal Data Center) was established three years later by an initiative from Hagstofa Íslands, Rafmagnsveita Reykjavíkur (Reykjavík Electric Power Utility), and the Medical Director of Health of Iceland as was described in an earlier article [3].

Fig. 1. IBM 285 Electric Accounting Machine at Hagstofa Íslands year 1949

J. Impagliazzo, T. Järvi, and P. Paju (Eds.): HiNC 2, IFIP AICT 303, pp. 225–229, 2009.
© IFIP International Federation for Information Processing 2009

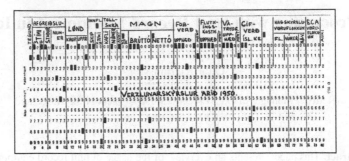

Fig. 2. Early form of the data registration using a punched card.   Hagstofa Islands: Import/export account 1950. (Author: Áki Pétursson)

Áki Pétursson (1913-1970) directed the use of this equipment at Hagstofa. He was trained at IBM Denmark and was the first Icelander to obtain such training and he directed Skýrr for the first eight years. Viggo Troels-Smith of IBM Denmark closed the first order for IBM punched card equipment for Iceland - the Hagstofa, in the year 1947. Later Viggo Troels-Smith became the director of IBM Denmark. An agreement was made in the year 1948 with Ottó A. Michelsen (1920-2000) to undertake the maintenance of IBM machines in Iceland. He became sales agent for IBM and later the director of IBM World Trade Company office in Iceland [1].

2 Rafmagnsveita Reykjavíkur and the Establishment of Skýrr

Rafmagnsveita Reykjavíkur (Reykjavík Electric Company) was founded 1921. In the year 1928, Rafmagnsveita started to use electromechanical accounting machines for accounting and processing accounts receivable and printing invoices. This type of equipment was used for quarter of a century until the advent of unit record equipment.

At this point, the leaders of Rafmagnsveita had been looking for improved ways to process the accounts receivable. In the year 1948 a "Hollerith system", that is unit record equipment based system, was ordered from IBM. At that time imports to Iceland were severely regulated by the government and the permission to import this "expensive" equipment for Rafmagnsveita was not granted. This situation remained unchanged for several years. Hjörleifur Hjörleifsson (1906-1979), a department head and later financial director of Rafmagnsveita, led this effort. He took great interest in automated data processing and he organised the founding of the Icelandic Data Processing Society in the year 1968; he became the first president of the society.

In the year 1950, Dr. Sigurður Sigurðsson (1903-1986) the medical director in Iceland for tuberculosis proposed that Heilsuverndarstöð ríkisins (State Health Institute), Hagstofa Íslands and Rafmagnsveita Reykjavíkur cooperated in establishing a common data processing centre. His proposal was accepted and a joint centre was established that later was named Skýrsluvélar ríkisins og Reykjavíkurbæjar (Skýrr). The government subsequently issued an import permit. Based on the order that Rafmagnsveita had placed with the IBM agent two years earlier, the institution ordered the following equipment: Tabulator IBM 405, Reproducing Punch IBM 513, Collator IBM 077, Sorter IBM 082, Interpreter IBM 552, and more. See Figure 3. The delivery time was two years and IBM delivered the equipment early in the year 1952 [2].

Fig. 3. The machine room of Skýrr at Rafmagnsveita company premises around the year 1955. Hafsteinn E. Gíslason (1914-1976) in the foreground and Guðmundur Sveinsson in the background.

In the fall of 1951, the preparation work for the unit record processing started at Rafmagnsveita. The customer register had to be punched on cards and the processing organized. An employer at Rafmagnsveita, Guðmundur Sveinsson (1907-2001), organized this work. When the equipment was delivered it was installed in office space at Rafmagnsveita. Some start-up difficulties were experienced but by mid year 1952 the invoices for both electric and hot water usage were sent to every household in Reykjavík – the old accounting machines became obsolete. Skýrr data centre had started operation.

In the beginning, Skýrr worked solely at projects for Rafmagnsveita (70%) and Hagstofa (30%). This changed as time passed and in few years Skýrr serviced numerous institutes of the State and City. The hardware was updated accordingly and the staff increased rapidly. See Figure 4.

At Rafmagnsveita the unit record equipment served to process the energy invoices for the City until the year 1964. That year Skýrr obtained the first computer in Iceland of the type IBM 1401.[2, 3] Then the data processing for Rafmagnsveita improved but the data entry and storage media continued to be punched cards and the processing sequential – based on batches of sorted cards. The real changes in processing came in 1968 when Skýrr obtained an IBM 360/30 with magnetic disks and tapes and an IBM 1403 line printer. The main files were now read to tapes or discs and all processing such as sorting and merging of files was greatly facilitated. A primitive version of disc operating system (DOS) controlled the system that made possible batch processing with limited multitasking and parallel processing and print queues.

The data processing at Skýrr grew without bounds in the first decade and faster than any one had foreseen. The space to house the operation had been increased by 500% by the year 1958 and the tabulators were by that time three with two of the improved type IBM 421.

Fig. 4. Eletrographic mark sensing technology was tried out in the first years at Skýrr to mechanise the energy meter readings for electricity and hot water in the homes. The inspectors were to mark the meter readings directly with special pencil on special cards that would subsequently be processed to become punched cards. The process was not reliable and it was discontinued. The author is seen inspecting rejected mark sensed cards in the year 1952.

Fig. 5. The IBM 1401 configuration that Skýrr installed in the year 1964 consisting of card reader/punch, the central unit, and a line printer

The use of punched cards dwindled quickly and file processing using punched cards came to an end. The punched cards were still used for a while as data entry media. Soon another innovation came to use - that is entering data on diskettes and later online data entry. The "old fashioned" technology based on punched cards disappeared quickly and by the year 1982, the unit record equipment was completely out of use at Skýrr. In conclusion, we can say that the period of data processing with unit record equipment lasted from the year 1949 to the year 1982.

References

[1] Áki Pétursson. IBM-vélar Hagstofunnar. Kafli í Afmælisrit til Þorsteins Þorsteinssonar á sjötugs afmæli hans 5. apríl 1950 / [nefnd skipuð af stjórn Félags hagfræðinga sá um út-gáfuna]. (The IBM equipment at the Statistical Bureau of Iceland. Chapter in Anniversary Edition for Thorsteinn Thorsteinsson on his seventieth years anniversity 5. April 1950. Editor Association of Icelandic Economists, in Icelandic.) Reykjavik, pp. 1–10 (1950)

[2] Kjartansson, Ó.: Upplýsingaiðnaður í hálfa öld. Saga Skýrr 1952-2002 (Fifty years of information technology: The story of Skýrr 1952-2002, in Icelandic) Skýrr, Reykjavík (2002)

[3] Benediktsson, O., Gunnarsson, J., Hreinsson, E.B., Jakobsson, J., Kaldalóns, Ö., Kjartansson, Ó., Rósmundsson, Ó., Sigvaldason, H., Stefánsson, G., Zophoniasson, J.: Computerisation of the Icelandic State and Municipalities: 1964 to 1985. In: Bubenko Jr., J., Impagliazzo, J., Sølvberg, A. (eds.) History of Nordic computing: IFIP WG9.7 first working conference on the history of nordic computing (HiNC1), Trondheim, Norway, June 16-18, 2003. Springer, Heidelberg (2005)

Computerized Typesetting and Other New Applications in a Publishing House

Timo Järvi

Professor (Emeritus), Computer Science, Department of Information Technology,
University of Turku, Finland
timojarvi@gmail.com

Abstract. The author was involved during years 1964-67 in a change process from manual typesetting to a computerized one. This paper describes the design and implementation of new graphical applications as well as the programming of IBM 1401. It also presents some reflections on the social affects of these changes.

Keywords: Computerized typesetting and hyphenation, Wedgeless line casting, Phone books, Phototypesetting, IBM 1401.

1 Introduction

In 1964, I became a summer trainee at the IBM Service Centre in Turku. I had studied mathematics at the University of Turku for three years. The studies included also computer-oriented courses such as algorithms, Turing Machines, structure of a computer, and programming. In addition, I wrote some practical mathematical programs in FORTRAN II and executed them on an IBM 1620 computer. During summer 1964, I programmed some business applications for IBM 1401. This paper describes my experiences, as I was involved full-time in the development of newspaper computer applications between the autumn of 1964 and the winter 1967.

2 Starting Situation

In the middle of the 1960s, large companies used computers; applying them to produce newspapers was a rarity. Even if a publishing house had a computer, it used the machine for business applications. In the USA, a handful of newspapers had started computer-typesetting experiments in the first half of the 1960s. Computer typesetting research projects were ongoing in American and European universities, but in Turku, we were not aware of them (see e.g. [1]).

In the spring of 1964, a delegation from Turun Sanomat (the main newspaper in South-West Finland) visited the *Graphical Fair* in Los Angeles, California, as well as six printing houses experimenting with computer typesetting and other technical novelties. After reporting to CEO Irja Ketonen, they made a decision to develop computer-typesetting applications in Turun Sanomat. The target was not only typesetting

J. Impagliazzo, T. Järvi, and P. Paju (Eds.): HiNC 2, IFIP AICT 303, pp. 230–237, 2009.
© IFIP International Federation for Information Processing 2009

the daily newspaper, but also phone books and other catalogues published by the company.

Turun Sanomat signed a contract with IBM Finland on 30 June of 1964 to lease an IBM System 360 computer, starting from the beginning of year 1966. Prior to that time, it used an IBM 1401 computer in IBM's local service centre to develop and run typesetting applications [3, 5].

3 First Applications

In Europe, the first newspaper, that published an article that was hyphenated and line set by a computer, was Turun Sanomat on 9 August 1964. This was only a modest start. In this experiment, a photocopy of a line printer resulted with only capitals used. At that time, the correct hyphenation of the English language was still a big problem. Hyphenation rules of Finnish, however, are very simple except for a few cases. An American linguist, Winthrop Vermillion, working for IBM had written a computer program to hyphenate and line set Finnish printer text. They fed the input using punched cards [3].

Turun Sanomat founded an electronic data processing (EDP) department. Keijo Ketonen, a son of the CEO, was the head of the department and MBA Kaj Arhippainen and I were system planners and programmers. Arhippainen had applications experience using unit record machines in a dairy, but he had not written programs. The first application we wrote, mostly as an EDP exercise for the company, was newspaper advertisement invoicing. It was a typical punch card application for IBM 1401, and we ran monthly. The first month of its deployment was October of 1964.

The second application, the newspaper distribution system, was more complicated. Newspaper deliverers mainly distributed Turun Sanomat in urban areas. In rural areas the newspaper was mailed. The deliverers had a ring of subscriber cards of their district, whereas the addresses of the mail delivery subscribers where written on so called Adrema metal plates and stamped each day on a special paper tape with a piece glued to every newspaper. All subscriptions had an end-of-year renewal. The switch from manual processing of subscriber information to automated processing was a big and uncertain step for the company, and especially for the small EDP department, and required careful planning. We deployed our system for the renewal of all subscriptions in the year shift. All subscriptions required processing in roughly thirty-six hours near the New Year Day.

Data of all subscribers (name and address) appeared in advance on a special mark sense card where details of the subscription could be added with a pencil. The company employed additional seasonal clerks to receive the subscriptions, pick the subscribers' cards, and mark the subscription details. This was because we calculated that we could not key punch the large number of cards (about 100,000) in the short time at the end of the year. An IBM 514 would punch the marked data. During the New Year's Day (newspapers do not appear on the 1st of January) the subscribers' cards were sorted by districts. In urban areas, the subscriber cards for each deliverer's area were printed using a simple program on 1401. The punched cards of the rural subscribers were first divided into four stacks of cards, which were then double collated (using an IBM Card Collator 077) into one stack so that every fourth card originated from the same district.

This stack was fed into the computer to print out four parallel address tapes so that the card reader and line printer speeds matched. We succeeded to get the last address tapes (foreign subscribers) at 5 a.m. on the 2nd of January.

During the first weeks of the year, we again sorted the cards of the rural subscribers into one stack so that the clerks in the office could add new subscriptions in the proper places. Earlier, Turun Sanomat kept on sending papers to former subscribers even a week or two after the expiration of the subscription, and patiently waited for renewals. Now, a huge number of phone calls came from last year's subscribers who had forgotten to renew their subscription.

After one month, the subscription situation was stable enough to transfer the subscriber file on disks. As there were two disk units with mountable ten surface disk packs, we designed a special triple index sequential (IS) file on both disks. An IS file can be accessed serially very fast as records are mostly in correct order on consecutive tracks. Random access is also possible, because a lookup table for the last records of each track exists. At that time, computer resources were very limited, and we had to exercise great care to be able to run our applications. For example, excessive disk head movement would slow down the printing of address tapes. We divided the rural subscribers into six sub files. Each sub file occupied three tracks on each cylinder and the remaining track served as a common overflow area for the cylinder. We reserved a few last cylinders for a general overflow area in case of the overflow from an overflow track. We needed the overflow areas for updating the files. Note that at that time we did not have terminals for the computer; we made the updates by searching manually the card of the subscriber, by key punching a delete hole on the card, and partly duplicating and punching the new information for the subscriber. We then fed both cards into the updating program that made the changes in the sub files (e.g. changing the address usually required moving the subscriber from one district to another). Using this configuration we could print six (maximum for the printer line width) parallel address tapes with minimum disk read/write head movement, thus leveraging the maximum printer speed. Due to updates the sub files gradually became out of pace so that the arm movement increased and slowed down printing. Thus, we had to reorganize the sub files periodically. This was easy because we could write a sub file read from one unit to the other one in the same way we did originally.

When the manual system was in use, the year shifts included plenty of overtime work in the circulation department. Though the clerks were a little unsatisfied for this, the overtime was a source of extra earnings, welcome during the Christmas time. Transfer to the computerized system with subscriber register on disks reduced the amount of overwork notably; causing some disappointment among the clerks for the loss of extra income.

4 The IBM 1401

We now describe briefly the IBM 1401 computer, the platform for our first applications. The smallest addressable unit of memory on the 1400 series was known as the "character" and consisted of eight binary bits (physically, eight ferrite cores). Six of the bits were used for character coding, using a system known as BCD based on the code used in IBM punched cards. The seventh bit was used as a parity bit, and the eighth as a "Word Mark". A "Word" on the 1400 series consisted of a variable number of consecutive character positions, the low order address one having the "Word Mark" bit "on". It was, therefore, known as a variable word length machine. Each machine language instruction constituted a "word" and could vary in length between 1, 4, or 7 characters, the first one carrying a word mark. An extra modifying character could be added to each of these formats. Data words were, of course, totally variable in length, and were processed character by character in sequence until the word mark was encountered [2].

We wrote programs using Autocoder, a symbolic assembler language. The variable length instruction started with a one character operation code which also had a word mark. As the opcode for addition was "1" this was utilized as a programming trick when increasing a loop counter by giving in the addition instruction the second operand address "*–6" (program counter –6). This referred to the opcode itself, which was now considered as a one character long number 1. Many other tricks made the programs harder to read for others.

In addition to the 1401 CPU the installation concluded a 1402 card reader-punch, a 1403 chain printer, and two 1311 disk storage drives with changeable 2Mw disk packs. The memory had 12,000 characters, but oddly a customer in the IBM service center was charged according to whether the program used 4, 8, or 12 k of memory.

5 Typesetting

Before computer typesetting could be attacked the technical environment had to be modernized. For text input, a special Fairchild paper tape punches were acquired with typesetting keyboards (which had more keys than a type writer). They had no visual output for the key punch operators. The operators quickly learned to read the punched tape codes to solve problematic situations. The mechanical line casting machines were equipped with paper tape readers which at least doubled their speed. A paper tape reader and punch were added to the IBM 1401 computer.

A line setting and hyphenating program acted as a starting point for our typesetting program. The paper tape input to the program was similar to input handled by modern text processing programs; that is, it had paragraphs of text without explicit line breaks with some special formatting codes (caps, italics, bold, font type, size, and end of chapter). For each row of line set text, the program calculated a suitable length and a place for hyphen if needed. It must be noted that newspaper columns are very narrow and Finnish words longer than English ones, so hyphenation is used often. To calculate the length of the present row we had tables of character widths for each font. In hot metal line casting spaces between words were actually special wedges which forced the letter matrices tightly between the borders of a row. These wedges had their minimum and maximum breadth so that a line must fit with minimums and exceed with maximums. If the latter was not achieved, special fixed spaces could be added between words.

We also improved the original hyphenating program by some rare letter combinations and special symbols. The idea was to only use such letter combinations for hyphenation that were always valid, and leave the ambiguous ones out. With this strategy, our program made hyphenation errors only in some compound words and foreign names. As a last part, we added special symbols to handle tables (e.g. stock markets and ice hockey or soccer standings) so that the columns would be straight.

Computer typesetting was gradually taken into production use during the spring 1965. Keypunch operators were employed to write reporters' text on punched tape. The tapes were collected and delivered to the nearby IBM service centre by a moped courier. The tapes were input into IBM 1401 which in turn output new tapes to control the line casting machines. These tapes were delivered back to the printing house and fed into line casting machines. One might wonder what the benefits of this complicated process were. First, the keypunch operators were much faster than the line casting machine operators, because they did not have to pay attention to separate lines and hyphenation. Second, the line casting machines could be kept operating at full speed, because they were not dependant on the operators writing speed. Third, the speed of line casting machines further improved because the expensive errors caused by too short or too long rows ceased to exist. Finally, we wanted to gain experience to be able to fully benefit from the company's first computer, expected to be delivered a year later.

6   The IBM System/360

IBM announced the System/360 computer in April 1964. As mentioned above, the agreement to acquire this computer was made only two months later. We started to study the new computer, which had an entirely different architecture, in spring 1965 as it was arriving at the beginning of next year. The 1401 only allowed one main program at a time but now also subprograms became available. At that time no courses about programming 360 were given, so we studied the manuals (indeed!). Naturally, there was room for misunderstandings which were later exposed. We wrote a few small test programs and travelled to Paris, France for test runs in the IBM European Test Centre in July 1965. The first thing we noted was that IBM had gone from the BCD to EBCDIC punch card code so that we had to correct quite a lot of special characters before we got the first translations of our assembler programs. After hard five days (computer time was available only by nights) we returned home with the first simple running programs. During the next fall and winter, we ported all our applications for 360 and tested them both in Stockholm, Sweden and Helsinki, Finland.

Meanwhile a computer room was built in the newspaper house. The System/360 had a mainframe with 32 kB main memory, a card reader and punch, line printer, 2 disk units, paper tape reader, and a specially made control unit for 4 paper tape punches, which were located beside the four automatic line casting machines. The new computer system was inaugurated on April 14 1966.

7   The Phone Book

In Finland, new editions of phone books were published yearly. At that time, the type matter of metal rows was stored and the corrections to a new edition were made by line setting the new rows and inserting them manually into the type matter and simultaneously removing the obsolete rows. This was both a time consuming and expensive process, and it required plenty of metal and warehouse space.

Our typesetting program could already handle tables, which is what a phone book basically is. Naturally for this application we added special features typical for phone books. We also printed the text with a line printer so that key punching errors could be removed before line casting, which was cheaper. We stored the whole text on disk making the yearly update an easy task. In fact, we started to make the updates regularly and the printouts were used by the telephone company's number service.

The first catalogue produced by this new method was the 1966 edition of South-West Finland's phone book. It was a success, and nine years later Turun Sanomat was printing all phone books in Finland.

It was easy to modify the program to handle other kinds of catalogues and Turun Sanomat begun to print many kinds of catalogues in Finland and abroad. This was in accordance of the goals the company set in spring 1964. For this purpose, the first phase of a new printing establishment was completed in spring 1965 [3].

8 Social Aspects

Adopting new technology can create resistance. In our case, there were two points that could have raised objections. The feeding of text was moved from expensive line casting machine operators to cheaper and faster key punch operators that belonged to a different labor union. Also the total amount of human work in the typesetting process was reduced and thus could have lead to unemployment.

In Turun Sanomat everything happened smoothly. There was a keen interest in the new technology and many employees took part in the development process. The changes happened slowly and gradually. The new technology gave the company new applications and market opportunities, which were exploited; production grew fast and more people were employed.

9 Wedgeless Line Casting

Sometimes the operation of the wedges failed in the line setting and caused a lengthy process to recover. A clever trick was designed to get rid of the wedges. As discussed above, the wedges compressed the letter matrices between the jaws of the machine so that both sides of newspaper columns become straight. There are other alternatives to tighten a row, as nowadays is well known from word processing programs, viz. aligning left (last row of a paragraph) or right, and centering. In these methods the opposing jaw or both move to tighten the row and the wedges remain in their minimum breadth.

The trick was to use centering for all normal lines and replace the wedges, i.e. the word space by exactly counted space or combination of spaces. To get the sides as straight as possible we added two special spaces to the line casting machine, one between the *thin* and *en* space and another between the *en* and *em* space. Our program counted the word spaces so that they differed from each other at most by the difference of two subsequent spaces from altogether five spaces, and the row had maximum length, i.e. no space could be replaced by the next thicker one. By this operation the line casting machine malfunctions decreased and the production speed increased. The maximum difference in line lengths was ca 1 mm, which did not disturb the reader.

10 Phototypesetting

The next idea was to get rid of the relatively slow line casting machines. Photomechanical composition had gained users in the USA by the middle of the 1960s. Turun Sanomat decided to adopt this technology, where a typesetting machine had drums of film which had all letters, numbers, and special characters on them. One changeable drum contained eight fonts. By varying the distance between the character on the drum and the film, it was possible to use the same negative image to produce a wide range of type sizes.

The necessary changes to our typesetting programs were small. Now the lines could be filled by given the exact width of space between the words in the line. As also the vertical place of a character was controllable, sub and super script became possible. Naturally, the whole type matter was output as film. This required offset printing, for which a new machinery was acquired later [3].

11 Design and Implementation of Applications

The design and development team for all of the applications described above was a group of two men. Several factors helped our small team to succeed. All programs were executed in batch mode, one program at a time. This made the programs simple, because there were no interactions with other programs. In IBM 1401 we used only main programs as the programs were rather short with few repeating parts. The first programs had straightforward logic which was not difficult to program.

The impacts of the new applications to work processes in other departments were manageable. New applications were adopted gradually, one at a time. For a single application, the number of people whose work was affected was moderate.

The idea of adopting new technology for printing came from the top level of company. We thus had full support from the company, and were provided the necessary resources to develop the applications, allowing us to concentrate on the technical problems. Furthermore, there was a sense of pride of the pioneering work, and excitement of the new computer technology. The latter may be much less of a motivating factor in systems development today.

Last but not least, it is important to acknowledge the help received from IBM's local system department. They gave advice in the beginning and took part in various negotiations. The testing trips were essential for our progress as well. To our most difficult questions we often found the answers in IBM's internal manuals that were made available to us.

12 Conclusion

The events described in this paper started a revolution in computerizing the graphical industry, according to the U.S. model, not only in Finland but at least in Scandinavia.

Those involved gave talks and wrote articles and we had interested visitors from Scandinavian countries [4]. In retrospect, the group of people realizing the first steps seems very small, compared to the magnitude of change. What contributed to the success, were knowledge, decisiveness, courage, and resources to make the needed investments. Of course, remarkable progress had taken place in the graphical industry after those early years, and progress continues. The key algorithms and techniques of typesetting, however, were there no later than three years from the initial decision to attempt to computerize typesetting. Those algorithms have since changed relatively little.

References

[1] Duncan, C.J.: Keynote Address. In: Proceedings of the International Conference on Computerized Typesetting, Washington D.C. (1965), http://www.cs.ncl.ac.uk/events/anniversaries/40th/webbook/typesetting/duncan_keynote.html (13.4.2007)

[2] The IBM 1401, http://www.columbia.edu/acis/history/1401.html (12.4.2007)

[3] Kalpa, H.: Juoksuflikasta vuorineuvokseksi; Irja Ketonen 1921-1988 (History of the CEO of Turun Sanomat, in Finnish). (Oy Turun Sanomat, Painopalvelut, Serioffset, Turku) (1995)

[4] Ketonen, K.: Turku tietokoneladonnan kärjessä (Turku leads computer typesetting, in Finnish). Graafikko 8/1965, http://www.saunalahti.fi/eeromari/graafinen/ts1.html (14.11.2008)

[5] Vahtera, R.: Matkan määränä kansan menestys (Turun Sanomat 100 years, in Finnish). (TS-yhtymä/Hansaprint Oy, Turku) (2004)

The Early Days of Computer Aided Newspaper Production Systems

Nils Enlund[1] and Hans E. Andersin[2]

[1] Royal Institute of Technology (KTH), Sweden
nilse@kth.se
[2] Helsinki University of Technology, Finland
hans.andersin@hut.fi

Abstract. During the years 1970-1973, the Laboratory of Information Processing Science at the Helsinki University of Technology carried out the Computer Graphics Project (CGP). The activities focused on the problems of producing newspaper text, advertisements, and complete pages using interactive computer graphics. The project and its commercial spin-off, Typlan, as well as the BUNPAPS continuation project 1973-1975, created a number of innovative, pioneering solutions for computer aided newspaper production, laying the foundation for the digitalization of media production.

Keywords: Newspaper production, page layout, text processing.

1 Computer Aided Newspaper Production in the Early 1970s

The 1960s were a time of great changes in newspaper production, an industrial sector that hitherto had been characterized by traditional technology and a production process with roots in Gutenberg's time. Offset presses that allowed high quality four-color printing were replacing letterpress printing presses. Offset also required the replacement of metal printing forms with photographically produced printing plates—a technology that paved the way for photocomposing machines, color separating image scanners, and page assembly by cutting and pasting film. Text galleys were still produced in manually controlled typecasting machines although a few printing companies already in 1957 had installed perforated tape readers to control the type casters. The speed had limitations, however, by the fact that the punch operators had to break their pace after every thirty or so characters to end the line and possibly hyphenate a word. The solution to this was the use of computer-based hyphenation and justification (H&J) systems that took unjustified text on perforated tape as input and produced a justified output tape with inserted hyphens and line endings. The first trials with computerized typesetting occurred in 1962 in the USA [24] and in 1965, IBM introduced hyphenation and justification software for its 1130 minicomputer [28].

In the Nordic countries, the Finnish newspaper *Turun Sanomat* was a pioneering user of computers in newspaper production. In 1964, the first H&J system in Europe, using an IBM 1401 computer, was installed. The system initially produced punched tape for controlling hot metal typesetters but in 1967, *Turun Sanomat* purchased the first photocomposition machine in Finland [20, 21]. The first photo composer in

J. Impagliazzo, T. Järvi, and P. Paju (Eds.): HiNC 2, IFIP AICT 303, pp. 238–249, 2009.
© IFIP International Federation for Information Processing 2009

regular newspaper production, a Photon 100, had been installed already in 1954 at the Quincy *Patriot Ledger*, although hot metal line casting machines remained in use at many newspapers for many years to come [27].

In 1970, more than fifty companies were delivering composition systems to the graphic arts industry, most of them North American [22]. The British manufacturer Comprite installed several newspaper systems, based on the PDP-8 minicomputer from Digital Equipment Corporation, in the Nordic countries, e.g., to *Hufvudstadsbladet* in Finland in 1969 [19]. In Norway, Comtec, a university spin-off, produced a similar paper-tape-in paper-tape-out system. In 1969, Hendrix Electronics introduced the 5102FD H&J system that allowed text input from paper tape to be displayed and edited on the screen of a video display terminal (VDT) prior to the output of justified paper tape.

A special problem was the computer-aided production of display advertisements, i.e., ads with a complex typographical design where many fonts and type sizes are used and where the text must be placed and adjusted to fit graphics in the ad. At the beginning of the 1970s, this type of ads could only be produced by separately composing the different text elements and then assembling them manually according to the advertiser's layout sketches. However, in 1972, Harris Corp. introduced an interactive VDT based ad composition system, Harris 1100. The screen would show an image in simulated stick characters of the ad as it would look when typeset. If the image did not conform to the layout sketch, the operator modified the typographical codes until she was satisfied with the result. The system then produced a punched tape for the photo composer. They manually pasted graphics. At the time, photo composers could only produce rather narrow film. Consequently, text blocks were set sequentially, cut out, and mounted according to the ad layout.

In 1970, the research institute of the American Newspaper Publishers' Association developed a computer program, LAYOUT, for the automatic planning of the placement of ads on newspaper pages [9]. They fed the dimensions of the ads on punched tape into an IBM 1130 where a FORTRAN program placed the ads in pyramid form on page templates. Layout sketches were output on a line printer and they became a basis for manually making up pages. The company Rocappi designed a system for automatic page make-up of simple book pages already in 1964 using an RCA 301 computer. British Printing Corporation developed during 1969–70 a prototype system for interactive layout of magazine pages [29]. The system used an IBM 1130 and an IBM 2250 interactive vector graphics terminal. The project was discontinued in 1970 and no one ever implemented the ideas.

2 Computer Graphics Project

2.1 Objectives and Resources

In 1968, Hans Andersin was appointed to the first chair of Information Processing Science at the Helsinki University of Technology. After a feasibility study financed by SITRA, The Finnish National Fund for Research and Development, Andersin initiated a research and development project, supported by SITRA and two major Finnish newspaper companies, *Helsingin Sanomat* and *Turun Sanomat*. The project was called the "Computer Graphics Project" (CGP). SITRA funded CGP for the period from February 1970 to September 1971. The Bank of Finland mainly financed the computer equipment [1]. The aim was to develop internationally marketable applications in the field of text processing, and the focus was on developing principles and prototypes for page make-up systems, editorial systems and document handling systems [3].

Digital Equipment Corporation provided laboratory equipment built around a PDP-15 computer. PDP-15 had a word length of 18 bits and was the first DEC computer using integrated circuits instead of discrete transistors. A separate input/output processor enhanced the performance of the system. The first delivered PDP-15 was installed at CGP in February 1970. The PDP-15/30 was equipped with a 20 MB DECdisc RP15/RP02, and with DEC's proprietary magnetic tape storage, DECtape. It also had a punched tape reader for the input of programs and data. The paper tapes were key-punched on a Teletype ASR-33. Programming was made in assembler. According to the "zeitgeist" of that time, the project staff soon decorated the CGP computer with a large peace symbol and it was nicknamed *Mirri* (in Finnish, *mirri* means pussycat and in Russian, *mir* stands for peace; see Figure 1).

The main interaction tool was an ARDS 100A VDT using a storage screen. The terminal drew vector objects between points on the screen in the manner of a plotter. The advantage of this was that all lines, regardless of angle, were sharp. The disadvantage was that character fonts had to be represented by stick characters and that raster pictures could not be presented at all. Another peculiarity was the long time constant of the CRT phosphorus: a once drawn figure remained visible on the

Fig. 1. The PDP-15 of CGP and part of the project staff. The authors of this paper are numbers five (Enlund) and ten (Andersin) from the left.

screen for a long time. To change the picture, it was necessary to wipe the entire screen and redraw the picture. The terminal had a primitive mouse for addressing points on the screen. Later, CGP acquired a DEC Graphic-15 system with a VT04 raster scan screen and a separate graphic processor. User interaction was by light pen or tablet.

2.2 Computer Aided Page Make-Up

One objective of CGP was to develop a system for interactive planning and make-up of newspaper and magazine pages. Initially, two separate solutions were planned, INE—Interactive Newspaper System—and IMA—Interactive Magazine System. Soon, however, the focus was directed toward the problems of newspaper page production. This was considered to pose a more interesting challenge because of the tight time constraints in the daily production cycle. Before long, it became clear that the ambitions were too high with respect to the available time and resources. The project therefore concentrated on defining detailed systems specifications for the INE and IMA systems and on designing a prototype system that would demonstrate the design concepts.

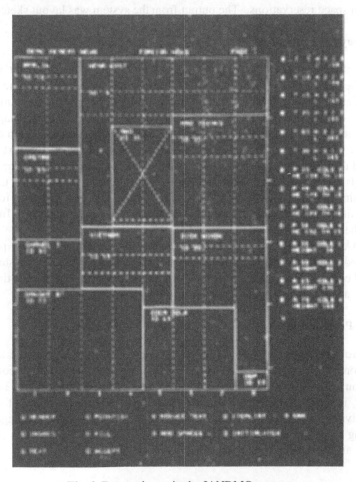

Fig. 2. Page make-up in the JANDMO system

This demonstrator was called JANDMO—short for January Demonstration System, since the solutions were to be shown to partners and funding organizations in January 1971. Because of delays in the delivery of the Graphic-15, they could not keep the deadline, but in February 1971, the first working prototype of a computer system for interactive make-up of newspaper pages was demonstrated to an enthusiastic audience.

JANDMO would let the user call up a list of available stories on the screen. From this list, the operator selected stories for proofreading and editing. He/she could assign a set of stories to a certain page, e.g., the sports page. An empty template, with only column guides visible, representing the page was then called up on the screen. The operator then interactively placed different text blocks of the stories—headline, lead-in, galley text—in the desired positions on the page (Figure 2). He/she divided the galley text into columns using a light pen to cut off the galley and move the tail end into the next column. The size estimates were approximate since no exact justification or hyphenation was possible. They represented ads and graphics by rectangular space reservations. The output from the system was layout sketches.

2.3 Display Ad Production

The CGP also developed a composing system for display advertisement where the user did the design of the ad interactively instead of by typographical encoding. In the IDA (Interactive Ad Design) system, the text blocks of an ad were named during text input—on punched tape or on the display screen. On the VDT, the shape of each text block was drawn, named, and placed interactively. The software then connected each block with the corresponding text, justified and hyphenated the text to fit the shape, and displayed the composed text using simulated characters. Corrections and adjustments had to be made by entering typographical commands into the text strings and repeating the process. Finally, the system produced a punched tape for a photo composer that exposed the composed text blocks in one single operation. Images and graphics then had to be pasted in manually.

The IDA system was an advanced precursor to the commercial ad production system produced by Harris Corp. in 1972 and which was to become the standard for display ad composition for many years to come. However, it took a long time before interactive ad design was implemented in professional systems.

2.4 Text Processing

A basic problem that had to be solved early in the CGP project was the automated hyphenation and justification (H&J) of text. In order to obtain a correct composition of lines on text, algorithms had to be developed for calculating the number of characters, in different fonts and point sizes, to be placed on each line of composed text, for dividing words according to the hyphenation rules of each language, and for distributing space evenly between words to fill the lines. The algorithms could then be used in all text-processing applications.

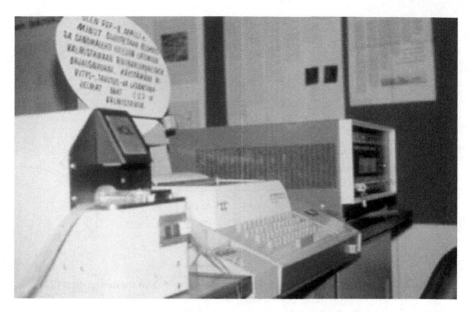

Fig. 3. The PDP-8/e based hyphenation and justification system at *Kaleva*

In 1970, CGP received a proposal from the newspaper company *Kaleva* to develop a simple H&J system for the production of galleys by tape-driven hot metal typesetting machines. In spring 1971, they built a system for the PDP-8 minicomputer (Figure 3). The entire software, including control and interrupt handling routines as well as input and output drivers, was crammed into the available 4K of 12-bit core memory. The system first used expanding space bands for justifying the lines in the typesetter but later had algorithms for justification without space bands—a more calculation intensive method that required the core memory to be expanded to 8K [30]. CGP had now found a commercially attractive product that they could sell immediately to other newspapers.

2.5 Integrated Newspaper Production Systems

The ambitions of CGP were high, aiming at designing and implementing an integrated computer based newspaper production system with a wide spectrum of functions such as text input, interactive editing, H&J, production of classified ads, composition of tables, display ad make-up, full page make-up, output of proofs and layout sketches, and online output to photo composers. The project could deliver proof-of-concept for many of these functions during the short project duration but newspapers would have to wait many years for such integrated newspaper systems.

Such an integrated production system must be built around a common database (Figure 4). Jules Tewlow first presented this idea in 1968 [31], but CGP was a pioneer in taking concrete steps toward an implementation. The vision of a totally integrated newspaper production system has not yet occurred. Instead, most newspaper production systems consist of a patchwork of systems and software from different manufacturers.

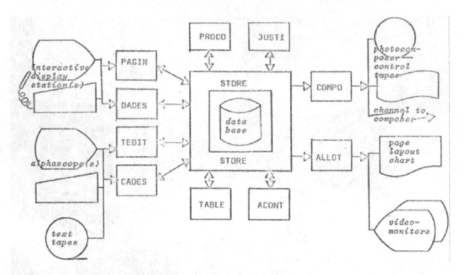

Fig. 4. The principles of an integrated text processing system for newspapers [22]

2.6 Continuation Projects

The SITRA funding ceased during the fall of 1971. The financing of CGP continued by means of minor commissioned projects and with earnings from commercial activities. A significant source of funding was Nordisk Avisteknisk Samarbetsnämnd (Nordic Newspaper Technology Association).

Research aiming at developing interactive newspaper production systems continued during 1971 and 1972 [4]. The group built an editorial system, SCANEX, for the PDP-15 computer and a Delta Telterm-2 alphanumeric terminal (unfortunately without Scandinavian special characters). They installed the first similar commercial editorial system, Hendrix 3400, in 1972 at the Detroit *News* [28]. Other continuation projects included a study on the use of simulation to study and optimize the operations of a newspaper [23] and a project for automatic indexing and retrieval of text in a newspaper archive [10].

3 Typlan: The Spin-Off Company

The CGP funding agreement required commercialization of the results. In 1971, 15 of the CGP project staff jointly formed a company, Typlan Systems Projects Oy Ab. The, mostly young, CGP researchers and a few close supporters owned one share each in the company. This led to that the firm was considered as "our own" company; motivation was high, though they kept salaries and costs low. The main product of Typlan during the first year of operation was the simple punched tape based H&J system developed for *Kaleva*. They also delivered similar systems to the Finnish newspapers *Etelä-Saimaa*, *Hämeen Sanomat*, *Kymen Sanomat*, *Lapin Kansa*, *Satakunnan Kansa*, and *Savon Sanomat*. The Finnish national news agency STT-FNB installed a system for "teletypesetting" of text.

The next product development step was to furnish the PDP-8 minicomputer with VDTs for online text entry and correction. Typlan's terminal based system was called Finntext and used VDTs from Hendrix and Delta Data. The first terminal based system in Finland was installed at the newspaper *Hufvudstadsbladet* in 1972. A few months earlier, the Norwegian company Comtec delivered the first similar system in Sweden to Värmlands Folkblad [19]. During summer 1973, Typlan installed a VDT based system at *Keskisuomalainen* in Finland. The earlier systems had had no means for storing the text files, but now they added disk storage. Typlan entered into cooperation with Hendrix Electronics Inc. and delivered VDT and database based systems to newspapers in the Swedish A-pressen chain. The enhanced Finntext system became a success and by the end of 1973, all the VDT and data base based typesetting systems in Finland were of this type [25].

The natural extension of the Finntext system was an adaptation to the requirements of newspaper editorial work. In the USA, the first experiments with text entry and editing by journalists had been carried out in 1972. The resistance from the journalists' union was solid. The European pioneer in editorial text processing was not a large newspaper publisher with strong negotiation muscles but, surprisingly enough, a very small local newspaper in Finland. The first editorial system in Europe was installed in 1974 at *Tyrvään Sanomat,* a local newspaper in Vammala that printed 8-10 broadsheet pages twice a week. The newspaper acquired a Finntext system consisting of a DEC PDP-8/e computer with 16 k of core memory, 1.6 MB of disk storage, two Delta Telterm 5200 text terminals, a tape reader, and a line printer. The computer was connected online to a Compugraphics 4961TL photo composer. Part of the text content of the newspaper was punched on paper tape by composing room staff but a large part was input and edited directly on VDTs by journalists who also entered typographical commands. After hyphenation and justification, the text was output on a line printer and proofread. Corrections were entered on VDTs by composing room staff that also initiated output to the photo composer. The system worked well and newspaper executives from all over Europe came to visit the small town of Vammala. A similar system was soon installed at *Etelä-Suomen Sanomat* [26].

Typlan delivered a number of Finntext systems in Finland and Sweden during the early 1970s. It soon became apparent that the PDP-8 was not powerful enough to cope with the increasing systems demands: a larger number of online VDTs, larger databases, and increasing functionality. In 1974, Typlan decided to move to the more powerful PDP-11 minicomputer from DEC. The platform change required software porting and reprogramming. SITRA granted financial support for the product development effort. At the same time, Typlan departed from the principle that only staff and close supporters could own (equal) shares in the company and shares were issued to 16 of the company's customers. In 1975, the new line of newspaper production systems, the Typlan Text-11, including both composition and editorial functionality, was ready. Typlan had moved from a university research project to becoming an internationally competitive systems manufacturer.

4 BUNPAPS

While Typlan struggled with commercial applications, CGP-initiated research into interactive make-up of newspaper pages continued during 1973-75 at Brown

University, USA. Hans Andersin and Nils Enlund were visiting researchers at Brown University, involved in a research project named Brown University Newspaper Page Production System, BUNPAPS. The U.S. State Department and an international group of newspaper companies funded the project: *The New York Times, Dagens Nyheter, Providence Journal, Chicago Tribune*, and *Detroit News* [7].

The objective of the project was to demonstrate the potential of interactive and algorithmic methods in newspaper page make-up. At this time, photo composers that could expose page-wide film had become available, and the idea was to increase productivity by outputting all text elements on a page in one single operation. Graphics would still have to be pasted in manually. Full-page output would be accomplished by first entering all text, including typographical commands, into a database. The text would be hyphenated and justified and the system would generate metadata on line endings and space requirements of the text blocks. This information would be input to page layout design software using heuristics and interactive graphics to create complete page layouts. The layout coordinates would then be merged with the actual text to control full-page output on a photo composer.

A prototype system was built around an IMLAC PDS-1D graphic workstation with a 16-bit processor, 8 k of core memory, and a 13-inch vector graphics screen (Figure 5). Interaction was handled using keyboard and function keys. The workstation was connected to an IBM 360/67 timesharing system. The mainframe held the database and executed most of the calculations.

In the prototype, page make-up was based on actual text material. The space requirements of the text were calculated without performing actual H&J. Only the outlines of rectangular blocks, linked to the text files, were shown on the screen. A text could flow between several linked blocks, from column to column, or from page to page. The text blocks were placed on a grid of columns on pages.

Fig. 5. The IMLAC PDS-1D graphic workstation of the BUNPAPS project

The significant innovation in the BUNPAPS system was a set of methods for placing elements on a page that was developed, implemented, and tested [5, 6]:

Manual placement of single elements, where the operator would enter the page coordinates of the upper left hand corner of a text block. Placing a story partly on top of an already placed one would make the underlying text flow away to accommodate the new item.

"Intelligent" placement, where the operator would only give approximate, simple commands concerning the placement of a text, e.g., "as high up as possible", "in a rectangle at the bottom right", or "floating over the elements already placed at the bottom of the page". The heuristic algorithms would obtain as good a fit as possible under the given conditions. Laying out a page was very fast and the results were often quite good and aesthetically pleasing.

Template make-up was useful because certain types of newspaper pages tend to follow repeating, relatively well structured, but seldom explicitly defined design rules. Such pages can be laid out automatically. A set of alternative, flexible design template structures were defined based on an analysis of actual pages. The algorithm would propose a template that would fit the available items. The operator could choose to use an automatically generated layout or to modify one manually [11].

Holefilling is a method for the automatic placement of editorial items on such pages of a newspaper that are dominated by advertising, leaving only a relatively small "newshole" for editorial content. The heuristic algorithms would fill this space as efficiently as possible [14].

The BUNPAPS project demonstrated that computer aided page make-up was a viable concept that could speed up the newspaper page production process. The project was the starting point for the later development of commercial page make-up systems [12, 13]. The concepts were adopted by Hendrix (later Hastech) when developing the first commercially available newspaper page make-up system, PagePro [17].

5 Consequences

During the second half of the 1970s, the work of the original CGP team and its followers moved into the realm of product development and commercial applications. Typlan continued the development on the PDP-11 based, and later the VAX-11 based systems for the newspaper and commercial printing industry and became one of the main systems suppliers to the European graphic arts industry [18]. They brought the principles of computer aided page make-up back from the BUNPAPS project and the company embarked, in cooperation with the Swedish company Teragon, upon a project to create a total integrated publishing system, TIPS. This was never completed. The emergence in the mid-1980s of powerful personal computers with standardized text processing, image processing, and page make-up software eventually put an end to the vision of a centralized newspaper production system. Integrated networks of specialized subsystems on standard hardware platforms became the preferred technology. However, the pioneering innovations of the 1970s were later incorporated into modern newspaper systems [15, 16, 17]. In addition, the early production systems implemented at various newspapers prepared the Nordic newspaper industry for the coming digitalization of the page production process [2, 8].

The staff of CGP, Typlan, and BUNPAPS eventually scattered. Some remained for many years with Typlan—Nokia later acquired the company—customers, competitors or other companies employed others, and some went into the academic world. Nevertheless, they all carried with them the creative enthusiasm of the pioneering years as well as a solid knowledge of systems design and of newspaper production. In addition to some of the central ideas of the projects, this might be the most important contribution of these early development efforts.

References

[1] Andersin, H.E.: CGP research in integrated newspaper systems, Laboratory of Information Processing Science, Helsinki University of Technology, Report 2/72 (1972)

[2] Andersin, H.E.: Textprocessing research – a service to the publishing industry. Data 6, 59–64 (1976)

[3] Andersin, H.E., Perilä, O., Perttula, P.: Interactive computer systems for the newspaper process. In: TAGA-71 Proceedings, Rochester (1971)

[4] Andersin, H.E., Hallivuori, M., Koski, T.H.A., Laaksonen, K., Leppämäki, K., Lundström, L.: System for computer aided newsproduction, Laboratory of Information Processing Science, Helsinki University of Technology, Report 1/72 (1972)

[5] Andersin, H.E., Enlund, N., Hopson, R., Millbrandt, W., Woodward, J.: Computer aided pagination of newspapers. In: TAGA -74 Proceedings, New York, pp. 230–247 (1974)

[6] Andersin, H.E., Enlund, N., Hopson, R., Millbrandt, W., Woodward, J.: Newspaper pagination by intelligent graphics. In: Automaatiopäivät-75 Proceedings, Espoo (1975)

[7] Andersin, H.E., Enlund, N., Millbrandt, W.: Pagination of newspages, Laboratory of Information Processing Science, Helsinki University of Technology, Report A-5/75, Espoo, 99 p. (1975)

[8] Andersin, H.E., Enlund, N.: Coping with technological change in publishing systems, PIRA Eurotype-Forum, Leatherhead (1977)

[9] Anon: LAYOUT computer program developed by ANPA/RI. ANPA/RI Bulletin 1075, 409–416 (1971)

[10] Björk, P.: Ett datorsystem för indexering och sökning i en dagstidnings klipparkiv, (A computer system for indexing and retrieval in a newspaper archive, in Swedish), MSc thesis, Laboratory of Information Processing Science, Helsinki University of Technology, Espoo (1973)

[11] Enlund, N.: Algoritmiska metoder vid paginering av tidningssidor (Algorithmic methods for newspaper pagination, in Swedish), MSc thesis, Laboratory of Information Processing Science, Helsinki University of Technology, Espoo, 104 p. (1974)

[12] Enlund, N.: Computer-aided layout design, Computer assisted page make-up. In: IFRA Symposium Report, IFRA, Darmstadt, 5 p. (1976)

[13] Enlund, N.: Computer aided page make-up. In: Computer Aided Printing and Publishing Conference Proceedings, London (1977)

[14] Enlund, N.: Improving man-machine communication using heuristic techniques. In: Interaktivnyje Sistemy, Akademija Nauk SSSR, Moscow, pp. 60–76 (1979)

[15] Enlund, N.: Electronic page make-up today, Special Report 129, IFRA, Darmstadt, 28 p. (1983)

[16] Enlund, N.: Electronic full page make-up—what took us so long? IFRA Newspaper Techniques, March 1990, pp. 7–12 (1990)

[17] Enlund, N.: Electronic Full-Page Make-Up of Newspapers in Perspective, Gutenberg-Jahrbuch 1991, Mainz, pp. 318–323 (1991)

[18] Enlund, N., Kallioja, T.: Tietokoneen käyttö lehden valmistuksessa (Using computers in newspaper production, in Finnish), Tutkimus ja tekniikka, Number 6 (1978)

[19] Friman, E. (ed.): Från handavdragspress till offsetrotation (From manual proofing press to offset rotary press, in Swedish), Hufvudstadsbladet: Helsingfors (1984)

[20] Järvi, T.: Computerized typesetting and other newspaper applications in a publishing house. In: Impagliazzo, J., Järvi, T., Paju, P. (eds.) History of Nordic Computing 2 (HiNC2). Springer, New York (2009)

[21] Kalpa, H.: Sanansaattajana Auran rannoilla – Turun Sanomat 1905-1985 (The messenger by river Aura – Turun Sanomat 1905-1985, in Finnish), Turun Sanomat: Turku (1984)

[22] Kautto, H., Perttula, P., Sulonen, R.: Interactive computer graphics as a new tool for newspaper editors, NordDATA-70, Copenhagen (1970)

[23] Koski, T.H.A., Louhenkilpi, T., Tuukkanen, A.: Simulating a newspaper system, Laboratory of Information Processing Science, Helsinki University of Technology, Report 2/73 (1973)

[24] May, J., Wrightson, W.S.: From lead to silicon—25 years of newspaper technology. In: IFRA, Darmstadt (1986)

[25] Palonen, O.: Tinapirusta toimitusjärjestelmiin – kun tietokone tuli lehtitalon sivunvalmistukseen (From printer's devil to editorial systems – when the computer entered newspaper page production, in Finnish). Tekniikan Waiheita 2, 20–29 (2005)

[26] Perttula, P.: Redaktionens och annonsavdelningens nya teknik för textinmatning, redigering och korrigering (New technology for text entry, editing and correcting in the editorial and advertising offices, in Swedish) 7:e Nordiska Tidningstekniska Konferensen, Lahti (1974)

[27] Perttula, P.: Kehittyvä tekstinkäsittelytekniikka, (Developing text processing technology, in Finnish). Insinööritieto Oy, Helsinki (1979)

[28] Seybold, J.W., Seybold, J.: Typesetting and pre-press technology. The Seybold Report on Publishing Systems 18, 3–23 (1985)

[29] Steuber, P.: A demonstration of magazine page layout using a graphic display terminal, Computer Graphics 70, Brunel University, Uxbridge (1970)

[30] Suistola, J.: Kaleva – sata vuotta kansan kaikuja (Kaleva – one hundred years as the voice of the people, in Finnish). Kaleva Kustannus, Oulu (1990)

[31] Tewlow, J.S.: Time-sharing and the newspaper of tomorrow: Part II – The newspaper of the future. ANPA R.I. Bulletin 951, 93–110 (1968)

Modernizing Text and Data Networks in the Early 1980s

Ossi Väänänen and Olli Mertanen

Turku University of Applied Sciences, Turku, Finland
ossi.vaananen@turkuamk.fi,
olli.mertanen@turkuamk.fi

Abstract. During the decades before the beginning of 1980s, there were just a few ways to transmit messages in electrical format. As personal computers were not available on everyone's desk and minicomputers were not meant for everyday working tasks, document creation was mostly manual. In early 1980s, people started to realize for the first time that the society around them had changed due to the increasing amount of computers and communication facilities. In this paper, some views have been presented from the perspective of young engineers at that time concerning the fast change in text and data networking that took place in the 1980s. The value of the paper is mostly in writing down these views and memories with some source reference material.

Keywords: Data communication, Telex, Network coverage.

1 Introduction

During the decades before the beginning of 1980s, there were just a few ways to transmit messages in electrical format. As personal computers were not available on everyone's desk and minicomputers were not meant for everyday working tasks, document creation was mostly manual work involving pen and paper tools very much. Handwritten texts were brought to the text handling centers for typing and messages to telecommunication centers for communication [16].

The foundation for telecommunication was on the Public Switched Telephone Network (PSTN) and similar networks for text transmission such as telex. New systems like teletex and fax-transmission and very first data networks used the same kind of circuit switched network technology as PSTN. There was a strong tendency to develop the computing and communication facilities and find more effective and cost saving systems to provide increasing productivity and profitability to industrial companies. The increasingly fast development of microelectronics and the extensive industrial growth in business created great pressure for renewing the ways to process larger amounts of data in computers and to communicate effectively between companies, authorities, and individual private persons.

The authors of this article were working in pioneering data communication and computer companies like Philips and Ericsson in the early 1980s. As information flow was manageable in those days, it was somewhat easy to follow the cutting edge of technological innovation and reach a substantial awareness of the current technological

J. Impagliazzo, T. Järvi, and P. Paju (Eds.): HiNC 2, IFIP AICT 303, pp. 250–257, 2009.
© IFIP International Federation for Information Processing 2009

structures. Computer and communication branch was easily at hand and you could make acquaintance with nearly everybody who was holding remarkable positions in at least local market place.

M.Sc. Ossi Väänänen is currently a research project manager and senior lecturer in Turku University of Applied Sciences. He is preparing his dissertation work on wireless learning environments. Dr. Tech. Olli Mertanen is currently working as vice rector in Turku University of Applied Sciences and is among the main drivers in many implementations of current and past day technologies.

2 Background

At the end of the 1960s and during the 1970s most of the communication happened in analogue networks; computers were just taking first steps towards mass handling of data and communication with each other. Anyway, there were remarkable developments done in communication environments as the coverage of PSTN and telex for text messaging were quite extensive in developed countries like Finland [8].

The usage of transistors and other electronic microcircuits was increasing in the 1960s but took more speed in the 1970s towards the 1980s. The fast development of microelectronics gave an irreplaceable present to the rest of the computer and communication industry; microprocessors. With the processors, the development of distributed multiprocessor systems started, and nothing could hinder the designing of complicated computer and communication systems. Microprocessors paved also the way towards personal computing [12].

3 The Technology of the Text Messaging

Most of the first text messaging networks were PSTN like transmission networks. The communicating parties were tied together either by having a permanent line or by switched circuit between them. Permanent circuitry was expensive and they only used them by large authority organizations or big industrial companies, but the switched network technology made the communication cheaper and available to all relevant business customers.

Telex network was a fruit of old traditional type of telecom infrastructure, fulfilling the basic text communication needs, though. Telex addressing was based on the telephone number type of addresses to customers individually. Despite of the limiting character set they offered an officially accepted trustworthy way to transmit short messages between organizations.

The transmission endpoints were distant typewriters communicating with each other on the separate network. In the early 1980s, these teletype writers using paper tape punchers and readers were already quite old-fashioned tools. The new versions of the machines had gradually started to get small displays, memory facilities, and floppy disk stations thanks to first microprocessors. They coded the small character set with 5 bits allowing about sixty different characters, which was a limiting experience even at that time. Furthermore, a relatively large amount of personnel was part of telex centers to type and print out telex messages manually. In larger organizations there were several (even twenty to thirty) separate telex lines and machines to take care of the increasing communication need. In 1985, there was still something like 1.5 million telex terminals world wide of which around 7000 were in Finland [15].

Personal data communication was in its infancy. They used PSTN for some individual needs with analogue modems providing slow communication links to central office computer centers and banking services. Both personal computers and the slow communication lines were extremely expensive to use at usual homes.

4 The Technology of the Data Networking

The data networking first began with some add-on technologies applied on the top of the PSTN network. Modems were particularly popular providing first slow communication links between central computers. On the other hand, they used the modem lines as part of the computerized system architectures like IBM´s SNA and Digital's Decnet. Data terminal concentrators connected remotely to mainframe computers via the modem lines.

The first attempts to communicate electronically between organizations began. Organizations had an urgent need to exchange bigger amounts of data between them and they searched with compulsion for automated methods to accomplish this task. The transferable data was punched to a paper tape at the sending computer centre and then transmitted via the telex network. The receiving data centre punched the resulting paper tape with a telex machine and inserted then the data to their computer. Thus, telex was probably the first solution for Electronic Data Exchange between organizations [1]. Of course, for years they had to use additional manual methods in the form of punched cards and card readers and manual posting of the tapes to the other end.

In the Nordic countries, they launched the first common Nordic Data Network at the beginning of 1980s and in 1981 in Finland. The network consisted of a circuit switched (datex) and packet switched (datapak) data communication service. Telecom operators were independently running the network and it was seen as a datacom "cloud" by the customers. For the first time the customers did not know how things worked inside the cloud. Terminal connected to channel unit or concentrator and reached the central computer by using multiplexed communication channels. On the edge, the user terminals had a standardized network interface and they used network terminals to connect them physically.

This was one of the first times to enjoy the fruits of standardization in data communication. However, it caused the customers some headache because they did not allow outsiders to carry their critical secret data. The 1970s was also the time where we saw the start of large standardization efforts of ISDN, which lasted longer than anybody expected and which did not reach its maturity until the 1990s [3,4,5].

5 Industry Applications as Driving Forces

The clear driving force and enabler of the innovations was the development of microelectronics. The use of microprocessors first occurred as individual small computers; however, soon an internal communication bus between different units tied them together. Multiprocessor systems were born. The architecture was clever because each processor unit could be dedicated to do its own specialized task and each was communicating with other unit when necessary internally via the system bus [13].

The new technology allowed for bigger and more challenging system designs for the new architecture. For example, an idea of removing bottlenecks in telex centers with huge amount of manual machines came about; multiprocessor equipment with several telex lines and many attached workstations was created. Thus, one multiprocessor switch could handle centrally the traffic of many old fashioned terminals. Messages were stored on system hard disk units. Core system units like memories and other critical units were duplicated in the new system architecture for reliability. Fewer people could take over the communication administration. The system sales strategies were also changed. Modern cost calculation methods and models helped the sales and extensive public marketing with leaflets and newspaper announcements were used to soften the customer companies [14].

The telecommunication operators were offering new data networking services with enthusiasm. They offered customers both circuit or packet switched services and they used the communication mainly to connect remote terminal and concentrators to the central mainframes. As the communication industry developed and the multiprocessor technology proceeded the vendors came up with wide area privately owned telecommunication system solutions. This alternative consisted of privately owned datacom nodes or switches using operator lines between them with no other services. The investment was profitable to many big companies at that time as the communication costs were high in comparison to turnovers and amount of transferred data.

Besides the wide area communication, local area communication was reaching its revolutionary breaking point. Local area networks (LANs) were born. LANs were based on the idea of providing a faster communication channel from personal computers to mainframe computers at the premises and they gave access to shared resources like communication lines, memories, and printers. Some competing solutions and operating systems were built providing a variety of features for computing and networking. The main solutions were Ethernet and Token ring networks with some minor alternatives.

Forerunners in computing and communication were the big international vendor companies like IBM, Digital, Honeywell and Philips and the main industrial customers from branches like banking, forestry, and metallurgy. These companies implemented substantial amounts of computers terminals and communication lines. For the first time, daily business operations moved over to computer-based systems. They handled documents and data in electrical format, saved them to computer memories and made rapid transactions between organizations possible. Some people talked even about paperless office.

Banks were acting as drivers in many technological areas. The bank systems involved the biggest computer centers; they were using substantial amounts of computer terminals at large central sites. Soon the demand for increasing distribution of data handling to small office branches required new means for data communication between central computers and terminal systems. Networking the branches was quite a challenge. Although the branches were small, they were technologically complex; devices as automatic teller machines used diverse networking protocols.

Circuit switched technology provided first means to connect remote terminals and computers together. As all permanent circuits and systems provided also a permanent cost, they made the first attempts to use packet switched systems. The idea was that while being able to share effectively the communication lines by high amount of users, organizations could save a lot of money. The data was packaged in standardized form such as X.25 and was transmitted to the destinations based on the individual packet addresses. The strange idea of forcing different users' data to the very same communication line at the same time was thus implemented. Furthermore, other vendor specific protocols for application specific mainframes and new LAN protocols were increasing the complexity [9].

High demands and expectations were directed towards the new system designs for banking and other industry branches. As technology was new, many problems in product development arose. Particularly the complicated multiprocessor system software with all its different modules created huge challenges for engineering skills and the time schedules for product delivery. Key customers bought many innovations nearly before the systems software designers and production personnel had heard about them. In fact, many designs were buried before they were really born at all.

Any the zeal to make use to new innovations was increasing rapidly and the ways to shape organizations and ways of working were changing accordingly [10]. Telefax and electronic mail were known also in early 1980s and soon databases and teletext appeared. Fax is a form of transmitting images via the telephone network; electronic mail is based on storing and transmitting messages to offline users. Teletext was one-way communication media used together with TV-broadcasting where the page-formatted information was retrieved from supplementary equipment integrated to a TV-set. One of the next waves was the videotex in which the text information was refined with some graphics. Some companies tried their first e-business and news distribution with videotex services on telephone and TV networks but many of them did not live for very long.

6 Future Views during the 1980s

In early 1980s, people started to realize for the first time that the society around them had changed due to the increasing amount of computers and communication facilities. This was changing the lifestyle and in homes, people had their first personal computers and microprocessor driven household machines. Advertisements were distributed to homes based on computerized database registers and visual world got first television and film animations. Banking and dealing with public authorities was more and more based on computer driven data handling, providing electronic accounting, data form editing, and bank transfer.

Future anticipations included views where everything was electronic and automated including money, post, newspapers, department stores, and offices. The worst fears were as bad as changing the work tasks totally and making them extremely difficult. The change would mean at least the necessity of learning constantly new things, having assignments with ultimate requirements of precision and the complex future work would provide less human contacts and lack any personality. Even wider views were presented e.g. by Daniel Bell in the 1970s, when he pointed out the critical change of society because of the changing role of information and knowledge, human roles and industrial production structures [2]. Many guesses turned out to be true but were also strongly exaggerated as we can see now [6].

New worries rose also for the first time as areas like data security and work ergonomics were lacking all basic knowledge at that time. Personal information including political, religion, conviction, health, creditability, criminal records, and punishments seemed to be compromised due to new ways of data handling [11]. People realized that the machines capable of storing substantial amounts of data would represent a major thread for their personal integrity. One could retrieve data in a non-visual form without physical access to the data storage; therefore, it was impossible to monitor what happened with traditional methods. In addition, there was some discussion of access rights to the intimate personal data of individuals. Nobody in fact understood that future internet would transmit simultaneously e.g. over 30 million people´s messages, not to talk about billions. And that even every child would have access to all kinds of data in the world [7]. In many countries, some form of legislation was set up quickly; but, for example, in Finland political contradictions prevented such legislation until the mid 1980s.

7 Conclusions

The 1980s started in a world where telecommunication spread widely in western countries and other developed areas. They used PSTN and telex for basic communication needs and the first local and wide area data networks were in the making. Teleoperators were managing most of the wide area communication services offered by them.

In early 1980s, the communication environment started to change due to increased variety of solutions offered for local and wide area networking; privately owned solutions were soon available. Complex multiprocessor system designs were utilized for the first time and the engineering staff was having hard times in trying to get the real time processing to work properly. Old solutions became better by refining their feature sets and many new solution evolved and ambitious efforts were made to standardize future networking solution. People started to use personal computing, communication, and home electronics for the first time and they felt some hesitation towards the future effects of IT to their foreseeable future.

In this paper, we have presented some views from the perspective of young engineers concerning the fast change in text and data networking that took place in the 1980s. The value of the paper is mostly in writing down these views and memories with some literature references. By now, we know that the development during the past few decades was quite amazing and was not foreseeable at those days. Even the wildest ideas presented in science fiction during that time belong now to our every day life!

References

[1] Auvinen, S.(toim.): EDI/OVT-ratkaisut liiketoiminnan menestystekijöinä (EDI-solutions as success factors in business), Suomen kuljetustaloudellinen yhdistys RY, Loimaan kirjapaino, Helsinki (1992)

[2] Bell, D.: The Coming of Post-industrial Society: A Venture in Social Forecasting. Basic books, New York (1973)

[3] Berndt, W.: The significance of standardization in the field of telecommunications for innovation, competition and world trade. In: 1986 Yearbook of the Deutsche Bundespost, preprint. Bad Windsheim (1986)

[4] Groebmair, K.: Integrierte Kommunikation: ISDN-Systems furs Buro (Integrated communication: ISDN-systems for the Office), Siemens Nathan International, Munchen (1985)

[5] Haglund, H., Kanervisto, J., Wirzenius, A.: ISDN näkökulmia (ISDN-views and scenarios), Tiedonsiirron yhteistyöelin: raportti 1/88, Kouvolan kirjapaino, Helsinki (1988)

[6] Henten, A., Kristensen, T.M.: Information society visions in the Nordic countries. Telematics and Informatics 17 (2000)

[7] IT-kommisionen: Informationsteknologien, Vingar åt människans förmåga (Information technologies. Wings for human capabilities), SOU (1994)

[8] Magnus, K., Lennart, S.(Red.): Världens största maskin, Människan och det globala telekommunikations systemet (The greatest machine in the world. People and the global telecommunication system), författarna och Carlsson Bokförlag (1995) ISBN 91 7798 990 2

[9] Marttila, H., Lautanala, K.: Tiedonsiirtopalvelujen valintaopas (The guide for telecommunication services selection), Tiedonsiirron yhteistyöelin, raportti 1/87, Painovalssi, Helsinki (1987)

[10] Mertanen, O.: Tietoverkkojen käyttömahdollisuudet keskisuurten ja suurten organisaatioiden dataliikenteen hoitamiseksi (The telecommunication network utilization alternatives for middle sized and big organizations), Licentiate thesis, Tampere University of Technology, Tampere (1985)

[11] Naisbitt, J.: Megatrends: Ten new directions transforming our lives, London, Futura (1984)

[12] Seppo, P.: Tietotekniikan artikkelisanakirja (Information technology article glossary), Tietoportti Ky (1985) ISBN 951-99683-5-0

[13] Queyssac, D.: Mikrotietokoneet 1 (Microcomputers 1). Infopress, Jyväskylä (1978)

[14] Riikonen, J., Kontinen, K., Lilius, R., Tuominen, P.: Toimistorutiinien päällekkäisyys (The routine overlap in offices), Suomen itsenäisyyden juhlavuoden 1967 rahasto: sarja B, no: 70, Kyriiri, 1982, Helsinki

[15] Sihvo, L.: Tekniikan käsikirja 3 (The technology handbook 3), Sähkötekniikka, K.J. Gummerus osakeyhtiö Jyväskylä (1968)

[16] Tuovinen, J.: Sähköpostin käyttömahdollisuudet ja vaikutukset yrityksissä (The utilisation of elecronic mail and the operational effects in enterprises), Nokia Campus –julkaisu 2/1988, Vientipaino, Helsinki (1988)

Glossary of Terms

Data communication: The transmission of machine readable code on a communication network.

Data processing system: Data processing system is a permanent set up of computer equipment for processing a relevant set of information handling tasks.

Microprocessor: The microprocessor is an electronic component where all logical operations are placed in one physical circuit that is microscopic in size.

Memory: Memory is data storage were machine readable code is saved for future use for short or longer times. The memory can physically as well be a magnetic tape or electronic memory circuit inside a computer.

Network Access: The network access is the way to connect the computer into the network. The network access can be wired or wireless referring to the physical form of the networking media.

Network coverage: The network coverage is the exact area where the signal from the nearest network station can be received. The coverage area is dependant on many things like the transmission power of the signaling system, locations of the neighboring stations and the physical structure of the network.

Online banking terminal: Equipment meant for public use to automate the personal banking operations with help of the bank personnel.

Telex: Text formatted data sent to a remote teletype terminal on a separate telex network. Very limited character set and the use of paper tape punch characterized the communication operation.

Lexicography for IBM

Developing Norwegian Linguistic Resources in the 1980s

Jan Engh

Oslo University Library, Norway
jan.engh@ub.uio.no

Abstract. In 1984, IBM and the University of Oslo set up a joint project, probably the first project of its kind in Norway. Its aim was to develop Norwegian language resources for IBM application software – for PCs, midrange computers, and mainframes. The primary objective: to create a "base dictionary" module that would drive language sensitive functions. The technology was based on simple character sequence recognition; its great asset being high compaction and rapid access to correct data. The module was to be built on documented linguistic forms. The dictionary should cover the general part of the vocabulary, and a broad coverage module was created for Norwegian Bokmål. Later, one module for Nynorsk was developed as well. At that stage, however, the project had become a regular IBM project. In the following years, other linguistic functions were added and eventually, the result served as the foundation for a grammar and for machine translation. The project was terminated because of the corporate financial crisis of the late 1980s. Later, the dictionaries were transferred to the University of Oslo. They are now an integral part of the basic infrastructure for Norwegian academic computational linguistics.

Keywords: Lexicography, Norwegian language, natural language processing, IBM, application software.

1 Introduction

In 1984, IBM's Advanced Office Systems Technology (AOST, Gaithersburg MA) launched an international corporate offensive to create language sensitive software after several years of development work for English (see [3] and [4]). As in the rest of IBM's Europe, Middle East, and Africa division, local managements in the Nordic countries were instructed to start development, if necessary in cooperation with the local universities.

Since IBM Norway had no staff with the necessary linguistic competence at the time, the natural choice was to turn to the University of Oslo for linguistic assistance. A joint project was set up with the specific aim of developing necessary resources for the Norwegian language and having them implemented and tested using relevant application software. Corresponding development was carried out for all the other major Nordic languages in the respective countries, although with great variation both as far as organisation and linguistic development etc. were concerned.

J. Impagliazzo, T. Järvi, and P. Paju (Eds.): HiNC 2, IFIP AICT 303, pp. 258–270, 2009.
© IFIP International Federation for Information Processing 2009

To my knowledge, this was IBM's first formalized software development contract with a Norwegian university. One University of Oslo research officer was assigned to the task as project leader (Jan Engh) that later involved several assistants. A steering committee was appointed, constituted by one IBM representative (Jan Hølen), and two representatives from the University of Oslo (Even Hovdhaugen and Jo Terje Ydstie) in addition to the project leader. The project took place on IBM premises and it was 100% funded by IBM, which also had the exclusive right to the research and development results.

2 The Project

The primary objective of the project, referred to internally as "the LEXIS project", was to create a linguistic component, a "base dictionary" module, for all natural language sensitive software. This module would function as an extensive "dictionary" for the analysis (recognition) of Norwegian word forms and for the generation both of alternatives to unrecognized possible words and of hyphenation points in word processing programs. Originally, the base dictionary module was intended for use in text-processing software only. Later, it was used for other types of application software as well and more components were added.

With a minimum of adaptation, the module was supposed to drive language sensitive functions in all of IBM's own application software for the embryonic PC market via midrange computers to the mainframes: Spelling checker, correct word form suggestions, and automatic hyphenation.

At this phase of development, all these functions were "unintelligent", based on simple character sequence recognition. The philosophy behind the base dictionary was that it would provide any program with documented information of the language in question. The coverage was extensive, and for instance rule-based hyphenation algorithms were to be used only for unrecognized character sequences. The great asset of the base dictionary concept was its compaction technology and the rapid access to the correct data, both extremely important factors at a time when the IBM XT (introduced 1983) came with a 256 kB memory working at a pace of 4.77 MHz.

The target group was *all* possible users. The dictionary component was not intended for office use only, but for school and everyday purposes as well. This was reflected in the coverage of the base dictionary. It should cover the general part of the vocabulary. IBM management had quite an optimistic view of how computers would penetrate into daily life.

3 The Base Dictionary

3.1 Vocabulary

The vocabulary of the base dictionary contained the core lexicon of Norwegian and as much more as practically possible. All and only the forms of the word types (lexemes) were included except defective forms, e.g. plural forms of most abstract words, such as *hat* 'hatred'.

In accordance with the company's policy of observing official standards and maintaining political neutrality, the official orthography as laid down by *Norsk språkråd* (The Council for the Norwegian Language) was adopted.

3.2 Architecture

The base dictionary consisted of three levels:[1] One "ultrahigh frequency" wordlist of 204 word forms was contained in the set of words generated by a "high frequency" dictionary, which in turn was a proper subset of the word forms generated by the main dictionary. In the original English version, the ultrahigh frequency list was supposed to represent approximately 50% of the word forms in a general text. The high frequency dictionary, in turn, should cover 85%.

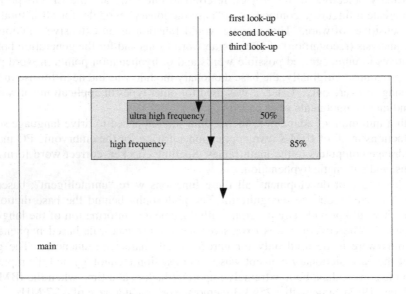

Fig. 1. Base dictionary architecture

This general architecture for Norwegian was adopted without modifications, despite the fact that it was based on frequency data for English.

3.3 Linguistic Interlude

The frequency assumptions were not the only aspect of the base dictionary concept showing that it had been developed for the English language. There was, in fact, a clear correspondence between the technical solutions adopted and the particular structural characteristics of English. Or, to put it differently: From a morphology point of view, English is, by coincidence, a "simple" language that happened to be adequately catered for by the current state-of-the-art technology.

---

[1] A detailed documentation of the input files formats, the development project history and the ensuing products can be found in Engh 1991[5]. See also [6].

A trivial point was the fact that the set of characters allowed in the input files was the one of English, A – Z. Since all other European languages use more characters, these had to be represented as double byte characters. Less trivial were the cases where the lack of English "simplicity" could be compensated for by quantity. English has only two noun forms, singular and plural[2] and a minimum of verbal forms.

singular	plural
car	*cars*

infinitive/present plural	*swear*
present singular	*swears*
past	*swore*
perfect	*sworn*

In linguistic terms, English has a poor morphology. Norwegian, on the other hand, has four noun forms and a few more verbal forms etc. Additionally, Norwegian orthography is characterized by a certain variability; that is, each "slot" in the paradigm may be occupied by more than one form, which means that for instance a number of nouns have many more than four forms.[3] Not only

		singular	plural
indefinite		*bil* 'car'	*biler*
definite		*bilen*	*bilene*

but even

	singular	plural
indefinite	*bok* 'book'	*bøker*
definite	*boka, boken*	*bøkene*
indefinite	*system* 'system'	*system, systemer*
definite	*systemet*	*systemene, systema*

or more, not to mention verb forms such as

infinitive	*sverge, sverje* 'swear (an oath)'
present	*sverger, sverjer*
past	*sverget, sverjet, sverga, sverja, svor*
perfect	*sverget, sverjet, sverga, sverja, svoret*
perfect plural/weak form	*svergete, svergede, svorne*

---

[2] The '*s* genitive is a suffix that can be added to almost every noun, and it is correspondingly easy to analyse and generate. This also holds for its Norwegian parallel, *s*, which may even attach to participle forms.

[3] And then there is the Bokmål/Nynorsk problem. Spoken Norwegian is one language with a number of dialects. However, there are two different ways of writing the language, Bokmål and Nynorsk. That is, Norwegian has two written standards. In the current setting, this means two separate base dictionaries etc. [19, pp. 53-57 and 98-104] describes the relationship between Bokmål and Nynorsk for those unfamiliar with the language situation in Norway.

However, this can be compensated for by just adding word forms and making the dictionary bigger. In principle, this has the effect that the (English) frequency considerations behind the tripartite architecture of the base dictionary become somewhat distorted. In practice, however, the Norwegian ultra high frequency list represented no problem. As for the high frequency dictionary, it had to be based on a rough estimate, since adequate frequency data for Norwegian was not available and could not be produced within the limited timeframes of the first project. Still, relatively infrequent genitive word forms, for instance, were simply omitted from the paradigms of the *lexemes* selected based on frequency data from many sources.

To some extent, a greater quantity can even compensate for the, in theory, infinite number of compound words of Norwegian. In written English, compounds are, in general, sequences of separate words, whereas Norwegian compound words, in contrast, constitute single complex words with other possible words as their constituents. In the English dictionary, *red* and *wine* has two entries, which also cover *red wine*. The Norwegian dictionary needs three entries: *rød* 'red' *vin* 'wine', and *rødvin* 'red wine' with the same inflected forms as *vin*. One apparent solution is to introduce a rule to combine constituents, which, in fact, was an option in the base dictionary format. There are, however, two main reasons why one should not adopt such a solution. One relates to possible applications (see below); the other is of a direct linguistic nature.

In addition to the simple juxtaposition type mentioned above, Norwegian exhibits far more complicated systems in multiple compounds (see [11, pp. 71f]). For instance, the emerging S and the disappearing E linking the main constituents pertaining to various different classes of lexemes: On the one hand, *vinglass* 'wineglass', and *krystallvinglass* 'wineglass made of crystal', but *rødvinsglass* 'glass for red wine' with an *s*. On the other hand, *lasteskip* 'cargo ship', and *diesellasteskip* 'diesel cargo ship', but *tørrlastskip* 'dry-cargo ship' without the *e*. No simple expansion of any dictionary can compensate fully for this type of occurrence.

3.4 Input Files

For both the main dictionary and the high frequency dictionary, the linguistic input files consisted of one stems file and several auxiliary files, of which the endings file was the most prominent (see [2]).

3.4.1 Stems File

From a linguistic point of view, a word is analyzed as a stem plus optional affixes (derivation or inflection). For instance, the Norwegian verb *bile* 'go by car; drive' contains the stem *bil* 'car' plus the infinitive suffix *e*. The noun *bile* 'axe', on the other hand, has the stem *bile*. Meaningfulness is a requirement. However, the base dictionary was *not* organized according to this linguistic principle. A stem in the stems file was a technical stem, which might or might not coincide with the linguistic stem. It had to be a valid word form, though, which meant that *bil* would represent both the noun *bil* and the verb and noun *bile* in the stems file. This had rather peculiar consequences for the analysis and inclusion of the Norwegian vocabulary, as will be shown below.

The stems file had the following format:

```
NORSK2    DICT      D1   V 150  Trunc=150 Size=33015 Line=7883 Col=1 Alt=0
====>
!...+...10....+...20....+...30.....+...50....+...60....+...70....+...80..
finn                       0   0NV.............O ØcING ØcV1 Øc11        07883
(---)
fins                       0   0JV............B                        07898
finsk                      0   0J.............A ØJ11                    07899
Finske_bukt                0   0N.............A ØF3B                    07900
fint_bygd                  0   0J.............O ØJ11                    07901
fint_føl_en_de             0   0J.............O ØJs                     07902
```

Fig. 2. Sample of stems file

Every record contained information about one "stem" and other word forms derived from the stem and the endings indicated. The stems were written from the first column, in EBCDIC with non-English characters represented as described in an auxiliary file. "_" represented a hyphenation point. (In later versions, the possibility of preferred hyphenation points was introduced.) In the following columns, additional information was stored. Columns 41-44 contained information about confusable stems, while column 45 was reserved for grade level information in the US English version. Columns 46-53 contained part of speech information ("N" for 'noun', "V" for 'verb', "J" for 'adjective' etc.), and column 61 was reserved for a word compounding flag. From column 63 to the end of the record, optional information was entered about the word forms that could be derived based on the stem.

As for the compounding flags, they indicate whether a given word form could appear as the constituent of another – compound – word. Additionally, each ending associated with the stem carried such a flag, indicating the combinability of the derived word form. Based on this information, compound words not represented in the dictionary were supposed to be recognized.[4] There was a limited set of possible combinability values: "B" 'back or isolated', "O" 'offset (i.e. cannot be a constituent of a compound word)', "F" 'front or middle', "A" 'anyplace', and four more. This was a simplistic, yet extremely powerful device – to the extent that it ought to be heavily restricted. Only a very limited use of the compounding flags was made for Norwegian. (With the extra precaution that the spelling checker of the application program would only consider words of considerable length as possible constituents.)

Column 63 etc. contained information about all the words derivable from the stem. Most of it in was provided in a shorthand writing as "implied endings", i.e. codes representing sets of endings. These implied endings were declared in the endings file.

3.4.2 Endings File
The endings of the endings file were technical suffixes, parallel to the technical stems of the stems file.

---

[4] Originally, this component was intended for both analysis and generation of compound words, e.g. even for the spelling aid window, see [13] and [14]. It was, however, completely unsuitable for the latter purpose, and was never used for generation in any software for Norwegian.

```
NORSK2   LEXISEND  A1  F 80  Trunc=80 Size=1494 Line=0 Col=1 Alt=0
====>
!...+....1....  +....2....+....3....+....4....+....5....+....6....+....7..

* * * Top of File * * *                                            00000
ØcJ1     e t ere est este s es eres estes                          00001
        >J AJ AJ AJ  J   J J  J     J                              00002
        >>O O  O  O   O    O O  O     O                            00003
ØcJ1s    e t ere est este es eres estes                           00004
        >J AJ AJ AJ  J   J J  J                                   00005
        >>O O  O  O   O    O O  O                                 00006
```

Fig. 3. Sample of endings file

Every three-line "paragraph" constituted the record of an implied ending set. In the first columns, the name of the set was given with an initial Ø character. From column 10, the endings were listed. On the second line, the part of speech for each stem plus ending was given (a word *pene* is an adjective, >J, *pent* an adverb or an adjective, >AJ, etc.). For practical reasons, they were both marked as offset, >>O.

3.4.3 Additional Auxiliary Input Files
Several additional auxiliary files were to be created. Some were of a linguistic nature such as those containing the 60 most frequent endings, information about hyphenation of endings, alternative representation of sounds, and characters, while others had a strictly technical content.

3.5 No Duplicates

The unfolded result (i.e. all the stems and the word forms generated by means of the stems and the endings) had to be free from duplicates. That is, one word in the sense of 'sequence of characters' should be represented only once, regardless of possible multiple meanings. This was important in order to save space, facilitating the compaction process and making recognition more efficient and precise. To implement the no duplicate requirement, a huge and complicated puzzle work was necessary. In fact, both the development of appropriate implied endings and the classification of the vocabulary by means of the result constituted a time-consuming activity. (See [5, pp. 12-18].)

4 Preconditions and Implementations

A complete development environment was provided by AOST for the developmental work, which was carried out on a 370 mainframe under VM/CMS. Initially, AOST even provided an electronic corpus, based on IBM business correspondence in Norway. Obviously, it was totally unbalanced and turned out to be of little value. Since no extensive machine-readable linguistic material for Norwegian was freely available at that time,[5] development continued by including all words found in accessible printed frequency material and words pertaining to all relevant lexical spheres (colors, parts of the body, kinship and construction terms etc.) were systematically entered. To extend the coverage further, the developers' private documents and all accessible company documents were regularly passed through the updated spelling checker to detect candidate words. Dictionaries were consulted, never copied. (It was a strict requirement that other authors' copyrights were not infringed upon.) Moreover, a considerable amount of information was required that could not be found in any dictionary such as defective forms. This was produced by the project group.

After successful test building, all source files were shipped to Gaithersburg for the final build and implementation in application software: *DisplayWrite* (later, even in lower end software such as *WritingAssistent* and in specialized composition software). Finally, the dictionaries had to be tested for each software release at IBM Norway. The project group established a special corpus of texts for this purpose.

5 History and Strategic Figures

The project started in the summer of 1984. The first phase ended one year later. The subsequent phases of the project were carried out as a regular IBM research and development project. Although the *formal* ties to the University of Oslo were severed, close informal ties were kept in view of recruitment. (24 linguists worked for the group, part-time or full-time for shorter or longer periods. (See [12].)

At the end of the first phase, the base dictionary contained 30,972 stems; the number of unique word forms generated was 292,190 - much more than existed at the base of the linguistic functions of any competitor at that time. Yet, this dictionary size was still far from ideal for a language considerably more inflected than English, although a significantly higher number of lexemes than 30,972 were covered due to the great quantity of homonyms. (The limited use of the compound recognition device expanded the total number of word forms covered even more.) Only Norwegian Bokmål was catered for during the first phase of the project. There were five subsequent Bokmål releases in all. The last main dictionary (1989) contained 51,292 stems, generating 487,166 unique word forms.

A parallel development program for Nynorsk started in 1988. Due to linguistic factors, the Nynorsk resources had to be created almost from scratch. No simple conversion of linguistic data from one written standard to the other was possible. The

---

[5] There were a few insignificant and scattered resources at the University of Oslo and Bergen in the early 1980s. However, they were inaccessible for an industry development project such as the one of IBM. Additionally, there was the machine-readable manuscript of *Bokmålsordboka* (a medium size monolingual dictionary) which was not yet finished in its first version [16],. However, *Bokmålsordboka* was inaccessible to the IBM project. Several years later, the right to use the electronic manuscript was acquired for IBM Norway internal use only. Still, it was never utilized for development purposes, only as test bed for a separate experimental linguistic database format, *WordSmith*, see [1].

second and final release for Nynorsk (1990) had a base dictionary of 92,787 stems, generating 360,680 unique word forms.[6]

6   The Need for an Implemented Morphology

In a subsequent phase, IBM wanted to develop new dictionary functions. Now, this was problematic, as the base dictionary was not properly organized from a linguistic point of view. That is, the information provided by the base dictionary did not indicate to which lexeme or lemma a given word form belonged. Cf. the case of *bil* 'car' and *bile* 'axe' above, which were recognized because of the very same "technical" stem. Thus, a genuine morphology and a corresponding lexicon had to be establish as a bridge between the word form recognition component of the base dictionary and, for instance, a synonym dictionary: Its main components were the lexicon input file and the inflection input file.

```
NOB_UTV  CLASS     A1  F 50   Trunc=50 Size=34 Line=0 Col=1 Alt=3
====>
!...+....1....   +....2....+....3....+....4....+....>

* * * Top of File * * *                                        00000
bygg                            800                            00001
bygg                            890                            00002
byggaks                         804                            00003
byggbrød                        800                            00004
byggdyrking                     900                            00005
bygge                           031                            00006
```

Fig. 4. Sample of lexicon input file

The structure of these files was very simple. In the lexicon input file, the lemma forms (the singular indefinite forms of nouns, the infinitive of verbs etc.) were listed with a code referring to an entry in a paradigm, which was given in the inflection input file. For example, *bygg* 'building; construction site' is inflected according to the paradigm Ø800, while *bygg* 'barley' is inflected according to Ø890, the verb *bygge* 'build; construct' according to Ø031 etc.

In its fifth and last commercial release, the Bokmål morphology contained 65,128 lemmata and 705 paradigms (1989). In the version ready when the entire project was terminated (1991), this had been expanded to a total of 121,577 lemmata. As for the Nynorsk files, the second and last release (1990) contained 110,412 lemmata and 576 paradigms.

The development software and the test-building environment for the morphology were developed in cooperation by AOST, the Centro Científico de IBM (Madrid), and by the Norwegian lexicography group during the first quarter of 1986. This subproject was carried out via VNET, IBM's own network system in the 1980s. VNET

---

[6] The low number of unique word forms compared to the number of stems is mainly due to the fact that only proper names have a genitive form in official Nynorsk orthography, not nouns in general as in Bokmål.

```
NOB6      TABLE      A1  F 50   Trunc=50 Size=7540 Line=782 Col=1 Alt=0
====>
!...+....1....  +....2....+....3....+....4....+....>
*neutr fullst N1 <tak>                                             00781
Ø800 Ø    NORNN                                                   00782
01                                                                00783
02 et                                                             00784
03                                                                00785
04 a,ene                                                          00786
05 s                                                              00787
06 ets                                                            00788
07 s                                                              00788
08 as,enes                                                        00788
```

Fig. 5. Sample of inflection input file

made it possible to run continuous working sessions between persons in different locations, in this case Bethesda (MA, USA), Madrid, and Oslo. In general, VNET was extensively used during the entire project period. There was contact between all the linguistic groups of Europe and the Middle East and the US laboratories more or less on a daily basis with a two-way flow of technical and linguistic information.

7 New Dictionary Functions

The implemented morphology made it possible to create a "morphology window", where the declension or conjugation of a given word form in a text could be displayed. This feature had a great educational potential, since the end user had the possibility to swap between linguistic modules (Norwegian, English, German, etc.). More importantly, the morphology paved the way for a synonyms function. Two extensive synonym dictionaries were created from scratch by the IBM Norway linguist group, one for Bokmål and one for Nynorsk.

The latter edition was the largest, containing approximately 25,000 entries, corresponding to a mid-size printed dictionary. The objective of the synonym dictionaries was to help the end user to write better Norwegian. There were two reasons why the synonym dictionaries had to be developed: The existing (printed) dictionaries had been edited mainly in view of solving crossword puzzles, i.e. not to help the users improve their writing. In addition, unlike the case with other language communities, IBM could not purchase them.

```
NYNORSK   IBM_SYN   A1  V 80   Trunc=80 Size=267 Line=91 Col=1 Alt=0
====>
!...+....1....+....2....+....3....+....4....+....5....+....6....+....7..
akta:j  gjæv, god, høgvørd.                                       00089
akte:v                                                            00090
    ta omsyn til, leggje vekt på, anse, ense, merkje seg,         00091
    vere merksam på;                                              00092
    ha stor vørnad for respektere, ære, heidre, vørde, tykkje om, 00093
    synast om;                                                    00094
    verdsetje, vurdere, mæte, skatte, estimere;                   00095
    vilje, emne på, rekne med å, tenkje, tenkje på, ha i sinne,   00096
    intendere.                                                    00097
    <C seg>                                                       00098
        vare seg;                                                 00099
        etle seg;                                                 00100
        vilje;                                                    00101
```

Fig. 6. Sample of synonyms input file

Additionally, rules for algorithmic hyphenation were implemented and a variation representation prototype was developed, exploiting the vacant grade level indicator for US English. It indicated to which level within a given written standards of Norwegian a word belonged, e.g. "radical" vs. "moderate" Bokmål. However, this particular feature was never implemented in any product.

8 Linguistic Challenges

During the technical development, the project group spent much time and effort clarifying the linguistic norm – not at all a trivial matter as far as the Norwegian language is concerned. One complicating factor was the inherent variability that characterizes Norwegian in contrast to most other languages, although the main cause was undoubtedly the surprisingly incomplete and incoherent standardization of the language in general. In innumerable cases, the *Norsk språkråd* had to be consulted – also for the benefit of Norwegian normative grammar. See [8]

9 Further Development and Market Considerations

The twin morphologies were later used as a basis for further "intelligent" linguistic functions (grammar and style critiquing) and stand-alone software (machine translation). That is another story (documented in [10]). Neither did materialize as products, due to the financial crisis that shook IBM in the late 1980s. At that time, entire development areas were eliminated, no matter their quality or state of progression. In the case of the linguistics development, one reason for its termination may have been that IBM's own word processing software, the *DisplayWrite* products, which never sold well, despite their comprehensive dictionary features. IBM sales representatives never understood this asset, and more importantly: They had no special incentive to promote them. The project failed to finance itself during the development period, and by the end of the 1980s, the days of very long-term investments in American software industry were gone.

10 Concluding Remarks

The entire IBM linguistic effort was a broad front offensive. At a time when other companies and academia contented themselves with creating linguistic toy systems that did not scale up, IBM went for full-scale development, covering language in general. At a regular pace, development advanced from the lexicographic basics to state-of-the-art computational grammar. (See[15]) Moreover, equally important, every language of at least the size of Icelandic saw almost parallel development. This was, in fact, the first worldwide investment by a private company in the area of multilingual natural language processing.

When IBM finally quit linguistic development for Norwegian, after almost 8 years of intense work (see [7]), AOST's successor sold the penultimate version of the lexicon and the morphology to a publisher, while IBM Norway transferred the most recent files to the University of Oslo for a symbolic sum. Today, they are part of the basic infrastructure of academic computational linguistics in Norway.[7]

Acknowledgments

I extend a special thanks to Diana Santos who read the draft and to Stig Johansson and Per Vestbøstad for clarification of facts.

References

[1] Baustad, J.: Automatisk analyse av maskinleselige ordbøker til bruk i en orddatabase (Automatic analysis of machine readable dictionaries for the creation of a word database). In: Fjeld, R.V. (ed.) Nordiske studier i leksikografi. Rapport fra Nordisk konferanse i leksikografi i Oslo, mai 1991 (Skrifter utgitt av Nordisk forening for leksikografi 1), pp. 423–431. Nordisk forening for leksikografi, Oslo (1992)

[2] Casajuana, R.: LEXIS input files. A comprehensive description. TESTBLD. A user guide. Unpublished paper, Centro Científico de IBM, Madrid (1989)

[3] Convis, D.B., Glickman, D., Rosenbaum, W.S.: Alpha content match prescan method for automatic spelling error correction. United States Patent 4, 328, 561 (1982)

[4] Convis, D.B., Glickman, D., Rosenbaum, W.S.: Instantaneous alpha content prescan method for automatic spelling error correction. United States Patent 355, 371 (1983)

[5] Engh, J.: IBM's Norwegian Lexicon Projects 1984-1991. Unpublished report, IBM Norge. Kolbotn (1991)

[6] Engh, J.: Leksikografi i IBM Norge (Lexicography at IBM Norway). In: Fjeld, R.V. (ed.) Nordiske studier i leksikografi. Rapport fra Nordisk konferanse i leksikografi i Oslo, mai 1991 (Skrifter utgitt av Nordisk forening for leksikografi 1), pp. 409–422. Nordisk forening for leksikografi, Oslo (1992a)

[7] Engh, J.: "Språkforskning i IBM Norge" 'Linguistic research at IBM Norway'. [Paper read at Møte om norsk språk (MONS) IV, Oslo 15.-17.11.1991] Printed in NORSKRIFT 72, 16–36 (1992b)

[8] Engh, J.: Linguistic normalisation in language industry: Some normative and descriptive aspects of dictionary development. Hermes. Journal of linguistics 1, 53–64 (1993)

[9] Engh, J.: IBMmorf. Bruksanvisning for IBMs leksikon og morfologi for moderne norsk (Manual for the use of IBM's lexicon and morphology of Modern Norwegian). Dokumentasjonsprosjektet, Universitetet i Oslo (1994a), http://folk.uio.no/janengh/IBMmorf.htm

[10] Engh, J.: Developing Grammar at IBM Norway 1988-1991. Unpublished report. Oslo (1994b)

[11] Engh, J.: Bindebokstaver (Binding morphemes). In: Gundersen, D., Engh, J., Fjeld, R.E.V. (eds.) Språkvett. Skriveregler, grammatikk og språklige råd fra a til å, pp. 67–72. Kunnskapsforlaget, Oslo (2001)

[12] Engh, J. [s.a.]: Natural language processing at IBM Norway, http://folk.uio.no/janengh/IBMnorsk.htm

---

[7] See [18], [17], [9], and the following pointers (1 December 2008): http://www.dokpro.uio.no/ordboksoek.html; http://www.hf.uio.no/tekstlab/innsyn/norsk.html; http://www.edd.uio.no/prosjekt/ordbanken/

[13] Frisch, R., Zamora, A.: Method for verifying spelling of compound words. United States Patent 4777617 (1988a), http://www.freepatentsonline.com/4777617. html (April 7, 2007)

[14] Frisch, R., Zamora, A.: Spelling assistance for compound words. IBM Journal of research and development 32(2), 195–200 (1988b)

[15] Jensen, K., Heidorn, G., Richardson, S. (eds.): Natural Language Processing: The PLNLP Approach. Kluwer, Hingham (1992)

[16] Landrø, M.I., Wangensteen, B., et al.: Bokmålsordboka: definisjons- og rettskrivningsordbok (A dictionary of Norwegian Bokmål: Definitions and orthography). Universitetsforlaget, Bergen (1986)

[17] Ore, C.-E.: Metaordboken - et rammeverk for Norsk Ordbok? (The metadictionary – a framework for Norsk Ordbok?) Paper read at the conference Leksikografi i Norden, Göteborg (1999), http://www.edd.uio.no/artiklar/leksikografi/ artikkel_Goeteborg.html

[18] Ore, C.-E., Kristiansen, N. [s.a.] (eds.): Sluttrapport 1992-1997 (Final report 1992-1997). Dokumentasjonsprosjektet, Universitetet i Oslo, http://www.dokpro.uio.no/ sluttrapp.pdf

[19] Vikør, L.: The Nordic languages. Their status and interrelations, 3rd edn. (Nordic Language Secretariat. Publication 14). Novus, Oslo (2001)

The Development of Software Testing
in Finland 1950–2000

Pentti A. Pohjolainen

Department of Computer Science, University of Kuopio,
P.O. Box 1627, FI-70211 Kuopio, Finland
papohjol@cs.uku.fi

Abstract. The paper presents the development of software testing in Finland. This topic has received little academic attention and it is frequently forgotten. The existing publications concentrate more on the history of machines and programming languages than on the history of the development of testing. The analysis made so far proves that the problems in the early times were very different from nowadays. For example, during the 1950s and 1960s, it was difficult to get computation time for testing. Meanwhile, during the 1990s, and after that, the greatest source of problems has been the complexity and the massiveness of programs. On the other hand, it seems that the education of testing has not been sufficient until the end of 1990s. Hence, the knowledge of diverse testing methods, test automation, and outsourcing are now better than in the past. In our research, we have interviewed over fifty persons. The interviewees vary from pioneers of Finnish computing, having tens of years career, to young professionals of testing. Their selection is from Finnish universities and over twenty companies in Finland.

Keywords: Development of testing, growth of testing, testing methods.

1 Introduction

We have found during this research how important and interesting area software testing is. In the beginning of many meetings, the interviewee has said, "I think that I have nothing to tell about testing". After a couple of hours, we see surprisingly that we have discussed all the time just about testing.

We have also found that no one ever researched the development of the software testing in historical perspective in Finland. Outside of Finland, we have found only one article [32], which tries to classify the development of testing in some kind of the stages.

Gelperin and Hetzel [32] have named five stages of the growth of testing: The debugging-oriented period before year 1956, the demonstration-oriented period between years 1957-1978, the destruction-oriented period between years 1979-1982, the evaluation-oriented period between years 1983-1987, and finally the prevention-oriented period after year 1988. This partition received a contradictory reception among the interviewees. Some of the interviewees considered the partition artificial, while others considered it correct.

J. Impagliazzo, T. Järvi, and P. Paju (Eds.): HiNC 2, IFIP AICT 303, pp. 271–282, 2009.
© IFIP International Federation for Information Processing 2009

We know that Martin Campbell-Kelly [30] has written about the early days of debugging, especially about Maurice Wilkes and his works in1940s. In this research we have inspected the development of testing, not the development of debugging, because people consider debugging and testing different things in software development since 1956 [32]. Of course, the very early testing method in Finland was debugging.

We have found also some writings of the development of software in Finland, for example Olli Varho's writing [43]. There are also some discussions about testing, but not about the development of testing. Later, in the 1990s, there were some Master of Science theses published, and SYSTEEMITYÖ [42] - a Finnish journal on software engineering was also founded. We can also mention some writers from that time, for example, Mika Katara, Mitro Kivinen, Erkki Pöyhönen, and Maaret Pyhäjärvi.

We decided to do this research with interviews, because there is no written material on the subject matter, the development of testing, in Finland. We selected the interviewees with a so-called snowball-technique. The first interviewee named two, three possible candidates, who gave new interviewees in turn, and so on. We then chose from these candidates only those, who had an important role in companies and universities, developing and executing software testing. The interviews took place all around Finland. The interviews were based on a questionnaire, free discussions, and recordings and we carried them out in face-to-face fashion.

In the beginning of an interview, we inquired personal data, education, and work experience. Secondly, we inquired when the interviewees had heard first time about software testing, what kind of teaching, books, and articles of testing existed at that time, and how the development of software testing changed toward year 2000 and after. We also asked which programming languages they used, how the programming languages affected the testing, who tested the programs, and how they carried out the tests. We also inquired how they documented testing, and the kind of testing methods used. Furthermore, we asked the interviewees, what they thought about the coverage, outsourcing, and automation of testing. The interviewees mentioned also some books about testing.

In this article, we present based on the gathered material the development of testing in decades from 1950 to the present day. Every decade constitutes a chapter of its own. We should note, however, that the presentation is not exhaustive of all the gathered material.

2   The Time of the Very Early Pioneers 1950–1959

In 1950s only one of the interviewees had heard the word testing – Hans Andersin [2]. Therefore, we base this work on his memories. At first, he remembered working in Sweden on the BESK-computer, which according to his opinion was at that time the fastest one in the world. He remembered a phrase in Swedish "testa programmen". They wrote the programs in machine language or later in hexadecimal format, so there was no need to write long instructions.

When you needed time for testing, you had to wait for your turn. When it was your turn, the program usually ran very unsuccessfully in the beginning. The process could stop anywhere and it would list the contents of certain registers. By investigating these listings, you tried to find out what had happened. When they found the error, the same process started again. The cycle repeated several times before the program was working properly. Testing was primitive. Of course, they had found possible errors visually before testing by a computer. The most effective way to avoid errors was to use pieces of completely tested and properly working programs.

The second computer in his memories was the IBM 650. By then, some systematic ways to find errors were in use. One diagnostic method was a debugging program called DDT, where the computer told all found illogical instructions. The program ran slowly and at the same time, it listed the erroneous instructions.

In those days, the training arranged by IBM for their customers was of good quality. The data processing literature affected somehow to methods of thinking. Development of testing was strong, even exponential, just like in the following decade. Systems designers and programmers did testing. The used programming language did not affect to the willingness to test, but testing was easier using certain languages. They wrote very few documents on testing.

3 The Time of the Early Pioneers 1960–1969

Punched card technology mostly governed the 1960s. Computer time was not available very much and testing was rather difficult. If you did not replace the erroneous card with the corrected one, you had to "batch" the instruction either in octal or hexadecimal code.

Compilation times were long, usually from 30 to 60 minutes. Most of the program listings also produced a listing in machine language (octal, hexadecimal). It was very slow and difficult to find out where the errors were. Nostalgia of 1960s is high because nearly all older ADP-people remember that time. It was the time of data processing old pioneers [12].

3.1 Some Memories from the Infancy

The following are some excerpts from the interviews.

"I was studying in the university, when I took my first course in programming. Linked up with it, there was a rather large practical work we had to do. At that time, nobody cared about the clarity of programs and still less we knew about testing. The process ended up as a long series of trials and errors: trying various input data, using core dumps when looking for bugs, and trying again. To what extent the program became tested, remains a total mystery - and this state of affairs continued to be a prevailing feature for a long period to come. It was also discovered that people tend to have a natural objection to find errors in their own programs." [1]

"It was in IBM, as I was a student in 1964, when a very unusual case happened. I worked as an operator and read at the same time the manuals of programming. Soon, I coded my own program. After the execution was correct, sometimes came up computational errors, sometimes all was correct. At last, I went to the present professor Markku Nurminen. We inspected the program together and agreed on that the computer operates incidentally wrong. After persuading the system analysts, we consulted the service. They tested the machine and found that there was one loose contact and therefore the result was sometimes right and sometimes wrong." [11]

"When I coded my first program I had no help. There was maybe one page of object code without any symbolic code in use. Of course, I thought the program works, so I threw all my documents into the wastepaper basket and went to the computer. Nearly nothing happened. I had to code the whole program again. One reason to all this was that the manuals were in Danish; I had mistaken some clauses." [15]

"The testing was familiar to me from the beginning of the decade 1960 in Kaapelitehdas in compiling statistical programs. Everybody believed, when coding his first program that it worked properly. There was no chance for a mistake. It was very humiliating to discover that the programs did not work as I had expected. Testing has always been to me going through trial and error. Sometimes when I had a very difficult problem, I had to go to get some advice from my colleagues. At the same time, as I explained my problem, it often happened that I myself solved it before my partner understood anything about it. It is useful to tell someone else about the difficulties; many times it helps you to get the idea of it." [19]

"Already in the basics of informatics was said that you must test - but not exactly how to do it. In practice you learned very soon that the basic things must be done carefully. There was no idea to go to the computer with poorly made program, because the available computation time was so restricted." [22]

"In the beginning, the programs were relative small so that there were no special problems in testing technique. Of course, everybody made errors except Ph.D in Mathematics Jussi Väisälä who coded correct code at the first time. It was very important to be careful in the programming because of the limited computation time." [25]

"First I remember the time, when there was no computer in our company. At that time, Hankkija did already have the kind of a computer that we had ordered. So we travelled 400 kilometres from Kuopio to Helsinki to test our programs in the night." [23]

3.2 The Development, Education, Methods and Literature of Testing

Only one of the interviewees, Hans Andersin [2], held the opinion that the development of testing in this decade was very strong. Probably the reason is that he can compare the decades of the 1950s and the 1960s. A few saw that testing has been sufficient. Most of the interviewees thought that the development of the software testing at this time was insignificant or missing. However, there was some development. Many researchers talked about the formal verification of programs. On the other hand, if you prove your program correct, someone else can ask, are your proofs correct. No doubt, one step in the development was the creation of the first Nordic computer science professorship in Tampere 1965. From my interviewees, Seppo Mustonen [19] was one of the establishers and Reino Kurki-Suonio [15] the first professor.

There was very little training for testing in the 1960s. The interviewees named only the training of IBM and the internal trainings in some other firms. Reino Kurki-Suonio [15] thinks that there was a lack of test training, because people perceived data processing more of a science than a practice.

The literature consisted mostly of the manuals written by the manufacturers, some programming guides and course publications. The first Finnish book mentioned in these interviews was by Eero Kostamo [37], "Automaattisten tietojenkäsittelysysteemien suunnittelu". In the book, there are surprisingly good instructions to do basic testing. We can see that there are instructions to use test cases - although they are not called "test cases", but the philosophy is the same. In addition, there are instructions to do desk checking and so called automated testing which means here that we use test tape where the program and the test cases are. They had to use the tape for the whole time of testing. Kostamo presents also main rules to document the correction of the errors. Other Finnish books were "Johdatus ohjelmointiin" of Reino Kurki-Suonio [38] and in Finnish translated book "ATK: automaattinen tietojenkäsittely" of Sven R. Hed [34]. In Hed's book, many pages cover testing. It is amazing how little education of testing occurred even in the 1970s, although some material appeared in Finnish already in the 1960s.

3.3 The Effect of the Programming Language, Who Tested and How Much, the Coverage and Documentation of Testing

The selection of the programming languages was, as early as in the 1960s, very wide. The interviewees named, for example, ALGOL, Basic, COBOL, FORTRAN, PL/I, SIMULA, and the assembly languages of the various data machines. The program testability of different languages varied. The more high-level the language was, the easier the testing was. These languages had such features, which guaranteed definite functionality. On the other hand, the programs coded by primitive languages were smaller and therefore easier to control.

Nearly all of the interviewees thought that the programmer himself tested his own programs. According to the interviewees, the time used for testing varied between 10 to 70 per cent from the programming time. Mostly it was between 50 and 70 per cent.

The coverage of testing was nearly an unknown concept. It was enough that the program worked. The documentation, if such existed, contained the storage of the program lists and they wrote it afterwards. Many programmers thought that documentation was unnecessary. One of the interviewees, Pentti Kerola [14], thought that documentation in this decade was sufficient. Most of the programmers thought that testing was a miserable thing.

4 The Time of the Early Professionals 1970–1979

In this period, testing was becoming easier and computers were becoming faster. They could make amendments to the programs using terminals. Compared with testing today, work was still very slow, but effectiveness was much higher than earlier [12].

4.1 Some Testing Experiences

The following are some excerpts from the interviews.

"I heard about testing when I entered to work in KELA at 1971. In my opinion, it was some kind of detective work. The test material was always too small. Therefore, errors were uncovered in the production run. That produced news in journals. Articles in the newspapers ensured that the same errors were not repeated." [18]

"My career began in Tampella, Tampere, but I heard more about testing in Softplan only after 1975. I remember the tight timetables and that the only chance to test was in the night. I tried to do my work so well that further testing was unnecessary." [21]

"One kind of test was when I started studying in 1972. I had never used a type-writer and I had to seek characters so long that the machine reached a timeout." [27]

"We have always had great hopes for testing to erase errors from programs. Sharers of the honour have always been around when everything was working, but when something went wrong the reason was in the faulty testing." [8]

In my first job in ADP department of a quite big company, practice was that the responsible person, who had changed or repaired a program, was on a standby at home also on weekends through the introduction of the program. I wondered that very much, because I thought that the programs had been tested before introduction so well that the project manager did not need to be on a standby." [3]

"Testing cycle was very slow, maybe two at most three times per day, so it was possible that you left your program for testing, but you got it back the next day. Therefore, desk checking was important. At that time, testing was batch processing, so you had no chance to debug. Tracing errors was very difficult." [4]

"It was not easy matter to estimate the time scale to make a program. Of course, testing was the last job and nearly all reserved time was already used. No small wonder was that we slept beside the computer many nights." [6]

"I remember when I coded my first programs, testing was to read dump and to debug. Overall, it was a boring job." [24]

4.2 Development, Methods, Literature, Coverage and Documentation of Testing; the Effect of the Programming Language, Who Tested It and How Much

Most of the interviewees agreed that the development of testing was slight or satisfying. Desk checking remained as a method. The new thing was that programmers began to think about "limits, loops, and whatnot", as Myers [41] presented in his book. Other writers in this period were for example Codd and Schaefer.[1] Some of the interviewees told that they had used prototypes and test beds.

Very few of the interviewees knew the names of the used methods. However, the methods used in Finland were nearly the same as outside Finland, although they came to use a bit later. Cited as an example, Moore [40] presented the method "State Test" as early as 1956 and Hirsch [35] presented the earliest known description of a software statement and branch coverage analyzer in 1967.

In this decade Systek, the State Computing Center (VTKK), and the Social Insurance Institution of Finland (KELA), developed actively testing in Finland. Education of programming and system design had started in many Finnish universities. Unfortunately, they nearly forgot the role of testing. One exception was ATK-Instituutti (The ADP Institute), where was a seminar of testing in 1970. Based on the seminar, there was a published report "Tietojenkäsittelysysteemin testaaminen" [29] in 1971.

Many of the interviewees saw that the proportion of testing in programming decreased. However, the volume was nearly 50 percent of the programming time. The mentioned languages were Algol 60, Mixal, and Lisp. Note that they published Lisp as early as in 1958. In this decade also designers tested, not only programmers. The

---

[1] These author names and those that follow may not be accurate but are based on the interviewees' memories only. Due to illness of the author of the article, we were unable to check the authors and to refer to their relevant publications.

programming language still affected testability. The coverage and documentation of testing was poor.

5 The Time of the Professionals 1980–1989

This is the preliminary time of PCs. They tested programs online. They delivered the preliminary tested version to a customer, who made the final testing. This decade started the customer oriented testing [12].

5.1 Beginnings of Testing

The following are some excerpts from the interviews.

"With my hobby, microcomputers, I came across the word testing. At first, I did not understand what it meant. When I coded my first little programs, I found that they were not always correct. Especially when I was young, I thought that testing was very difficult. At last, in the same decade, I made with my partners a test bed for testing programs automatically in C-language. It was quite a novel thing at that time." [5]

"My diploma work was a system for city of Oulu, to provide rented flats. I remember that we tested it very well. However, the end-users were very old people. We found that the usability testing was not sufficient. Generally, I have liked testing." [16]

"In the late 80's the testing of embedded telecommunication software was usually quite on ad-hoc type of work. A very essential improvement for the testing process and practises was proposed by Hannu Honka [6] for Nokia. I had a possibility to contribute to the testing of protocols for the first GSM base station in the world in the beginning of 1990's. Based on that experience, the systematic and automatic software testing approach proved to be an essential improvement for the testing practises." [17]

"I say that my testing was in the beginning quite much of trial and error. I knew no methods or operation models; they came later." [28]

"When I worked in Softplan in Tampere, Pasi Kantelinen wrote there a little guide for testing. In my opinion, these instructions are valid still today. Many times we tested together with the customers and that was productive." [10]

5.2 Development, Methods, Literature, Coverage and Documentation of Testing, the Effect of the Programming Language, Who Tested It and How Much

Most of the interviewees thought that the development in this decade was good or almost satisfying. Now, testers started to design test cases systematically. The V-model came to use as well as the black-box, white-box, top-down, and bottom-up techniques. For example, Harlan Mills [39] presented the top-down technique as early as 1970 in IBM.

They greatly discussed software engineering in the literature in this period. The interviewees remembered authors like Pressman, Sommerville, Gilb, Jackson, and

Kaner. It should be noted, however, that for instance, Gilb wrote already in the 1970s.

One thing, which only a few of the interviewees mentioned, was test automation. Mark Fewster and many others worked hard with this problem in the 1980s [31]. We suppose that this was an unknown thing to many testers in Finland.

Very interesting thing was that one of my interviewees [26] got education in testing in the school (Linnanpellon lukio, in Kuopio) in the 1980s. That was exceptional.

As new languages, interviewees remembered the publication of ADA, C, C++, and Pascal. Note that C and Pascal appeared in the 1970s. In the 1980s, they mentioned testing groups for the first time in these interviews. Based on the interviews, it is easy to see that there was some development in testing. The coverage and documentation of testing became a little better. The proportion of testing was between 30 and 50 per cent of programming time.

6 The Time of the Young Professionals 1990–1999

During this period, customers learned to use PCs. They tested the programs as before. Computers or terminals were on user's desk, and users knew what they really wanted. Computers were becoming more and more effective. Programming and testing was becoming easier, because of the new programming languages and macro-oriented languages. In fact, most testing was customer oriented. Customers received "almost a complete system" and started to use it. In guarantee time, the customer told about program errors that they had found. Programmers corrected the errors and they delivered the new version to the customer. The programs were larger than before and they were more complex, which was a problem [12].

6.1 Happenings and Memories between the Years 1990 and 1999

As an example, one of my interviewees, Juha Itkonen [9] became familiar with testing for the first time in Helsinki University of Technology, where courses on testing appeared. They had a testing course together with University of Helsinki already at the end of the decade.

"I got practical experience as an assistant researcher in VTT. Then, the eyes-opening-experience was that everything did not work in practice, although I had tested it well in my own opinion. It was enough that, when other people in VTT started to experiment with the program, errors appeared. I was aware of that testing is something else than just experimentation." [9]

"I remember that I was studying on a software engineering course and there was quite a lot work to be done. We had programs, which we had to test. There was CTC (Coverage Analyzer for Testing programs in C-language) indicator connected to the programs. Passing the task (obtaining a high enough coverage) was far from trivial." [13]

"When I began to test, I used to do it according to given instructions. In other words, I stared into the screen from day to day. The idea, what testing was, sprang up, when I myself picked up the baton what I tested and how. The point of view that the experienced tester could be better than a novice is completely wrong. The own capacity of the people is always higher than guidelines which somebody else has dictated. I suggest all to do instructions of their own and after that to ask comments from somebody else to them." [20]

Additionally, another interviewee [7] thought that too many rules, how to do testing, is not good.

6.2 Development, Methods, Literature, Coverage and Documentation of Testing, the Effect of the Programming Language, Who Tested It and How Much

The development of testing in this decade was good, some say even excellent. New methods were for instance the management of testing and quality management. Notable was that there were now some real attempts to automate testing in Finland. For instance, Edward Kit [36] said, "The time for test automation is now".

In the literature, the most notable Finnish book was Ilkka Haikala's and Jukka Märijärvi's "Ohjelmistotuotanto" [33] in 1995. In this book, there was an entire chapter dedicated for testing. Software engineering was discussed much in the literature in this period. The interviewees remembered authors like Kit, Beizer, Hetzell, Marick, Gilb, Whittaker, Fewster, Graham, Bach, Pettichord, Whittaker, Dustin, Rashka, Paul, and Kooman.

Testing groups began to work, particularly in big companies. Java, Visual Basic, and Python were some of the new languages introduced in this period. Testing was 50 per cent from the programming work. Documentation and the coverage of testing developed a little.

7 The Time from the Year 2000 until Today

This is the time of PC computers, used as stand-alones or as terminals to the central computer. There is no lack of computer time. They could test programs easily online. The customer's word was the final acceptance of the new computer system [12].

Many interviewees thought that the development of testing has been now very strong. Automation has developed furthermore. A quite new activity, outsourcing of testing, has increased exponentially. There are in Finland software houses that develop almost only outsourced testing. Also, Test Driven Development (TDD) and agile programming take root - testing is no longer only the last stage in programming. In TDD, the tests derived from the requirements, and only after they satisfied the requirements did the coding begin.

Although almost all think that development goes ahead just right, there are also different opinions. For example, Eerola [3] thinks that we tested before the millennium so much that after it, everybody thought that testing was complete and the correctness of programs was on a sufficient level. They forgot that testing is a continuous and evolving process and hence testing decreased catastrophically to Eerola's mind. The same thing has happened with other approved practical methods and ways of action, too. We do the good thing once and then we forget it. Another reason, which has decreased testing, is the downtrend of the software industry, which wants to economize on testing costs and to shorten time to market programs.

8 Conclusion

In this paper, we argued that the various testing methods had been available years before they came in use in Finland. Many methods had been in use, but the interviewees disagree about, when the methods came to use in Finland.

We know that there are some publications about testing published already in the 1950s outside of Finland. The quantity of literature has increased every decade.

We argue that we waked up a little late in Finland. In the year 1958, when we got our first computer, it is my opinion that we trailed maybe ten years behind the global state of development of the software testing. In addition, that was nine years after Wilkes [44] gained his historical insight in 1949 that "a good part of the remainder of my life was going to be spent in finding errors in my own programs". Now the situation is much better. We can say with a good reason that we have reached the global state of development.

Many of the interviewees think that TDD is the greatest revolution since object-oriented programming. Testing coverage increases little by little along with the documentation. Nowadays, testing and testers have respect for example in Qentinel Oy, which is one of the leading companies of outsourced testing in Finland.

Worth noticing is that the first testing experiences of almost all interviewed have happened through trial and error. Although training has increased remarkably in the decades 1990 and 2000, it does not reach beginner testers. Could we think that we should introduce testing more systematically already in the first programming course?

Acknowledgments

I thank warmly all interviewees for their time, interesting meetings, and their employers for great flexibility. Special thanks to the Department of Computer Science, University of Kuopio, which sponsored this research. I wish thank PhD Mauno Rönkkö for his reading and comments. I also wish thank PhD Petri Paju for his good literature references.

The interviewees in alphabetical order: Alakangas Tarja, Alanko Timo, Andersin Hans, Andersson Thorbjörn, Eerola Anne, Eriksson Trygve, Haglund Henry, Haikala Ilkka, Hannula Esko, Honka Hannu, Honkasaari Terttu, Hotti Virpi, Hyvönen Mervi, Itkonen Juha, Jantunen Pekka, Jokiharju Tuula, Järvi Timo, Karhula Tarmo, Kaseniemi Mauno, Katara Mika, Kerola Pentti, Kinnunen Pirkko, Kivinen Mitro, Kurki-Suonio Reino, Käckman Tarja, Laiho Matti, Lappalainen Vesa, Latvakoski Juhani, Lehtinen Heli, Liinanto Erkki, Mustonen Seppo, Poutanen Olavi, Pyhäjärvi Maaret, Pääkkönen Tuula, Pöyhönen Erkki, Roine Kirsti, Röyskö Kirsti, Sakkinen Markku, Stenius Mårten, Sulonen Reijo, Tarnanen Pentti, Tervonen Ilkka, Tienari Martti, Toroi Hannele, Toroi Tanja, Torvinen Seppo, Tukiainen Petteri, Törn Aimo, Vanhatalo Hilkka, Verkamo Inkeri, Yksjärvi Jorma.

The employers in alphabetical order: Avain Technologies Oy, Bestsel Oy, City of Turku, Enfo Partner Oy, Financium Oy, Finish Tax Administration, F-Secure Oyj, Fujitsu Services Oy, GE Healthcare, Haaga-Helia University of applied sciences, Haglund Networks Ltd, Helsinki University of Technology, Nokia Mobile Phones, Nokia Multimedia Computers, Nokia Technology Platforms, Qentinel Oy, Social Insurance Institution, State Technical Research Centre, SYSOPENDIGIA Oyj, Tampere University of Technology, Testwell Oy, TietoEnator Oyj, TKP Tieto Oy, TS-Yhtymä Oy, University of Helsinki, University of Jyväskylä, University of Kuopio, University of Oulu, Åbo Academy University.

References

Interviews

[1] Alanko, Timo, University of Helsinki
[2] Andersin, Hans, Helsinki University of Technology
[3] Eerola, Anne, University of Kuopio
[4] Haikala, Ilkka, Tampere University of Technology
[5] Hannula, Esko, Qentinel Oy, Espoo
[6] Honka, Hannu, State Technical Research Centre, Oulu
[7] Hotti, Virpi, University of Kuopio
[8] Hyvönen, Mervi, Social Insurance Institution, Helsinki
[9] Itkonen, Juha, SoberIT, Helsinki University of Technology
[10] Jokiharju, Tuula, Nokia Multimedia Computers, Tampere
[11] Järvi, Timo, University of Turku
[12] Karhula, Tarmo, Pensioner, Kuopio
[13] Katara, Mika, Tampere University of Technology
[14] Kerola, Pentti, University of Oulu
[15] Kurki-Suonio, Reino, Tampere University of Technology
[16] Käckman, Tarja, Nokia Mobile Phones, Oulu
[17] Latvakoski, Juhani, State Technical Research Centre, Oulu
[18] Liinanto, Erkki, Social Insurance Institution, Helsinki
[19] Mustonen, Seppo, University of Helsinki
[20] Pyhäjärvi, Maaret, F-Secure Oyj, Helsinki
[21] Roine, Kirsti, Bestsel Oy, Tampere
[22] Sulonen, Reijo, Helsinki University of Technology
[23] Tarnanen, Pentti, Enfo Partner Oy, Kuopio
[24] Tervonen, Ilkka, University of Oulu
[25] Tienari, Martti, University of Helsinki
[26] Toroi, Hannele, GE Healthcare, Kuopio
[27] Vanhatalo, Hilkka, Fujitsu Services Oy, Helsinki
[28] Yksjärvi, Jorma, SYSOPENDIGIA Oyj, Helsinki

Literature

[29] ATK-Instituutti: Tietojenkäsittelysysteemin testaaminen (The Testing of Data Processing System). ATK-Instituutin kannatusyhdistys, Helsinki (1971)
[30] Campbell-Kelly, M.: The Airy Tape, An Early Chapter in the History of Debugging. IEEE Annals of the History of Computing 14(4) (1992)

282   P.A. Pohjolainen

[31] Fewster, M., Graham, D.: Software Test Automation. Effective use of test execution tools. ACM Press, New York (1999)

[32] Gelperin, D., Bill, H.: The Growth of Software Testing. Communications of the ACM 31(6), 687–695 (1988)

[33] Haikala, I., Märijärvi, J.: Ohjelmistotuotanto (Software Engiueering). Suomen atk-kustannus, Espoo (1995)

[34] Hed, S.R.: ATK: automaattinen tietojenkäsittely (ADP-Automated Data Processing). Tammi, Helsinki (1966)

[35] Hirsch, I.N.: MEMMAP/360. Report TR P-1168, IBM Systems Development Division, Product Test Laboratories, Poughkeepsie, New York (1967)

[36] Kit, E.: Software Testing in The Real World. Addison Wesley, Reading (1995)

[37] Kostamo, E. (ed.): Automaattisten tietojenkäsittelysysteemien suunnittelu (The Engineering of the Automated Data Processing Systems). Systemisuunnittelukurssin opettajakunta, Helsinki (1963)

[38] Kurki-Suonio, R.: Johdatus ohjelmointiin (An Introduction to Programming). Tampereen yliopiston tutkimuslaitos, Tampere (1966)

[39] Mills, H.: Software Productivity. Dorset House (June 1988)

[40] Moore, E.F.: Gedanken-Experiments on Sequential Machines. In: Automata Studies. Annals of Mathematics Studies, vol. 34, pp. 129–153. Princeton University Press, Princeton (1956)

[41] Myers, G.: The Art of Software Testing. John Wiley & Sons, New York (1979)

[42] Systeemityöyhdistys SYTYKE: SYSTEEMITYÖ. Sytyke ry, jäsenlehti. Helsinki (1993)

[43] Varho, O.: Automaattisten laskukoneiden yleispiirteet. Teknillinen aikakauslehti 2/1959, 25–29 (1959)

[44] Wilkes, M.: Memoirs of a Computer Pioneer. MIT Press, Cambridge (1985)

An Early Danish Computer Game

The Case of Nim, Piet Hein, and Regnecentralen

Anker Helms Jørgensen

IT University of Copenhagen, DK-2300 Copenhagen S Denmark
anker@itu.dk

Abstract. This paper reports on the development of Nimbi, which is an early computer game implemented at the Danish Computer Company Regnecentralen in 1962-63. Nimbi is a variant of the ancient game Nim. The paper traces the primary origins of the development of Nimbi. These include a mathematical analysis from 1901 of Nim that "killed the game" as the outcome could be predicted quite easily; the desire of the Danish inventor Piet Hein to make a game that eluded such analyses; and the desire of Piet Hein to have computers play games against humans. The development of Nimbi was successful in spite of considerable technical obstacles. However, it seems that the game was not used for publicizing the capabilities of computers – at least not widely – as was the case with earlier Nim implementations, such as the British Nim-playing computer Nimrod in 1951.

Keywords: Computer game history, Piet Hein, Nim, Regnecentralen, Nim.

1 Introduction

On 9 July in 1962, Regnecentralen in Copenhagen employed Søren Lauesen, a nineteen-year old mathematics student. Søren Lauesen – now professor and my colleague – recently told me about his first project: The development of a computer program playing a variant of the ancient game Nim. Before I embark on the story let me introduce the other players: the French-American mathematician Charles L. Bouton, the British game playing computer Nimrod, and the Danish inventor and poet Piet Hein.

2 Nim and Its Players

The game Nim has been played since ancient times. Its origin is obscure, but some hold that it originates in China [12]. The game is simple:

> "Initially we have any number of heaps, each containing any number of tokens (usually matches). In the simplest form, two contestants play alternately, and may pick up as many matches as they wish at one time from _one_ pile, but they must take at least one match. The aim is to avoid taking the _last_ match of all[1]." [2, 304].

---

[1] In another version the player who takes the _last_ token wins.

J. Impagliazzo, T. Järvi, and P. Paju (Eds.): HiNC 2, IFIP AICT 303, pp. 283–288, 2009.
© IFIP International Federation for Information Processing 2009

The game has two definite advantages. Firstly, we can play it with almost any object (stones, matches, coins etc.) and in any numbers. Secondly, in spite of its basic simplicity, it remains intellectually challenging even for experienced players as the complexity can be increased by adding heaps and/or tokens.

In 1902, the French-American mathematician Charles L. Bouton of Harvard University published an in-depth mathematical analysis of the game, based on binary numbers [1].

> *"It is the writer's purpose to prove that if one of the players, say A, can leave one of a certain set of numbers upon the table, and after that plays without mistake, the other player, B, cannot win. Such a set of numbers will be called a safe combination"* [1, 35].

Bouton succeeded and provided a simple method that enabled players to analyze the game. By conceiving the heaps as binary numbers and applying a simple adding rule, the player can easily tell whether a position is safe or not. This contrasts the earlier state of affairs, where an experienced player could overview only simple Nim games with relatively few heaps and tokens.

Fig. 1. The game board of Nimrod, the Nim-playing computer

In 1951, the British computer company Ferranti developed the Nim-playing digital computer Nimrod, see Figure 1.[2] Nimrod was designed to illustrate the principles of automatic computers in general and was the first computer exclusively designed to play a game [2, 201]. Nimrod appeared for six months at the Exhibition of Science during the 1951 Festival of Britain in London and took on all comers [2, 286]. It was later on display at the Trade Fair in Berlin. Germans had never seen anything like it and came to see it in thousands. It was necessary to call out special police to control

---

[2] From http://jwgibbs.cchem.berkeley.edu/nimrod/desk.html

the crowds. The machine became even more popular after it had defeated the Economics Minister Dr. Ludwig Erhardt in three straight games [2, 287].

As to Bouton's work, the Danish poet, inventor, and mathematician Piet Hein was put off by it:

> *"Bouton's thorough analysis of the game, that instantly in principle destroyed the ancient game, called for a response ... that could reestablish the lost dignity as an unbeaten game."* [6, 5].

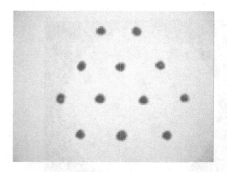

Fig. 2. The layout of the Nimbi game

Piet Hein even referred to Bouton's work as the "murder on Nim" [5]. Piet Hein intended to create a variant of Nim that would bring the game beyond such analyses while retaining the simplicity of the game. He succeeded in 1945, see the game board in Figure 2 [6]. Note that each token is a member of three lines (laterally, diagonals up-left and up-right) and how the shape is a triangle with the corners cut off. The rules of Nimbi are the following:

> *"A move consists in removing one or more tokens from the board. If more than one token are removed, they must be consequtive on the same line. The one removing the last token has lost."* [5]

This game was published in an article in Scientific American in 1958 [4] and has been the subject of mathematicians' analyses under the name Nimbi [3].

3 The Development of the Computer Game

Since the invention of the game in 1945, Piet Hein had a dream of programming a computer to play the game against humans. This dream came nearer when Norbert Wiener introduced Piet Hein to Niels Ivar Bech, head of Regnecentralen. This happened when Norbert Wiener stayed in Piet Hein's home in Rungsted the preceeding summer while finishing the book God and Golem, Inc.

> *"The game problem appealed immediately to Bech's taste for diverse tasks, to create a meeting place, where non-professionals could get contact, even dialog, with a computer and get a convincing direct impression of (a minimum) of computers' level of intelligence"*. [5]

The game was so complex that Piet Hein did not know how to make a winning strategy, so he thought that computers could be useful here [10]. Søren Lauesen was asked to develop this game only one week after his employment. The project began in July 1962 and was completed in August 1963 with close collaboration between Søren Lauesen and Piet Hein. The game was implemented on the Gier computer, the first transistorized computer developed in Denmark [7]. The development entailed many challenges, among these the central game algorithm, the input/output, and the board representation in Gier.

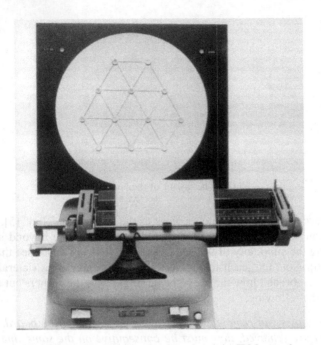

Fig. 3. The Gier Nimbi game board and the IBM console

The heart of the game is the data structure representing the game and the algorithm enabling analysis of positions and moves. Søren Lauesen reported that after several days of pondering on how to find the right move in a given situation, the solution dawned to him on a ferry crossing the Great Belt. It is based on a mathematical analysis with safe positions.

The input/output was designed as a 2+3+4+3 hexagon board, see the Figure 3.[3] The tokens were buttons with lights that players could press when human players made their moves. Søren Lauesen reports that there were extensive discussions with hardware engineers on this issue.

Another major design problem was how to represent the 12 board positions in Gier. This was handled by letting bits 28-39 in the multiplication register represent the positions as on/off. This special solution evidently implied writing the program without multiplications!

---

[3] From http://www.datamuseum.dk/site_dk/rc/NIB/kap19.shtml

The final program was but a mere four pages of Gier assembly code and four pages of tables [8]. In addition to playing the game, the program also provided a log of the game played, printed on the typewriter. If a game was interrupted, the program could tell if it was theoretically possible to win the game [9].

4 Perspectives

We now discuss two wider aspects of the development: the role of games in computer publicity and the synergy between computers and games. The predecessor of the developed Nim game variant, Nimrod, created much publicity for Ferranti and for computers in general in 1951. According to Piet Hein's son Hugo Piet Hein, Regne-centralen did use the computer game for promotional purposes. However, it did not seem to have attracted significant interest by the public. In 1951, computers were strictly confined to highly specialized calculation tasks in specialized application domains that were unknown to the public at large. Ten years later, that picture had changed somewhat, even in Denmark. Apart from the general increase in public awareness, computers gained much public exposure when Regnecentralen provided successful computer support for the Danish parliament election on 15 November 1960, which was broadcast on television [11]. This publicity aspect had an interesting side effect. When Regnecentralen brought up the question of charge for the development expenses, Piet Hein allegedly opposed it. He argued that Regnecentralen had to see the game as a publicity opportunity.

Games have always fascinated people and computers have played a major role here in the last decades. The Nimrod and Piet Hein's Nim variant are early examples of computer games simulating traditional board games such as tic-tac-toe, draughts, and chess. Later, simple computer games in their own right appeared such as Space War and Pong. These games utilized the graphical and interactive capabilities of later computers. In the next decades, computer games underwent an immense growth technically, culturally, and financially. Computer games have evolved into a set of genres of its own–from simple strategy games like Tetris and PacMan to game worlds such as Civilization, Everquest and World of Warcraft. These are rich digital societies that mirror real life in many ways – probably far beyond the imagination of the creators of the early computer games of the 1950s and 1960s.

References

[1] Bouton, C.L.: Nim, a game with a complete mathematical theory. Annals of Mathematics, Series 2 3, 35–39 (1901-1902)
[2] Bowden, B.V. (ed.): Faster Than Thought – A Symposium on Digital Computing Machines. Sir Isac Pitman & Sons, London (1953)
[3] Fraenkel, A.S., Herda, H.: Never rush to be the first in playing Nimbi. Mathematics Magazine 53(1), 21–26 (1980)
[4] Gardner, M.: Mathematical Games: Concerning the game of Nim and its mathematical analysis. Scientific American 198(2), 104–111 (1958)

[5] Hein, P.: Hjertets renhed [The Purity of the Heart]. In: Svejstrup, P., Naur, P., Hansen, H.B. (eds.) Niels Ivar Bech – en epoke i edb-udviklingen i Danmark [Niels Ivar Bech – an epoch in the EDP development in Denmark]. Copenhagen, Data, 93-96 (1976), http://www.datamuseum.dk/site_dk/rc/NIB/kap19.shtml (accessed December 10, 2006)

[6] Hein, P.: En variant af spillet Nim og et udkast til en maskine, som spiller det ny spil mod en menneskelig spiller [A Variant of the Game Nim and Draft of a Machine that Plays Against a Human Player]. Unpublished memo, 12 pages (undated)

[7] Klüver, P.V.: From Research Institute to Computer Company: Regnecentralen 1946-1964. IEEE Annals of the History of Computing 21(2), 31–43 (1999)

[8] Lauesen, S.: Nim simulering [Nim simulation]. Gier assembler program. Regnecentralen, Copenhagen, 8 pages (1963)

[9] Lauesen, S.: Brugsanvisning for NIM-brædtet [User's Manual for the NIM Board]. Regnecentralen, Copenhagen, 1 page (1963)

[10] Lauesen, S.: Compiler-gruppen: Teknisk perfektionisme kontra nytte [The Compiler Group: Technical Perfectionism versus Utility]. In: Isaksson, H. og Pedersen, O. (eds.): Regnecentralen – dansk institut for matematikmaskiner [Regnecentralen – Danish Institute for Mathematics Machines], pp. 53–64 (2005), http://www.itu.dk/~slauesen/CV/RChistorie.pdf (accessed December 6, 2006)

[11] Melbye, A.: Valgudsendelser i tv [Parlament election broadcasts on tv] (2002), http://www.datamuseum.dk/site_dk/rc/NIB/kap22.shtml (accessed December 16, 2006)

[12] Spencer, D.: Game Playing with Computers. Hayden (1968)

Demoscene Platforms: A Case Study on the Adoption of Home Computers

Markku Reunanen[1] and Antti Silvast[2]

[1] University of Art and Design Helsinki
markku.reunanen@iki.fi
[2] University of Helsinki
antti.silvast@iki.fi

Abstract. This paper discusses the adoption of new technology by a hobbyist community known as the demoscene. The demoscene is chiefly a European community that originates from the mid-1980s and continues to exist even today. During its twenty years of existence, the demoscene has had to react to several changes in the field of information technology, in particular new hardware and software platforms. Based on the contemporary communication found in disk magazines and Internet forums we present case examples of the transitions and analyze the adoption processes. At large, the observations made serve as examples of the rich and unexpected ways in which the home computers were domesticated since the early 1980s.

Keywords: Demoscene, Computer hobbyists, Diffusion of innovations, Multimedia.

1 Introduction

The demoscene is a community that creates digital art with home computers. It has its roots in the late 1970s home computer revolution and software piracy. The demoscene—or just *the scene*—has traditionally been a male-dominant hobby, popular in Europe and especially in the Nordic countries. The aim of this study is to provide the reader an overview of the community and its relationship with the ever-changing world of computing. Ultimately, the demoscene and its practices serve as examples of the rich and unexpected ways of living with computers, never anticipated by the original manufacturers.

Any new technology needs to fit into already existing relationships and practices. In the context of the demoscene, a typical example of this would be a new computer like a Commodore 64 or Amiga or PC appearing in the market. By studying how the demosceners react to new platforms, we aim to show that new computers do not get judged only by technical features or market price. Rather, the reaction to new computers has to do with inclusion: it is important for the sceners to estimate which material objects and persons can belong to the scene and which cannot.

The demoscenes' communication has not been studied from this perspective before. On a different level, our study aims to describe a self-reflective community of technology users. We claim that communities of computer users are actively debating about those social relationships, practices, and technologies that account for the community itself.

J. Impagliazzo, T. Järvi, and P. Paju (Eds.): HiNC 2, IFIP AICT 303, pp. 289–301, 2009.
© IFIP International Federation for Information Processing 2009

2   Starting Points for the Study

To understand the demoscene and its development it is necessary to place it in a historical context. The contemporary technology and its possibilities are fundamental for such a culture. However, they alone do not explain why an international community of demo groups would emerge in the late 1980s. In the following, we present the reader a historical overview of the era and position our work in the context of demo research conducted by other researchers.

2.1   Historical Frame

The home computer revolution of the late 1970s and the early 1980s was a necessary precondition for the birth of the demoscene. Affordable computers appeared in stores and for the first time in history were available to the masses. This commercial and technological development was not enough in itself—there had to be a need and interest to buy one. The early attitudes towards computers were often controversial: advertisements and governmental plans typically emphasized educational values, whereas in reality gaming was the most popular use from the very beginning [18]. The loose attitudes towards copyrights lead to an extensive software piracy, which in turn lead to the birth of the *pirate scene* with its *crack intros*, later evolving to computer demos [14, 17]. *Cracking* in this context refers to the removal of copy protections of commercial software.

The first popular home computers such as Sinclair Spectrum and Commodore VIC-20 did not yet feature extensive sound or graphics capabilities. The low amount of memory was also a limiting factor. The first demoscene computer was Commodore 64, introduced in 1982, featuring advanced graphics and sound for its time. Its popularity was not shadowed until the late 1980s. For example, in Finland C64 was advertised as "Tasavallan tietokone"—"The Computer of the Republic" [18]. The other 8-bit computers of the era such as MSX and Amstrad CPC sold well in certain countries but did not attract the early demosceners in great numbers, presumably due to their lesser popularity and a weaker pirate scene.

The following important model of Commodore computers was Amiga 1000 introduced in 1985, followed by Amiga 500 (1987), which was a more compact and affordable model suitable for home users [1]. From the home computer perspective, the major competitor was Atari ST, released in 1985, which was able to sustain a modest demoscene of its own. Commodore retained its position amongst the hobbyists with its Amiga line of computers until the early nineties. By that time, the border between home and business computers had mostly faded away. IBM PC compatibles started appearing at homes and after the Commodore bankruptcy in 1994 [1] there was little commercial competition left. We examine the effects of these changes on the demo hobbyists in further detail in Section 4.

2.2   Related Work and Criticism

As we have overviewed in our online demoscene research bibliography [15], media researchers, sociologists, and cultural historians have already shown some interest in the demoscene. For the purpose of this article, we separate these studies to two domains. The first way of researching the scene has been to view it as artistic activity, which makes it the subject of art research. "Demoscene culture", in this use, is likened to other artforms, or it is even elevated to an artform of its own. This has meant looking at the demoscene as "art of the real-time" [20, 14], as a form of musical hobby [12] or as an emerging digital art form [19]. There is also a second way to measure the culture in the demoscene: as a particular way of life. This perspective relates to sociology, cultural studies, and cultural history. The researchers have discussed demoscene as youth culture or counter culture [17], multimedia hacker culture [6] or as a gendered community [9].

We admit that these studies have opened up demoscene for discussions in the mentioned research domains. In doing this, they have however taken a very abstract and often an outsider perspective to the scene. Another major pitfall of these studies has been the tendency to write "the history of the winners", often based on anecdotal evidence. Narrowing the research to famous groups and competition winners leads to a biased view of the phenomenon, since the majority of members and artifacts of the scene fall outside this winners' category. Overall, we feel that the real live action of being in the scene has been neglected thus far. In this article, we stress that the demoscene is always something active; as community, it is a collection of social relationships, practices and technologies [10], whose composition must be discussed by the members in order to keep it afloat.

3 Material and Methods

There is a wide variety of artifacts produced in the context of the demoscene. Examples of these are *demos*, *intros* (small demos), *disk magazines*, text files, pictures and tunes, which have already been studied [17, 20]. Additionally the communication between the scene members produces messages in modem-based bulletin board systems (BBS), newsgroups, disk magazines and message boards. The demoscene artifacts too convey meanings, but to understand the cultural values and reasons for phenomena it is reasonable to choose communication, because in it the active construction of common meanings is made more explicit. Various Internet archives such as demo sites proved to be a valuable source for the desired material—gathering the same information fifteen years ago would have required a great deal more time and an extensive network of contacts in the community.

The skipping of material on Atari ST, MSX, Sinclair Spectrum and other small scenes was a conscious choice. Firstly, the three most active platforms (Commodore 64, Amiga, and PC) and their changes are easier to study due to the good availability of source material. The material also represents a wider population. Secondly, since our focus is on transitions and reactions instead of the particular properties of the different scenes the actual selection of platforms is fairly insignificant.

3.1 Disk Magazines

Disk magazines—or *diskmags* for short—are interactive electronic magazines, which were originally distributed on diskettes in copy parties. The structure of a diskmag roughly mimics the structure of an ordinary magazine or a newspaper: there is an editorial, news, rumors, advertisements, interviews, and articles on topics that interest the readers. *Charts* are an important part of diskmags. In the charts, the most popular groups, coders, swappers, musicians, graphics artists ("graphicans") and demos are ranked either by voting or according to the editor's personal preferences.

Several properties of diskmags make them a valuable source for researchers. Sceners write them to sceners, meaning the topics reflect the interests of the community. For the same reason the opinions stated are typically not tuned down to please the outsiders. The articles are also contemporary, providing a peek to the phenomena of the time not colored by nostalgia, which would be the case if we interviewed the writers today. The rumors and speculation in diskmags are especially useful for tracing contemporary understanding and debates. Those seeking for historical facts should however note that the mags' factual content is not very reliable, because it is characterized by differing interpretations and competition of groups and cliques.

For this study we chose four diskmags as the main sources of information. The large amount of diskmags made the selection a difficult one but based on the opinions of hobbyist sources, we picked Sex'n'Crime (Commodore 64), Zine (Amiga), R.A.W. (Amiga), and Imphobia (PC). The 45 issues analyzed cover the period from 1989 to 1996. In the 1980s there were earlier disk mags as well but the period covered by Sex'n'Crime (1989–1990) is of particular interest because of the Commodore 64–Amiga migration. At the other end of the span, mid-nineties, the diskmags started to lose their status as a communication channel because of the Internet.

3.2 Supporting Material

Since the mid-1990s, the scene has increasingly started to use the Internet for the exchange of thoughts. Already in 1993, there was an article about the net in the Imphobia diskmag. To support and contrast the observations made from the diskmags, we used the ample archives of Usenet newsgroups *alt.sys.amiga.demos* and *comp.sys.ibm.pc.demos* as supporting material. Especially the latter newsgroup was highly active up until 2002: according to Google Groups, there were over 10,000 messages yearly during the most active period [2]. Reading and analyzing all the messages would have been a colossal task so we chose to limit the scope to relevant topics dealing with the adoption of new technologies.

Two additional resources used were competition results from the four biggest yearly *parties* (scener meetings) and *pouet.net*, a popular demoscene website. In contrast to the qualitative data of diskmags and newsgroups, the data obtained from competition results was quantitative by nature. The parties chosen were Assembly (Finland), The Party (Denmark), The Gathering (Norway) and Mekka & Symposium (Germany), during the period 1992–2002. Before 1992 the parties were smaller in scale and organized more often, according to Polgar [14] and the reports found in the Sex'n'Crime diskmag. The sample obtained from the party results consisted of 2094 productions.

3.3 Methods

Our observation of the text articles and discussions was based on distinctions and associations. We observed the construction of oppositions: what kinds of practices belong to the scene and which outside the scene? What associates with "elite" sceners (*i.e.* valuable), what with "lame" uses and users of computers (*i.e.* not valuable)? What marks the boundaries of the scene use and other use of computers?

When dealing with the quantitative data of the party results and productions the goal was to facilitate visual interpretation. Five variables were chosen: amount of Commodore 64 demos, Amiga demos, Amiga intros, PC demos and PC intros each year. We obtained the totals by summing the quantities from each party. Unfortunately, the limitations of the data set reduce the accuracy of the result. Firstly, the competitions in some Assembly parties were limited to only 15 entries because of a preselection. Secondly, Mekka & Symposium party appeared only in 1996 so its contribution is not present in the earlier totals. The latter weakness is somewhat countered by the effect of Mekka & Symposium growing from a small party at the expense of The Gathering and The Party.

4 The Major Transitions

The notion of a *major transition* here refers to a significant development in the information technology industry and the reactions of the demoscene to it. This section is divided according to the dominant platform of the era. It should be noted that this division is merely a simplification of the actual events: the different eras are overlapping and greatly more complex and detailed than what the threefold model would suggest.

In his book on the diffusion of innovations Rogers presents five distinctive groups of adopters: innovators, early adopters, early majority, late majority, and laggards [16]. Our observations of the transitions of the demoscene revealed a similar pattern: innovators try out a new platform early on but the demos they make are mere curiosities at that time. Influential persons and groups—early adopters—migrating to the new platform eventually start dragging the early majority with them. The late majority adapts because of practical reasons and only the laggards remain opposed to the transition. The retro movement has its point of reference in the past. In the demoscene circles, the phenomenon is now called "oldschool" or "oldskool" (also used by Tasajärvi *et al.* [20] to refer to the first era of the scene).

4.1 Commodore 64

Our most important source, Sex'n'Crime, was a Commodore 64 diskmag published by the group Amok during 1989–1990. The first impression the reader gets from Sex'n'Crime is that the Commodore 64 cracker/demo scene of the late 1980s was a hostile environment. Numerous accusations, rumors, and news about wars between groups appear practically in every issue of the diskmag. The rhetorical style found in the articles is emotionally loaded (both positive and negative) and occasionally downright harsh. As an example of the style, in Sex'n'Crime #21 (1990) *OMG/Amok* responded to a letter to the editor like this:

> *"Dear Roy of Dynamics, let me say this from the bottom of my heart: you are lame!"*

The ranking of individuals and groups in the charts was a controversial subject, sparking heated discussion in the following issues. In some letters and interviews, you can sense dissatisfaction with the ongoing wars and unfriendliness but overall these opinions did not constitute a significant part of the discourse. The distinction between the legal and the illegal activities was vague: cracked games, police raids, pirate software swapping and legal demos still went hand in hand in 1990. Gruetz-macher provides a slightly different interpretation [4], claiming that the illegal and legal scene activities slowly drifted apart in the late 1980s.

The emergence of the Amiga line of computers in the mid-eighties naturally received attention from the Commodore 64 sceners. This was the first technological transition the young scene had to face. Surprisingly—in comparison to other changes documented in the following subsections—the reactions expressed in Sex'n'Crime were chiefly positive or neutral. Polgar, however, reports that there was opposition as well [14]. In the news section of Sex'n'Crime the gradual transition becomes apparent during 1989–1990 (news of people "going" to Amiga) but it was not portrayed negatively, while the style of the diskmag otherwise was controversial. An important factor was that while new, the Amiga was still a product of the same company as the familiar Commodore 64.

4.2 Commodore Amiga

Amiga 500 was the second major hardware platform of the demoscene, following the success of the Commodore 64. Similar to Commodore 64, Amiga started as a uniform platform where the software would run the same on all setups. However, later the newer models such as the Amiga 1200, released in 1992 with its new AGA (Advanced Graphics Architecture) chipset and faster processor fragmented the platform. Starting from 1992 both the R.A.W. diskmag and the *alt.sys.amiga.demos* newsgroup contain a multitude of messages about the incompatibility problems related to the new chipset—a new challenge that was there to stay. Another source of problems was the difference between the PAL and NTSC Amigas, which hindered the exchange of demos between Europe and the United States.

There are notable differences between the two diskmags analyzed: Zine, published from 1989 to 1991 was still extensively connected to the cracker tradition, whereas R.A.W. (1991–1996) was chiefly demoscene-oriented and more refined in its appearance. The historical connection between the two communities remained at least through swapper activities. As an example of this interplay, the contact section of R.A.W. #5 (1993) still featured numerous advertisements for illegal swapping.

The first major transition faced by the Amiga sceners was the AGA in 1992 and the following two years. Incompatibility of software was only one facet of the transition. The opinions found in R.A.W. and the newsgroup varied from excitement to extreme resistance. The positive arguments were based on the new possibilities offered by the new hardware, whereas the opposition claimed that there was no challenge in doing demos on such powerful computers. Another argument used was the high price of the new machines, which placed them out of reach of many users and even lead to a supposed split of the scene. *Rufferto/Covert Action Team* summed up the views of the opposition in R.A.W. #6 (1993):

> *"OK, you'll be able to do much better and faster routines, but everybody knows, that you're not one of the best coders then, you just have got one of the best Ami-gas!"*

In hindsight the real threat to the Amiga was neither the AGA nor the accelerator boards but the IBM PC. First in 1993 and increasingly thereafter the community members expressed concern of the future of their platform—earlier the status of the Amiga scene had been so strong that people would look down upon any rivals. In the heated newsgroup posts and diskmag articles there were numerous arguments for and against PCs. Interestingly even in the Amiga forums you could find favourable mentions of the PC, while the consensus was against the transition. A platform war kept raging in diskmags and newsgroups (including *comp.sys.ibm.pc.demos*). Some of the most common, often contradictory, arguments for and against the new platform were:

o Amiga demos are better designed and programmed.
o PC hardware is not uniform.
o Windows/MS-DOS sucks, Amiga has a better operating system.
o PC owners are followers of big companies.
o Amiga has coprocessors for sound and graphics—either a positive or negative feature.
o PC has more computing power / PC has too much computing power.
o PC/Amiga owners just play games—used by both sides.
o PC is more suitable for texture mapping.
o PC has better graphics modes because of SVGA (Super VGA display cards).
o Developers are leaving the Amiga, PC has more software.

Polgar [14] and Saarikoski [17] provided further discussion of the Amiga–PC clash. In addition, Saarikoski's remarks on the Finnish "machine wars" of the 1980s provide some means for understanding the juxtaposition [18].

4.3 IBM PC

The demoscene that formed on the IBM PC and compatible machines since the early 1990s cannot be treated as one single scene only. During its seventeen years, the PC demoscene has faced changes that can be compared to complete platform transitions.

Imphobia was an influential diskmag published in 1992–1996. The development of the magazine closely resembles the course of Zine and R.A.W. on Amiga: the early crude magazine evolved into a well-edited and impressive publication. In the early issues until 1993 references to software piracy could be found but after that the focus of the diskmag soon changed to the legal demoscene. The underdog status of the PC scene in comparison to Amiga was generally recognized and dealt with in varying manners: either by acknowledging the situation or by coming up with emotional or rational counterarguments. An interesting finding is that since Commodore 64 was not considered a threat any more, the writers considered it either outdated or— increasingly by time— held the coders in high regard for pushing the old computer beyond its limits.

A controversial theme occurring frequently in our source material was the increasing computational capacity of the PC. While some regarded it as an opportunity to make better demos there were opposing voices too, complaining that the 486 or Pentium did not require any skills from the programmer. These discussions started in Imphobia and *comp.sys.ibm.pc.demos* in 1993 and continued until at least 1995. Another, fiercer hardware-related disagreement concerning sound card support took place in 1994–1996. This time the controversy was about demos that only supported Gravis Ultrasound, which had gained a strong following among the PC sceners.

A new kind of transition started in 1995 (first mentioned in the newsgroup already in 1994) with the introduction of Windows 95. Until then Windows had been running on top of MS-DOS, the predominant operating system of the PC scene. This shift was technically different to the previous ones since it was about software, not hardware. The future of MS-DOS looked uncertain, which called for a reaction from the community. The response was highly emotional and at first mostly negative. We must specifically mention one of the many arguments used in the discussions: the emergence of Windows 95 would mean an end to direct hardware access, which had been a principal technique used in demos from the earliest days in order to achieve the best possible performance. Losing this control over the machine did not suit the existing practices. During 1995–1998, the *status quo* did not yet change, with most demos still released for the accepted MS-DOS platform. Several options such as OS/2, Linux and even an own operating system "DemOS" were considered but eventually the PC scene followed the industry and mostly migrated to Windows towards the end of the 1990s.

4.4 Chronology of the Transitions

The qualitative results gained from diskmags and newsgroups presented in the subsections above illustrate the mechanisms and characteristics of transitions. The weakness of such analysis is that we cannot perceive the magnitude and speed of migrations. To illustrate the chronology of events we plotted the data collected from the party results of 1992–2002 in time/productions coordinate system for visual inspection (Figure 1).

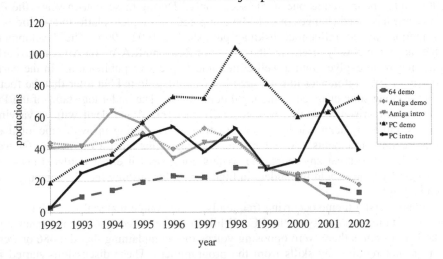

Fig. 1. Party productions by year

Certain properties clearly stand out from the diagram and support the previous observations: until 1995, the PC scene was less productive than the Amiga scene; after 1996 the positions changed permanently. The drop after the peak year 1998 coincides with the Windows migration, presumably indicating the challenges involved in such transition. The decay of Amiga productions starts in 1998 and the trend continues during the following four years. Perhaps the most surprising observation is the Commodore 64 renaissance of the late 1990s. We can explain this phenomenon by the increase of Commodore 64 sceners attending the big mainstream parties, the decay of illegal activities, and the introduction of suitable competition categories in the parties. Additionally, such activity on an almost 20-year old machine reveals the strength of the retro/oldschool attitudes among the demoscene.

5 Practices and Distinctions

The demoscene reacts to large transitions through its own practices and its interpersonal relationships. The mechanisms both limit and enable the adaptation of new platforms. The same limitations and strengths apply when demoscene has to confront larger issues than the scene itself. Similarly, Rogers notes that the structure of a community can facilitate or impede the diffusion of innovations in a system [16].

5.1 Skills

As Turo-Kimmo Lehtonen [10] points out, the existing attachments between users and their technologies always both limit and enable new technologies. In the demoscene, an important form of attachment are the skills of a scener. Similar appreciation of skills is apparent in other male-dominated hobbyist communities as well [21, 11, 5]. Technical features of a new platform do not automatically lead to success. Quite the contrary, too efficient a computer can undermine the skills needed to make demos. "I don't like lamers who require a hyper-fast PC to do little things like 24 faces glenz" (Imphobia #7, 1993), a commentator notes of the PC. "I think using AGA just shows that you are incompetent to do really innovative things on normal machines" (R.A.W. #6, 1993), another comments on the AGA technology on Amiga. However, this relation can also turn upside down: once the new computer starts to enable scene skills, it can be "a waste of talent" to stay with the old computer like the Amiga (*Tsunami/VD* in R.A.W. #9, 1995).

The same applies to using new "too easy" tools, even with existing computers. The use of so-called *demo-makers*, tools that require little or no programming skills, was routinely frowned upon according to our data. Also certain interpreters like AMOS, a form of the BASIC programming language, were seen as not belonging in the scene: "We'll see a whole bunch of AMOS coders, but they hardly fit in our scene, do they?" (R.A.W. #3, 1992). Nevertheless one could accept "easy" tools in the future, once they start to better enable scene skills. The role of the Flash scripting language for making demos is a topical debate on this.

Sceners often describe bad skills as something of a child's play. Since people frequently refer to demosceners as kids in the media [3], this distinction carries some irony. According to one diskmag, bad demos look like a drawing competition at a kindergarten (R.A.W. #6, 1993). Another Amiga owner mentions that he would never buy a PC, "because this is indeed a computer for only playing, little children and for hardworking businessmen" (R.A.W. #3, 1992). Therefore, the demoscene skills are not child's play, but they are not hard business either.

The most severe sign of no skills is ripping other demos' source code, graphics or music. The following newsgroup posting by *Lancelot/Aggression* in 1993 notes:

"ANYONE WHO COPIES PICTURES IS A LAMER!!! As a gfx-artist I am very well aware of how difficult it is to make a good picture. The reason why paintings are copied is that IT IS SO MUCH EASIER."

This frowning upon ripping is not a question of artist's copyright—with the demoscene's extensive cracking past, that would not be very believable. Rather, ripping is not a scene practice because it is too easy. The writer positions himself inside the scene: he is an artist and knows how difficult it is to make something that requires skills.

5.2   Elites vs. Lamers

The discussions we observed show that sceners put great efforts to define what they are not. This is marked by the distinction between "elites" and "lamers". Comparably, the early MIT hackers of the 1960s divided users to "winners" and "losers" [11]. The dictionary definition of "elite" points to the ambivalence of the concept. In common use, elite is a group of people considered best in particular society. However, in its original use in the late 18th century, elite was a noun of process: it meant "selection" or "choice". Similarly, in our data, many argue that it should go without saying what describes elite and lame. Nevertheless, the sceners still constantly debate this description. There seems indeed to be an active selection and choice of whom and what deserves to be elite, and even on what counts as a satisfactory test for that (see also Kline & Pinch [8]).

The lamer has certain motivations, skills, and qualities. Firstly, the lamer is motivated by aims to be something that is not his essence. He would like to be famous or is trying to be better than he is. According to one account,

"The most typical lamer type is the guy in a group nobody knows because he has no contacts, moreover no coders, musicians, gfx... But this kind of lamers would like to be famous. But he isn't because he can't do anything." (Zine #02, 1989)

The same account already points to lamer's skills, which we also covered in subsection 5.1. The lamer "can't do anything (related to the scene)". Other accounts mention that the lamers are constantly asking for advice on coding routines. Even more severe forms of lame skills are the buying or ripping of content made by other groups. Finally, lame qualities include having, aside little contacts, little ideas and personality: "it (lameness) is your personality or better the missing of it" (Imphobia #3, 1992). With all these connotations, it was a powerful metaphor to call a new computer lame.

In our data, there is much more emphasis on defining lamers than on defining elites. There are many entire diskmag articles devoted to the motivations, skills and qualities of a lamer, none for the elites. This may reveal that the scene does not need to observe in detail the normal conditions. Rather, it needs to keep an eye on every-thing around the scene: all those changes that appear abnormal and even threatening to the scene's existence. For this purpose, the elites need the category of "the others", the lamers. As *Domino/TRSI* puts it in R.A.W. #06 (1993), "What's the point in be-ing elite if there are no lamers?"

5.3 Confronting a Changing World

We have underlined that demosceners have an active and self-reflective relation to new computers. They often consult other sceners and try to determine whether a new computer counts as viable for making demos. Similar patterns are apparent for exam-ple in studies by Lehtonen [10] and Rogers [16]. Most sceners are not enthusiastic early adopters of new technology, but want to use computers for certain ends instead. This means defining whether the computer in question is elite or lame and whether it enables scene skills to flourish. The sceners in our source material strived to create and maintain a critical distance to the new computers. The users were thus retaining a degree of control over technological change [10].

However, the degree of control over change was not high. The technological sphere still has an autonomy of its own. Similarly to the average consumers [10], the sceners were simply subjected to the arrival of Amigas and PCs—the scene could mediate the arrival, but not prevent it. Consequently, in our data, the sceners always eventually adopted the newest computers and technologies. In addition, while argu-ing about computers on more general level, the sceners often chose the same language as their environment: the language of the markets and companies. In a diskmag entry, "the death of Amiga" was said to result in "the stupid PCs and the videogames in charge of the computer and entertainment scene" (R.A.W. #3, 1992). One commenta-tor even claimed that Microsoft was "The innovative engine of the entire software industry. Does Microsoft support the Amiga? Microsoft supports any machine worth supporting" (R.A.W. #8, 1995).

As we observed in subsection 5.1, the scene activities are sometimes contrasted to "hard business". However, the sceners can still use the arguments of markets for their own purposes. This inconsistent relationship with business describes the scene in rela-tion to technological change. Internally, the scene can observe anything according to its own binary oppositions between *elite* and *lame* and *skillful* and *non-skillful*. Nev-ertheless, it cannot change the much larger spheres like the global markets of com-puters and the mass media. If the sceners want to discuss computer business, they can do nothing but communicate accordingly.

6 Conclusion

The transitions we have described illustrate the role of active communication in the domestication of home computers from the late 1980s to the late 1990s. People will reject a new platform at first if it does not fit the current community practices, no mat-ter how technically advanced it is. One might expect that technically proficient and active people such as the demoscene members would be among the innovators or early adopters of new technology, but our study disproves such assumptions. The ad-aptation of community practices in the case of demoscene takes considerable time and largely follows the same pattern as any diffusion process.

What appears in the mass media as harmless adolescents making audiovisual presentations hides an elaborate system of interpersonal relationships and practices. Thus portraying this complex community as a mere monoculture of nerds or a preschool for IT business [7] is an oversimplification. The conflicts both inside the scene and with the outside world may rather rudely affect the persons involved, because they are so deeply involved with the system. The emotional tone of the discussions also reveals the intimacy of computer as an object.

References

[1] Bagnall, B.: On the edge: the spectacular rise and fall of Commodore. Variant Press (2005)

[2] Google: Google Groups, comp.sys.ibm.pc.demos (2007),
http://groups.google.com/group/comp.sys.ibm.pc.demos/about
(accessed April 14, 2007)

[3] Green, D.: Demo or Die! Wired, issue 3.07 (1995)

[4] Gruetzmacher, T.: PC Demoscene FAQ, plain text version (v0.83) (2004),
http://tomaes.32x.de/text/pcdemoscene_faq.txt (accessed April 14, 2007)

[5] Håpnes, T.: Not in Their Machines. How Hackers Transform Computers into Subcultural Artefacts. In: Lie, M., Sørensen, K.H. (eds.) Making Technology Our Own: Domesticating Technology into Everyday Life, pp. 121–150. Scandinavian University Press (1996)

[6] Inkinen, S., Salmi, M.: Media aseena ja työkaluna – hakkereita, teknohippejä ja koneromantiikkaa uuden median verkoissa (Media as a weapon and a tool – hackers, techno hippies and machine romanticism in the networks of new media). In: Tarkka, M., Hintikka, K.A., Mäkelä, A. (eds.) Johdatus uuteen mediaan (Introduction to new media), pp. 90–91. Edita (1996)

[7] Kauppinen, J.: Demoskenen alakulttuurista nousee suomalaisen it:n kärki (The leading Finnish IT springs from the demoscene subculture). Aamulehti 7.7.2005, p. 20 (2005)

[8] Kline, R., Pinch, T.: The social construction of technology. In: MacKenzie, D., Wajcman, J. (eds.) The Social Shaping of Technology, pp. 113–115. Open University Press (2004)

[9] Kurki, R.: WE ARE! Tutkimus postmodernista identiteetistä sukupuolittuneissa yhteisöissä (A study on the postmodern identity in gendered communities). Lahden ammattikorkeakoulu (Lahti Polytechnic) (2002)

[10] Lehtonen, T.-K.: The Domestication of New Technologies as a Set of Trials. Journal of Consumer Culture 3, 363–385 (2003)

[11] Levy, S.: Hackers. Dell Publishing (1994)

[12] Lönnblad, H.: Kahden tietokonedemon vertaileva analyysi (A comparative study of two computer demos). Musiikin Suunta 19(2), 28–34 (1997)

[13] Nordli, H.: The Net is not Enough: Searching for the Female Hacker. Norwegian University of Science and Technology (2003)

[14] Polgar, T.: Freax. The brief history of the demoscene, vol. 1. CSW Verlag (2005)

[15] Reunanen, M., Silvast, A.: The Demoscene Research Bibliography (2007),
http://www.kameli.net/demoresearch (accessed October 25, 2007)

[16] Rogers, E.M.: Diffusion of Innovations, 4th edn. The Free Press, New York (1995)

[17] Saarikoski, P.: Valtavirtaa vastaan—Demoscene suomalaisen kotimikroilun historiassa (Against the mainstream–Demo scene in the history of the Finnish homecoputer hobbyists). Lähikuva 3/2001, pp. 54–65 (2001)

[18] Saarikoski, P.: Koneen lumo. Mikrotietokoneharrastus Suomessa 1970-luvulta 1990-luvun puoliväliin (The Lure of the Machine. The Personal Computer Interest in Finland from the 1970s to the mid-1990s). Nykykulttuurin tutkimuskeskuksen julkaisuja 83. Jyväskylä (2004)

[19] Shor, S., Eyal, A.: DEMOing: A new emerging art form or just another digital craft? (2002), http://rhizome.org/thread.rhiz?thread=8522 (accessed April 15, 2007)

[20] Tasajärvi, L. (ed.): Stamnes, B., Schustin, M.: Demoscene: the Art of Real-Time. Even Lake Studios & katastro.fi (2004)

[21] Turkle, S.: The Second Self: Computers and the Human Spirit. Simon and Schuster (1984)

IT Museums and Related Projects
in the Nordic Countries

Summary of a Panel Discussion

Jaakko Suominen[1], Kimmo Antila[2], Peter Blom[3], Ola Nordal[4],
and Outi Penninkangas[5]

[1] University of Turku, Department of Digital Culture
jaakko.suominen@utu.fi
[2] Museum Centre Vapriikki, Tampere
kimmo.antila@tampere.fi
[3] IT-ceum, Sweden's Computer Museum, Linköping
peter.blom@itceum.se
[4] Norwegian University of Science and Technology (NTNU)
ola.nordal@hf.ntnu.no
[5] Media Museum Rupriikki, Tampere
outi.penninkangas@tampere.fi

Digital heritage is cultural heritage!
— Outi Penninkangas

Abstract. Following some museum related papers presented at the conference, the panel discussed the challenges of IT museum projects in different Nordic countries. The panel provided examples on individual museum projects as well as university based models and IT related exhibitions in regional museum institution. The panel focused on questions on preserving and presenting hardware and software as well as financial issues of museum projects, and the paper introduces shortly the discussion between the panelists and the audience.

Keywords: IT museums, Exhibitions, Digital cultural heritage.

1 Introduction

Information technology is important part of cultural heritage in the Nordic countries - like in many other regions and states in the world. The consequential position is not only result of success of some internationally important and active companies, such as Nokia and Ericsson. Nowadays, when information technologies seem to be necessities in our everyday life, we need historical understanding of it. How the increase of importance and popularization of the information technologies have taken place? What are the historical processes producing that IT-oriented situation? Who have been the key actors in this change? How do we use history as an increasingly important element in constructing our relationship with emergent information technological innovations? If we think about contemporary culture of digital technology and its future, we see processes of using and recycling past as an emerging trend in the future [9].

J. Impagliazzo, T. Järvi, and P. Paju (Eds.): HiNC 2, IFIP AICT 303, pp. 302–309, 2009.
© IFIP International Federation for Information Processing 2009

Museums have an essential role in dealing with questions of information technology and its history. However, there are certain challenges, when one introduces information technology to museums – not only as a pedagogical tool for presenting other issues – but an object and topic of technological cultural heritage. Who should take the responsibility to preserve and present history of computing and information technology, since they are quite new phenomena and not largely included in traditional museum exhibitions? Moreover, how should we do that?

For answering those questions, we organized a panel for the HiNC2 conference. The panel was a good addition to some conference papers, wherein they discussed the questions of museum work (see for example [10]). The panel focused on two major issues: 1) Questions of collecting, preserving, and exhibiting: relation between hardware, software and other materials, and 2) questions of funding: how to finance projects, how to institutionalize them and how to share knowledge about the best and the worst practices dealing with financial and other issues.

2 Panelists and Their Projects

The panel discussion started, after the short introduction by the chair, **Jaakko Suominen**, with talks of panelists, where they introduced themselves and their museum projects. We selected the panelists, not only for gaining some sort of Nordic variety, but also for getting experiences on different kinds of museum projects.

Kimmo Antila works as a curator of museum centre Vapriikki, in Tampere, Finland. According to Kimmo Antila, the centre's concept is unique, because it presents quite widely different issues from history and archeology of Pirkanmaa and Tampere regions to industrial specialties, technology, and modern art and design. With its 360,000 items, the centre is one of the largest museums in Finland and probably best known from its major exhibitions of foreign cultures (such as China). In his preliminary talk, Antila wanted to underline questions of modern and contemporary technology in museum collections and exhibitions. When Antila started his work at the centre in 2004, he was a little bit amazed when he discovered that most of the installations about technological history focused on the first industrial revolution (before modern information technologies for example) and its machinery. He argued that presenting more modern or contemporary technology is more or less problematic for most of the museums. The other key argument Antila presented was that computing relates to so many different branches that people should noticed it, for example, when one is making an exhibition about textile industry. The use of computers and the new information technology is part of one period of (industrial) history in general.

In addition to Vapriikki, Antila mentioned the Helsinki Museum of Technology[1], which is a major player of the field as well. Helsinki Museum of Technology has also some machinery related to Finnish computing history, such as the early Finnish ESKO computer from the 1950s (on ESKO, see e.g. [6]) and Siemens 2002 mainframe installation used by the Finnish Cable Works in the early 1960s. The museum also has contracted computing museum collection of Jyväskylä (see [10]). Whereas Jyväskylä has focused on academic computing and mainframe installations, Helsinki museum of technology tries to concentrate on more modern information technology and smaller computers as well.

---

[1] http://www.tekniikanmuseo.fi/

For conclusion of his introduction, Antila mentioned that Finnish research on history of computing has been very active lately. The research has helped making links and creating cooperation with museums. The co-work will be important and strengthened in the future.

After Mr. Antila's introductory remarks, the panel moved on to the next speaker, Mr. **Peter Blom**. He worked as a curator of IT-ceum, Sweden's Computer Museum, located in Mjärdevi Science Park, Linköping. The museum opened in 2004; its location is in Linköping because many important Swedish IT-related corporations operated in the area, e.g. Saab, Luxor, Facit, and Ericsson. The Linköping Municipality, Linköping University, and Saab finance the museum, and for the seasonal exhibitions, it has had partners ranging from non-profit foundations to the Nintendo Corporation. At the core of the museum is the main exhibition, "50 years of Computing in Sweden", covering the period from the Second World War to today. Like Kimmo Antila, Blom pointed out that the museums of history of technology and science are usually interested in older periods, and therefore the role of the IT-ceum is somewhat different. Blom underlined, for example, that most of the IT-pioneers are still alive so one can get first hand information on the issues of computing, which is not a case with many other technologies.

We can also see the IT-ceum's different role in its mission. Peter Blom noted, that IT is changing society rapidly (or society changes IT rapidly) and the museum hopes that people can make choices about their future by knowing and evaluating the past and the present. Therefore the museum wants to present the latest discoveries and technologies as well. IT-ceum has done that, for example, by making exhibitions on the latest technological discoveries cooperating with the Swedish Defence Research Agency. In addition, co-operation exist with Swedish national science museum and other major players.

IT-ceum is very keen on dialogue with schools in the area; it is trying to create a neutral discussion base for the public about IT-related issues. The museum has lately had exhibitions on visual digital culture and digital games. These areas, which have probably been some times in the computing marginal, have provided opportunities for testing the limits of computing. Today, they form a major part of digital culture.

The next speaker came from Norway. **Ola Nordal** is currently writing a book on the IT-history of the Norwegian University of Science and Technology (NTNU) in Trondheim. He has also participated in a project dealing with collections of the university's computer items, which they nowadays display in a small scale. Nordal mentioned that there is no such thing as a computer museum currently in Norway, although the Norwegian Museum of Science and Technology in Oslo[2] has some objects of Norwegian IT history in its permanent exhibition. In addition, the Norwegian Telecom Museum[3] has some artifacts and exhibitions on computing. There is no organized collecting of computing material in Norway, and Norwegian University of Science and Technology's 1000 object collection is one of the largest IT-related museum collection in Norway. The collecting started in the 1980s and the 1990s by some enthusiasts of the Department of Computer Science. They wanted to preserve valuable historical IT items, such as two Danish GIER computers that were used by the university in the early 1960s (see [3]; 2005 [8]; [5]).

---

[2] http://www.tekniskmuseum.no/
[3] http://www.telemuseum.no/

The museum project has some short-term and long-term goals. Museum project will organize, document and make catalogues about the collection as well as exhibit collections. Long-time goal is to gain a status of national computing museum or built up technical or university museum of Trondheim, where they would install the collection. Now, the project is preparing a number of small exhibitions displaying functional computers, so visitors can experience the tactility, feel, and sound of the equipment - and not just see a "dead" computer on display.

Outi Penninkangas, Curator of Media Museum Rupriikki, Tampere, began her talk by describing daily routines of her museum. Rupriikki started its work at 2001. In the first phase, the local media and communication firms such as the Aamulehti newspaper and Elisa telephony operator cooperated with City of Tampere and University of Tampere to organize it. Officially, they opened the museum to the public in 2003 for promoting history of communication and role of media in society. Different types of communications such as history of newspapers, telephony, radio, television, as well as information technology divide Rupriikki into sections. IT section of the museum was co-produced by the Department of Hypermedia Studies at the University of Tampere, and the section was focused on three different topics were IT-related issues are essential: work, home (daily life) and gaming, which is also one of the research focus areas of the Hypermedia Laboratory. The purpose of the IT section is, for example, to visualize to visitors questions of the Internet, change in computer memory capacity, personal computing, and in gaming cultures. Due to rather limited collections of computer objects of Tampere museums, the local microcomputer club (Pirkanmaan mikrotietokonekerho) donated the IT artifacts. After its opening, Rupriikki discovered the great challenges of exhibiting IT related issues interestingly. Therefore, today, the museum is trying to find new ways of cooperation for improving its exhibitions. Museum needs academic connections but also help provided by the local computer hobbyists. One current project by an enthusiast is to produce a system where the public can come to the museum with their old data in floppy disks. During their visit, they will transfer the data to usable, modern format, stored in CDs or DVDs. The project is still under construction.

In addition to basic IT exhibition, Rupriikki has some special, thematic exhibitions. Curator Outi Penninkangas mentioned two projects in particular. In 2006, Rupriikki organised an exhibition focused on Commodore computers, which were most important home computers in Finland and in many other countries as well, especially during the mid-1980s. The proposition for the exhibition came from a local computer vendor, Triosoft. It was among the earliest firms in Finland starting business with Commodore hardware and software (such as games) in the early 1980s. In the beginning, the museum was a bit skeptical of how to get working computer installations to the exhibition, but the project proved to be a great success. With the help of ten working Commodores loaded with games and other software, museum gained new audience, which has never before visited in Rupriikki – or in some cases – any other museum after visitors' childhood. The visitors were fascinated with the possibility of using machines, playing games, hearing sounds and trying to remember how it was like to program some BASIC code with their own Commodore 64 machines.

Another project Penninkangas mentioned was the 10th anniversary exhibition for the Mindtrek conference. The idea of the exhibition came from the conference organizers, who provided some documented material and multimedia works produced for

Mindtrek competition during its ten years history. The works consists of e-learning applications, multimedia art, internet solutions, as well as games. During that project, the staff of Rupriikki realised again big challenges of presenting history of information technology and software. Although the multimedia works can be only ten years old, it could be difficult to find working hardware and right operating systems for the presentation, in order to create authentic surroundings for the experience.

3   Hardware, Software, and Documentation

Lately, interest towards questions of history of software and software cultures has emerged in academia (for the emergence of software issues, see for example [1, 4, and 7]). Therefore, we wanted to touch upon relation between hardware, software and other forms of computing in this panel as well. The panelists were asked several questions by the chair: How to choose what to preserve and what to present? Could you comment on the relation between hardware and software in IT-history and IT-history oriented museums? Is there anything new in these topics to discuss?

Outi Penninkangas opened discussion by mentioning Police Museum of Finland in Tampere, which will open in 2008. The museum will present the whole information system used by police in the earlier days. That sort of presentation of the information system was a good idea in Penninkangas' opinion due to the fact that police work has been changing, like many other types of work, since computers arrived at their workplace. TietoEnator, a Finnish-Swedish firm which has made the information system, is participating in the museological documenting work of the system.

Peter Blom wanted to emphasize that the question of preserving and conserving does not relate only to software: hardware will not last forever either. Lots of interesting software is stored on tapes, and it is difficult to run them anymore. Moreover, if one manages to transfer the old software to new data systems there is still the open question of how to present it. Therefore, it is a problem of many dimensions, which IT-ceum in Sweden is trying to solve in its exhibitions. Mr. Blom referred to Outi Penninkangas' earlier speech and nodded that it is very nice to get enthusiasts, who can help with these kinds of issues.

Ola Nordal pointed out that software also is a hardware problem - and a literature problem. One needs three things to make the software run; 1) the actual software media (disk, tape, cards, and so on), 2) a machine that can operate the software, and 3) the documentation of the software. Therefore, the philosophy of the Trondheim collection is to try to collect all three, not only the boxes.

Kimmo Antila referred to a new project about Finnish innovations. The project will put a strong emphasis on regional innovation systems and major important innovations in the Tampere region. Antila revealed that most of them are IT-related: mobile phones and different kinds of software. In his opinion innovations systems are, as an exhibition topic, very hard issue to work with. Therefore, museum needs close cooperation with researches who had been involved with the innovations and projects. It is almost impossible for museum curator to analyse the theme or get anything out of manual by him/herself.

Mr. Antila mentioned also his own research and publication project about history the Digital Media Institute in Tampere University of Technology. The institute was a vital actor in the 1980s and the 1990s pushing towards lots of research and development projects with companies, and Antila used oral historical methods in his studies about the institute.

After the panelists' addresses, the audience had an opportunity to comment on issues mentioned. One audience remark was to put emphasize on questions of programmers and ideas behind the old software, which could be demonstrated without actual software itself. Another point was that one can use emulators for running old software, we do not need old functional hardware in every case.

John Impagliazzo asked about Danish and Icelandic projects related to computer museums or to the preservation of computer history; participants from those countries completed the Nordic museum picture by telling briefly about their national projects. In Iceland, there is a special interest group on history in data processing society. The group is for instance encouraging people to write down their memoirs on computing. In addition, the group is planning to conduct interviews with some veterans in companies (in steel industry for example) and computer related institutions.

A Danish colleague told about a huge cellar in Copenhagen, which is full of old equipment, software, manuals, and other material. The project group has already created a virtual museum onto the internet[4] and has received some funding from local authorities. They hope that opening of the museum will occur in next few years.

4 Financing the Projects

One key factor of the museum project is funding. Panelists were asked to tell about good practices, how to finance museum related projects and how to secure continuation in difficult situation where number of museums is large. Would it be possible to combine local, national, and international funding in private and public level?

Peter Blom started his answer by mentioning that one way is to seek national status of a computer museum, but this kind of process would take five to ten years. Therefore, IT-ceum in Sweden is trying to find alternative ways to get funding. Currently, they have three major partners, who are not eager to finance the project for years. Therefore, the seeking of other solutions is essential. One resolution is to put exhibitions on the road, which is a good possibility because the museum is in Linköping, not in Stockholm with a large population, other tourist attractions, and huge number of potential museum visitors. Touring helps also getting funding from private partners, who are happy if the exhibition gets a wider audience. Moreover, this is one way to obtain the omnipresent national status of a computer museum.

According to Ola Nordal, Trondheim does not have finance strategy yet, but if the collection is well documented and catalogued, it is lot more difficult to squander it and probably easier to get funding for it. Nordal was quite optimistic about getting funding, because history of computing is relatively interesting topic currently compared to many other areas of cultural or technological heritage.

Outi Penninkangas added wisely, that before receiving governmental funding one have to admit that digital heritage is part of our cultural heritage. She stated that museums in Finland are somewhat lazy in applying funding for governmental sources for these sorts of purposes. Ministry of Education in Finland has, for instance money for

---

[4] See http://datamuseum.dk

information society projects for museums, but so far there has not been much interest of executing history of computing related projects.

Kimmo Antila admitted that he is quite doubtful with the idea of getting sponsorship money, although they had managed to gain small sum of private funding for some projects. For constant work and big exhibitions, one has to have public finance for international, national, or regional sources or from some private foundations. For example in Finland, there are several private foundations, which support industrial heritage and history of technology research projects and exhibitions, including history of computing. Antila agrees with Outi Penninkangas in the issue that major governmental bodies do not see yet the importance of history of modern technology.

The audience participated actively in the discussion with the panelists. Oddur Benediktsson from Iceland claimed Nordic or European level cooperation, which could most likely help in getting projects financed. Peter Blom answered and told a little about financing of Nordic bodies for their projects. He emphasized that it is important so seek funding from a right stock and from right places.

Kimmo Antila started to think about possibility of using culture and knowledge export funding sources. He told about a Korean colleague he met at the International Committee for the History of Technology (ICOHTEC) conference who was interested in Nordic IT history. These factors were combined, particularly in a book by Manuel Castells and Pekka Himanen [2]; the combination would be used in showing international importance of the Nordic social and technological model.

Emmi Tittonen described briefly financial issues of the Jyväskylä museum project in Finland (see also [10]). After struggling some years for getting money for rents the project received some funding from the Ministry of Transportation and Communication for documenting work. When museum collections moved to another location, the Ministry of Education and the City of Jyväskylä, and some other governmental bodies helped in covering the expenses. Still, it is difficult to get money, even for the rents, and the museum activists have to seek different possibilities for funding.

John Impagliazzo asked, if the national IT societies have active role in preserving IT heritage, which they have in USA, for example. He believes that the societies would make good players to lobby for historical research and preserving projects. Per Lundin and other Swedish colleagues briefly mentioned the Swedish research project connected to Swedish IT society. The project has also some sponsors.

A colleague from Denmark, participating in Danish computer museum project asked if the panelists had experiences of some sort of "interface problems" with well-established national science and technological museums. Kimmo Antila answered that he does not believe that there would be such problems in large scale. Antila demanded building of the Nordic network of museums related to history of computing. That kind of network is needed for comparing and sharing experiences in the situation, where we have shared problems and similar goals to aim in different countries. Even though one has to admit, that museums also compete with each other (at least in national level), the co-work is essential.

5 Conclusion

The panel discussion showed that there is a huge need for work related to computing history. The work needs not only historical, technological, and museological efforts, but also public relations and discussion. Hence, we hope the panel motto "Digital heritage is our cultural heritage" to become a common and shared conception. For gaining these objectives, we will need more international cooperation. Probably the next HiNC conference will reveal how we have succeeded in these attempts.

References

[1] Campbell-Kelly, M.: From airline reservations to Sonic the Hedgehog: A history of the software industry. MIT Press, Cambridge (2003)

[2] Castells, M., Himanen, P.: The information society and the welfare state: the Finnish model. Oxford University Press, New York (2002)

[3] Espelid, T.O., Maus, A., Nordbotten, S., Skog, K., Sølvberg, A.: Research and curricula development at Norwegian universities. In: Bubenko, J., Impagliazzo, J., Sølvberg, A. (eds.) History of Nordic Computing. IFIP WG9.7 First Working Conference on the History of Nordic Computing (HiNC1), Trondheim, Norway, June 16-18, 2003. IFIP International Federation for Information Processing, vol. 174. Springer, New York (2005)

[4] Mackenzie, A.: Cutting code: Software and sociality. Peter Lang, New York (2006)

[5] Nordal, O.: Tool or Science? The History of Computing at the Norwegian University of Science and Technology. In: Impagliazzo, J., Järvi, T., Paju, P. (eds.) HiNC 2. IFIP AICT, vol. 303, pp. 121–129. Springer, Heidelberg (2009)

[6] Paju, P.: A failure revisited: The first Finnish computer construction project. In: Bubenko, J., Impagliazzo, J., Solvberg, A. (eds.) History of Nordic Computing. IFIP WG9.7 First Working Conference on the History of Nordic Computing (HiNC1), Trondheim, Norway, June 16-18, 2003. IFIP International Federation for Information Processing, vol. 174. Springer, New York (2005)

[7] Parikka, J.: Digital contagions: a media archaeology of computer viruses. Peter Lang, New York (2007)

[8] Sanders, N.: Making computing available. In: Bubenko, J., Impagliazzo, J., Sølvberg, A. (eds.) History of Nordic Computing. IFIP WG9.7 First Working Conference on the History of Nordic Computing (HiNC1), Trondheim, Norway, June 16-18, 2003. IFIP International Federation for Information Processing, vol. 174. Springer, New York (2005)

[9] Suominen, J.: The Past as the Future. Nostalgia and Retrogaming in Digital Culture. Fibreculture, issue 11 (digital arts and culture conference (perth) issue) (2008), http://journal.fibreculture.org/issue11/issue11_suominen.html

[10] Tittonen, E.: Increasing the Museum Value of Information Technology Objects - The Case of the Finnish Data Processing Museum Association. In: Impagliazzo, J., Järvi, T., Paju, P. (eds.) HiNC 2. IFIP AICT, vol. 303, pp. 45–54. Springer, Heidelberg (2009)

University Education on Computers

Summary of a Panel Discussion

Reino Kurki-Suonio[1], Oddur Benediktsson[2], Janis Bubenko Jr.[3],
Ingemar Dahlstrand[4], Christian Gram[5], and John Impagliazzo[6]

[1] Tampere University of Technology (Emeritus), Finland
reino.kurki-suonio@tut.fi
[2] University of Iceland
oddur@hi.is
[3] Royal Institute of Technology (Emeritus), Stockholm, Sweden
janis@dsv.su.se
[4] University of Lund, Sweden (Emeritus)
[5] Technical University of Denmark (Emeritus), Copenhagen, Denmark
chr.gram@ddf.dk
[6] Qatar University, Doha, Qatar
john@qu.edu.qa

Abstract. Following a session on university education, this panel discussed early Nordic visions and experiences on university computing education, contrasting them to today's needs and the international development at that time. This report gives short papers by the panelists (their opening statements), and a brief summary (the chair's interpretation) of the views that were raised in the ensuing discussion.

Keywords: Nordic university computing education, university computing education.

1 Introductory Remarks

More than forty years have passed since computer science and related topics were introduced as academic disciplines, even though universities had already used computers for some time and students had already experienced programming courses. The first professors in these fields had started their work in computing practice more than forty-five years ago. To obtain a quantitative idea of the way the world has changed since then, notice that the factor computed by Moore's law for forty-five years is no less than one billion; that is, it is a factor of ten to the ninth!

Trying to imagine ourselves in those times, we remember also that computers were centralized facilities, operated by special personnel in the batch mode. Computers were far too expensive and it was difficult to justify their use for educational purposes or for computing-related research; they were primarily purchased for more "serious" use as tools in number crunching and/or administrative data processing.

Another major difference is that in its infancy the world of computing was still rather homogeneous. Until the mid-1970s, "all" computer people – system and application

J. Impagliazzo, T. Järvi, and P. Paju (Eds.): HiNC 2, IFIP AICT 303, pp. 310–321, 2009.
© IFIP International Federation for Information Processing 2009

developers, academicians and practitioners – gathered at IFIP world congresses, for instance, and they were still listening to each other with interest and with more or less good understanding. In other words, the many disciplines that were inspired by information technology were just emerging and had not yet developed their separating paradigms, no specialized conference or workshop series existed, and the gulf between theory and practice was still narrow.

This panel presentation has provided a spectrum of viewpoints of computing at universities from different countries and from different periods. The overall collection total of these points of view has created an interesting dialogue useful to computing history and history specialists.

2 Early Development in Finland

My own university career started in 1965 at the University of Tampere and continued from 1980 until 2002 at Tampere University of Technology. In both places, I had the privilege of developing degree-based education in computing from scratch. When I became involved with this, I had five years experience in application design and implementation as well as in programming education at Finnish Cable Works, one of the roots of today's Nokia. My ideas of computing education were, however, strongly influenced by a post-doctoral year at Carnegie Institute of Technology (now Carnegie Mellon University), where the computer science department was just beginning to start in a formal way.

As discussed in more detail in [8], in Finland the first chair in computing was established by a surprise move in 1965 by the University of Tampere – then still a School of Social Sciences – at which point I suddenly found myself involved in designing an academic curriculum for an emerging discipline. This activity was not a result of gradual development. Since we did not have much of a model to use, I had a rather free hand in the curriculum design.

Contrary to what we had heard about the controversy between a tool and a discipline in Norway [10], this was not a problem in Tampere since the university did not have natural sciences or technology with large number crunching needs. Later, however, this controversy was strongly reflected in the acquisition of computers, as is apparent in [11]. In any case, in computing education we were definitely going for a new discipline, which we felt to be of fundamental importance to human civilization.

For the core of this discipline, I considered expressing of complex algorithmic processes. It was clear that, as an academic discipline in an area with much practical importance, the curriculum should combine practical skills with theoretical understanding. Of course, this "motherhood" statement was never easy to implement, since "one man's theory is another man's practice". In addition, much of what practitioners criticized as being too theoretical in our curriculum is now pure practice.

Although the field then was much more homogeneous than today, computing practice had two important lines of separation: one between *scientific computing* and *administrative data processing*, and the other between *programming* and *system analysis and design*. In my mind, the emerging discipline should do away with these differences. I felt that the discipline is much more fundamental than using computers as tools in certain applications, and that results in its core areas are application-independent.

Additionally, I also strongly opposed the common view of practitioners that programming is a low-level activity of coding, or the technical mastery of one or more programming languages.

In designing and then implementing the curriculum, my colleague, Miikka Jahnukainen, assisted me. He had already been involved with a plan to educate system analysts and designers for administrative data processing. We felt that it was a good idea to expose the students to our complementary views on what was most essential for the students. I could concentrate on algorithmic processes, data structures, principles of programming languages and operating systems, and other aspects of the young computer science, whereas Jahnukainen's approach better prepared students for the more mundane practices of the ADP departments and led to the Scandinavian direction of "systemeering". However, to my disappointment, the two views seldom merged successfully in the students' minds. My idealism was also shaken by the experience that so many of the students – especially ones who wanted to specialize in administrative system design – had tremendous difficulties in passing the courses that I considered to be the core of the discipline.

In any case, when further Finnish universities followed us in starting their computer science and related departments, we had already gained some experiences that they could utilize, in addition to the international models that then started to be available.

3   A Swedish Perspective

In the early days of computing, the 1950s and the 1960s, researchers and practitioners had different visions about computing in the future. Swedish researchers' vision was the continued use of large computers, precise application problem formulation in high-level, declarative languages followed by "code generation" and optimization. We believed in the development of advanced tools for design and generation of information systems. We also believed we would/could develop a comprehensive "theory of information systems development". However, we totally underestimated the complexity of such an undertaking. It is important to note that, in the 1960s, our vision of future information technology did not include (1) personal and personally owned and portable computers, (2) data communication development and the internet, (3) security threats and problems, and (4) the development of commercial off-the-shelf (COTS) software and hardware. We could hardly have imagined that these things were possible.

Today, university education in information technology has become specialized in many different directions such as theoretical aspects (computer science), databases, information systems, software engineering, requirements engineering, human-computer interaction, and many other specialties. However, in most of these specialties we still consider certain fundamental topics as essential. Some of them include modeling of "object systems" (applications) using different types of models (conceptual, object-oriented, process, rules, etc.), programming languages of different kinds, algorithms and data structures, mathematics and logics, and design, testing and proofs of programs.

Major changes during the last twenty years that have affected the needs of academic computing education are the personal computer and advances in software and hardware technology, advances in telecommunications, the internet technology including search technologies. These developments have changed our vision of the way we can build future systems and the way our vision affects the way future systems may influence our daily lives.

What should be the proper role of computer science and other theoretical bases in computing education and research today? The complexity of systems is increasing. Systems increasingly experience "bad input" and hostile attacks. The need to build systems with "a correct and safe (robust) behavior" is increasing. The need for interfaces designed in such a way that non-computer experts can use them is obvious.

As a contrast, the use of formal methods, mathematics, and logic in computing education seems decreasing. In some Swedish colleges, for dubious reasons, some advanced theoretical topics in computing have been "dropped" in order to attract more students to information technology. We should never forget that systems and program development is much more than "front page design". Unfortunately, few companies of today understand the importance and need for higher-level theoretical knowledge within the computing field.

4 University Computer Science Education in Denmark

4.1 The Very Beginning

Before 1962, no regular curriculum in computer science existed at universities. However, we do know that universities offered several extra courses for both students and academic staff. Some of the topics included programming in assembly language, Algol or FORTRAN, which departments then supplemented with courses in numerical technical calculation.

The first regular courses for students emerged in the early 1960s at the universities and they centered on departments of mathematics; at the technical universities, they centered on departments of electronics. As an example, the first computer-related course at Copenhagen University was "Mathematics 4", and the contents of the course (a) Programming in Algol, (b) Numerical analysis of problems in linear equation solving, numerical integration, and root finding.

4.2 The First Plan

Through his work on compiler construction and on EDP applications, Peter Naur became convinced that some common basic principles lay behind all data processing and use of computation. In 1966, while he worked as a senior consultant at Regnecentralen, he published a red booklet with 64 pages called "A Plan for a Course in Datalogy and Datamatics" [9]. The booklet outlined what a general course in computer science should contain. The preamble stated that "Datalogy is as fundamental as language and mathematics in education", and some knowledge of programming must be taught early. The plan proceeded by describing in some detail six major areas:

o Concepts and methodology for datalogy; computers; data processes.
o Single data elements; dealing with data representation; numbers and arithmetics; classification and choices.

o Medium size data sets; problems concerned with searching and sorting; sequential analysis of text; arithmetic expressions; list structures.

o Communication between man and computer; format of input data; output representations; dialogue between man and machine.

o Large data sets and file transactions; processing efficiency; utilization of sequential secondary storage; searching on secondary storage media.

o Development of large programs; consideration of safety problems; ways to plan and develop large programs.

Using this plan as the list of contents, Naur and a group of colleagues at Regnecentralen planned to write a textbook containing eighteen chapters. It was our conviction at the time that new textbooks were essential; the management at Regnecentralen supported this belief. In 1967-69, the group wrote thirteen of the planned eighteen chapters; however, they never finished the last five chapters. The project stopped because in 1969, Copenhagen University appointed Naur as professor in Datalogy. At the same time, Regnecentralen moved toward a more business-oriented direction. However, the material they developed influenced the computer science curricula created in the late 1960s.

Table 1.

Typical 2007 Courses	Corresponding Titles 1968	Remarks
Intro to Mathematics	(same)	
Linear Algebra	(same)	
Advanced Algorithms	(same)	
Compilers	(same)	
Types and Programming Languages	Programming Languages	
Functional Programming	LISP	LISP was the only functional language
Advanced Databases	Databases	
Operating Systems	(same)	
Object-oriented Programming and Design	Design of EDP Systems	The term "object-oriented" was not invented, but design was dealt with much the same way as today
Optimizing in Production Planning	System Analysis, Optimization	Not exactly the same course, but much of the same flavor
Computer Architecture	(same)	Very similar courses, even if technology differed
Man-Machine Interaction	Input/Output Formatting	The term "interaction" in today's meaning was not possible; the emphasis was on user-friendly input/output
Artificial Intelligence	(same)	Courses existed in late 1960s, but the contents were much different from today's courses

4.3 Comparison with Today

The tables below show a comparison between computer science courses of today and courses in 1968. The column "Typical 2007 Courses" contains course titles from a typical computer science curriculum 2007. The column "Corresponding Titles 1968" shows, where similar courses existed already around 1968 and where methods, principles, or technology were still under development.

Table 1 mentions some of today's courses, which are more or less similar to courses that already had existed in the late 1960s. Table 2 contains several modern courses that had no obvious parallel in the old days. For many of the courses, the technology was not yet available; for other courses, the theory was still under development; in a few cases, the topics simply did not exist in the 1960s.

Table 2.

Typical 2007 Courses	Corresponding Titles 1968	Remarks
Intro to Graphics		No graphical media existed
Intro to Image Processing		No means for image manipulation existed
Logic: Models and Proofs		Prolog courses began to appear in curricula in the 1970s
Software Engineering		The term was not invented until 1968
Computation and Deduction		Theoretical computer science courses were not established
Cryptography and Security		Problems around secure EDP were not yet on the agenda
Reversible Computation		Theories were not developed
Algorithmic Geometry		Mathematicians had not yet started to use computers in geometry
Data net	(Data Transmission)	The term "data net" was not invented, but one-to-one transmission was used and taught
Intro to Distributed Systems		Distributed systems were not invented
Chip Design	(Circuit Analysis and Design)	Systems and methods for chip design did not exist
Robot Experimentation		Robots did not really appear in courses until the 1980s

5 Experiences in Lund

In 1985, I entered academia at Lund Technical College (LTH), so I did not take part in the early build-up, except for programming courses in machine code and later Algol. When I did become a teacher after much practical experience in industry, I found that the education offered at LTH was at a strong level, both practically and theoretically. In the 1960s, I had thought that getting research started was more urgent than mass education because computer scientists outside the Stockholm area had a rather poor job market. The question always had emerged as to whether computer science was a science in its own right. My response is emphatically "yes". This is the first time in civilization that we learn to instruct a completely obedient apparatus, and we are finding it surprisingly difficult. Our department at LTH offered programs in both numerical analysis and in computer science, but that was for historical reasons.

Our students sometimes complained that they wanted to learn C++ because that was what industry used. Actually, industry asked the faculty to teach students foundations and problem solving; for commercial usage, industry was prepared to teach specialized topics themselves. A computer scientist should know the difference between a good method and a poor one, even if he or she must use the latter for a while. We had a seminar once at a national conference; it started out with the question: Does computer science build upon its foundations such as computability, program proving, and the Turing machine? I do not think it always does.

6 The Start of Computer Science Education in Iceland

With the acquisition of an IBM 1620 Model 2 computer in 1964, the University of Iceland entered the computer age. Programming became part of the engineering curriculum in the following year. The programming language used was FORTRAN II. Programming became a required component of an "applied mathematics" course in the engineering curriculum. At that time, only the first three years of the engineering studies could be completed in Iceland; students would go abroad to finish their studies.

In the academic year 1972-73, a new three-year sequence of study, the BS in Applied Mathematics, became a curriculum in the Mathematics Department at the University of Iceland. The core curriculum consisted of mathematical analysis, algebra, and statistics, in addition to computer science, numerical analysis, and operations research. The curriculum was partly based on the recommendations of the ACM Curriculum Committee on Computer Science "Curriculum 68: Recommendations for the Undergraduate Program in Computer Science" [2].

Computer science became a separate three-year BS degree program at the University of Iceland in 1976. The Mathematics Department housed the degree program in computer science; the program remained there for the subsequent ten years, before becoming an independent department.

The following table shows the first computer language taught to engineering and science students at the university and the computer systems used.

Table 3.

Period	Computer system	First language
1965 – 1975	IBM 1620	FORTRAN II
1976 – 1978	IBM 360/30 and PDP 11	FORTRAN IV
1979 – 1982	DEC VAX-11	FORTRAN 77
1983 – 1986	DEC VAX-11 and PCs on net	FORTRAN 77 and Modula-2
1987 – 1990	DEC VAX-11 and PCs on net	FORTRAN 77 and Turbo Pascal
1990 – 1996	Unix servers and PCs on net	C++ and Turbo Pascal
1997 – 2006	Unix servers and PCs on net	Java and MATLAB

It was noted that the first computer language taught at a university could have a profound effect on the students involved, since the first language often becomes a tool used for the entire working life.

7 A U.S. Perspective with International Overtones

During the 1950s and the early 1960s, the United States began to generate courses associated with data processing primarily targeted toward technical (two-year) colleges. By 1965, ACM had published a paper that was a preview of the well-known Computing Curriculum'68. By the 1970s, we witnessed literature regarding graduate and undergraduate information systems programs, which culminated with Computing Curriculum'78. By the 1980s, we saw literature on discrete mathematics and programming courses, now coined as CS1 and CS2 as well as curricula recommendations for information systems and computer engineering.

7.1 The "First" U.S. Computer Science Department

It is always dangerous to speculate "firsts" when it comes to history, particularly computing history, because many institutions of higher learning explore innovative learning and teaching, particularly during the 1960s. Notwithstanding, it does appear that Purdue University was a leader at least in one area. The Purdue website states:

"The first Department of Computer Sciences in the United States was established at Purdue University in October 1962. There are three natural phases in its history. In the 1960s the effort was to define courses, degree programs, and indirectly the field itself."

During that time, the university hired five faculty members in the first year for its graduate program, which was part of the Division of Mathematical Sciences within the departments of mathematics and statistics. At first, computer science was an option in the mathematics and later became a separate B.S. degree in 1967.

7.2 Emergence of a National Computing Curriculum

By the mid-1960s, much activity ensued in curriculum development. ACM had established a Curriculum Committee on Computer Science (C3S). This group had been considering curriculum problems for approximately three years. During the early part of this period, the committee held a number of informal sessions with computer people at various national meetings. In the latter part of this three-year period, ACM formally organized the committee, where it made a definite effort to arrive at concrete suggestions for a curriculum. In 1965, the group published a paper [1], which became the precursor to Curriculum'68.

Other movements began to emerge during the 1960s. In February of 1967, the President created a Science Advisory Commission (SAC) that focused on the use of computers in higher education. The Computer Sciences in Electrical Engineering (COSINE) Committee explored the ways in which computer science would be part of electrical engineering that then led to the establishment of a Commission on Engineering Education in September of 1967 in Washington DC [5]. The question of recognition became a topic of discussion concerning whether the emerging discipline of computing was legitimate in its own right. Lofti Zadeh placed a marker on that topic with his landmark paper on the subject [12].

7.3   ACM Curriculum'68

The synergies that existed in the mid-1960s gave rise the very well known publication of the ACM Curriculum'68: Recommendations for Academic Programs in Computer Science. It was no accident that Curriculum'68 closely resembled the degree program at Purdue; indeed, Purdue was a test bed for developing recommendation. The published computer science curriculum contained three divisions for computer science that included:

- o Information Structure and Processes (data structures, programming languages, methods of computations),
- o Information Processing Systems (computer design and organization, translators and interpreters, computer and operating systems, special purpose systems), and
- o Methodologies (numerical mathematics, data processing and file management, symbol manipulation, text processing, computer graphics, simulation, information retrieval, artificial intelligence, process control, instructional systems).

Curriculum'68 also included recommendations for mathematics and the sciences. From the mathematical sciences, the curriculum recommended elementary analysis, linear algebra, differential equations, algebraic structures, numerical analysis, applied mathematics, optimization theory, combinatorics, mathematical logic, number theory, probability and statistics, operational analysis. From the physical and engineering sciences the curriculum recommended general physics, basic electronics, circuit analysis and design, thermodynamics, system mechanics, field theory, digital and pulse circuits, coding and information theory, communication and control theory, and quantum mechanics.

Curriculum'68 enjoyed a high degree of initial success. Many universities, nationally and internationally, that had an interest in establishing a computer science department began using it as a reference, at least as a starting point. However, it was not long before the recommendation showed some of its frailties and began to receive criticism. By 1974, published documents called for a revision of Curriculum'68 [6]. This paper claimed among things that the 1968 report did not address the nature of computer science, it did not address the subject matter for a complete bachelor's program, and it did not address articulation between technical and university programs. In addition, specific courses mentioned such as discrete structures, switching theory, and sequential machines seemed isolated, and many courses *not* mentioned in the 1968 report already existed in many computing programs.

A follow up article in 1976 [7] addressed what a computer science major should be able to do rather what courses a student should take. These attributes included an ability to (1) write correct, documented, readable programs in a reasonable time, (2) determine whether written programs are reasonably efficient and well organized, (3) know what types of problems are amenable to computer solution, (4) make reasonable judgments about hardware; and (5) pursue in depth training in one or more application areas. The strong undercurrent toward curriculum reform soon led to a formal revision of the battered 1968 report.

7.4 ACM Curriculum'78

To address the needs of the computing community, ACM created a new committee to overhaul the former curriculum report. The committee created a new report called Curriculum'78 [3] and developed themes of concentration that included computer programming I and II, computer systems, computer organization, file processing, operating systems and architecture, data structures and algorithm analysis, programming languages (overview and theory), computers and society, database management systems, artificial intelligence, algorithms, software design, automata, computability, formal languages, and numerical mathematics. Curriculum'78 was similar to Curriculum'68; however, the new version stressed greater adherence on software and treated hardware in a more general way. Many universities around the world adopted the framework Curriculum'78. After three decades of use and the development of new technologies, with few modifications, many computing programs in existence today reflect a strong association with the curriculum report from 1978. The curriculum seems to have endured the test of time.

7.5 Further Evolutions

Despite its level of success, Curriculum'78 soon was to come under scrutiny and would not be satisfactory to the greater computing community. The 1980s witnessed a flood of new curricula recommendations, particularly from the Data Processing Management Association (DPMA), which today is the Association for Information Technology Professionals (AITP), and from the Computer Society of the Institute for Electrical and Electronic Engineers (IEEE). Some of these reports include:

o DPMA Educational Programs and Information Systems (1981).
o ACM Information Systems Recommendations – Undergraduate & Graduate Programs (1983).
o IEEE Computer Society Model Curriculum – Computer Engineering (1983).
o DPMA Information Technology and Systems (1984).
o DPMA Associate (Two-Year) Level Model Curriculum – Information Systems (1985).
o DPMA Model Curriculum – Information Systems (1985).

The mid-1980s witnessed great debates on the subject of computing. Some of the debate centered upon whether computer science was indeed a science as opposed to being a part of engineering or a mathematics discipline – or neither of these. The culmination of the debates resulted in a new computer science curriculum recommendations called Curriculum'91 [4]. The next fifteen years saw major changes in curricula development on all computing areas. The details of these developments are beyond the scope of this narrative.

8 Discussion Summary

Arne Sølvberg from the Norwegian University of Science and Technology, Trondheim, briefly commented on the background of Norwegian computing history in the discussion. He identified two important Scandinavian sources of inspiration in the early development: work on programming languages and compilers by Peter Naur's group in Denmark, and Langefors' approach to information systems engineering in Sweden. As a major change to the early situation, Sølvberg indicated that computing departments are now well established and they no longer have to defend their existence. Although there is not so much change in the foundational courses, we find that much of the earlier curriculum content appears in other disciplines, which has an effect on the relationship of computing departments to other departments.

This led to a discussion on some factors that call for changes in today's programs and may even affect their viability. We see diminishing numbers of students and increased problems in getting good ones; we must address the interdisciplinary nature of computing and students' ability to use computers, even though they need not know how they work inside. As a response, people suggested that we must create new kinds of programs, where computing may be combined with other areas such as art. Instead of programming languages, we may have to use multimedia as the central role in the new computing approaches.

A brief exchange between Ingemar Dahlstrand and Janis Bubenko, Jr., brought up a contrast that is important in computing education. In computer science, we are interested in making the machine do exactly what we want it to do, whereas in system design a major problem is to determine what we want the computer to do.

Regarding new kinds of programs, Enn Tyugu referred to specialized computing programs, as those in bioinformatics. Christian Gram mentioned the rise of "IT high schools" and an IT university in Denmark where "computer science" becomes an add-on to a professional education in another area.

As for the diversity of computing-related programs, John Impagliazzo mentioned that according to a survey conducted a few years ago, universities in the U.K. have more than five thousand different titles for names of computing programs; the ACM/IEEE Computing Curricula 2005 discusses only five basic models for them: Computer Science, Computer Engineering, Information Systems, Information Technology, and Software Engineering. Bud Lawson emphasized that from the viewpoint of systems engineering, traditional programs concentrate just on how to deal with computers, which is only one component in total systems.

The discussion ended with an understanding that the relatively homogeneous early views on university education in computing are transitioning by tremendous diversification. Instead of trying to place the study of computing into a well-defined place in a structured classification of university disciplines, we now need to view it as an interdisciplinary area. Such a transition would require important organizational changes that will bring specialists together from different kinds of computing-related areas and that will encourage interaction and cooperation among them.

References

[1] ACM Curriculum Committee on Computer Science: An undergraduate program in computer science—preliminary recommendations. Communications of the ACM 8(9), 543–552 (1965)
[2] ACM Curriculum Committee on Computer Science: Curriculum 1968: Recommendations for the undergraduate program in computer science. Communications of the ACM 11(3), 151–197 (1968)

[3] ACM Curriculum Committee on Computer Science: Curriculum 1978: Recommendations for the undergraduate program in computer science. Communications of the ACM 22(3), 147–166 (1979)

[4] ACM/IEEECS, Computing Curricula 1991, Report of the ACM/IEEE-CS Joint Curriculum Task Force. IEEE Computer Society Press [ISBN 0-8186-2220-2] and ACM Press [ISBN 0-8979-381-7] (February 1991)

[5] Coates, C.L., et al.: An Undergraduate Computer Engineering Option for electrical Engineering. Proceedings of the IEEE 59(6) (June 1971)

[6] Engel, G., et al.: Initial Report: The Revision of Curriculum 1968. ACM SIGCSE Bulletin (September 1974)

[7] Engel, G.: The Revision of Curriculum 1968: An Abstract. ACM SIGCSE Bulletin (July 1976)

[8] Kurki-Suonio, R.: Birth of computer science education and research in Finland. In: Bubenko Jr., J., Impagliazzo, J., Sølvberg, A. (eds.) History of Nordic Computing, pp. 111–121. Springer, Heidelberg (2005)

[9] Naur, P.: Plan for et kursus i datalogi og datamatik. A/S Regnecentralen, Copenhagen (March 1966)

[10] Nordal, O.: A tool or science? The history of computing at the Norwegian University of Science and Technology. In: Impagliazzo, J., Järvi, T., Paju, P. (eds.) HiNC 2. IFIP AICT, vol. 303, pp. 121–129. Springer, Heidelberg (2009)

[11] Nykänen, P., Andersin, H.: Scientific computers at the Helsinki University of Technology during post pioneering phase. In: Impagliazzo, J., Järvi, T., Paju, P. (eds.) HiNC 2. IFIP AICT, vol. 303, pp. 116–120. Springer, Heidelberg (2009)

[12] Zadeh, L.A.: Computer science as a discipline. Journal of Engineering Education 58(8), 913–916 (1968)

Author Index